No Distance Between

Charles A. Sullivan

iUniverse, Inc.
Bloomington

No Distance Between

This is a true story, told to the author's best recollection. Some names, places, and details have been changed to conceal identities and maintain story continuity.

iUniverse books may be ordered through booksellers or by contacting:

iUniverse
1663 Liberty Drive
Bloomington, IN 47403
www.iuniverse.com
1-800-Authors (1-800-288-4677)

ISBN: 978-1-4502-7852-2 (sc)
ISBN: 978-1-4502-7853-9 (ebk)

Library of Congress Control Number: 2010918823

Printed in the United States of America

iUniverse rev. date: 4/4/11

To Ann, my loving wife,

and

To Ann, my little friend.

LOVE
IS ALWAYS
ORIGINAL

Photographs courtesy of Paul Shambroom

Working with Ann in a counseling situation was the single most grueling experience of my professional career. Committing myself to helping her pick herself up from deep within herself was the single most challenging and truly awesome undertaking I ever had addressed. Seeing her emerge as a woman who believed in herself as a person of worth and value was the single most thrilling experience of my life. The accusation that I was "after her body" was the single most unkind attack that ever had been directed against me. I never forgot it, not even after we made love together for the first time—and not even after the fiftieth time.

ACKNOWLEDGMENTS

I am just as ignorant, stubborn, and uncomfortable today about accepting and utilizing computer technology as I was twenty-five years ago when I first wrote every word of this book by hand on lined composition paper and then hunt and pecked more than 500 double-spaced pages of manuscript on my typewriter.

The difference between then and now, however, is that today's publishers don't want a typewritten hard copy; they require a computer generated word document burned on a disc that can be imported into a desktop publishing software package and then converted into a portable document file. I don't even know what all that means.....

With my wife's assistance and her general knowledge of computers, I was able to type my manuscript into a word document, but that's as far as I could go. I needed the expertise and willingness of someone who was computer literate, knew the intricacies of formatting, and had the patience to deal with my ignorance. I needed Cheryl.

When Cheryl S. LaMarr, a neighbor and true friend of my wife and I in our Florida community, learned that I was writing a book, she volunteered her computer savvy and the technical support I needed to prepare my manuscript for submission to my publisher. Cheryl's tireless efforts to format text to my specifications—not always the same one day as they were the day before—and her never-ending willingness and ability to bail me out of one technical problem after another, is a labor for which I am humbly grateful. It is with pleasure that I acknowledge the generous contribution of her time, energy, and patience with true appreciation. Many thanks, Cheryl.

One cannot even imagine the difficulty my wife, Ann, encountered as she copy read the content of this book, word by word, line by line, chapter by chapter, over and over again, as I described in graphic terms my love relationship and lovemaking episodes with another woman—of the same name. It had to hurt. I know it did. Although I offered to spare her from that task, she accepted it and served me well, not only looking for, finding, and correcting punctuation and grammatical errors, but frequently offering on-the-money content suggestions and advice. Thank you, hon. I love you so much.

AUTHOR'S WARNING

If you really think Jack and Jill went up the hill to fetch a pail of water, perhaps you shouldn't read this book. If you are happy and content with children's nursery rhymes, all is well. Understand, however, that this book is no nursery rhyme or fairy tale—and it certainly is not for children. It is an honest and explicit disclosure, large portions of which have been written in graphic detail.

This book was not written to win applause, to enthrall a reading audience, to be a commercial success, or to earn literary credit. It was written to fulfill a promise made to a dying person. I hope you love the story as much as I loved writing it and as much as I loved the person about whom it was written.

I ask only that you not criticize this book *after* you have read it, labeling it pornographic, dirty, disgusting, filthy, or vulgar. If you believe, because of your culture, upbringing, or religious beliefs, that sexual activities, the body's sexual parts, or the sex act itself are any of these things, you are herewith *forewarned*. It is best that you close this book and seek the alternate entertainment of an instructional visit to an ostrich farm where those of closed minds or limited vision can satisfy themselves by burying their heads in the sand.

I believe that both the narrow minded *and* the broad minded reader will be shocked by parts of this book.

Shock is an acceptable response; shock is justifiable. I further believe that if you think that loving and intimacy are vulgar, or if you think that the graphic words used to describe loving and lovemaking are disgusting or pornographic, you will not be pleased with this writing.

If you think the beauty of lovemaking is personal and should be quartered behind the closed doors of the bedroom, perhaps the beauty of nature along with the beauty of humankind's creativity should be similarly shielded, the beauty of a sunset not to be painted, the beauty of a mountain not to be photographed, the beauty of a symphony not to be heard, and the beauty of a poem not to be written, none of these to be shared with anyone.

If you think that going beyond shock is going too far, I can think of no good reason for you to select this book for your reading enjoyment. You would be just as entertained by the erotic "beyond shocking" make-believe happenings of a novel, the real-life beauty of this writing best left to those who can see beyond the words and appreciate the deep feelings and the genuine respect and love which fostered the herein described events and experiences. To those of you in this latter category, I am humbled by and grateful for your understanding, and to you I say, enjoy!

INTRODUCTION

Truth is like the stars; it does not appear except from behind obscurity of night.
—Kahlil Gibran

The taboos of adultery, rape, incest, and promiscuity have fallen one by one to the author's pen, but never have the scurrilous little secrets within the hallowed halls of a school been revealed so graphically by one of its own.

Business tycoons, corporate moguls, politicians, professional athletes, religious leaders, television stars, and Hollywood celebrities each have had one or more of their number write of transgressions of the flesh and of their venturous affairs and illicit encounters. Now it is a teacher who dares to shake and topple the institution of education from its lofty and unsullied pedestal in a love story which eventually moves innocence and professionalism to a frenzy of steamy and erotic activity.

In this explicit, first-person account of human frailties falling victim to circumstance, a teacher tells the true story of his special friendship and intimate relationship with a student, and reveals his shock at learning that the course they traveled together was neither a unique nor novel pathway but a heavily traversed and well-worn thoroughfare.

The touching of this untouchable subject, the breaking of this unbreakable barrier, and the telling of this untellable story is related here as it happened, by one who made it happen, by one to whom it happened.

CHAPTER 1

Introducing the accusation, Ann, the place, the time, the historical setting, and the Alternative School.....

The accusation came early—shockingly early, much too early—a crocus showing its pointed bud before the passing of winter in violation of Nature's order. It stunned me, angered me, numbed me, hurt me, and broke me. It sure as hell wasn't a fuckin' joke.

Like a dagger, that accusing finger was unwavering, swift, piercing, and, in many respects, final. It was no accident, no mistake, and no veiled or cloudy threat of mysterious origin or questionable intent. That accusing finger was direct and cutting, a weapon of lethal impact. Let it be certain—the person behind that accusing finger wasn't kidding around. She was deadly serious.

For me to be on the receiving end of that pointing finger was no light matter of painless consequence. It wrenched my family, severed me from many dear and long-time friends, exacted its toll on my physical being, and scrambled my brain. It damn near cost me my job. It said I wasn't a very good teacher or counselor. Even worse, it said I wasn't a very good person. How good a teacher, counselor, or person could I be, after all, if I were playing around with a student—a thirty-six-year old teacher, counselor, and married man fooling around with an eighteen-year old female student?

And *that* was the accusation.

****

"What the hell's the matter with you?" I shot back with infuriated rancor, my eyes bulging in disbelief. "You think I'm fuckin' crazy?"

"I'm just asking," she said stabbingly.

She wasn't apologizing, I knew *that* for sure.

"*You're* fuckin' crazy," I raged.

"The way things look, I just—"

"I don't give a shit how things *look*," I interrupted with sting and disgust as I turned to leave. "You're sick, woman! 'Am I after her body,' " I repeated with caustic scorn. "What kind of asshole question is that? If you had any idea what that kid's been through, maybe you'd do something to help instead of running off at the mouth and being so suspicious." I hardly stopped to take a breath. "Christ, she's been in this school since September, and you still don't know one fuckin' thing about her."

I threw my hands up in despair. I was steaming, my blood boiling like a tea kettle of provoked water enraged to furious turmoil by a scorching flame. I wanted to keep ripping into her, make her pay for it, and return the insult. Like an unfairly blamed schoolboy, pounced upon by a playmate for having allowed the ball to hop over the playground fence, I wanted to punch her in the face and beat the living crap out of her. But I wanted to get out of there, and away from her, even more.

Fran had whisked me into the closet we had converted to use as a darkroom for our photography class and had confronted me with the accusation. Was she speaking for herself or for all five of the full-time teachers who, with me, comprised the professional staff of our Alternative School? It didn't make any difference. I felt sick. I just wanted to get the hell out of there.

I flung the door open and left her standing alone as I stepped into the chilly hallway and looked around. The afternoon was late, and most of the kids, except the "regulars," had left for the day. Julia, Lois, and Dawn were engrossed in animated conversation on the stage, our lounge area. Marlene and Freddy were playing ping-pong in front of the stage, while Arlene watched from the sidelines.

"Hey, Charlie, watcha doin'?" called out Arlene. "Ya want winners after me?"

My heart was pounding, my thoughts in ragged disarray, fractured and scattered like an elegant piece of Limoges China dropped on a tile floor, but I still had enough wits about me to sweep together the necessary words for a disguising response.

"Yeah, maybe a little later," I answered in hollow-hearted reply.

Two staff members, Marilyn and Lisa, were working at the table in the side conference room. I instinctively looked for Ann. That was dumb. I knew she already had left. But I looked, anyway—a habit. Then I turned quickly and took the few steps to the office. I closed the door behind me and flopped heavily into the chair behind my desk. I just sat.

How the hell could this be happening to me?

****

I had met Ann for the first time the previous spring. It was mid-May. I remember it vividly. It was Monday, May 14, 1973, downstairs on the first floor of Teaneck High School in Teaneck, New Jersey. I had come down from the Guidance Office on the second floor in search of a student who had cut Mrs. Heafy's physical science class the Friday before. Heafy wanted me to talk to the kid and see what the problem was.

The bell had just rung for sixth period, and a tall, slim girl in jeans rushed down the corridor toward me. An attractive girl with long, shiny, brown hair almost to her waist, she had a worried look about her.

"You're Mr. Sullivan, aren't you?" she inquired intently.

"Uh huh," I nodded.

"You think I'll get accepted into the Alternative School? I turned in my application, but I haven't heard anything yet. You know when they're gonna decide? I *really* wanna go, ya know. I hope I get in," she spurted in quick, begging sentences before continuing with a frown. "I'm gonna be a senior next year, and I can't take another year in this place. You know when they're gonna let us know?"

A smile had begun to crease my face before she had reached the midpoint of her exuberant burst. I toyed with the idea of pulling her leg and telling her she had been rejected because she was too excitable, but I just laughed.

"I'm pretty sure you'll be accepted," I said with designed reassurance. "If all our applicants are as enthusiastic about the A-School as you, we'll have one heck of a group, right?"

"Oh, that would be super. I'm so excited! When will we know for sure?" she pressed.

"It won't be long," I answered. "I think everybody will be notified very soon, probably by the middle of next week. We're still takin' applications, ya know. The deadline isn't 'til Friday."

"Yeah, I know, but I'm really anxious. Okay," she sighed with a spin, apparently resigned to another week of wait. "Thanks a lot."

"Hey," I called as she was about to hurry away. "What's your name? I don't know—"

She turned back with a quick, effusive motion that spoke silent appreciation for the opportunity to identify herself, to say who she was and be recognized, be remembered.

"Ann Jordan."

"Ann…..?"

"Jordan—Ann Jordan. Yesterday was my birthday. I'm eighteen now."

"Oh, wow, that's really neat," I exclaimed, not quite certain why such detail had been offered. "Happy birthday! See, now, next year, I bet we'll be celebrating your birthday in the A-School," I laughed.

With crossed fingers, we were looking for a hundred students, give or take, to start our new school. The way our applications were coming in, I expected we'd be close to our target number by week's end and probably accept everyone who had applied.

"Oh, I can't wait," she bubbled. And she was gone.

****

There was still a heck of a lot of work to be done through June and the summer months before the Alternative School could open in September. But we had come a long way from the time the original proposal had been put on the table before the Student-Staff Senate almost fourteen months ago, and there had been three months of preparation before that.

I was involved from the beginning, but it hadn't been my idea. Credit for introducing the alternative school concept to our school district belonged to Paul McGarvey, a young man who recently had joined the high school faculty. He had just completed a summer of intensive graduate-level course work at the Institute of Open Education at a small college outside of Boston.

Paul introduced the concept of alternative education to our school district in an in-service workshop offered to interested faculty members. Not many were interested. The response was.....underwhelming. Little more than a handful participated and all, including myself, were generally ignorant of alternative education concepts.

While Paul may have been the general contractor for the Alternative School foundation, or at least the footings, Marilyn Franck, an energetic and spirited social studies teacher who enjoyed an excellent rapport with students, was the bricklayer. At about the same time Paul was conducting his in-service workshop, Marilyn, a more active member of the Student-Staff Senate than I, had been involved in a number of gripe sessions with students. Out of these informal "Why do we hafta....." and "Things would be a lot better if....." free-flowing exchanges emerged a resolute conviction shared by all: "There's gotta be a better way."

Marilyn cradled this infant idea, conceived in expressed student need, and carried it to the workshop where the handful of participating teachers wrapped it in the swaddling clothes of Paul's concepts and turned it back for nurturing and development to a newly organized Senate Committee on Alternative Education.

While Marilyn received some degree of unsolicited recognition for her work and effort, Paul never got any credit for laying the conceptual foundation, for providing the skeleton around which the meat would be fashioned, and for stimulating the imagination and motivation of others, including myself, who eventually took the ball and ran with it.

The widespread development and proliferation of Alternative Schools in the early 1970's was an outgrowth of the free-school movement of the late 1960's, with a few notable differences. Alternative Schools were the publicly funded, defensive, Johnny-come-lately trailers of the privately financed free-schools that had been the vanguard of academic change. Alternative Schools were the public sector's acknowledgment, most often reluctant, that schools within "the system" had to do something about the shocking degree of tension, alienation, and apathy that the increased social awareness of the times had revealed to be rampant throughout the nation's public schools.

This sorry state of affairs had found expression in the disturbing and frenzied protests, unrest, and violence of the period. Those who recognized the problems that faced public education urged changes in the school environment as well as a review of traditional educational goals, objectives, values, and processes. They also advocated the adoption of alternative learning concepts. One of the popular ideas was to establish Alternative Schools as small learning communities which would encourage students to exercise initiative and assume responsibility, provide them with a greater role in determining their own educational destiny, and give them choices from among a variety of learning experiences. These innovations all were designed to help students understand what education was supposed to accomplish.

It surely didn't take me long to latch on to the concepts. I had graduated from college with a Bachelor's Degree and a teaching certificate and had started my first teaching job a few days before my twenty-first birthday. Initially as a classroom teacher of social studies, English, and journalism, then as a counselor, and later in an administrative role, I had ample opportunity to witness the sterility, the rigidity, and the irrelevance of the system. I saw how the autocratic bureaucracy of the system turned kids off of education instead of on to it, made kids hate learning instead of love it, caused kids to close up instead of open up, and put more emphasis on passing and failing than on learning and growing. More often than not, the system fostered—even demanded—conformity, and stifled—even punished—originality. Worse still, it unconsciously conditioned students to function as if all learning began and ended with the ringing of a bell (in school), in small groups called classes (in the daytime), between eight in the morning and three in the afternoon (on weekdays only—but not during the summer), if they all dressed properly (no shorts or jeans, please), and if they were acquiescent, quiet, and obedient—particularly quiet. I mean, how the hell could bodies learn anything if they didn't keep their mouths shut? Learning always takes place in silence, right?

I not only witnessed the crap, I was part of it. I wasn't happy about being part of it, but I was part of it. It took a long time before I would admit to my role as an abetting agent, even to myself. Hey, I had seen the other side, too. I had seen good teachers who cared about kids and knew, understood, and empathized with the complexities of what it was like to be a young person. I had seen teachers stand as excellent role models for young people. I had seen students respond to teachers and emulate the noblest of their character traits. I had seen teachers work tirelessly to pull the best from students, to motivate and stimulate their young minds, and to instill in them an everlasting curiosity for discovering and trying new things. I had seen teachers help kids develop confidence in their abilities and in themselves.

In the best of times and in the best of places, however, the percentages weren't good. There were far too many instances when education, or what was being done in the name of education, missed its mark. The process often became so impersonal, perfunctory, and perfidious that it alienated those it should have been inspiring. The architects and engineers of the process often became so mired in stagnation that their clients choked on the stale air and clamored for an open window.

The time was ripe for change. What worked for some, even if they were the majority, didn't work or wasn't working for a lot of others. And *they* were the ones who started rattling the bars. The quiet ones copped-out, walked out, and dropped out. The louder ones cut classes and raised hell. They protested, sat-in, and took over. They yelled and were violent. They cursed and spat. They marshaled their forces, recruited supporters, and swelled their ranks with the disenchanted, the disillusioned, the disappointed, and the angry. They yelled "Fuck you!" out the windows. They wrote "Fuck you!" on the walls. They told teachers and administrators who evidenced difficulty hearing their complaints to go fuck themselves. It was Vietnam all over again. But this time it wasn't a rebellion against the politics of a government. It was a protest against the school as an institution—as they saw it, a tired, old, deaf, intransigent, insensitive, and bureaucratic institution.

Students petitioned for semester courses, mini-courses, and relevant courses. They wanted fewer requirements, easier requirements, or no requirements. They pushed for a say, a stake, a role in their own education. They demanded their teachers be human and humane, interested and interesting, motivated and motivating—*people* first, teachers second. They insisted on people who weren't so engrossed in their subject matter and so pompous in their learned state that they often forgot what they were supposed to be doing with their acquired knowledge. They wanted people who didn't consider history, chemistry, and mathematics to be ends in themselves; instead, they wanted people who understood the unique historical, chemical, and mathematical needs of the uncultivated and unsophisticated adolescents—many with limited tolerance and less enthusiasm—who sat before them each day. What all these kids really were saying was, "There's gotta be a better way."

It was a simple, yet ironic, message with which the educational establishment had to grapple. For years the professional literature and journals had gushed their educational jargon of sanctimonious goals—recognizing individual differences, meeting individual needs, teaching the whole child, and individualizing instruction. The not-so-sanctimonious fulfillment of those goals hadn't gone much beyond "tracking" the smart kids in smart classes, the slow kids in slow classes, the middle kids in middle classes, and all of the kids in "group guidance." So much for individualization. Even pinning a sweet-sounding or sweet-smelling label to each elementary school group—bluebirds, robins, daisies, butterflies—couldn't cover the stink of an unfinished task carelessly left too long unattended on a back burner until teachers and parents, and even the kids themselves, could detect the unmistakable stench of rotten eggs.

So, now kids were picking up on the same theme. "We're all different. We're Black, we're white, we're bright, we're slow, we're timid, we're aggressive, we're confident, we're insecure, we're happy, we're sad. Why the hell, then," they screamed, "should it surprise anyone that we just might be different, also, in the *ways* we *learn*? How about giving us some choices," their reasoning followed, "that offer us different ways to learn, so we have some flexibility in choosing those ways most suited to our individual needs and our unique personalities? We don't *all* have to do the *exact* same things in the *exact* same way at the *exact* same time in order to learn the *exact* same lesson!"

They were right. How could anyone argue with them?

Their communication may have been garbled, their means inappropriate, and their actions crude, but they sure as hell were right. What was somebody, what was anybody, going to do about the fact that people learn in different ways?

Surely, the whole system didn't have to be scrapped. Maybe it didn't even have to be changed. Maybe it could be left intact and continue to serve well those it did serve well. Maybe the only thing that had to be done was to provide some additional choices, some other ways, some alternatives that could be selected by those who were not being served well and whose needs were not being met by the existing system.

This was the philosophy I came to embrace, the philosophy of alternatives, of choices, of choosing. I accepted it, I espoused it, I believed it, I loved it, I extolled it, I wrapped it, I packaged it, and I sold it. I didn't do it all by myself. We did it together. The small group of teachers who had participated in that first in-service workshop with Paul, with some additions and deletions along the way, eventually became the high school's Student-Staff Senate Committee on Alternative Education, then the Alternative School Steering Committee, and finally the Alternative School staff.

Yes, I embraced it, I believed it, and I loved it. There was no way of knowing that, in a very short time, it would become so much a part of me that I would accept it as a lifestyle and, with all of its implications and far-reaching consequences, I would live it.

CHAPTER 2

The Alternative School really started at THE PICNIC.....
so, what happened at the picnic?

> **"As everyone knows, the Alternative School started at the regular high school in a committee formed by the Student-Staff Senate. But as only we know, the Alternative School *really* started at THE PICNIC."**

That's what the kids inscribed in their yearbook, the Alternative School's yearbook, at the end of the A-School's first year. THE PICNIC is *really* where the A-School began.

It was a sunshine day in June, a picture-perfect day for an outdoor get-together in the park. Had it been raining, or even snowing, it probably wouldn't have made much difference. This was *it*, finally! This was an afternoon of celebration for a group of people eager to celebrate, a real student body and real teachers together for the first time. It had taken a hell of a long time to birth this baby, and now everyone shared in the excitement of creation. But eighteen months of labor pains had been more than just a strain.

The seven teachers, five students, and one administrator who had served on the Alternative School Steering Committee had battled and hassled, internally as well as with external forces, with problems of philosophy, budgeting, curriculum, staffing, student selection, ideology, school board politics, State Department of Education approval, and neighborhood opposition to our proposed site location. Even though the latter issue was yet to be resolved, the other areas of intense concern had been addressed one by one. They were now, for the most part, behind us. Today, they were all but forgotten. Today, there would be no struggles with anyone, no fights, no knotty problems to solve, no grand strategies to plan, and no disquieting, upsetting, disturbing, or unsettling surprises to cause headaches or diarrhea. Today, the unfinished work was left to hang in suspension.

Today was picnic time, alternative style. Bring your own picnic lunch, kids, and the staff will bring the punch. We'll meet in the park, and we'll just have a grand old time getting to know each other. And, don't forget—bring a large, empty, 46-ounce juice can with you.

To each of the one hundred and five kids who had applied, the staff had sent a letter of acceptance and an invitation to the picnic. Then, we held our breaths, parents of a child about to take its first steps, a toddler released and let go to stand on its own. We didn't know if our baby was going to make it or not in a world as much filled with the enticing invitation of smooth pathways, clear sidewalks, and open roads as with the threatening peril of jagged rocks, cracked concrete, and yawning potholes. We moved over the next few days in a mix of contradictions—positive but uncertain, intrepid yet afraid, confident and hesitant at the same time—not knowing whether our child would stand or fall, walk or stumble.

Except in a few isolated instances, we didn't know the students, and they didn't know us. The regular high school was a large one with well over a thousand students and more than a hundred teachers. In many cases, the group of students who were to become the students of the A-School didn't know each other; in fact, "they" as a group hadn't even existed a few weeks before. "We," who were to become four of the teachers of the Alternative School, officially had been designated as such only two months before, and there were still two more teacher appointments to be made to complete the staff.

"Any news?" Fran shouted to me as soon as I was within range.

"Nope, nothin' yet," I called back as I ambled down the grassy incline to the table under the trees where the tall brunette, probably in her early thirties, sat.

The news Fran wanted to hear was the news all of us were waiting to hear—that the Alternative School had a home. We had the students—one hundred and five strong, a representative cross section of the regular high school population, a good mix of Black and white, male and female, college-bound and non college-bound students, a distribution as close to perfect as anyone could have hoped to achieve. We had the staff—four teachers hand-picked from the Steering Committee by the principal, four pioneers of sorts, enthusiastic and raring to go. I had been appointed Coordinator, or director, of the A-School in mid-April, and I now was involved in the screening of applicants for the two remaining staff positions. But we didn't have a home.

"We're not gonna hear anything before next week, if then," I continued with a sigh. "They're gonna have another hearing on it, I'm sure."

"*Another* hearing?" Fran exclaimed as I sat down across from her. "Jesus!"

I understood her alarm and her frustration. Since being introduced to the sometimes turbulent, often unpredictable, and always illuminating world of local politics in early May, the Steering Committee had three times gone before the township Board of Adjustment. The Church Street residents and those in close proximity of our proposed home in the basement of St. Paul's Lutheran Church were opposing our request for the variance we desperately needed. They had joined together, pooled their resources, and hired an attorney, digging in for a fight to the finish. They were furious that a school—an Alternative School, no less—loomed as a threat to intrude upon and disrupt the tranquil quiet of their neighborhood community.

"They're gonna fight us 'til the day we open," I said wearily. "They're just gonna keep the pressure on and hope we'll give up and go somewhere else. They're gonna do everything possible to tire us out and wear us down."

"I'm so tired now I can hardly think straight."

"We're all draggin' our asses," I responded with a conceding nod. "I'm so exhausted I could go to sleep right here, right now."

"Whaddya think's gonna happen?" Fran pressed with a wince that revealed her fear of what I might say.

"In the end, finally, ya mean?" I questioned with a raised eyebrow. I smiled. "We'll get the variance. Relax. We'll get it, as sure as God made little green apples!"

I looked around the small picnic area. A half dozen or so picnic tables had been pulled close together under the trees. People gathered in clusters, some sitting on the grass with their lunches, some standing at the end of the table upon which the coolers had been set.

The day was sunny and delightfully warm, perfect for short sleeves and jeans. A number of girls in cut-offs or shorts and halters took advantage of the relaxed atmosphere to lie in the sun and get a leisurely start on their summer tans. Some of the kids preferred to stretch out in the shade, picking stout tree trunks against which to rest their heads, propped just enough not to miss anything. Others sat cross-legged nearby. There was quiet conversation in one group, laughter and clowning in another, and excited buzzing in another. There was something for everyone, a veritable smorgasbord of social offerings to satisfy the moods and tastes of all. People sampled freely, moving with fluidity from one group to another and one conversation to another, a living kaleidoscope of continually changing configurations. Ronnie, Michelle, and Harold were making the rounds trying to recruit enough players to get a softball game underway, while Larry and Freddy already were out on the field tossing a Frisbee back and forth. Everything I saw was exciting, especially the turnout. There were kids all over the place.

"We *have* to get it," I repeated with conviction, not altogether certain whether my assertiveness was designed more to convince Fran or to assure myself. "What the hell are we gonna do with all these kids if we don't? I'm glad you and Marilyn took care of getting things set up for today. I couldn't get here any sooner. Jesus, look at all the kids. Everything seems to be going okay, huh?"

"I think we're gonna run out of punch," Marilyn said in high-spirited response to my query as she joined us. Obviously pleased by the size of the crowd, there was more delight than concern in her voice, until she saw Fran's troubled look. "Any news, Charlie?"

"No, I just told Fran. We're gonna have to sweat it out."

"How can we run outta punch? We had enough to float a battleship," Fran exclaimed.

Marilyn waved her arm in a presenting sweep. "I know, but, look. There's gotta be more than seventy kids here already, and they're still coming. And they're bringing their empty juice cans! I can't believe they're all coming! Look at the pile of cans over there."

"That's great!" I said as I surveyed the colorful mixture of large soup, fruit, juice, and vegetable tins that had accumulated on the ground behind one of the tables. "Maybe we should have told them to bring *full* juice cans. You didn't tell anybody what the empties were for, did you?"

Both women shook their heads.

"We didn't say a word," Marilyn replied with a smug smile.

"Good, we'll sweat out the variance, and let the kids sweat out the cans."

****

"You guys gonna play ball?"

I had seen Michelle jogging toward us, and I knew her approach presaged an invitation. Her enthusiastic bounce as she pounded her fist repeatedly into the pocket of the fielder's mitt on her left hand spoke her eagerness for an acceptance from the three of us who sat talking.

"Yeah, Fran and Marilyn will," I volunteered impishly as I nodded toward the two women who looked as if they didn't have enough energy to stand up. "They'll make a great double play combo in the infield."

"And Charlie will pitch," Marilyn countered quickly with a wry smile.

As much as the three of us wished to be good sports and appreciated the offer to be included, we invoked joke and jest among ourselves to beg off, promising "maybe later" to save face. Michelle enjoyed the entertainment of watching teachers needle each other, before skipping away in search of other, more likely, prospects.

Play softball? The whirlwind activity and maddening excitement of the past three months, together with its accompanying exhaustion, had exacted its toll on all of us. Not one thing had happened easily. Each move we had considered, each decision we had made, and each forward step we had taken had required careful deliberation, lengthy discussion, and painstaking preparation. Each part of the process had been totally consuming of our collective energies, patience, and mental resources. We were virtually at the breaking point, dog-tired and still pressing. There always seemed to be things to do, people to see, places to go, items to check, and deadlines to meet. At the end of the day there always seemed to be enough unfinished business to keep the head spinning until two o'clock in the morning, though the body ached with the fatigue of overtax and cried for the respite of sleep.

Putting together a school would have been a monumental undertaking even if we had had little else to do, but we all had our regular teaching jobs as well. Marilyn, Fran, and Lisa were classroom teachers with daily lesson plans and preparations to make, papers to correct, and tests to grade. Marilyn had her social studies classes, Fran taught English, and Lisa was a teacher of French, Spanish, and Russian. I was a counselor serving the year as acting director of guidance. The end of the school year, with its things to complete and loose ends to tie up, was squeezing all of us.

We had gotten through the weeks leading up to the picnic on nothing but adrenalin. The pressure and demand of what seemed to be unending A-School work had created enough hyper-activity to keep the heart racing and the feet moving from one meeting to another and on to the next. We had met with Rev. George Slater and the congregation of the Lutheran Church. We had met with college admissions personnel at nearby Fairleigh Dickinson University. We had met with township officials, newspaper reporters, school administrators, nervous parents, prospective students—anyone with whom we *had* to meet, anyone who wanted to meet with us. We had taken our act on the road, visiting several existing Alternative Schools in New Jersey and New York, trying to learn from their successes and mistakes. We had met with each other in staff meetings *ad infinitum*.

Play softball? All we wanted was one day, even half a day, to relax. We all needed the reprieve of a picnic—just a happy, exciting, high-flying, hectic, emotionally overwhelming, exhausting picnic in the park—so we could all catch our breaths!

* * * * * * *

"What's with the cans?" asked Julia, holding an empty Sacramento tomato juice can aloft.

"What's with your can, Julia?" shouted Peter from a few yards away.

"Fuck off," Julia retorted. She didn't bother to turn a look at the tall, dark haired boy with sideburns and a thin mustache who had seized the opportunity to call unasked for attention to her more than ample bottom.

"Maybe they're for paint or some kind of arts and crafts project," chirped Judith thoughtfully, ignoring the intervening exchange.

"Nah," said Eddie with a dismissing wave. "Arts and crafts are for kindergarten." He wasn't going to allow such a logical explanation snub out the chance he had been waiting for to clown. "The cans are for panhandling. We're each gonna go door-to-door on Church Street and take up a collection."

"For what, to pay the teachers?" Richard quipped.

"No, so we can buy a year's supply of good grass," Eddie responded with a broad grin.

A couple of kids in the group laughed. Some looked over quickly—lightning flashes of panic—to where I was sitting to see if there would be a reaction to the comment. Others threw a sideways glance toward Marilyn, but she was deeply involved in discussion with a group sitting at another table. The teachers tried not to be the focus of attention, but, invariably, wherever a teacher happened to be, a small circle of kids formed in orbit. Marilyn, too, was being pressed about the mystery of the empty cans and why everyone had been asked to bring one to the picnic.

I heard Eddie's bid for attention, but I offered no response. I took it more as a wisecrack than as a challenge. There seemed little to be gained by dignifying it with a reply. It was best to let it rest without conferring unmerited distinction upon it or attempting to discredit it. Louise and I had been talking about the kinds of English and history courses that might be available to students in September and whether any would carry Honors credit, at the same time lending an ear to the nearby banter and chaffing about the juice cans. I was sure she had heard the remark about the grass, too, but she ignored it as I did. We continued our academic discussion, and I just made a mental note of who the wise guy was.

"Maybe they're not for anything," offered Lois. "Maybe they just want to test our creativity and imagination."

"Look," said Eddie, still seeking an opening to spoof. "The way things are goin', we may not end up in the Church in September. We may end up in some building with no toilets and have to use the cans to take a leak."

About a dozen and a half kids had joined the lively exchange. The chatter of speculation increased in quantity and volume as those on the fringes of the group tossed their ideas into the circle. Each quip and tongue-in-cheek comment seemed to cue a quick response or trigger a ripple of chuckles or a roll of boisterous laughter.

"Ask Charlie," someone yelled from the group at what seemed like the height of the can-you-top-this game that had evolved.

"Yeah, Charlie, what are we gonna do with the cans?" called out Judith. She took a few steps toward where I was sitting. A big smile lit her face.

Judith was a cutie. I liked her a lot. She was one of the few kids I knew. She had worked in my office for a year during her free period when she was a sophomore. This past year, even though she had no free time to work, we had stayed close. We had spent many lunch hours and a lot of after school time talking in my office about everything and anything, but particularly about the Alternative School as it developed from a theory in the head of a dreamer to a reality. She had been one of the first to apply. Now, she stood in front of me, her eyes sparkling and her face beaming, spunkily taking advantage of the edge she had on others, her friendship with me, to teasingly confront "da teach" as a nose-to-nose equal, calling me to account with the pluck and poise of a proud peacock.

She fingered the "JUDITH" name chain around her neck with her left hand and, as I stood up, she flipped a can to me. The gang of kids surging behind her grew quiet.

"Okay, Charlie, why did we hafta bring these dumb cans with us?" she posed, grinning her delight.

"They're to save fat," I said quietly.

"Fat?" she asked incredulously, cocking her head to the side.

Everyone leaned forward like branches of a willow responding to the gentle push of a summer breeze.

"Yeah, you know, like during World War II."

The puzzlement showed on Judith's face and in the squinting eyes and wrinkled brows of all the freshly scrubbed faces neatly assembled in the semicircle in front of me. They were innocently unaware that they were about to be sold a bill of goods as easily as McDonald's could sell a hamburger.

"Yeah, kitchen fat was important for the war effort," I continued. "It was used in the making of soap and munitions. Housewives were encouraged to save their waste fat in a tin can and turn it in….."

Sitting ducks. I had 'em—could have heard a pin drop, even in the soft grass.

"…..Every Thursday morning the radio announcer would come on the air and say, 'Okay, ladies, today is Thursday, and you know what Thursday is. Thursday is the day to bring your fat can down to your friendly local butcher. He can hardly wait to get his hands on your fat can.' "

The intensity with which everybody had been listening was broken with the laughs of those who had gotten the pun. Some issued derisive groans, disappointed and chagrined at the ease with which they had been duped. Others scratched their heads, still waiting for the punch line.

"Yeah, 'bring your fat can down to your friendly butcher,' " Lois mocked with a dispassionate choke.

"That's your first alternative lesson," I winked with a devilish front. "Just because someone is in a position to capture your attention doesn't mean he's not gonna bullshit you. It's a good thing to keep in mind the next time you see a television commercial, right?"

"C'mon, tell us," Judith pleaded.

"Geez, I don't know," I replied, continuing the subterfuge. "I just got this invitation to come to this picnic and be sure to bring a big juice can. What else do I know?"

It was obvious I wasn't going to tell. The chatter gradually resumed as the large group fragmented into smaller groups of threes and fours. Some drifted away to other areas, still speculating on what mysterious use the juice cans were to be put. I overheard bits and pieces of conversation coming from different directions. There was hopeful talk about plans, dreams, and expectations for the next school year, still a summer away. There was excited talk about looking forward to next September and the dramatic opening of "our" school. There was heavy talk about making new friends, working together, and being a big family. I tingled all over.

Judith grabbed me and pulled me off to the side, out of range of the few who dawdled nearby, ambivalently considering their next doing.

"You're a big tease, ya know that?" she gushed impishly.

"Hey, you were pretty cocky there," I retorted with pretended alarm. Then with a laugh, "You thought ya had me, didn't you? I couldn't let ya get away with that."

"Yeah, I know," she grinned admittingly. "But I gave it a good try, didn't I?"

"Nice try, Judith. Close, but no cigar," I winked. "Just a little *short*."

Her face screwed up tightly in twisted pain, much too exaggerated to be real, but not enough to conceal the dulcet smile that slipped through the creases. She huffed with abnormal vehemence and spitefully turned her back to me before halting momentarily. Then, nose in the air, she bolted away with bristling swiftness to punctuate the deliberateness of her abandon. Yes, I *was* a tease. She knew my last words were calculatedly chosen to address themselves as much to her short physical stature, about which she often was gibed, as to her efforts to confront me.

I turned and sat down, very satisfied with myself that I had resisted the temptation to let the cat out of the bag about the cans. When everyone arrived at the A-School in September, they were to find more than a hundred cans lined in rows sixteen across and seven high, nailed to boards and hung on the wall, open-end facing out, ready for use, a personal and individual mailbox for each student and teacher in the Alternative School community.

* * * * * * *

"Do you remember me?" whispered a squeaky little voice, mimicking that of a child, in my ear.

I turned abruptly.

"Do you remember little Annie?" Again the voice squeaked its question with the tentative sidle of a four-year old.

I couldn't keep from laughing. Here was this tall, lean, long-legged girl standing next to me, talking like a baby. It broke me up.

"Oh, yes," I squealed, returning the imitation. I tried to keep a straight face, but I couldn't. "I remember little Annie."

We both laughed together, and she sat down beside me on the bench, assuming the same position as I, back to the picnic table, facing out. I immediately caught a fresh scent as if she had stepped out of a shower only minutes before, although I knew that wasn't the case.

I had seen Ann earlier in the afternoon, recognizing her immediately as the enthusiastic and spirited girl so eager to be accepted into the A-School she could hardly wait for the application deadline to come and go. I had wondered if she'd approach me today, but she seemed to be deliberate in maintaining a cautious distance, always there on the fringe, not too far away, but not too close, either. Her contact with me in the hall at school had been at her initiative and without hesitancy. Today, until now, she had appeared to be restrained by a timidity that kept her just beyond contact, slightly out of range. A couple of times I thought I caught her staring at me. Maybe she caught *me* staring at *her*.

I found myself inquisitively attentive to her whereabouts and her activity. When she dropped from sight, I immediately looked to locate her. There was something, I don't know, something about her—magnetic and needy, bold but shrinking, trivial but compelling. Her eventual approach, masked in the diminutive voice of a child, occurred at one of the infrequent times I was alone, off to the side by myself, and not engaged in conversation or involved with a group. I was aware that I had manipulated my position, apart from others, to permit it.

"I like your hat," she said, this time in her natural voice.

She seemed a bit nervous, although there had been no trace of uneasiness when she was playing "little girl."

"It's my favorite," I responded with a smile, adding quickly, "It's also my only."

It was an English-style, canvas, golf cap with narrow blue, red, and white stripes. It didn't look bad—a little garish, I suppose. I'd never confess to anyone how old it was. The flimsy inside lining was falling apart, and the leather sweatband was stained and cracked, testimony to how many times I had mowed the front lawn in the blazing sun. From the outside, however, it just had a comfortable, well broken-in look. To the top, toward the front, I had pinned a large, plain, white button on which I had written "Charlie" in script with a magic marker and the numeral "3" beneath my name.

In advance of the picnic, the teachers had randomly arranged the students into six groups of seventeen or eighteen, with a teacher assigned to each group. These were to be our Seminar, or homeroom, groups in September. Our distribution of name tags with Seminar numbers on them allowed everyone at the picnic to identify who was to be in whose group. The button on my cap was my name tag.

"Does that mean you're the teacher for Seminar 3?" she asked, pointing to the button.

"Yup, that's me." I leaned forward and looked around at her shirt, a white knit tennis shirt with a placket front. "Where's your tag?"

"I think I lost it when I was playing Frisbee. I'm in group five," she said dryly. "Who's the teacher?"

"I don't know. Nobody knows," I responded genuinely. "Marilyn is group one, Fran is two, I'm three, and Lisa is four. Five and six are gonna be the new teachers. I don't think they're gonna be from the high school. I think they're gonna be hired from the outside."

"Oh," she mused pensively. "That's what I heard the other kids saying."

She crossed her right leg over her left knee and held her ankle, both hands clasped between the bottom of her jeans and the top of her white sneakers. She sat in circumspect silence.

I knew all along she was in Seminar 5. Of the one hundred and five students in the A-School, I knew only six from prior contact. Brenda and Bob I knew as members of the Steering Committee. Judith, my little office helper, I had known for some time. Betty and Donna had been my counselees two years before. And, of course, I knew Ann from our three-minute encounter on the first floor of the high school a month ago. When the students had been divided into Seminars, I naturally was aware of what happened to the six I knew. Donna was the only one assigned to my group. I knew Judith was in group two. And I knew Ann was in group five.

"Hi, Ann," greeted Lois as she sat down next to Ann on the picnic bench. "Hi, Mr. Sullivan—Charlie?"

"Hi, Lois, Seminar 1," I returned, reading her name tag. " 'Charlie' is just fine with me. I don't need the 'Mr.' stuff."

"Watcha doin', Ann?" the freckled girl asked as she lit a cigarette.

"Just restin'. I'm tired of running around. Hey, look who's coming, the Barefoot Contessa."

"Sleeping Beauty," Lois squibbed.

Rita, who had kicked off her shoes and had been relaxing with two other girls under a tree a few yards away, was walking in our direction. The pretty girl in shorts and a plaid shirt joined us. She straddled the end of another bench across from me.

"I wasn't sleeping," Rita chirped.

"Oh, shit, you're in group four," Lois exclaimed, as her eye caught Rita's name tag. "I'm in group one with Marilyn. Geez, I wish we were both in the same group. I wish all *three* of us were together," she added between hasty puffs, looking sideways to include Ann. The three girls obviously knew each other.

"Yeah, me too," said Rita wistfully.

"That would be a trip, wouldn't it?" Lois boomed with exuberance. "Can you imagine the three of us—"

The small talk was the same, but the ambience of the situation had changed. I felt emptiness in my gut, a vacant hollow in the pit of my stomach. The tentative conversation Ann and I had begun was being snuffed out before it could develop substance, a candle wick's first flicker unkindly whiffed away by an intruding wind before having had the chance to reach full glow. My spirit shrunk in a splash of cold water. I felt bleached and removed from the present chatter and voided from the previous exchange. Strong feelings, they were, for such a small occurrence, I know. Lois kept plowing right along.

"Ya know, I just *knew* I'd be in group one. One is my lucky number. Almost everything important in my life has a one in it. So, now I'm in group one with Marilyn. I just saw Ricky, and he said—"

I looked off to my right, my attention diverted, my mind wandering from the chitchat in which I temporarily had lost interest. My lucky number was seven. I watched with fascination as the Frisbee soared majestically in the distance, the group of kids on the field scrambling, hands outstretched and bodies extended, to reach its point of landing, Larry leaping high above the others to snare the gliding missile on his finger tips. His display of mid-air ballet brought cheers and applause from those on the sidelines.

God, they sure could make that thing fly! It was just a simple toy, but it was a masterpiece of aerodynamic genius, the strangest bird that ever could be, with no wings to flap, no beak to peck seeds, and no legs to perch on apple tree branches. They flung it outward and upward with a wrist-snapping flick, and away it went, rising, rising, breathing with the whiffle of an asthmatic, climbing, whistling, singing the song of high-voltage electric wires strung in a fire-break up the side of a mountain, soaring, up and up and up to kiss a cloud, cresting to float in equipoise, a canoe in the sunny calm of midday on Greenwood Lake. Then, down, drifting downward, a magic carpet of today's summer dreams in doomed descent toward tomorrow's winter, dipping from immortality, speed skating on a thin sheet of ice at tree-top level, then losing momentum, lowering, and sinking. Summers don't last as long as they used to. When I was a kid, summer seemed to last forever. Remember how the ice cream man always wore a white suit? He always looked so clean. I used to run like hell to get a dime from my mother when I heard the jingling bells, panicked he'd drive away too quickly and not be back until next summer. And he was old. What if he died before then? Now the ice cream man is a long-haired teenager with dirty fingernails and acne, wears dungarees, and drives around with his girlfriend in the front seat of the truck. You can hear the stereo when he turns into your block. Down, down, lowering, sinking, skimming, and shivering. Caught! Plucked from flight, halted, unfulfilled, unfinished, interrupted, and grounded. Caught and brought down.

Damn, how they could throw that thing! They could throw it a mile and bring it down on a pin point. When I try to do it in the back yard, the friggin' thing usually hits a tree trunk ten feet away or crashes into the side of the house. I *never* can get any lift on it, no matter how I hold it or how I throw it.

"My lucky number is three," Ann said quietly as she stood up.

"It's okay for us to say 'Marilyn,' isn't it?" questioned Lois as she leaned forward toward Rita. "All the teachers have their first names on their tags," she continued as if to provide justification for a positive response. "And Mr. Sullivan said it was fine with him if—"

Skillfully interjected, Ann's remark slid past Lois and Rita whose conversation went forward without interruption.

Ann's quiet declaration caught me by surprise. I felt my face flush red, my senses stunned by the sudden rush of conflicting feelings. I was sorry she wasn't in my group, happy she wanted to be there, but embarrassed she had been so revealing. I didn't want any of the three to show.

Ann took a few steps, crossing between the two gossiping girls, before turning back to me with a sheepish smile.

"You won't forget we have a date to celebrate my birthday, will you?"

I grinned back awkwardly.

A date to celebrate her birthday? Where in blazes did *that* come from? I remember I said we'd— She *couldn't* have taken that to mean *we* would celebrate her birthday. I—I just meant that—

Again I felt a terrifying race of hotness within my veins.

Ann had turned away and had walked some distance before I realized how dumb I must have looked sitting there with that false smile and that confusion painted crimson across my face. I got up stiffly and walked in the direction of the cooler, leaving Lois and Rita to their own entertainment.

".....and I don't give a fuck," Brian expounded with vehement gusto, his back to me, his arms flailing.

My sudden departure from Lois' rambling chatter and amateurish puffs of non-inhaled smoke inadvertently had placed me in the midst of another conversation. As Brian wheeled, he found himself unexpectedly confronted. His irreverent comment dangled in a limbo of intimidated embarrassment.

"It's okay to say 'fuck' in this school, isn't it?" the small, good-looking boy asked with obvious fluster. The guilt-provoked question didn't seem to be directed to anyone in particular. There were five or six other fellows standing around the cooler, but he was looking at me.

"I mean, we're not even really in school yet, really. This is just a picnic, right, not a school, really?" he flustered, looking for affirmation and a way out of what he must have thought was a ticklish situation.

"Who the fuck cares what the fuck you say," Eddie replied brazenly from within the group.

Everybody laughed, but there was still a lot of uneasiness among the guys who had clearly had their free-wheeling conversation upset by my urgent but ill-timed need for a drink, or something to do, or some place to go, or somewhere to hide.

"I don't care if you say 'fuck' as long as you don't say 'you' after it and address it to me, or say 'it' after it and have it mean the school," I shot out quickly. I was surprised at my ability to recover from my own uncomfortableness enough to put so many words together with any semblance of coherence. "Now, get the fuck outta the way so I can get a drink," I laughed, as I poked Brian playfully in the stomach. I pushed through the gathering to the pile of paper cups on the table.

They all roared. My hand shook as I pushed the button and watched the steady stream of icy fruit punch fill my cup.

I just can't believe she could think *we* were going to celebrate her birthday, I thought to myself.

I was thinking the same thing two hours later when I returned to the same spot and the same table. Now in shadow, the grass was well trampled and soggy beneath the spigot that had faithfully dispensed its refreshment to the end. I tilted the cooler forward to drain the few drops remaining, waiting with interminable patience for the final drip, unwilling to admit that the jug was empty and the picnic over.

Where the hell did she get off thinking—?

I looked around. The afternoon was getting late. Many of the kids already had said their goodbyes. A good number still hung on, clinging to the moment and reluctant to leave. The chatter had subsided, the dusty bat and ball had been tossed in the grass under a table, the Frisbee was gone, Ann had left, the jugs were empty, and a half-dozen wire mesh park baskets overflowed with brown bags, used cups, paper plates, and sandwich remains. The kids who stayed milled aimlessly, players on a stage refusing to acknowledge that the final curtain had come down. The picnic was over, but it had been everything we had hoped it would be. It had been our first real undertaking, our first step, our first test, our first big success, and the fist day of the rest of my new life.....

CHAPTER 3

The A-School opens, students sign up for a "Discovery!" class, and suddenly there's a disaster looking for a place to happen.....

> **"County Court Judge John T. Mooney, sitting in Superior Court yesterday, denied a temporary injunction requested by 51 township residents who were seeking to stop the district's Alternative School from opening Wednesday."**

The Alternative School opened Wednesday, September 5, on schedule. We always knew it would. We weren't sure *where*, but we knew it would.

Now, with September gone and October waning, property values in the Church Street vicinity hadn't plummeted, and not a single one of the neighborhood children had been raped. Bushes and shrubs hadn't been uprooted, and lawns in the area, rather than being gouged with tire tracks and strewn with rubbish, looked very much the way suburban lawns along tree-lined streets should look under streams of late autumn sunlight.

The Church Street residents had waged a bitter and vociferous battle against our variance request before the Township Board of Adjustment in the spring and then before the Town Council throughout the long summer. Now, in October, not only had their worst fears not been realized, but the absence of noise, congestion, and litter had left the neighborhood as void and empty as the newspapers were of A-School news.

We had been a hot item for the local press through June, July, and August. Now, we were as forgotten as the headlines which had flourished only a short time before:

"NEIGHBORS BATTLE ALTERNATIVE SCHOOL"

"ALTERNATIVE SCHOOL VOTE PUT OFF"

"ALTERNATIVE SCHOOL DECISION MAY BE CHALLENGED IN COURT"

"ALTERNATIVE PROGRAM THREATENED; SUIT FILED TO OUST SCHOOL"

If the neighborhood and the newspapers now were void and empty, the A-School wasn't. It was busy, active, bustling, fresh, alive, and vibrant. It was full of kids learning how to make decisions, mistakes, and progress; learning how to govern themselves, enjoy themselves, and discipline themselves; and learning how to work together, think together, and live together. Most of all, and best of all, it was full of kids *learning*. They even were learning how to die together, or rather, learning together how to die, in a course being taught by Lisa, "Death and Dying," one of the most popular of our fall trimester offerings.

By almost any and every standard, the A-School kids were giving a good accounting of themselves. George, who had failed physical education at the regular high school last year, was logging more hours of independent study physical education activity than anyone else. He always was on the look to grab three or four other kids to go down with him to the elementary school playground at the corner to play basketball. When he wasn't able to persuade, convince, entice, cajole, or connive anyone to go with him, he went himself to shoot baskets or jog, even on days when it was drizzling.

Quiet Beth, known to be timid and hesitant both in classroom and social settings, was now talking, laughing, making friends, and having the time of her life. Loudmouth Jill was learning how to shut up. And when she forgot, she was told, by six teachers and a hundred and four students, each of whom took special relish in providing a less than subtle reminder. Eddie had found out, as much to his surprise, I'm sure, as to everyone else's, that "fuck" wasn't the only expressive word in the English language. He now was using "piss" with regularity. Tom and Frank were taking a night course in Arabic at the University. Arlene was taking three different art classes with Ben, one of our two new teachers. Carla, not generally regarded as outgoing or assertive, was more and more frequently demonstrating real leadership characteristics in Seminar 5 with Janis, our other new staff member.

And my little friend, Ann—poor Ann. Ann was riding a roller coaster. She was up, and she was down. Sadly, for Ann, there were more downs than ups. Ann didn't see lawns along tree-lined streets under streams of late autumn sunlight. She wrote the words of a poem on a piece of white composition paper and left it for me in my juice can mailbox.

The wind has been swirling round and round
And the leaves are dancing upon the ground;
I wish they'd settle down,
Rest a while.
It's a cold, damp, and lonely night;
The clouds are crying at its sight
But their tears were froze to ice;
What a shame.
Lost! Lost in this maze and I'm growing so weary.
Please help me home
Where I can rest.

I didn't know if it was an original piece or if she had picked up the words of a song, as she frequently did, from the radio. I never asked. If one were to judge a poet's skill and measure a work by the poignancy with which its message was delivered, Ann's poem was a masterpiece. Its artistic imagery mirrored the desolate and forsaken spirit of the Ann I had come to know over the past two months.

* * * * * * *

I had signed up to teach only one course in September. My responsibilities as Coordinator hadn't been very clearly defined. By the end of the first day, however, it had become evident what was expected of me, what my role included, and what my title meant, whether I liked it or not. It meant moving man, interior decorator, set designer, prop man, handy man, sign maker, custodian, foreman, typist, secretary, receptionist, mimeographer, record keeper, accountant, administrator, disciplinarian, supervisor, counselor, attendance officer, change-maker for the Coke machine, ass-kicker, the guy with the fuckin' list of students, the guy with the fuckin' list of courses, the guy with the fuckin' list of things to do, the guy with the fuckin' screwdriver to fix the fuckin' refrigerator, and the fuckin' guy who forgot to bring the fuckin' toilet paper so the fuckin' kids could wipe their fuckin' asses. Hooray, we had the toilets; nobody had to pee in the juice cans! It meant Charlie—friend, soother, and healer. It didn't mean God. At least three kids told me during the first hour of the first day that I wasn't fuckin' God. Yes, the first day had been very defining. One class was going to be enough to teach.

I called the course, "Discovery!" None of the kids knew what the course was going to cover. When they asked me, I wouldn't tell them. I knew, but I didn't want to scare anyone. Seventeen of them took a leap of faith and signed up, anyway. Ann was the first to put her name on the sheet.

I designed the course as an intensive experience in *self*-discovery and self awareness. It was meant to stimulate personal growth through participation in exercises which required honesty, trust, risk-taking, self-disclosure, the open expression of feelings and emotions, and the giving and receiving of verbal and non-verbal communication as well as positive and negative feedback. It was a tough course. Damn tough. I know. I didn't teach the course in the traditional sense of a teacher teaching. I *took* the course with everyone else, one of eighteen students who sat on the floor in the foyer at the bottom of the stairs in the rear of the basement three days a week. We taught each other and learned from each other. It was the most challenging course I ever took, and it was the best, despite the sometimes uncomfortable floor.

We called the "home" of our Alternative School "the basement." Actually, it was the large, finished, multi-purpose auditorium, complete with stage, below St. Paul's Lutheran Church. The A-School featured bare-bones, no-frills education. Classes met wherever there was room. Teachers left their good clothes home with their last names. Jeans were fine for sitting on the floor.

I really got to know Ann in "Discovery!" class. I got to know everybody, and everybody got to know everybody else. We were a little family inside a bigger family. But I really got to know Ann.

We all had a rough time in "Discovery!" class, particularly at the beginning. The things we did together necessitated invariant patience, understanding, sensitivity, caring, and a genuine and compassionate concern for each other's needs and feelings. And this was being done, mind you, within a larger environment in which people called each other "asshole" with regularity and told you to "fuck off" or "shove it" at the drop of a hat. But the ultimate requirement and essential ingredient for each participant in "Discovery!" class was the inner strength and self-confidence that it took to survive when things got rough and tough. A person's self-esteem and positive self-image were the only props one could use for support when there was no one else and nothing else upon which to rely.

Everyone had trouble with the tasks and exercises in the course in varying degrees, depending on the amount of self-confidence and self-esteem that each person possessed. Ann had the most difficulty. Of all the students in the course, she had the least amount of feelings of self-worth. I gradually came to realize that, of all the students I had ever taught or counseled, of all the people I had ever known, young or old, Ann had the least amount of positive feelings about herself, the lowest self-esteem.

It came out a little at a time, piece by tragic piece, in class and out. The poem wasn't the first hint. Had the poem been an isolated incident, I wouldn't have given it a second thought. But over the past six weeks there had been several poems, many long talks, and an abundance of pathetic evidence that told me Ann's world was not a happy place, despite the carefree and lighthearted characterization she staged for everyone to see.

* * * * * * *

"Hi, Charllllieeeee!"

"Jesus, now what?" I muttered to myself.

I had so much work to do I didn't know where to start. If I didn't get a chance to sneak off some place and put a dent in the backlog of bloody paperwork that was piling up—

"Hey, Charllllieeeee, wait up."

I knew it was Ann, tagging after me like a puppy. She had been attaching herself to me as a stray would follow the hand-out of a befriending stranger. It seemed she was begging notice and attention at every turn and being overly grateful for the candid talks we had been having, particularly in the comfortable and relaxed quiet of the lounge at the end of the day. There was something uniquely attractable about her that made me like her in spite of her persistent neediness. There was something very pathetic, almost waifish, about her that made me feel sorry for her. She evidenced a haunting need, yet a cringing reluctance, to break through a barrier that prevented her from expressing herself and feeling free to share anything but the most superficial information about herself and her life. There were too many statements that seemed to burst halfway to daylight only to have their conclusions swallowed back into the night of her unspoken soul. It was easy to get involved in some heavy personal counseling with her. I used every opportunity we were together to probe and support. Despite recent successes in getting her to "open up," however, some situations didn't lend themselves to counseling, at least not at the time they were happening.

"How ya doin', kiddo," I called over my shoulder, slowing until she reached my side. "Where've you been?"

"Charllllieeeee, where ya goin' in such a big hurry? Julia said you were lookin' for me."

"I was heading for the office so I could shut myself in for an hour and get this stuff done," I answered, waving the folder of loose papers I was carrying. "Where—"

"I thought—" she stammered. "I saw Julia, and she said—"

She started to giggle. Then, in an exaggeratedly pronounced, deep, husky voice, almost a burp, she eructed, "Were you lookin' for little Annie?"

I stopped and turned to her. I looked right into the eyes of her silly grin. Just what I thought. Stoned. I knew it. She was stoned out of her fuckin' mind.

"Yes, of course I was lookin' for you. Where the hell have you been?" I asked in a hushed tone. "You're fuckin' wrecked."

Her squinting response was a question and a statement at the same time.

"I was out in the car?"

She frowned with a hurt look like a little kid caught with her hand in the cookie jar.

"Out in the car?" I shook my head and looked around. "C'mon."

I took her arm and walked her quickly across the basement, retracing my steps of a few moments before. I pushed open the door to the back foyer, our "Discovery!" classroom, and nudged her through. We both sat down on the steps. I didn't say anything.

"I like it here," she said quietly as she looked around the familiar little alcove.

"I like it here, too," I snapped. She was talking about the room; I was talking about the school. "But I'm not gonna last here very long. You're gonna put my ass in a sling."

"It's so nice, and warm, and cozy," she swooned with a melancholy expression, her elbows now propped on her knees, her chin in her hands, her glazed eyes fixed in a straight-ahead stare.

She didn't seem to understand my uncomfortable predicament.

The only light in the foyer came through the small window in the door at the top of the stairwell. The dimness lent an aura of closeness and a mystique of security to the small enclosure. It *was* nice and cozy. That's why I had picked it as my classroom. Warm? I could feel the heat on the back of my neck, nervous perspiration and a flushed embarrassment, the kind of warmth that sneakily assaults from behind, moving surreptitiously upwards along the spine from the middle of the back to the nape of the neck, reddening the complexion and pulsing an overabundance of heated corpuscles to the tips of the ears.

"Ann, I can't keep hiding you every time you get zonked," I said almost pleadingly.

This wasn't the first time she had come to school stoned and had to be shuttled out of sight. She smoked almost every day, but she usually concealed it well. A dexterous pot-head who hid behind a smoke screen, she cunningly foiled others by projecting herself as a naturally giddy scatterbrain filled with idle chatter and silly gibberish. The Ann everybody saw and knew was, more frequently than not, a stoned Ann. But some days, when she was able to get her hands on *really* good weed, she couldn't hide it. Her flight was about as inconspicuous as a red kite against a sky of white clouds.

"I'm sorry, Charlie. I don't wanna get you in trouble, really."

"I know, but, everybody's lookin' for you. How could you come to my class this morning and then not show up for English? Everybody knew you were here, and then Rita couldn't find you, and neither could Fran. Then *I* couldn't find you. Shit. I told Fran that maybe you went home. I thought maybe you weren't feeling well."

"That's what happened, Charlie," she blurted apologetically. "I *didn't* feel well. That's the truth. My cramps are killin' me. I just got my—my female thing, you know. I'm a mess. I hadda go down to the store. Here, change places with me, will ya. I can't hear on this side."

"Whaddya mean?" I queried as I got up and she slid over. I was still blushing a little from her straightforward admission that she had her period. I sat down on the other side of her.

"I'm deaf on that side. Born that way. Didn't ya ever notice how I always try to position myself on your—"

Christ. Every time I talked to this kid, she dropped another piece of bad news on me. Initially, I suspected she was doing it on purpose, a deliberate mention of adverse circumstances designed to evoke sympathy. But I came to know this wasn't the case. The revelations always occurred in the same inauspicious manner, spontaneous matter-of-fact tidbits that inadvertently popped into the middle of a conversation. There was never any accompanying complaint—no bitching, no moaning, and never any feeling sorry for herself, just something old-hat to her but shockingly new to me. She wasn't keeping totals, but I was. And everything was adding up lousy.

Two weeks ago, she had lost her wallet. Then, a woman in the Acme parking lot had backed into her car and dented the fender, and her father had given her hell. In one of our afternoon talks, she had mentioned being in a leg brace from the age of one until she was five years old because of a birth deformity in her hip. The kids had made fun of her when she started school. Last week I had to bust her chops because she and Mike and a few other students had come to our A-School hike and overnight camp-out in Harriman State Park by themselves, instead of with the rest of the group. To make matters worse, they hadn't even signed up that they were coming. A few days ago, kids fooling around in the lounge had knocked into her, spilling a full cup of soda down the front of her new, green sweater. Her father was driving her crazy, finding fault with everything she did or didn't do. The day before yesterday she had left her fifth piece of depressed poetry in my mailbox. Yesterday—God, yesterday—she had had a tough time in "Discovery!" with an exercise in receiving non-verbal communication. She tried so hard to read what Steve was trying to "say," and when she couldn't, she became flustered and frustrated, coming apart at the seams when she overheard someone say she was dense. Today, she had her period, she had cut Fran's class, she just told me she was born deaf in one ear, and she was wrecked. This kid was a walking disaster looking for a place to happen! Unfortunately, she was "happening" in the middle of my fuckin' school.

And now we were sitting on the back stairs, and I was trying to figure out what the hell I was going to do with this ball-buster.

"I think you better go home, kid."

I tried to say it softly and with sympathy. It didn't work. It was like trying to tell someone that their pet dog had been run over by a car and hoping they wouldn't be upset.

"Oh, shit, Charlie, don't send me home. I can't go home. Please don't do that to me," she sputtered.

"I'm not *doing* anything to anybody. I'm just tryin' to save your ass—and my ass."

"But I *can't* go home."

Silence.

"Charlie, I *can't* go home. It's almost lunchtime. My father's gonna be comin' home for lunch. He's been on my case all fuckin' week. He hasn't said one word to my mother all week long. You know how he gets. He doesn't talk to her, but he jumps all over me for everything."

Yes, I knew. She had told me often. She never cried, winced, or moaned. She just told me in her matter-of-fact, that's-the-way-things-are, what-else-is-new way, relating the hurtful stories of his deflating comments and fault-finding attitude toward her. Her recounting of his belittling and ego-crushing criticisms had made *me* wince and almost cry.

"I only had a few tokes in the car. I'm okay. No one will know anything. I'll go to Marilyn's class after lunch, okay?"

"C'mon," I said, getting up from the stairs with my folder, now bent in half and heavily creased down the middle.

She cowered from my reach, shrinking back as I extended my hand to pull her up.

"I'm not gonna send you home," I said reassuringly.

How could I send the knucklehead home?

"Ya wanna go to McDonald's and get a hamburger?" I asked.

She looked up, relief spreading across her face, a convict spared execution by the last minute stay of the Governor.

"Oh, thank you, Charlie, thank you, thank you. You're just—"

"C'mon, asshole," I interrupted jauntily. "Up on your feet."

"You're the best friend I ever had, Charlie. I really—"

"C'mon, c'mon," I urged, not ready to hear the rest. "I gotta get you outta here and get something into your stomach."

We hopped the steps together, two at a time, and slipped out the back door to the parking lot where she managed—just—to make it to my car without falling on her face.

"I'm sorry—"

"Shut up!"

We went to McDonald's and had burgers, fries, and Cokes in virtual silence. It was the quietist lunch I had all week. The cheapest, too. She paid. I wasn't gonna pay for her friggin' lunch.

CHAPTER 4

Getting to know Ann: her low self esteem, her rejection of professional help, the missing "warm fuzzy," and that blouse.....

If I were getting to know Ann, she was getting to know me, too, but only what I wanted her to know—that I cared *about* her, yes; that I cared *for* her, no. I wasn't an idiot. I let her know me in ways that would facilitate the serious counseling in which I had become engaged with her and to which I was fully committed. It was classic cyclical counseling, but it was ripple counseling as well. Ann, this pebble of a kid, had landed in the middle of my lake with but a tiny plunk. And each time I addressed myself as a counselor to the small circle that spread outward from her entry, I found another, and another, and yet another, each ripple a wider, broader, and more encompassing problem with which to deal. I became increasingly worried about her, this little pip-squeak who seemed to walk every path hand-in-hand with Misfortune.

It wasn't the stupid little things that happened from day to day. It wasn't the accidents, the coincidences, the disappointments, the squabbling with her father, the dented fender, or the spilled soda. Heck, those things are part of every adolescent's life. It wasn't even the childhood leg brace or the deaf ear. It was her handling of these events and circumstances that troubled and concerned me. Her response to them wasn't normal. Bad enough it would have been if she had internalized and personalized these occurrences, which she did, but, further, she *accepted* them as her fate, predestined and inevitable. *That* was the problem, the dangerous part—her bland, unquestioning acceptance and her acquiescent ownership. She believed that the trouble, the problems, and the misfortune that came to her *belonged* to her because that was what she was worth. If people shit on her, if tragedy befell her—well, so what else was new? That's what happened to people who were worthless, worth shit.

The feelings she had about herself, and the way she thought of herself, came from deep within. I couldn't help but note early the irony of the situation.

She had friends, people who liked her, people with whom to do things, and people who enjoyed sharing time, ideas, stories, and experiences with her. One could see it at the A-School every day. There was no obvious reason for anyone to think she was anything but a socially well-adjusted adolescent. But, deep inside, she was friendless, alone, unattached, and isolated.

She had a home and a family—a mother, a father, two brothers, a sister, an aunt, a cat, and even a maid, all part of a financially secure, well-respected, chicken soup household to care for her, to wait on her, and to soothe, comfort, and support her. But, deep inside, she was homeless, adrift, a wandering stray, a waif.

She possessed personal qualities many other people only could have wished to have. She was considerate, fun-loving, full of life, and loyal. She was exceptionally thoughtful and warmly caring, the kind of person who wouldn't hurt a flea and who, literally, would give someone the shirt off her back. But, deep inside, she was stoic, staid, and somber. She thought she was worth shit.

If the way she perceived herself bothered me and caused me concern, the ironies were doubly vexing and much more difficult to explain or comprehend.

Working with Ann in a counseling situation was the single most grueling experience of my professional career. Committing myself to helping her pick herself up from deep within herself was the single most challenging and awesome undertaking I ever had addressed. Seeing her emerge as a woman who believed in herself as a person of worth and value was the single most thrilling experience of my life. The accusation that I was "after her body" was the single most unkind attack that ever had been directed against me. I never forgot it, not even after we made love together the first time—and not even after the fiftieth time.

* * * * * * *

I gave her as much time as I could, every minute I could afford, minutes I couldn't afford, and then a little extra for good measure. It seemed we talked endlessly, before school, after class, at lunchtime, after school, and any other time between when she came to me upset or depressed, troubled or perturbed, with urgencies real or imagined. I did my best to read the need and meet it.

She knew I was her friend. She knew I cared. She knew I would listen. She knew I would protect her. She knew she could trust me. And she knew I would never betray her trust. She also knew that I would make her do her homework, kick her butt when she messed up, wouldn't let her use me as an excuse, and that I'd tell her the truth even if it hurt. We talked about everything from Kahlil Gibran to smoking pot, from sex to her summer camp experiences, and from her parents to my wife and kids. We talked about therapy.

She really could have used—she needed—some professional therapy.

"I don't need a fuckin' shrink," she had blistered in rebellion at my initial mention of it. "I'm not crazy. You think I'm crazy?"

"Of course not. I didn't say you were crazy," I replied with coolness, attempting to defuse her charged reaction. "I said it might be good if you had someone you could talk to on a regular basis, by appointment."

"Can't I talk to you?"

"Yes, of course. Don't be silly. You know you can talk to me. You can talk to me anytime ya want. But I'm not a therapist. I'm a counselor."

Her uncertain look asked for further clarification. Maybe I was getting through.

"I can talk with you, but I can't treat you. A therapist is a doctor. A therapist can prescribe medication if it's needed. Depression can be treated. And, sometimes, like when you're really in the pits, it might be good if ya had something to sorta get ya through, ya know? I know some good people. I could—"

"I got everything I need to get me through," she obstructed.

"What, your stash? That's not gonna help."

"It helps."

"For a while it might, when you're flyin', but when ya come down?"

"I don't come down. I'm high all the time."

Shit. She had all the answers, even if they were lousy.

Every time I mentioned it, she bucked the suggestion. Who was going to pay for it, her father? When was she going to find the time? She could always get some Valium from her father's drug store, right?

"Don't start fuckin' with that stuff," I ordered threateningly. "That's all ya hafta do, mix tranquilizers with pot. Ya might just as well stick your head in an oven and turn on the gas."

"I'm not stupid. I don't mix them. I alternate."

"Beautiful."

I couldn't get my foot in the door. I *did* know some good people. I tried to find an opening to break through her resistance. I offered to pay for it out of my own pocket. I told her I'd go with her if she wanted me to. I promised she could stop going if she didn't like it or if she didn't think it was worthwhile.

It was like talking to a stone wall. She was obstinate, adamant in her refusal, constant on her course of resistance, and blind in her immature rationale. Therapists were "shrinks," in the same way that policemen were "pigs," and she couldn't get sufficiently past the derogatory labels to grant any measure of respect or competence to either group.

I pleaded, without success. I pressured as much as I dared, pulling back only when the extent of her anger threatened the continuance of the open communication she had established with me.

She had gotten into the habit of sending me notes via the school's internal communications system, the juice can mailboxes. Sometimes her notes contained afterthoughts of our conversations or things she felt more comfortable writing than saying. Most often, however, they were tiny thank-you-for-being-so-patient-with-me or thank-you-for-listening messages scribbled on the back of a gum wrapper or matchbook cover.

The first note I sent to Ann was after a "Discovery!" class in which she accidentally had been left out of a "boosting" exercise. It had been Ronnie's turn to give positive reinforcement, a "warm fuzzy," to each member of the class at the very end of the period, but he had left Ann's name off his list. Every kid in the class had one nice thing said about him or her in front of everyone else before they left the room, except Ann. She sat waiting for her "warm fuzzy," but it never came. She was devastated, but she didn't say a word.

> **I'm sorry you didn't get your "warm fuzzy" today like everyone else because you deserved one as much as anyone else. A day without a "warm fuzzy" is like a day without sunshine. So, Ann, here is your "warm fuzzy" for today:**
>
> **YOU ARE SUNSHINE**
>
> **Charlie**

She waited for me in the lounge after school again that afternoon. More or less, it had become a regular practice, although neither she nor I ever planned it that way. A dozen or more kids customarily would stay after school, the number gradually dwindling as the afternoon wore on. But it was almost mid-November now, and, with daylight savings time no longer in effect, it got dark earlier and the number of late-stayers had dropped sharply.

Ann usually waited for me on the stage, chatting with Lois, Carla, Dawn, Jeff, Brian, or Julia, the most regular of the regulars, or playing ping-pong with Marlene, Freddy, Arlene, or Harold. Sometimes, if I ran late—I almost always had some amount of office work to do after school—she would leave a note in my mailbox and go. Most of the time, however, I'd find her sitting in the big, red, over-stuffed living room chair the kids had found on the curb on special garbage pick-up day back in September. They had lugged it in, with other assorted pieces of discarded furniture, for our lounge. Wasn't that a strange twist of fate? The neighborhood people who had fought us tooth and nail were the ones who unknowingly provided the furnishings for our home, free of charge.

I checked the mailbox on the way out of the office. No note. As I walked to the stage where I knew I'd find her sitting in the big, red chair, I wondered what we'd talk about today. Yesterday we had gotten into some heavy stuff about controlling one's own destiny.

Before I even reached her, she was purring.

"Your note was *so* beautiful, Charlie. I love you for it," she squealed in her "little girl" voice. Then, she continued, "I almost never get any mail. When I got your note, it just made my whole day worthwhile."

She had waited to tell me that. That was the only reason she was here so late today. I had hoped she would stay and wait. I was glad she had. It was so late that everyone else had gone.

"You *are* sunshine," I said with feeling as I sat in a chair across from her. "I don't know how the hell your name could have gotten left off that list. I'm really sorry."

"It wasn't your fault," she said, pulling her knees up in front of her, wrapping her arms around them, and leaning forward. "You really think I'm sunshine?"

"Yeah," I answered. "You're bright and warm and toasty, aren't you?"

"Do you know how that makes me feel when you say that?"

I laughed.

"Yeah, I guess. Sorta like a toasted marshmallow, right?"

"No, Charlie, really."

Uh, oh—this was serious. She wasn't laughing.

"Do you know how that makes me feel, really?"

I looked at her closely. I looked right into her glittering eyes.

"Yes, I know exactly how it makes you feel," I answered with glowing certainty. "It makes you feel like jumping into the car, driving home, changing into a blouse that makes you look pretty and feel good about yourself, and then racing back here to school and hopping into that big, red chair so you'll be all ready when I come out of my office."

She blushed brightly. Never before had I seen her blush. It was a big, big step, and I was thrilled. Only two weeks before, we had had a serious talk about emotions, and she had told me how difficult it was for her to express her feelings, her person held in paralytic siege by unvented sentiments, a clutter of unrevealed and undeclared emotions imprisoned and suffocating within her. People who think they're worth shit don't go around expressing their innermost feelings. Now, however, she sat there, blushing crimson, a huge smile on her face and a tear in the corner of each eye, a rose in bloom at the dawning of a new day, freshly blessed with two glistening pearl's of morning's waking. I was tickled, too, that I had guessed *exactly* what she had done.

"Oh, you noticed," she bubbled. "I'm so happy you noticed, and I'm so pissed I didn't get away with it. Damn it," she said emphatically, slapping her knee with the palm of her hand. "You notice everything!" There was as much lightheartedness in her voice as there was amazement. "How did you know?"

"Well, when you've seen the same blouse a dozen times," I laughed, "you just sorta notice it's the same old thing."

I never had seen the blouse before. It was a long-sleeve, light blue, nylon blouse with a high ruffled collar and covered buttons. It was very attractive and quite revealing. I knew she never wore a bra. Really, with this blouse, she should have. It wasn't tight, but it was—I didn't want to stare.

"C'mon, Charlie, you bust me every chance you get. This is almost brand new. You know you've never seen it. I've never worn it to school before."

"I know, I just—"

"It does make me feel good about myself. Ya like it?" she asked coyly.

"I like it a lot," I admitted with an accepting nod.

"I knew you would." She gave me an exaggerated wink and a thumbs up sign with one hand. "I was trying to control my own destiny."

It was my turn to blush. She was cute, the little rascal. I barely had noticed. I mean, I knew she was cute, but I never thought of her as *being* cute, if that makes any sense. Maybe during our frequent talks—or when I was kidding her, or scolding her, or drying her tears—I should have spent more time looking and less time listening. Oh, how I had listened! A dollar for every hour I had listened could have eased me into the cushy world of early retirement! And all the time, she was a cutie. Ain't that a grabber? Cute blouse and all, and cute little—

I smiled and looked up. It was a shame. I hated to leave so soon, but—

"Well, now I gotta control *my* own destiny, kid," I said with a stretch. "I gotta get goin'. It's really late, and I'm beat. Ya mind if we cut it short today? I'd like to stay, but—"

"No, I gotta get goin', too," she said. Never, when I said I had to go, did she try to drag things out, stall, delay, or impede my departure. "It *is* late. I think my father's expecting me to make some deliveries for him."

"I gotta get home and figure out how the hell I'm gonna get back here tomorrow morning," I thought aloud.

"Why? Whaddya mean?" she asked.

"I gotta bring my car to the garage for repairs. I need a new generator, probably an alternator, too. I haven't figured out how I'm gonna get back and forth tomorrow. I haven't figured out how I'm gonna pay for it, either," I lamented.

"I'll pick you up," she volunteered without hesitation.

I picked up my briefcase and took a deep breath, trying to assess her unexpected offer. I didn't know if—well.... It would solve my immediate problem, but I didn't want to create another one. There didn't seem to be—

"What time should I come for you?"

.....she went all the way home to change into that blouse.....

"Do you know what time you'd have to get up?" I asked dissuadingly.

I lived at least twenty minutes away, and I was well aware that getting her bones out of the sack in the morning wasn't one of her favorite activities. Like me, she would put off getting up until the last possible moment, usually just seconds before the bladder was about to burst.

"It doesn't matter. What time?" she asked again, pressing for an accepting response.

I hesitated briefly, but not long enough to lose the lift. Why not? I needed the ride, badly.

"It really would be nice, Ann. Thanks."

"Are you kiddin'? It'll be nice to do something for you for a change. You're always doin' something for me, all the time you spend, and everything. What difference does it make what time I get up?"

She meant it. I could tell she was excited and enthusiastic with my acceptance of her offer.

And it wasn't the worst idea for me to be dependent on her for a change.

CHAPTER 5

"I can't believe we're doin' this. We're goin' to the zoo!" The beautiful zoo experience and its horrible aftermath.....

Ann didn't come inside. My wife, Pam, heard the beep of the horn at exactly seven-forty, right on time. Ann never had been to the house before, but she had met Pam and my ten-year old daughter, Jayne, on the A-School hike and camp-out a month before. Pam knew all about Ann and accepted my counseling involvement with her sympathetically. The stories of Ann that I shared with Pam made her an empathetic supporter.

"Ann's here for you, hon," she called from the kitchen.

"Okay, I'm headin' out."

I grabbed my briefcase from the hallway and went into the kitchen to kiss her goodbye. I headed back through the living room, out the front door, and down the front walk steps to the car.

Ann was radiant—excited, bubbly, and spirited. I could tell she had had a smoke on the first leg of her early morning jaunt, from her house to mine. Pleasantly buzzed, she chattered incessantly the entire twenty-minute trip to school in a rolling commentary about the pleasant weather, kids from school, Marilyn and Fran, her camp experiences in New Hampshire, her father's drug store, costume jewelry, and any other thing that chanced to pop into her daffy head. She interrupted her loquacious monologue only long enough to hum or sing a few lines from a show tune or curse a slow driver.

At seven-forty the following morning, we were doing it all over again. My garage man hadn't completed the work on my car, and I had been forced to make last minute arrangements with Ann for a second day of chauffer service.

It was a gorgeous day, unusually mild for the season, even nicer than the day before. As we drove down Forest Avenue toward Route 4, I had a difficult time plotting out the day ahead in my mind, the task to which I usually pledged my behind-the-wheel thoughts each morning. Not being the driver was distracting. Freed from the conditioned routine that forced unconscious repetition and precluded originality, my mind gave space to outrageous thoughts in the same way a humble shopkeeper might splurge his thinking upon finding himself the holder of a winning million dollar lottery ticket.

"U-J-Z-9-0-6, you have an eight-thirty this morning?" I asked with the rhythmic crackle of a ham radio operator, addressing her by the license plate number of the maroon station wagon she handled with familiar ease.

"An eight-thirty?"

"An eight-thirty class, you got?"

"Oh, no—no class until Seminar," she replied.

Yesterday, she had to be in school the same time as I. Today, she had rolled out of bed before she otherwise would have had to, just to pick me up. I felt a little guilty. She had offered the first day's ride. I had begged the second.

"So, ya wanna stop for breakfast?"

"Stop for breakfast?" she asked in surprise, questioning the question. "You mean, and not go to school? What about you? Don't you hafta open up?"

"Marilyn has keys. She can open up. I know she has an eight-thirty class. I've opened up every day since September. It won't hurt for her to do it one time. We hafta go to school, but we can go late. I don't have anything 'til Seminar, either."

"Oh, that's neat," she exclaimed excitedly. "But I just had coffee before I left the house. My mommy is *so* good to me," she swooned in dreamy appreciation. "Let's go to the zoo, instead!"

"The *what?*"

"The *zoo*—the children's zoo in the park, right here!"

She was bouncing up and down behind the wheel with animated anticipation, a puppet jiggling out of control at the end of a string. We were just coming up on the entrance to the county park.

"Turn left!" I yelled commandingly, swept with the contagion of her exuberance. Her idea was even better than mine!

She slowed a little and cut the wheel sharply. Jesus, she made the left turn from the right hand lane!

"Yippeee!" she shouted.

"Jesus Christ, be careful! You know what the hell you just—"

We were both laughing and jumping like two little kids playing in a brand new sandbox.

"This is a pisser!" I said in amazement as we drove through the park entrance. "I can't believe we're doin' this. *We're goin' to the zoo!"*

****

Ann parked the car in the empty parking lot. We walked across the tracks of the children's train ride and into the zoo section of the park. The first thing she spotted was the raccoon cage. Our jovial mood of just a few minutes before acquiesced to the tranquil and serene surroundings, and we talked in hushed voices.

"They're just like the ones that come right into my cabin, you know, in New Hampshire, where I go to camp each summer," she whispered. "They're such cuties, aren't they?"

The place was sedately quiet, no movement or activity except for a few young attendants who moved from one small, fenced-in enclosure to another, busying themselves with their morning clean-up and feeding chores. Most of the leaves already had fallen from the trees, and the sunlight streamed brightly through the bare branches. The droplets of early morning moisture glistened and sparkled on every blade of grass, on every tree trunk, and on the leaves strewn along the pathways. There was crispness in the fresh, still air that was briskly invigorating and crispness under foot as we strolled slowly among the corn flakes Lady Autumn bounteously had spread upon her breakfast table. We indulged ourselves heartily, feasting our senses on the sounds, sights, and scents of Nature's gourmet offerings. We nourished ourselves on delectable treats garnished with the diamond chip sparkle of a billion jeweled dewdrops that seemed to surround us in a fairyland of sugar crystals.

We walked to the left, over the gently arched wooden footbridge, pausing for a moment in the center as the frenzied scurrying and splashing of a flock of wild ducks in the small stream below broke the stillness. We moved on, through the farmyard section of the zoo with its cows, chickens, pigs, sheep, and the two Nubian goats with their noses poked through the slats of the split rail fence to have their heads patted and their necks scratched. We obliged, wishing we had something to feed them, too.

I felt like a royal sovereign in an enchanted kingdom, surveying the livestock of the realm, a princely escort to a fair damsel whose hand I dare not hold lest the laws of the province be violated and the movement be misread. Damn! I wanted to hold her hand or put my arm around her or do something. So, what would be wrong if I took her hand? How awful? Would that hurt someone? What damage would be done by a gesture that simply says, "I like you; you're a nice person?" Would there be something wrong with an innocent, silent token of affection? Wouldn't that be normal and natural?

Yeah, sure. Who was I tryin' to kid? Just a little token of affection, huh? From a male to a female, from a married man to a single girl, from a teacher to a student—Christ, a beautiful morning, a heavenly paradise, caring thoughts, sensitive feelings, and harmless intentions, in a screwed up world that was going to force me to jam my hands into the back pockets of my jeans and assume an air of nonchalance and casual indifference. I was going to have to stuff my feelings and emotions up my rear or down my throat—anywhere—as long as they didn't show, weren't exposed, and were hidden as if they were something of which I should be ashamed.

I wasn't ashamed, but I did what I *had* to do. I bit my tongue and jammed my hands, feeling only my own rump through the inside of my back pockets, fingering the two quarters in the left pocket, slipping the two coins gently between my finger tips, sliding their smooth surfaces silently, softly, one onto the other. I pressed them together and squeezed them tightly, George Washington's metallic image the unlikely benefactor of the felt warmth I had to divert from its intended and proper recipient.

We had made a small circle, and now we crossed back over the stream, using the covered bridge this time, passing a covey of geese and continuing along the pathway past the monkey cage.

"You better stop playing with that, or you'll get acne and go blind," Ann gurgled to the monkey who seemed to be enjoying himself.

I laughed. Ann's recently emerged fresh and blatant humor begged apology from no one and offered no one safe quarter. I gave her a poke in the ribs, and we moved on past the llamas and the ostrich-like rheas.

I could see in the back, behind the enclosures, the brightly painted engine and railroad cars of the kiddy train, retired for now, a splash of color standing against the muted browns and grays of the season. The train looked as if it were savoring the restful quiet and peace that it never had the luxury of enjoying during the spring and summer when kids and tiny tots, ice cream cones in hand and stuffed dolls under arm, piled onto the wooden bench seats of its string of cars. It looked as if it were enjoying this picturesque, late fall morning as much as we were.

On the way out, we chirped and chattered to the yellow-crowned Amazon parrot in the standing bird cage, seeking a squawking response. We reluctantly had to settle for a quick flutter of his brilliant green neck feathers and the disinterested tuck of his head beneath his wing.

We returned to the car and resumed our drive to school in silence, both aware that we had shared a spiritual, almost sacred, experience together.

At two-thirty that afternoon, the zoo was the furthermost thing from my mind. I was in the office where I had just gotten off the phone, the small room so noisy I barely could hear myself talk. Five or six of the kids were in heated debate over menu items for the Thanksgiving feast being planned for next week. I had to make another call, and I was just about to clear everybody out of the office when I looked up and saw Ann in the doorway. Tears streamed down her face. I moved quickly to her, leaving the discussion about whether we should have sweet potatoes or mashed potatoes, or both, behind me.

"Ann, what's the matter?"

"You're not gonna fuckin' believe this," she stammered as I put my arm around her shoulder and backed her out of the doorway.

We headed across the basement to the privacy of the back stairway.

"I didn't tell my father I was takin' the car this morning. And he wanted to use the car today to go play tennis. And when he found out the car was gone, he had a shit-fit. And when I got home for lunch, he was waitin' for me. I mean, he was like a fucking lunatic. And now I can't have the car for a week. And my Seminar got on me because I was late. And my mother was on my father's side. She really wasn't on his side; she just didn't say anything. Everything is all fucked up. I don't even have any good weed left. I was supposed to get some this afternoon, but now I don't even have the car. He got so pissed, just because I took the car. I *always* take the car. He *knows* I take the car. He didn't tell me not to take it today. Fuckin' shit!"

It came in one continuous stream, mixed with tears and sputtering, from one end of the basement to the other. We went through the rear door and sat down on the stairs. We just sat there. I handed her my handkerchief. She wiped her eyes, and we sat.

So excited she had been about doing me a favor, and now she had lost her car for a week. We had had such a beautiful morning together, and now she was in tears. I was as crushed as she was and feeling responsible. We didn't say much. There wasn't a heck of a lot left to say. I wanted to hold her and tell her I was sorry. I wanted to kiss her. I wanted to die. And I didn't want her to feel like a piece of shit. Christ, we had come so far from that. I didn't want to lose it now. I couldn't go through all that again, not from scratch. Christ, *please*—

I kept my arm around her shoulder and stroked my fingers through her long, dark brown hair and let her cry it out.

The next morning, I found her note in my mailbox.

Dear Charlie,

It's been a rather trying day. With the sole exception of the stop we made on the way to school, and a few other rare moments, it's been one big shit brick. Those few other rare moments were you.

It wasn't you who got me in trouble, Charlie. Your auto repair man screwed me, my Seminar screwed me, and I screwed me. Not you. I know you feel bad and you feel like it's your fault. All I can say is please don't.

As far as my punishment goes, it was quite mild compared to what it might have been.

Hell! Not having the car is going to be a hassle, but it's probably the best thing that could have happened. I mean, most of the problems I have with my parents revolve around that car.

Well, that's a tiny piece of all the things I wanted to tell you, but I'm just too zonked to continue. Please excuse the obscenities all over our friend, Mr. Gibran's beautiful stationery. They were just the most expressive words I could find tonight.

Tomorrow will be better.

Love, Ann

It wasn't as bad as I thought it was going to be. Any note from Ann that ended, "Tomorrow will be better," was good stuff.

I didn't overlook the fact that the note was signed, "Love, Ann." I wasn't sure what kind of stuff that was.

* * * * * * *

But the zoo episode wasn't over.

I hadn't given it much thought over the weekend, and when I returned to school Monday morning, I had a lot of other things on my mind. It was going to be a three-day week, with school closed for Thanksgiving on Thursday and Friday. Tomorrow night, Tuesday, was going to be our big Thanksgiving feast.

I worked through the morning, mostly on odds and ends, notes, the bulletin board, phone calls, the last of the Early Decision transcripts, and other assorted items that I wanted to get out of the way so there wouldn't be unfinished business left hanging over the holiday.

After Seminar, I was ready for a break. I collared Harold coming out of Ben's Seminar. Harold always was good for a game of ping-pong. A skilled player and a good sport, he'd take on all challengers, including me, even though I wasn't in the same league. If I really exerted myself, if my game were "on," and if I were lucky, I could stay close to him. Unfortunately, it was a rare occurrence when all three of the ingredients I required for a fighting chance came together at the same time, and he usually disposed of me before working up much of a sweat. Despite his penchant for more formidable competition than I could provide, he always was sport enough to give me a shot, or maybe he just got a sadistic thrill out of beating the crap out of me over and over again.

Today I exerted myself, but it didn't make any difference. It was no contest. He slammed me so many times in the first couple of minutes I thought I had walked into the middle of a turkey shoot. It wasn't until I was on the short end of a 9-2 score that I got my first slam point.

"Your turn to chase," I heckled as he turned to retrieve the ball which had rolled to the far wall.

"Did you have a good time with Ann in the zoo?" I heard the soft whisper in my ear.

I didn't turn immediately. The comment caught me off guard, and I felt my face flush. When I did turn, Julia was already hurrying off. She obviously hadn't asked the question to get an answer.

I lost the next seven points in a row. By the time I recovered, the game was all but over. At 21-8, I put my paddle down on the table.

"Ya wanna go again?" Harold asked mischievously. "I still have another forty-five seconds."

"You're too fuckin' hot," I snapped. "I'll wait 'til ya cool off. Then, I'll take ya left handed. What the hell did you eat for breakfast this morning, buckshot?" I muttered over my shoulder as I walked away from the table.

I didn't know where to go first. I wanted to get hold of Julia, but I wanted to see Ann, too. I looked up on the stage. Neither one was there. I didn't know if either one had a class now or not. Probably not Julia—I had just seen her. Ann, who knows? I stuck my head in the office as I passed by. Nobody. I bounded up the stairs toward the front door and looked around the corner; nobody on the upper steps leading into the Church, either. I pushed open the heavy front door and felt the rush of cold air. Only a few days ago the weather had been beautiful. I stood there for a moment, the door ajar, but there was no one in sight. Fuck! I let the door close with a clunk, and I turned back down the stairs. Why the hell had she opened her mouth to Julia?

I went out to the basement again and walked toward the back, past the dividers that had been arranged to form classroom size cubicles along the wall. I peered into the first section, Janis' parapsychology class, and there was Ann, sitting in the circle of kids. Crap, now I'd have to wait for her to get out.

I went back to the office and puttered around, restless and disgruntled. I couldn't get down to anything serious. I was upset and angry, a caged lion held from its prey, able only to pace back and forth in thwarted, frustrated wait.

When she came to her mailbox a half-hour later, I grabbed her.

"Hi, Charlie, how ya doin'?" she greeted in high-spirited fashion.

"Did you say anything to Julia about us goin' to the park, the zoo?" I launched.

"Huh?"

"The zoo. Did you tell Julia about us goin' to the zoo?"

I hadn't even taken the time to say, "Hi."

"Yeah, I guess I did. Uh, yeah, I told her we stopped there."

"Why the fuck did you say anything?" I bristled invectively, sitting down on the edge of the table in front of the mailboxes.

"Uh, I don't know. Wasn't I supposed to? I mean, I didn't know it was a secret or anything," she spurted, joining me.

"Well, it wasn't a *secret,* but—"

Yvonne and Beth walked past on their way to the office, and we lowered our voices.

"She asked me how come I was late for Seminar, so I told her. I didn't think there was anything wrong."

"So, now, she asks *me*, 'Did you have a good time with Ann in the zoo?' like it was a big fuckin' joke or something."

"Oh, shit, Charlie. I'm *sorry.* I guess I shouldn't have said anything. I didn't think anything was wrong."

"Nothing's *wrong.* It's just—you can't just blab anything to anybody. Shit, man, ya gotta keep your fuckin' mouth shut. She doesn't know what happened in the zoo. She can think anything; she can say anything, and it's lousy. It looks lousy. It's not a case of whether anything's wrong or not. It's a case of trust."

"Trust?"

"Yeah, trust. It's like, when you tell *her*, it's a betrayal of trust, a betrayal of me."

"Shit, Charlie, I told her we stopped at the zoo. Period. It can't be *that* bad. I didn't reveal any atomic secrets or anything," she fired back at me.

It didn't sound so bad when she put it that way. I wondered why I had gotten so pissed.

"Well, it's still better to keep your mouth shut."

I got up and walked away to end the conversation. I had to go somewhere to cool off and give the matter more thought. I left her sitting by the mailboxes. She could give it more thought, too.

She stayed around after school that afternoon as usual, sitting in the red chair while I worked in the office on a time schedule for our second trimester courses. When I finished, I walked out to the stage. I offered her a ride home, but she said she'd walk.

"Oh, come on," I prodded. "You don't wanna walk."

"Nah, I'm in no rush," she replied with cool disinterest. "When I get home, I'll just get axed for something *else* I did wrong, so what's the big hurry?"

I got the dig. Smart and sharp.

She picked up her jacket and a book from the floor next to the chair, and we shuffled across the stage and up the steps to the front door. Everything was very tense and detached. She went through the routine motions with an undisguised stiffness and a spiteful silence that screamed the hurt inside her. Stubborn ass that I was, I ignored it, outwardly holding to the rightness of my anger, inside not sure whether I was right or not. I starved for a face-saving way out, an accommodation of some sort that would fall short of an outright apology.

"Le'me give ya a ride, okay?"

No response.

Damn her! She was milking the silence for every bloody drop of pain she could squeeze out of it. I thought she was shitting me about walking, but all of a sudden I wasn't so sure. If she walked, it would hurt like hell—not her, me.

"All right, I guess, if it's okay with you," she accepted after the extended pause.

"Sure, it's okay. You don't wanna walk," I reasserted. "It's chilly, and it's late….."

She stared at me blankly, knowing full well that neither the temperature nor the time had anything to do with my offer or her delayed and extracted acceptance.

We made the drive in silence. No talk. No chatter. No joint. The only thing we shared was heavy silence, hanging like a dark cloud overhead, threatening a soaking downpour to mat fallen leaves into soggy piles, blocking storm drains and causing rushing swirls to flood along curbsides and into dipped intersections.

In front of her house, her vacuous and uncertain "Goodbye" hit me like a thunderbolt. She lingered for a moment before turning away quickly so I wouldn't see the tear that trickled down her cheek.

God, *now* look. What a fuckin' mess. Everything was all screwed up. Everything was wrong and begging correction. I leaned over and kissed her clumsily on the back of the neck as she stepped out of the car without a word and hurried up the driveway.

On Tuesday morning, I got her note in my juice can mailbox.

> **Dear Charlie,**
>
> **Thanks for the lift! I forgot to say that, didn't I? I guess I really wasn't crazy about the idea of walking home. It was important to me that you knew I wasn't just hanging around for the ride.**
>
> **I was sure that any trust there was between us was all over. It was like a hurricane swept through my soul and destroyed everything inside. I despised myself for ruining the best thing I had,**

and that was my relationship with you. Knowing you has been constant growing and learning. I try to absorb everything you say and—(is emulate the right word?). Well, I guess I got off to a pretty shitty start. Hey! This is *not* a butter up job. I've never dug so deeply into myself.

The memory of what you said to me when we were sitting by the mailboxes will sting for a long, long time. It hurt so much. Betraying *you* (God, I hate the word betraying) was the worst thing I could do.

Well, you live and you learn. At least it finally dawned on me that I'm gonna have to keep a helluva lot more inside. Yes, tomorrow morning Annie starts a new chapter.

When you dropped me off, I saw a tiny ray of sunshine coming through the clouds after the hurricane. I can never thank you enough for that.

I can't believe after all that's gone through my head there's not about 40 pages to this letter. This is about my 12th attempt, so if it looks like Chinese, forgive me! I hope this summarizes how I feel.

Love,

Ann

It wasn't a bad note, except for the part about despising herself and keeping more things inside her. Hell, I had been working my butt off to get her to like herself and to get things out, and now, I mean, if you tell someone to keep their fuckin' mouth shut, what can you expect, especially if she likes you and wants to please you and thinks you're her best friend. I had nobody to blame but myself.

We talked about it that afternoon in the lounge. I tried to negotiate an acceptance of my anger and justify the unbending position I was taking. I just made things worse. It wasn't easy trying to explain that some things were okay to let out, but other things weren't, and why it was okay to spill everything if you were talking to me, but keep your mouth shut as far as anyone else was concerned, especially when I couldn't think of one good reason why. The logic escaped me. It escaped her, too. It wasn't logic. It was foolish. The more I tried to explain the whole situation, the more unexplainable it became. Exasperated and frustrated, I was ripe to pounce on something else. When she made a slightly sarcastic remark about how well she was getting to know me, and how she thought she could predict how I was going to react to something, I attacked with vengeance.

I was at my worst as a counselor and as me. I had been trying to be manipulative and, when that didn't work, I had become childish. Everything was all fucked up. Why was it so hard for me to say I was wrong? Shit. I let her go home feeling confused and hurt. I went home feeling guilty as hell, disappointed and disgusted with myself, and very lonesome, like I had just lost my best friend. Unfortunately, I brought these lousy feelings with me when I returned to school that night for our Thanksgiving feast, so the gala event wasn't as exciting for me as it was for everyone else in attendance. Ann and I generally avoided each other, and I spent most of the evening circulating with Pam and eating so much that I felt as physically uncomfortable and overwhelmed as I did emotionally.

I didn't know what I was going to find in my mailbox on Wednesday morning. I knew I'd find something, but I didn't know whether I wanted to or not.

You don't understand!

A friend of mine once said to me that she knew me "like a book." It really bothered me for a long time because I knew there was a lot more to me that she never saw. I hope you didn't interpret what I said as thinking I knew you like a book. Of course, there's a million things I'll never know about you. What I meant is that I find you really interesting and I like you a lot, so I try to listen to everything you say. I try to know you through that.

God! I wish I could put into words what's going through my head but it's just too dangerous.

Now **can I go to sleep!?!**

Love,

Ann

P.S. Are we still friends?

ZZZZZZZZzzzzzz

"Are we still friends?" I said to myself in amazement. Shouldering the guilt that rightfully was mine to bear, she was worried that *I* might not want to be *her* friend. Jesus, a bastard who treated her the way I had for the past two days didn't deserve such a friend!

I stuffed the note in my pocket and hurried out to the basement. I couldn't wait to see her. Marilyn had opened up early, and quite a few kids already had arrived.

"Have you seen Ann?" I asked Marissa as she passed by.

"Yeah, she's right up there, or she was a minute ago," the tall girl answered. She pointed to the piano on the stage, but there was no one there now.

I hopped up on the stage, anyway. Instinctively, I glanced to the big, red chair, turned away from where I was standing. I could see the top of someone's head. I walked around to the front of the chair and looked down at this little kid with a bashful smile on her face, an anxious look in her eyes.

"I was hiding," she said in her "little girl" voice. "I knew you'd find me, if you wanted to…."

"So, how's my little friend, today?" I chuckled.

"Your little friend is just fine—just like a toasty marshmallow!" she squealed as she jumped up and threw her arms around my neck.

"I'm sorry, Ann—about everything. I'm so sorry. I was just so stupid and—"

"We're still friends, right?"

"If you don't choke me to death, we're gonna be friends for a long, long time. How's that?"

"That's neat-o, just neat-o!"

CHAPTER 6

One day she was sitting on top of the world and singing a loving song; the next day she was in shambles at the bottom of the barrel telling me a story I didn't want to believe.....

God, she could sing!

I had heard her sing before, in the car and around school a little, but now I heard her *really* sing.

It had been one of those sluggish December days for me, the kind that starts at seven-thirty in the morning with the slow, uncertain grind of your engine as you sit shivering behind the wheel, your fingers crossed, and your breath fogging the windshield. Officially, it wasn't even winter yet, but the frigid bite of the wind and the heavy overhang of bleak clouds, the sun trying to break through a gun metal gray sky, announced the season's early arrival with unmistakable smart, and I knew things were going to get worse before they got any better.

A lot of kids were staying late after school again. There wasn't much doing anywhere else. As far as general attitude was concerned, A-School students, like students in any school at this time of year, were trapped in the no-man's-land between Thanksgiving, which had come and gone with its turkey feast and all the trimmings—including, if I remember correctly, *baked* potatoe*s*—and the Christmas holiday, still a trifle too far away to spark any excitement.

But as far as school activity was concerned, the A-School lived. We had concluded our first trimester courses, and a whole new array of second trimester classes had begun. The kids were excited about putting on the school's first stage presentation, *The Prime of Miss Jean Brodie,* for which cast tryouts were starting. Ping-pong had become so popular, and the games so clamorous and disturbing to classes in session on the basement floor, that it had to be banned until after three-thirty.

My work in the office was keeping me at school long into the afternoon, even with the addition of Betty, the mother of one of our students, who unselfishly volunteered her time and energy as our unofficial secretary and our official comic relief. Betty was as sharp as a tack and as fast as the crack of a whip, a clown but no fool. Affectionately called Betty Boop, she was a treasure, a much needed help to me, and a friend to all. Even with Betty's assistance, however, there were certain things, such as high school permanent record cards, college applications, recommendations, and transcripts, that I had to take care of myself.

It was after five when I decided to pack it in for the day. I knew a lot of kids had stayed late. I had heard their racket earlier. But now, as I walked out of the office, the general noise level had subsided. I could hear singing, and I muttered under my breath why they had to play their radios so offensively loud.

When I reached the front of the basement, I stopped dead in my tracks. I couldn't believe my eyes or my ears.

There was Ann, strutting the stage as if she owned it, punctuating her words and lines with stops and turns, belting out a song with all the gusto, pizzazz, distinctive facial expressions, and charismatic body movements of Barbra Streisand, the super show-stopper she idolized.

"Oh, my man, I love him so.....he'll never know....."

Holy Christmas! Everybody stood and watched. Halfway through the song, they even stopped playing ping-pong, the ultimate tribute! I walked to the center of the basement floor and sat down on a folding chair, clutching both sides of the metal seat with my hands, staring straight ahead. It simply was an incredible performance!

"Holy shit," Brian whispered next to me. "Look at that."

".....for whatever my man is.....I am his.....for—ev—er more."

Her last notes blended into the clapping and cheering of the group of amazed spectators. It wasn't exactly a standing-room-only audience, maybe eleven or twelve kids and myself, but damn! We all knew we had been treated to a stunning show, like hearing Barbra Streisand herself. But it wasn't Barbra; it was Ann!

Everything started to fall into place, a jigsaw puzzle assembling in my mind, the straight-edge pieces now beginning to fit together and frame new meaning. All the shows she always talked about, the shows she had been in at camp in New Hampshire where she went each summer, first as a camper and later as a bunk counselor and water ski instructor—*The Wizard of Oz, Guys and Dolls, Sound of Music, Pajama Game*—I couldn't remember them all now. And the shows in town with the Jewish Community

Center Players—Rosemary, the lead in *How to Succeed* two years ago, and Grandma Tzeitel in *Fiddler* last year. And for the past month she had been going to rehearsals every night with the Teen Drama Group at the Hackensack Y with whom, last January, she had played Sandy, the lead in *Grease.* Son-of-a-bitch! She had told me all the stories a hundred times. I had listened, but I hadn't paid much attention. Camp shows were camp shows. I knew she had to be good. I mean, for someone her age to get lead roles with the Community Center Players, an experienced adult group, and to play a *grandma* last year at age *17*, she had to have something going for her. But I had no idea, no idea at all, she had *that* kind of voice and *that* kind of stage presence.

"That felt.....good!" she heaved, trying to catch her breath.

She had hopped down from the stage and had crossed over to where Brian, Marlene, and I were sitting, other kids stopping her along the way to congratulate her, say nice things, and slap her on the back.

"Really good, really good, really good," Brian applauded.

"Great, Ann," Marlene seconded.

"Wow, you can *really* sing," I exclaimed, shaking my head in wonderment.

She beamed back, as proud as punch. This fucked up kid, who thought she was worth shit, was dynamite. Placed on a stage, she had the confidence and poise of a professional. Put in a role, she forgot who she was or who she thought she was. She could be anyone she wanted to be. She was like three different people—the Ann I knew, the Ann everybody else knew, and the Ann on stage who could adopt a character and make herself it.

"That's my favorite song. I love all of Barbra's songs, but that's my absolute favorite," she exuded.

"That was something else," I whistled, still a little dumbfounded. "You're really *good.* I've heard you sing before, but never anything like that."

"Oh, I love you; you're the tops, Charlie. Tell me again how good it was."

She said it in the mimicking "little girl" voice she now used less frequently than she previously had.

Now, I understood. Now, I knew. How could I have been so *dumb*? How could I have been so dumb *for so long*? The kid was on stage. She had her own portable stage built into her head. She could pull her stage out and hop up on it anytime she wanted. If she played the role of a little girl, she didn't have to be Ann. She didn't have to be nervous, she didn't have to feel insecure, she could say I was the tops without being afraid or embarrassed, and she could say, "I love you," right in front of everybody and get away with it. Son-of-a-fuckin'-bitch!

"I love you, too, you little knucklehead," my little boy's voice squeaked in humorous reply.

So there—I could do it, too. I could say anything *I* had a mind to. But the joking words were hardly out of my mouth before I felt a sobering sweep of guilt. *It wasn't a game.* She was doing what she *had* to do. *I* could make a *game* of it, but to *her* it was a way of surviving; it was who she was, and it wasn't a very good idea for me to toy with that.

I backed off.

"What kind of voice is that, your singing voice? What's it called, musically?"

"I'm a lyric soprano or mezzo soprano, with a range from D below middle C to high C. That's the official poop," she laughed, but there was a lot of pride in her answer.

"Well, it was unbelievable, that's all I can say. I wish I had it on tape."

"I *have* it on tape—not that, but that song," she said excitedly. "I did 'My Man' when I was in junior high—remember, Brian?—in the spring musical review. We did all the songs from *Funny Girl.* I had a solo. My mother taped it."

"I remember," Brian nodded vigorously. "How could I forget?"

Ann grinned from ear to ear and swished her hair, a smiling daisy with an upturned face dancing atop a slender stem.

"Man, I'd sure like to hear it," I said.

"Me, too," said Marlene with enthusiasm. "Can ya bring it in?"

"If you want," Ann beamed, her pleasure obvious. "You both can listen to it, if ya want. I think it was great, but my father said he didn't think it was that hot," her voice trailed.

So, what else was new?

"You gotta be kidding," Brian said with alarm. "It brought down the house. There were a thousand people in the audience."

I looked up. It was gone. The exuberance was gone. Her face was blank. She wasn't on stage any more. Ann was back.

"C'mon, kid. Ya have the car, or do ya need a ride?"

"I guess I could use a lift," she said glancing at her watch. "Holy shit, I didn't think it was so late."

"Then, smile, and go get your coat. What about you two?"

Marlene and Brian both nodded acceptance.

"And don't forget your books," I added before Ann had time to step away.

"Me?" she questioned with a laugh and a broad grin. "No homework for me tonight. I've got a rehearsal for *Sweet Charity*. I gotta be in Hackensack by six-thirty. I'm not even gonna have time to eat."

At least she was smiling, again.

****

She was singing a different tune the next day. This time she wasn't "on stage," she wasn't smiling, and the song grieved the sorrow of a requiem. It hadn't started out that way.

It was late in the afternoon again, so late that almost everyone already had gone, except for two or three kids hanging around the ping-pong table with their coats on, ready to leave. Ann was in her red chair, and I was sitting across from her. We had been talking quietly for about ten minutes. Shortly after the others had gone up the stairs and the door had clunked shut behind them, our conversation had turned to Mike.

"We were sorta like—well, we're definitely good friends. We have so much in common—the acting, the music, and all. I mean, if you're not into the theatre, you just can't understand it. We talk about tryouts, rehearsals, cast parties, auditions, disappointments, you know. We really like each other." She hesitated. "We made love together."

I nodded.

She fiddled with her sneakers and kicked them off.

"A little while back," she said, shaking her head from side to side. "We tried, but, I don't know, everything was really strange. The next thing I know, he had a *boyfriend*," she muttered. "I mean, we're still good friends, but—"

"Nice."

"Yeah, nice," she choked. "It made me feel like….."

"Don't say it, damn it. Don't you dare say—"

"…..like a piece of shit," she concluded, defiantly. "Sometimes it's better to just say it and get it out, Charlie. That's what you've wanted me to do, right?"

She was right. I guess I was trying to save *myself.* Who was I trying to kid?

"I know," I confessed.

"It's really hard for me to deal with," she said dryly. "Now, sometimes, I see him at parties with his boyfriend, Johnny."

As she talked, she had been squirming and shifting herself in the chair, pulling her legs up beneath her and curling herself tighter and tighter into a ball. Now she sat sideways in the chair, almost in a fetal position, facing away from me. I knew she was crying. I pulled my chair closer to hers and reached out. I put my hand on her foot and gave it a squeeze.

"I know it hurts, kid."

"It hurts so much, Charlie, you can't even begin to know," she rejected between breathy intakes.

"I know."

"No, no, you don't. You don't know, not everything, not anything."

There was a long pause before she uncurled herself and turned around again toward me. She sat rigid in the chair, a coiled spring. Her voice was terse.

"You wanna know? You *really* wanna know everything, and know how much I hurt?"

I swallowed deeply, but there was nothing to swallow. My mouth was dry. The moisture was in my palms. I saw her brush away the tears from her eyes, but her cheeks were still streaked. She sniffled.

"Whatever you wanna tell me. If you wanna get it all out, that's okay," I offered.

I provided the opportunity. That was the easy part. I feared what I might be in for. I didn't know what to expect. I knew she had the guts to tell me anything. I didn't know if I had the guts to hear whatever was coming.

"Whaddya wanna know first? Ya wanna know how I was raped when I was fourteen? That's nice, too, huh?"

I didn't answer.

"A couple of summers ago, my girlfriend and I were hitching down the shore, and these two guys picked us up." The tears streamed down. "That was my introduction to the beautiful world of sex, in the front seat of a fuckin' car, having my head pushed down on this freak's cock. I wanted to bite his fuckin' cock off, but it was too disgusting, so I just choked on it."

I didn't say anything. I couldn't. I was frozen.

"And I could hear my girlfriend screaming in the back seat. Everything—everything happened so damn fast. The next thing—the next thing I know, I'm being yanked and pulled and dragged over the seat, and I'm in the back and this fuckin' bastard is—he's on top of me, pulling my pants, yanking and shoving and pulling and pushing, pushing his hand in my face and smothering me with my own underpants, and groping and grabbing and shoving himself inside of me and hurting me—the fuckin' asshole—hurting me something awful, and laughing, and then cheering, 'Yea!'—the fuckin' bastard."

She sat glaring and crying, her fingernails digging into both arms of the upholstered chair, her nostrils dilated, her eyes bulging, and her chin set firmly as if chiseled in stone, cold and ragged, a sculpture of agony. She was feeling it all over again—the hurt, the anger, and the humiliation. My knees buckled as I got up awkwardly and sat down on the arm of the chair next to her. I put my arm around her shoulder. I released her clutch on the chair. I took her trembling hand in mine and rested it on my trembling knee. We were both a mess.

"It was awful. He got what he wanted—even more. He took it—thought it was funny I was.....new. Yeah, a big joke it was. The fuckin' guy cheered when he broke me. He shot his fuckin' stuff, and then the bastards threw the both of us out on the side of the fuckin' road, like two bags of garbage."

She sat stiffly for a moment longer. Then she just swayed and let herself topple sideways against me. She leaned forward, resting her forehead on my knee, exhausted, embarrassed, and sobbing. She stayed like that for quite a while as I rubbed her back and tried to soothe her.

My heart ached, and my insides revolted. I felt nauseated. My mind strayed, trying to get away, trying to run like a frightened child fearing further punishment. My eyes darted in a desperate search for a hideaway, a distraction, a place to go where I didn't have to think about it, a haven safe from instant replays and the cruel remembering of her words.

I looked around the stage. The faded lithograph, a seascape, hung at a careless angle on the wall—wrong—its beat-up frame crying to be straightened. The couch—the couch was wrong, too. It didn't look like it did yesterday. It didn't look soft and comfortable like the handsome back seat of a spiffy sedan. It looked awful, a pitiful castoff, threadbare and worn, raped of its past elegance, dumped on a curb, swept up by ghoulish scavengers, and yanked, pulled, pushed, shoved, and dragged into a church basement to have greasy potato chips and slimy liquids stain its spotted and frayed covering, to be uncaringly smirched and scuffed by dirty sneakers, to be ripped by ball point pens protruding from back pockets, and to be damaged and humiliated. The soda machine was wrong—a fickle robot with mechanical innards that one day could be trusted to answer the call of your last coin with a gush of carbonated respite and the next day left you standing empty-handed, cheated, hurt, and angry, wanting to smash your fist against the false promises inscribed on its shell and kick its carcass across the room until it apologized for its cruel violation of trust. It was wrong—wrong, wrong, wrong! The chair was wrong, too, its broken lower rung hanging limp, like it was waiting for someone to cheer, "Yea!" And the fuckin' bookcase next to it—an untidy receptacle for the leftovers of yesterday's lunch, a dung heap of brown paper bags and crumbled balls of waxed paper that made its shelves choke and gag in disgust.

I couldn't get away from it. The heartache was everywhere. Everything had been raped. I couldn't escape the hurt, the crying, and the humiliation. Everything was filthy, like the rug. Wrong, everything wrong. The inside of the refrigerator smelled like worn underpants. The bastard! He took her and broke her and fucked her. Why did he hafta fuckin' fuck her, the fuckin' fuck-head?"

"So, then, I met this guy at camp….."

Her head was still down, and she spoke softly and haltingly into my knee, her voice muffled but calm. Her words were forced between labored breaths.

"…..who I really liked a lot, and we tried—we tried to make love, and he had a lot of trouble, and he couldn't—he couldn't do it, and he said there was something—something wrong with me. He said I was…..too small."

Her back heaved under my hand, and she broke down again, her body trembling and lurching as she tried to catch her breath and cry at the same time.

"And then Mike and I—we get together, and then he starts—the fuck—he starts going out with….." She raised her head to scream out the last few words, "…..a fuckin' *boy*!"

She rested her head back down on my knee.

"Ssshhhhhhhh, baby," I said. "You're okay."

I rubbed both of my hands back and forth over her back, and I leaned over and kissed her neck. I didn't know what else to do. I felt helpless.

"Now you know how I hurt? I hurt so fuckin' much, I can hardly stand it. I don't even wanna live. I wish I were dead."

I looked down at the back of her head, at the bent-over back of this poor, pathetic creature clinging to my leg. She had bared her soul, and now she sobbed quietly, emotionally drained, embarrassed, and broken, her stem snapped at midpoint, her face downward, a flower wilted. Tears rolled down my cheeks, too. She didn't deserve this. Yesterday she was the happiest I ever had seen her, singing, shining, and sitting on top of the world. And now she was in shambles at the bottom of the barrel.

As I sat looking at her, I remembered when first she had mentioned her childhood leg brace to me. Her leg and hip treatment had involved extensive X-rays, and her mother had made a casual remark to her, only a month or so ago, about having children, and whether she even could. She was shattered then and shattered now. I hoped she didn't remember, but she did.

"So, whaddya think?" she asked as she bolted to an upright position and looked at me. Her eyes were puffy and swollen, her face wet, her voice shaky. "I was raped, I'm too small, I turn guys gay, and I might not be able to have children, anyway. I'm good enough to get fucked over, but I'm not good enough to get fucked. Ain't that a pisser?"

It was the first time I heard her really feel sorry for herself. I couldn't blame her. Shit, it had to be better than holding it in. It took everything I had to stifle the urge to respond with impulsive stupidity. It was *killing* me. I wanted to tell her she wasn't raped. I wanted to deny the undeniable, to tell her she was wrong, to disbelieve the truth—the horrible, sickening truth. It was dumb and idiotic. I couldn't believe my own thoughts. I felt the victim of a strange juxtaposition of mental processes: my thinking was rational enough to know my thoughts were irrational. I wanted to tell her it didn't happen. I wanted her to *believe* it didn't happen.

I struggled to keep my mouth closed, to disengage my tongue, to dare not utter the frenzied and absurd jumble of my brain's rage, so I wouldn't sound like a complete asshole. I wanted to tell her she wasn't too small, that I *knew* she wasn't too small. How the fuck was *I* supposed to know how small she was?

The craziness whirled in my head like a wad of soggy garments tumbling out of control in a clothes dryer stuck in the spin-dry cycle. Somebody turn the fucking thing off! You can have all the children you want. You don't turn guys gay. I'm not turned off. You're good enough to get fucked. I'll fuck you. You're not too small. Look, watch, you'll see. Holy shit! Around and around, faster and faster, my head whirled in a blur of insanity. I gotta hold on, hold things together. Is this what it's like to go off your rocker? Grab hold. I gotta get back. Push the OFF button. OFF, damn it! Easy, Charlie, ya can't give what ya can't give—and you're not gonna fuck anybody, asshole. Hold on, that's it. Slow, baby.....slooooow. What a trip! That was a fuckin' ride. That was nuts! Thank God *that's* over. Whew! But you *would* fuck her if it made her feel better, wouldn't you? Shut up! It's OFF. Shut the fuck up. I pushed OFF! Breathe, settle down—easy, now. That's it, nice 'n easy.

"And there's one more thing, too," I managed to choke from a parched throat. I had to say something. I couldn't just sit there.

She looked at me, out of countenance, a mixture of puzzlement and surprise furrowing her brow.

"Like what? There's more?" she questioned with skepticism.

"Yeah, there's more. There's one thing more," I replied softly. "You forgot to add to your list that you're one fine person, one of the nicest people I've ever known."

Jesus, I didn't know whether she was so much down on herself that she'd just say, "So, who the fuck cares?" or whether it would make any difference to her one way or the other.

"Thank you, Charlie," she whispered appreciatively.

The tears started again, but there was no difficult breathing, no bodily convulsions, no head down embarrassment this time. She just sat there facing me, the droplets rolling down both sides of her face and dripping from her chin.

"Thank you," she repeated. "You're the tops."

No, I wasn't the tops. I was a damn fool for not throwing my arms around her, kissing her, and telling her I loved her. But I was scared, and married, and I didn't think I loved her.

It would have been worth the lie, anyway.

CHAPTER 7

Prelude to Christmas and the first annual A-School holiday party: Whoever heard of a party with good weed and no Ann. She was what?.....

With the end of first trimester courses came the end of "Discovery!" No one wanted it to end, but it did. Courses for the second trimester began on schedule, but there were still a lot of kids who talked about reviving the "Discovery!" class. It seemed quite out of the question, really, since everyone had a new schedule, and there was no time in the day when all eighteen of us were free at the same time. That had been my only stipulation when the issue of continuing the course had been belatedly raised: all eighteen had to be able and willing to continue together.

Dear Charlie,

Somehow, three days of every week never feel complete anymore. "Discovery!" really started off my day in the right way. I would walk out of class with a warm feeling. Now, "Neurotic Personality" just gives me

> **the shakes. I know it is impossible to hold regular classes during the day (at least this trimester) but maybe we can meet at night. I know others feel the same way. It was the one class where everyone was important. Let's try!**
> **Barbara**

"Hey, Barb," I called across the basement. "Got your note."

"Good, hold on a sec—I'll be right there."

Barbara was a good kid. Christ, they all were good! We had *some* group, not just in "Discovery!" class, but in the whole school. I looked around at the kids in the basement as I waited for Barbara. There wasn't a bad egg in the crowd. Man, they were different—all different and very different—but what a bunch! That's not to say we didn't have a few who broke the rules from time to time and had to be disciplined, but what group of a hundred and five teenagers doesn't have a few like that.

Barbara was a quiet leader. She wasn't the *most* popular student in the school, but she was well-liked and respected. She was the kind of kid who got things done without a lot of noise or gaudy fanfare. She was a pretty girl, a friendly person, and an enthusiastic student. She didn't hang around a lot after school—I think she had a part-time job—but she was involved, and she took the A-School seriously.

"I don't have any problem with a class at night," I said as she approached. "I think it's a great idea, but I don't know about everyone else."

"I'm pretty sure they'll go for it," she responded happily. "I've already checked with a few, but I wanted to make sure it was okay with you before I went any further."

"If you'll do the checking, it's okay with me, as long as everyone agrees on the same night." I shook my head, doubtfully. "I don't know, Barb. I think it's gonna be tough. The only night I *can't* make it is Thursday. Any other night in the week is fine. But, don't forget," I cautioned, "You gotta come back to me and say, 'Everybody, *everybody* agrees on such and such night,' okay?"

Two days later she came back.

"Everybody agrees on Sunday night."

"Everybody?" I questioned, seeking absolute assurance.

"Everybody."

"Okay, we're on—every Sunday night, from seven o'clock until whenever, for, uh, as many Sundays as everyone wants," I outlined spontaneously.

"That's the deal?" she questioned, now *her* turn to seek absolute assurance.

Was there anything else to add? No, nothing I could think of.

"That's the deal," I confirmed.

"Then that's the deal!" she flourished with obvious glee.

We both laughed and shook hands heartily, like two wily businessmen who had just agreed on the selling and the buying of the Brooklyn Bridge, and she hurried away to spread the news.

* * * * * * *

Christmas was weird at the Alternative School. Everybody looked forward to the vacation, but it wasn't like in the regular school where you couldn't wait to get the hell out, and you wished you never had to come back. Christmas at the A-School meant a branch from a fir tree jammed into a bottle on top of the bookcase in the lounge. It meant less people going out to Blimpie's for hero sandwiches and more people bringing in colorful cookie tins or holiday wrapped boxes with exotic homemade treats and sweets to share with each other at lunchtime. It meant kids asking if they could get physical education credit if they went ice skating at Rockefeller Center. It meant a general outpouring of love, warmth, and giving within an environment where "asshole" still remained as much a term of endearment as one of degradation. And it meant mailboxes stuffed with Christmas cards and notes of holiday greetings and wishes of good cheer. It meant a note from Lisa:

> **Dear Charlie,**
>
> **A note to say how glad I am to be working with you this year and how happy I feel to know a person as unusual and wonderful as you.**
>
> **Thanks for all your support.**
>
> **Peace, health, and happiness to you in the coming year.**
>
> **Have a *restful* vacation.**
>
> **Much love,**
> **Lisa**

And there was a note from Judith. Judith, my best student friend coming into the Alternative School, the only one who knew me well enough to stand up with a twinkle in her eye and confront me about the empty juice cans at the picnic on that sunny day back in June.

But now, after almost four months of A-School operation, Judith believed she had become a casualty of all my office work and, especially, of all the time I had devoted to Ann. Despite the fact that she and I frequently had seen each other and talked together, and we both had served on the Steering Committee for the first trimester, and I had spent a lot of time with her when she was working on her applications for college, things weren't the same. She believed she was the victim of my neglect and had been hurt by it very deeply. It took a big person to leave me a note before the holidays:

> **Dear Charlie,**
>
> **Whatever has happened these past three months is over, "the storm has ended," as they say. I think you understand what I mean, and right now I can't really verbalize it. As I told George in Seminar last week, not all worthwhile experiences are easy to go through and I think I speak from experience.**
>
> **Anyway, a BIG thanks for your college application help; because of it, things were a lot easier on me than on most. But, more importantly, thanks for everything—and if you know what rest is (sometimes I wonder), try and get some this vacation. I'm leaving tomorrow for grandma's, so merry Xmas and happy new year and I'll see you in January.**
>
> **Judith**

> **For all the times you missed lunch because of me, for one reason or another.....**

A Snickers bar, my favorite candy treat, was attached.

It meant a quick, last day of school, note from Barbara:

> **Dear Charlie,**
> **I didn't have a chance to say good-bye—so bye-bye. Have a happy!!**
> **Love—**
> **Barbara**

It meant an unsigned note in Ann's unmistakable handwriting on a spiral notebook page that echoed the past and presaged the future, revealing her to be caught somewhere between:

> **I feel so deeply for you, Charlie. That's what's so dangerous to put in words. I don't know why, but I've been taught to suppress those kinds of feelings.**

And it meant, above all and best of all, that when we all came back from vacation on Wednesday, January 2, we would have to wait only two more days for the first annual Alternative School holiday party at the house of Betty Boop!

****

There wasn't supposed to be any pot at the party, but the place reeked. They handled it discretely, out on the front stoop, in the bathroom, and upstairs in the bedroom. It never was in sight, but it was there. The pot was there, but Ann wasn't, and that in itself was an ironical twist. Whoever heard of a party with good weed and no Ann? Even my wife, Pam, noticed Ann's absence.

By now, Pam was a familiar face to the A-School kids. She had gone on the hike and camp-out, and she had gotten dressed up in costume like everyone else and had been at the Halloween party when the ping-pong table had collapsed with an overload of sitters. She had helped with the Thanksgiving feast, and now she was with me at Betty Boop's party. We drifted, sometimes together and sometimes separately, from one platter of food to another, from one raunchy joke to another, from one room to another, and back to the punch bowl and the noise, chatter, and traffic in and out of the bathroom. A round trip took about a half hour; we went around more than once.

"No, I have absolutely no idea where the hell she is," I answered with agitated concern.

"Nobody does," said Pam. "Are you worried?"

"I wasn't an hour ago, but I am now," I acknowledged, looking at my watch. "It's twenty after ten, for cryin' out loud."

Pam nodded. She knew well of Ann's erratic behavior and generally dispirited state. When Ann had expressed misgivings about the approaching holiday season and the absence of any family plans to celebrate the New Year, I had mentioned it to Pam, and we had decided to set an extra place and invite Ann to our house for our traditional dinner on New Year's Day. Ann came, in a *dress,* mind you, with an appropriate box of candy, as happy as a lark. I don't even think she was stoned! She stayed to help with the dishes and play with my kids until late in the evening. That had been only a few nights ago. Tonight there was a bash, and she was nowhere to be found.

"I'm not afraid she's gonna miss the party," I continued. "This fuckin' thing will go on forever."

"Charlie, come here," Julia called from the kitchen.

"No way, sweetie," I called back over the din. I suspected what probably was going on in the small kitchen off the dining room, and it was best I didn't see it or get involved. They had been trying to turn me on to grass for the past two months. "No way."

"No, really, I'm serious. There's someone on the phone for you. I don't know who it is. C'mon," she pleaded.

Surprisingly, there was no one else in the kitchen when I got there. Julia handed me the phone and waited a second, then left.

"Hello?"

"Hello, this is Terri," I heard on the other end of the line.

"Terri?"

"Terri, Ann's friend."

"Oh, yeah, Terri. Hi, Ter, what's up?"

"Listen carefully, and take it easy."

"Something's happened to Ann, hasn't it? I knew it. What happened?"

"Listen to me—"

"I'm listening!" I yelled back. "What the fuck's the matter? What happened, for Christ's sake?"

"Ann called me from New York. She told me to call you. She didn't know the number there, and she had no way to look it up. She was arrested."

"She was what?"

"She was arrested. They took her to a police station. She's gotta go to night court."

"What the hell did she do?" I queried as I clenched the receiver and shouted into the mouthpiece.

"I'm not exactly sure. She was upset and crying. I think she got caught selling pot to someone."

"Holy fuckin' Christ! I don't believe it!" I turned to Pam who had followed me into the kitchen and was at my side. "She got arrested."

"Listen, she's got a lawyer," Terri continued. "They assigned her a lawyer, and she's gettin' out. She said to tell you that she's gonna get there, so wait for her."

"She's comin' here? Oh, Jesus. Okay, all right. Holy Christ."

"Don't be mad at her, okay, Charlie? She's pretty upset and scared."

"Okay, thanks. I'll wait. Thanks, Terri, thanks a lot. Yeah, no, I won't. Okay. Terri? Ter? Shit."

I slammed the receiver onto the wall hook.

"Can you fuckin' believe that?" I said to Pam who was now holding me and trying to cover my mouth. "Can you fuckin'—"

"Take it easy. Everybody will hear," she cautioned.

"Can you fuckin' believe that asshole got arrested? Holy good night."

****

Ann walked through the front door at a quarter after one. The party had moved into high gear, latecomers now indistinguishable from those who had arrived early, both groups glowing equally, the indulgence of good food, rich desserts, spiked punch, and heavy smoking turning inhibitions aside.

"Hey, look who's here!" someone shouted.

There was so much noise, only a few people heard. But I had been waiting for two hours or more, biding in quiet suffer, just to hear those words. It didn't seem like two hours; it seemed like two *years*.

She played her entrance like an Academy Award performance.

"Hello! Hello!.....How the hell are ya?.....Watcha doin', sweetie?.....Hi, there, sports fans.....Yeah, better late than never.....Any food left for little Annie?.....Hello, hello, hello.....So, what's been goin' on?.....Remember, now, no pot.....Ha, ha, ha.....No, no thanks.....wait 'til I take my coat off.....Up your ass, Richard; stick it where the sun don't shine.....Yeah, I thought it was next week."

She weaved her way through the crowd like an actress at a premier, acknowledging everybody, answering everybody, sassing everybody—never stopping—kissing everybody, and raising her middle finger high in the air with a raucous laugh when she spied Julia. She didn't miss a trick. With every hug and every turn, she scanned the room, surveying the scene, and I knew she was looking for me.

I hadn't missed a trick, either. Pam and I had situated ourselves in the farthest corner of the living room, away from the door but still within sight of it. I knew that after Ann had made her grand entrance and had sweet-talked her way through the mob, she could leave everybody behind and get to me in the quiet corner, and I could find out what had happened.

"What in God's name happened to you?" I begged in a whisper after she had concluded her greetings with appropriate aplomb.

"Are you okay, Ann?" Pam questioned. At times like this, Pam was always more compassionate than I.

"Yeah, I'm okay," Ann lied, biting her lip to hold back tears. "Did Terri call you?"

"Yeah, about two hours ago. I didn't—"

"Ya think it would look bad if we all went out for a walk?" she choked. "I don't think I can fake this much longer."

"Good idea," I answered as I got up and grabbed our coats from the end of the sofa. "Let's get the hell outta here."

The three of us made our way through the crowd of kids and out the door. Pam sat down on the front steps.

"Go ahead," she said, "You two take a walk. I'll wait here."

Damn, it was cold. It was like stepping out of a furnace and into an icebox, stepping away from cramped bodies, exhaled breaths, and enclosed warmth and into the bone-chilling shiver of freezing pre-dawn—into a murky, foggy, frozen daiquiri of heavy sweetness that nipped the senses and stung the lips.

Ann and I walked to the corner and turned left up the block.

"Oh, Charlie," she blurted, "It was fuckin' awful. I was in a cell. They put me in a fuckin' cell. They locked me up with a half dozen prostitutes. They were kids, teenagers, and they fuckin' thought I was one of them!"

She started to cry.

"What happened?" I asked slowly, emphasizing each word. "*What happened?*"

"I 'turned on' this guy in the park. I mean, I drove into the City to make a buy, and then, when I was in the park—this guy looked like a kid. He didn't look like a narc."

"Where was this, Washington Square Park or Bryant Park, behind the library?"

"Bryant."

It didn't make any difference. They both were cesspools, one as bad as the other.

"You went to Bryant Park and 'turned on' a narc. Beautiful! He looked like a kid, huh? Did ya think a narc wore a police uniform and a sign around his neck, 'Beware of Narc'?"

I didn't know whether to laugh or cry. How could anyone be so fuckin' stupid? Bryant Park was an inglorious patch of lawn which gave credence to the old line about the grass always being greener over the septic tank. A vest-pocket park, its boundaries were too porous to hold back the seepage of moral degeneracy from adjacent 42nd Street. Its debasing element of dope pushers and pimps turned every tree and bench into a mart for the exchange of money for drugs or sex. Noted for its illicit traffic and its no-questions-asked transactions, the park was a favorite buy site for kids from New Jersey who came to the City by car through the Lincoln Tunnel or by bus into the Port Authority Terminal.

"Yeah, the fuckin' bastard busted me and took me to the station house, and I got locked up with a bunch of prossies for three hours waitin' to go to night court."

"Holy shit."

"And they fingerprinted me and took mug shots and made me feel like a fuckin' criminal. And they took my pot. I just paid—"

"But ya got out."

"Yeah, they gave me a lawyer, and he told me not to worry. When we went to night court, he told me to keep my fuckin' mouth shut, and he'd get me out. Charlie, I had to give him your name as my guardian."

She reached into her coat pocket and took out a lawyer's business card and a yellow form from the Criminal Court of the City of New York. She handed them to me. The card identified Richard B. Weitzen as a Legal Aid Society attorney at law. The form was the defendant's copy of an order adjourning court action in contemplation of dismissal in six months provided the defendant was not guilty of a further violation during that period.

"Holy Christ."

"But you only have to be my guardian for six months."

"Great."

"He gave your name to the judge….."

"Holy shit!"

"…..and your address."

"Holy shit, my address, too?" I moaned in disbelief.

"Shit, Charlie. I can't let my parents find out."

The urgency in her voice provided the emphasis and punctuated her exasperation.

"Christ, why didn't you just tell 'em I was a teacher so I'd lose my job and get the whole fuckin' thing over with," I said cuttingly.

"I did," she said quietly. "I had to."

"Oh, my God!"

She had been crying off and on, but now, as we reached the corner and turned left again, the freezing cold and the reliving of the story got the best of her. Her body trembled and shook. I watched the quivering of her lips, and, when the tears started to flow, I took her in my arms and held her close to my chest.

"Please don't hate me, Charlie. I'm so sorry."

"I don't hate you, Ann. How could I hate you? I just feel so sorry for you. I want everything to be okay for you. I don't want you to be in trouble. I want you to sing. I want you to be happy."

She wiped her eyes on my jacket and looked up at me. God, I wanted to kiss her.

"Will ya kiss me, just one, teeny-weeny, little kiss?" she asked softly, still shivering against me.

I was shaking, too, with cold and with fright.

"A teeny-weeny, little kiss? No, I don't think so. I'll kiss you like sunshine," I said.

Oh, God, did *that* ever sound corny—like soap opera fluff that makes you gag or want to puke. But it wasn't. It was honest. It was how I felt.

"I'll kiss you like sunshine kisses the leaves," I whispered.

I did.

CHAPTER 8

There was uneasiness at my house, and there was uneasiness at Ann's house, but all was well at the Alternative School. And then there was the night of the snow storm.....

The party was the blast everyone had expected it to be, so much so that Kohoutek was all but forgotten. Despite the advance publicity and the media-hype that the newly discovered comet had received, I hadn't given it a second thought. For me, the excursive and non-celestial events of the evening had overshadowed Kohoutek's heralded arrival. It was hard for me, therefore, to share the indignant frustration that the rest of the world felt when the comet, expected to be one-fifth as bright as the moon and to be seen within a meteor shower, turned out to be a major astrological disappointment and a colossal dud for the millions who had watched for it in the northern winter sky.

I had more important things to worry about, disappointments and concerns that were closer to home.

A year and a half of self-indoctrination while putting the Alternative School together, now followed by more than four months of functional operation, had taken its toll. It had become increasingly difficult for me to isolate the concepts of alternatives, which I so fervently espoused as applicable to education, from insidiously creeping into my thoughts as they pertained to my personal life. Even the burdensome work load and the fast pace of my days weren't enough to knock me out at night. I sat up late on the living room couch, musing alone in silence, nothing in particular but everything in general. When I finally went to bed, I couldn't sleep. It didn't happen continuously. It was sporadic, but it was haunting.

I loved my wife. I loved my two girls, Jayne, who would be eleven in April, and Sandra, who would be four. After a number of years of apartment living, Pam and I had bought the one house in town that we wanted to own. We had seen it and liked it and then, all of a sudden, it was on the market. We knew the owners, we made an offer, the offer was accepted, and we bought it on the spot!

Pam worked part-time jobs from time to time, and the extra money, combined with my regular salary, made ends meet. We never had much left over, but we never were in need, either. Pam was a member of the local Women's Club, and much of our social life revolved around the organization's regular and seasonal activities. We went to the dinners and parties, and we bowled on Thursday nights in their mixed league, right through the summer.

I knew I wasn't the easiest person with whom to live. I knew at the time that I was jealous, possessive, and controlling, but I thought I was at least a decent father and husband. We did things and went places together as a family, and in fifteen years of marriage I never had cheated or coveted another woman. I didn't feel a restlessness to go on to someone else or some other place. I felt stagnant, apathetic, and listless. I was going through the motions in robot-like, regimented fashion. I was living a lackadaisical and lackluster, servile and sterile, humdrum and ho-hum life, and I detested it. At one point, I sat down and scratched out a list of all the things I had done that day, that week, and that month, and a list of all the things I wished I had done that day, that week, and that month. There was no agreement between the two lists.

Pam and I discussed my languid feelings several times without resolution. We even made up a joint list of all of our couple friends. It started out as a joke, but it was serious. After we each had taken turns crossing off the couple, or the male or female half whom one of us wasn't that crazy about, we were left with only one complete couple, Barbara and Harry, whom both of us thought were pretty neat. That was it, one couple. I felt stuck and trapped. Just as in education, what worked for some, even if they were the majority, didn't work or wasn't working for a lot of others, including me.

I found myself giving a lot of private, quiet, late-night thought to divorce and all of its ramifications, but I never breathed a word to Pam; nevertheless, it was constantly on my mind.

****

"Yeah," I said, almost unconsciously, without looking up from my desk.

"Charlie, I got a problem."

"Yeah, me, too. Not enough hours in the day."

"No, really. Can I talk to you?"

"Ann, I just can't. Not now, okay, really."

I *never* had put her off before. I always had given her the time. But there had to be a first time. Today I was snowed under. It was five-thirty. The second of four, big deadlines for the mailing of college applications, January 15, was tomorrow. I *couldn't* miss the deadline. I hadn't had a good night's sleep in a week. The place was quiet, and I wanted to—I had to—finish everything, or bring it home to complete.

"Please?"

"Geez, Ann, gimme a break, will ya?" I said with exasperation. "You're not the only one with problems, ya know. I got problems, too—my own."

It was an unkind thing to say. I was sorry before I even finished. It was a perfect example of what was happening to me. I was feeling so much pressure that I felt I couldn't even afford the time to be kind, or nice, or even civil. Pam felt it at home; so did my kids. The staff and kids at school felt it, too. And now, Ann.

I thought for a moment she might run away in tears, and then I'd have a real mess on my hands.

"Ya wanna know something?" she challenged.

I was in for it now.

"I'm sorry, Ann. I didn't mean—"

"No, no, I mean, I never thought about you having problems. Is there—can I help with anything?"

Her response surprised me. It wasn't what I expected it to be.

"No, kid, thanks. I'm sorry. I didn't mean to say that to you, especially like that."

She shrugged. "You wanna talk?" she questioned, sympathetically. Then, without waiting for an answer, she pressed. "Why don't you tell me *your* problems for a change? You listen to all *my* problems, and I always feel better after—"

"My biggest problem is I have too much fuckin' work to do and not enough time to get it all done. You gonna help with that?"

"No, I guess I can't help with that. So, what's your second biggest problem?"

"You don't wanna hear about my other problems, believe me. My other problems are—"

"Are what, bigger? More important?" she quizzed.

"No, no, they're sorta, you know—they're sorta….. personal."

"Like mine aren't?"

Boy, she was sticking it to me!

"No, but mine have to do with things, you know, like at home and all. They're just not—"

"Pam?" she asked, with a squint of her eyes that hinted surprise and disbelief.

"Sorta, yeah, I guess," I admitted sheepishly.

I put my pen down on the desk.

"Oh, wow, I didn't know *that,*" she gasped in hushed amazement. "Whew."

No, of course not. She wasn't supposed to know. Nobody was supposed to know. I just—I got caught. One weak, unguarded moment, and I let it slip. We both ignored the red ballpoint pen that rolled to the edge of the desk and dropped to the floor. In the awkward quiet of the room, it sounded like a bomb had exploded in a garbage can.

"But how could—I mean, I don't wanna pry. It's not my business, but everything seems to—everything looks okay. Are you pulling my leg, Charlie?"

Shit, one fuckin' slip of the tongue.

"No, I'm not pullin' your leg," I said in a somewhat resigned tone.

"Wow—"

"It's—it's nothin' serious. It's just—everything's not what it's supposed to be, or maybe everything's the way it's supposed to be, and I don't like it. I don't know. It's nothin' to worry about."

My words dropped like pebbles into an abandoned well, falling to the bottom of a stone-walled shaft with hollow plunks that reverberated in the dark emptiness, the pallor of their dull echo matched by the blank stare in the eyes that seemed to look right through me.

"Boy, the two of you always look so happy."

"That's what everyone sees, and that's what everyone is gonna see," I defended, trying to withdraw behind a parapet of strength, a victim of my own errant tongue.

"Ya really had me fooled. I don't know what to say. If there's anything I can do—"

"Thanks, kiddo. I don't think there's much anyone can do."

She turned to leave and moved toward the doorway.

"Don't go," I said. "Um, this is just between the two of us, okay?"

She blanched like an almond, scalded.

"Did I ever say that to you?"

I looked at her apologetically. Cut down, but good. Never once had she asked for my trust. She knew it was there. I was embarrassed to have questioned hers.

"No, kid."

The hurtful expression left her face as she smiled.

"Never," she said softly, in quiet answer to her own question, as if to accentuate my reply.

I gathered the papers from my desk and shuffled them into my briefcase. I picked up the pen and stuck it into my pocket.

"Let me give ya a ride home. We can talk on the way. What's the problem? No, le'me guess," I said with a stopping hand. "It's your father, again, right?"

"No kidding, who else?" she replied as she closed the office door behind us. "It's my father, *still* and *always*. I don't even want to talk about it."

She didn't. I let the silence hang in stark openness as we walked to the car, resisting the temptation to fill the extended void with idle talk. When she was ready, she'd say what she had to say. In the meantime, I was too tired to speak, too tired to question, and too tired to think. I didn't even try to beat the light at the corner. I was too tired to drive. I'd listen. That's about all I was good for. I'd wait. I'd wait for the light, and I'd wait for her. When she was ready, it would come in a torrent. Before the light changed or after I made the turn? Before or after? Let's play a game. Before? Or after? Before? Before, of course.

"I'm just not enough," she began. "I'm not smart enough, and I'm not good enough. At work I'm not fast enough. At home I'm not responsible enough. I'm not mature enough. I'm not enough enough."

Pause.

"There's no way to meet his expectations, ya know what I mean?"

No reply necessary—rhetorical question.

"My sister couldn't, my brothers couldn't, my poor mother can't, and me," she huffed frumpishly, "I'm so far away from meeting his expectations, he'll be finding fault with me 'til the day I die. Even then he'll be complaining it's costing him too much to bury me."

"Nice thoughts."

"Charlie, do you *know* how much I try to please him?" she begged my understanding. "You *know* how much—oh, fuck. What's the use?" Her sputtering annoyance halted with a flailing surrender of her arms.

I waited for the silver gray Dodge and the dark blue panel truck to pass as I readied to make the turn onto Saffron Road. My left directional signal clicked its violent intrusion into the vacant quiet, the green arrow flashing in insolence on the dashboard at the most ironic time, the most inelegant place. Her father's drug store was on our right, right there in front of us, on the corner. Her father probably was there now, and this was her street, a turn of the wheel away, her house a short block and a half down on the right, set back from the road.

"Isn't there anything—there's gotta be *something* he's happy with about you, something he's satisfied with, isn't there?"

"No."

It echoed, the resounding reflection a dozen times louder that the original declaration. No hurt. No anger. There may have been a hint of resignation, but mostly there was nothing but abject finality.

"No, there's nothing in my life that means anything to him. My friends are jerks, my stereo is too loud, I smoke too much, my hopes are pipedreams, and I'm dumb. To my father, my life is just a pinball machine that keeps gobbling up his money and lighting up, 'tilt.' "

Fuck.

****

January faded into February and then into early March, with many things changing and many things remaining the same. The most significant constant was the A-School itself. Nobody seemed to tire of it. The novelty never wore off. Even through the winter doldrums, enough was happening to keep everybody's interest kindled and enthusiasm peaked. The cold weather seemed to serve as a cohesive agent rather than as a disjunctive force, with more kids staying inside and finding things to do together in a clubhouse kind of atmosphere. Every corner nook, every foyer, every stairway, every group of chairs, and every quiet spot became a cozy hideaway to sit and chat and pass the time.

As people had gotten to know one another beyond the superficial level over the past half-year, conversations and friendships had become more substantive than trivial, a greater tolerance for individual differences had emerged, and close personal friendships in pairs and threesomes had given way to fours and fives. Intermingled with the fun and nonsense and games and guffaw characteristic of any large group of teenagers, there was much clear and heartwarming evidence of growth, maturity, learning, and development, although to hear them talk among themselves, one would have had serious doubts.

Their language was absolutely atrocious. They communicated at a base level, their skills in verbal intercourse most often reflecting more emphasis on intercourse than on verbalization. With unrestrained generosity, they bestowed the capacity for sexual activity on every imaginable object: the fuckin' table, the fuckin' tree, the fuckin' steps, the fuckin' car, the fuckin' film, the fuckin' book, the fuckin' this, and the fuckin' that. Their generosity was exceeded only by their inquisitiveness ("What the fuck do ya think you're doin'?"), their search for truth ("Don't fuckin' bullshit me!"), their tolerance of the behavior of others ("I don't give a flyin' fuck what you do."), their sexual creativeness ("Fuck my ass."), their sexual courageousness ("Fuck my nose."), and their earnest desire to remain virginal (Don't think you're gonna fuckin' screw me."). I almost fell off my chair the day I heard an exasperated Julia, begging Eddie to leave her be, express the courtesy for which A-School students had become universally known and loved: "*Please* go fuck yourself, Eddie."

Student mastery of the "c-k" words—the seven monosyllabic, sexually explicit terms ending in "c-k"—permitted those of either gender to let loose a verbal barrage of colorful if indelicate words—dick, fuck, suck, lick, crack, cock, and prick—in response to any situation, good or bad, happy or sad. But they were only words. Except for one or two, they could be included on any third grade teacher's spelling list, right? The girls were as bad as the guys. And it had a contagious character. It wasn't unusual for staff members to use the same acquired terminology among themselves or *with* students or *to* students. If a student told a teacher to "fuck off," it was just a demonstration of A-School freedom of speech. If a teacher told a student to "fuck off," the student paid attention!

In addition to the late-stayers, the kids who regularly stayed after school to play ping-pong or hang around to talk in the office or in the lounge, there were other subgroups of A-Schoolers who never changed from month to month, particularly the so-called "feet people," the car-less students who remained resolute and constant in their search for a ride. A large portion of that group were those ever desperate for a lift to the regular high school where they took their science courses, utilizing the main building's lab facilities. It was a walkable distance in good weather, but in the rain or cold the kids happily piled into cars for the short but welcome drive.

Anyone with a car, student or staff member, was open to be tapped for taxi service. I had a car full of kids almost every time I had to make a trip to "the portables," two pre-fabricated classroom buildings which the A-School used as an annex or "second" home. Located on the grounds of one of the nearby elementary schools, the portables housed some of our regular classes as well as our always eventful, often chaotic, and usually controversial Town Meetings. The Town Meetings met for an hour and a half every sixth school day as the one-person, one-vote, self-government component of the A-School.

If the kids weren't trying to bum a ride to the high school or to the portables, they were trying to get to other places. During the second trimester, the bowling group I had organized for physical education credit three days a week relied on wheels for the trip to the bowling alley in Foster Village. And the kids who didn't "eat in" at lunchtime always were eager to break up the day with an outside excursion to Friendly's, McDonald's, the pizza place, the deli, the diner, or to Burger King if they could convince me or someone else to go out and warm up the car.

Ann usually went with me to the portables, to the bowling alley, and to lunch. Then, of course, there were our Sunday night "Discovery!" classes, Ann again a loyal companion.

We met every Sunday night for more than two and a half months as Barbara had successfully arranged. We never started any class until everyone was there, and I don't remember anyone ever being late or missing a class.

Ann was always the last person to leave at the end of the evening even though it didn't always appear that way. Sometimes she'd say good-bye before everyone else had gone, go out, drive her car around the block, park on the street, walk back, and let herself in when the only car left in the Church lot was mine. It was an outgrowth of an accidental situation, a one-time occurrence when she had left for the night but returned in search of a lost glove that had fallen out of her coat pocket. But it became routine. We never talked about it; she just did it, and I didn't question it. It was just an attempt to keep ugly rumors from starting rather than trying to hide something. There was nothing to hide. It was the only thing we ever did to cover our uneasiness at having the amount of time we spent together be seen and misinterpreted by others. We'd sit and talk for hours, until one or one-thirty in the morning, sometimes later. It wasn't much different than staying after school to talk on a regular school day, except "after school" on Sundays meant after eleven o'clock.

One snowy, Sunday night the group broke up early because of the weather, but Ann and I stayed as usual. By the time she left at a quarter past one, the unplowed roads were blanketed with a treacherous accumulation, and the snow still was coming down heavily. I cautioned her to be careful. She had played out a joint, and I knew she was stoned. Watching her car skid and slide out of the parking lot, I made my own decision not to even attempt the drive home. I called Pam and then made myself comfortable on the couch in the lounge and spent the night at school.

When I looked out the door the next morning, I was glad I had stayed. At eight o'clock, when nobody showed up at school, I had second thoughts. I wondered if schools were closed for the day. By eight-thirty, I stopped wondering. I knew my mistake. Teachers, like kids, wait all winter with hopeful anticipation of a "snow day" and a bonus vacation. So, here was that eagerly awaited, much longed-for day off, and here I was, snowed in at school! I called Pam to let her know I was okay. Then I called Ann to share my misfortune and find out how she had made the drive home the night before.

"Oh, Charlie, I can't believe it. You stayed there overnight? If I had known you were gonna stay, I would have stayed, too."

I have no recollection of my verbal response to Ann's bold statement. Whatever words I groped to put together are forever lost to memory. I was overwhelmed by the surge of hotness that raced through my body, my first real, honest–to-goodness, sexual response to Ann. My reply must have been a hastily contrived sputtering of something completely asinine. I only recall thinking I'd better get off the phone as quickly as I could.

CHAPTER 9

Ann's progress signaled it was time for me to step back. Despite a secret, a dream, and the words of a song on a piece of paper, I would step away......

I was very satisfied and contented with Ann's progress over the past few months. If the A-School was the most significant constant, Ann was the most notable change. After verbalizing and ventilating much of the baggage she silently had been carrying within herself for such a long time, she was more vibrant and alive with enthusiasm and optimism that ever I had known her to be. She laughed and smiled much more readily. She walked tall with her head up instead of with rounded shoulders and her head down. She was much more verbal, and she took less shit from everyone, including me. She knew she wasn't worthless; if nothing else, I had made damn sure of that. Her writing was no longer that of a disillusioned and drifting person. She took control more often, not perceiving herself as a helpless victim of someone else or of whatever circumstances chanced to come her way. She felt better about herself, her body, and her head. She wasn't hiding behind her little girl's voice as frequently as she had been. She had developed a healthy degree of resiliency, and she needed it. Everything *wasn't* perfect; there *were* disappointments and setbacks from which she had to recover and rebound.

She had worked hard for months on an oil painting in the art room at the portables. One day, when she went to class, the canvas was gone. She and Ben and some of the kids turned the place upside down, but the almost finished painting she had planned as a gift for me was never found. Its disappearance remained an unsolved mystery and a bitter displeasure. She never believed that the painting had vanished at the hands of a person who was jealous because it was intended as a gift for me, but I never believed otherwise.

She tried out for the Spring Musical at the regular high school, but she was from the A-School; she wasn't one of the "in" group. She wasn't in the chorus or the choir, and the musical had been selected, as it often was, with a consideration of the voices available to and familiar to the director. In effect, the choices for the leading roles had been predetermined. Ann knew the inside politics of the selection game, but she knew as well that she could sing circles around the person who had been picked for the female lead. She was right, and she was pissed.

There also were disappointments from which *I* had to recover. On one occasion, exasperated by what appeared to be Ann's ever increasing dependence on marijuana, I had taken her stash and thrown it out the car window. Another time, I stole the little cosmetic pouch in which she carried her stash, wrappers, clips, and roaches and took it home with me. No matter what I did, how much I counseled, what I told her, how long we talked about it, or what I said or did, I couldn't curb her seemingly insatiable appetite for grass. It got worse instead of better. Even before a show, when she did everything possible to get her voice in top shape, she smoked. She gave up regular cigarettes, but not her joy butts.

Before Ann's self-esteem had improved, when she still was regarding herself as little or nothing more than worthless, there were three occasions when Terri or one of her other girlfriends had telephoned me in panic, fearful that she might be acting out a subconscious death wish. The first call jolted Pam and me out of bed in the wee hours of the morning to scour the streets and backyards of Teaneck until just before dawn, freezing our asses off. We never found her. She ended up in the house of a friend after walking around aimlessly for hours, stumbling from yard to yard in a foggy stupor, unable to find her own house.

Two weeks later, I found the little air-head just in the nick of time, alone in the back seat of her car in the Acme parking lot two blocks from home, swallowing her tongue and turning blue. She had tripped on acid and gone into convulsions. If I hadn't gotten there in time to pull her tongue out of her throat, she would have choked to death. I was furious and scared shit. When she came to her senses, I shook her, literally grabbed her by the shoulders and shook her, until her teeth chattered.

"What the fuck are ya tryin' to do, get me stuck with a corpse on my hands?" I screamed at the top of my lungs, my face beet-red with anger. "No more fuckin' acid, ya hear! Never again, you shit-head. No more acid!" I repeated. "You're so fuckin' stupid, I don't know—"

"I promise—"

"You promise? You better fuckin' promise!"

I was fighting a losing battle. A week later, I had to pull her off Route 4 where she was walking the center white line at one o'clock in the morning, headlong into on-coming traffic, stoned beyond belief and singing her head off. At least it wasn't acid. It was weed, but at least it wasn't acid. To my knowledge she never used acid again. Maybe she did, but not that I ever heard of or saw.

Since those hair-raising incidents, however, Ann's self-control and sense of responsibility had improved markedly. I knew some of the progress and improvement was a result of the substantial amount of time and attention I had been giving her. I knew a lot of it was the result of my chewing her out, yelling at her, and threatening to take her to the hospital emergency room and letting her parents come and get her if I again found her endangering herself. I had threatened, also, to withdraw myself, to stop spending time with her, and to wash my hands of our relationship if she didn't control herself and behave more reasonably and with more maturity. I knew I sounded more like her father than I wanted to, or than she wanted me to, but I knew something else, as well. I knew she liked me. I knew she liked me a lot. I wasn't dumb. I could read the signs, and I had played them for all they were worth, straining to get the most mileage from each one. It had worked. The improvement had been substantial, and I was pleased.

And now it was time to step away. I knew what she could do with the support and encouragement I had been providing for her and the demands I had been making of her, but it couldn't go on that way forever. As with a person temporarily on crutches, a time comes when one has to take the support away, at least some of it, gradually, carefully, and gently, to see if the patient can stand alone.

So, tomorrow I'd give it a try.

The next day, I found I wasn't quite ready for what "tomorrow" had brought. It brought Ann, bounding into the office just before lunchtime, flying higher than a kite, singing, yackety-yacking, and clowning. She danced over behind the desk, flicking the calendar on the wall with her finger as she passed, tripping over a box of books that had come down from the high school, before leaning on my shoulder and whispering in my ear.

"I have a secret to tell ya. Wanna go to lunch?"

"Sure," I answered. "Is that the secret, you wanna go to lunch?"

"No, Charlie-nut. Ya wanna go to lunch, and then I'll tell ya the secret," she giggled.

"What's the matter with you? Did you hit your funny bone when you got outta bed this morning, or did you just have one of your silly cigarettes," I teased.

It was good to see her in such happy spirits, but I suspected her joviality was more likely linked to my second conjecture than it was to my first. I thought she was buzzed.

"No, honest! No funny bone and no weed," she exclaimed indignantly. "Well, maybe just a quick hit or two," she admitted when she saw me smile and look at her with a doubting stare over the top of my glasses. "C'mon, let's go, go, go."

We went to Libanoti's, an Italian place on the border of Teaneck and Bergenfield. We never had been there before, but we had passed it several times on bowling days and always said we'd give it a try.

I was puzzled that she didn't say anything further about a secret, and it wasn't until she had finished her veal parmigian and spaghetti that I broached the subject.

"So, tell me a secret."

"Whaddya mean?"

"I thought ya had a secret you wanted to tell me."

"Oh, I don't know, now. I—I don't know whether I should tell ya or not."

"I thought you were all hyped about somethin'. I thought that's why ya wanted to go to lunch," I challenged.

The disappointment showed in my voice, I'm sure, if not on my face.

"Yeah, but if I tell ya, it won't be a secret any more, will it?" she cooed.

Was she debating with me or with herself?

"Well, okay, I'll tell ya. I guess I can. I really want to, but I'm a little afraid. Maybe I'll just tell you part," she said cheerfully, apparently happy at working out a compromise in her own head.

I couldn't figure it out. She had been so excited an hour ago about a secret she wanted to tell me, a jack-in-the-box straining her spring to jump a surprise in my face, but now so reluctant I almost felt guilty trying to prod it out of her.

"Okay, shoot. Secret, part one, first installment."

She hesitated for a moment. Then she pushed her plate aside, crossed her arms in front of her on the table, and leaned forward.

"I had.....a dream.....about you.....last night." She spoke so softly I had to read her lips to understand what she was saying.

I was a good lip reader. I got the message. I got it all. I wished I hadn't eaten all the bread in the basket. I felt like I had to stuff something down my throat—fast. I wiped my mouth with my napkin, folded it neatly in half, and tucked it underneath my fork next to my plate.

"Oh, yeah?" I said with as much nonchalance as I could muster. It wasn't enough. My voice broke. Two lousy words and my voice had to break. Damn. And this was the day I was going to gently take a crutch away! I could forget that bullshit, now. It was going to be, "Save *yourself* day, Charlie. Grab your ass, and run for your fuckin' life."

"Yeah," she purred. "Isn't that somethin'?"

Her voice didn't break.

Christ, I needed time to think. If this asshole ever spilled what she dreamed, I was dead. What would I do? What would I say? I knew what she dreamed. I had to try and stop it—bluff, and go for broke.

"So, what was the dream about?"

I had to bet my balls she didn't have the balls—

"Uh, I'm not sure I can tell ya."

Good, I thought. Let's get back to school.

"Sure you can," I fronted, faking enthusiastic curiosity while steadying my left knee from shaking under the table. "Wasn't it a happy dream?"

"I *can* tell ya if I want, but I don't know if I *want* to," she teased, her eyes twinkling.

The little bitch! She wasn't satisfied she had me by the short hairs. Now she wanted me to beg her not to cut off my balls. I couldn't push my luck. How far, how much, could I bluff? She was holding all the high cards, and all she needed was a little encouragement to play them.

"You really don't hafta tell me anything, ya know. It's *your* secret," I conceded.

"I really do wanna tell you. It wasn't exactly happy. It was.....nice, yeah, nice. But it's a little embarrassing to talk about," she blushed.

She didn't try to hide it. She didn't have to. She was the dealer. The fuckin' little tease had caught me with not a single chip to play. The best I could do was appeal to her sense of timing and hope I could come back, double or nothing. I'd let her hold the ace, but I had to kill the trump card. I had to gamble.....

"Well, ya told me the secret about havin' the dream," I commended. "Maybe you can, you know, tell me all about it later on. Ya don't hafta tell me everything now, all at once. Part one now, and part two some other time."

I could tell by the look on her face she was gonna buy it. Hallelujah! She knew damn well I knew what the dream was about, anyway.

"That's a great idea, Charlie. Why didn't I think of that? I can tell ya all about it later. We gotta get back soon, anyway. I don't wanna start it if I can't finish," she rationalized as if that wasn't the way she had planned it all along. "We got time for another Coke?"

"A Coke? Sure, we got enough time for *that.* Go ahead," I said, relieved but still jittery. "Have another Coke."

Have anything ya want. Have a sirloin steak. I can't get up right now, anyway. Have a lobster or a filet mignon. Have anything your sweet little heart desires. Just let me *out* of here!

It was a hell of a lot easier sticking crutches under someone's arms than it was taking them away.

****

I had an appointment with Dr. Franklin, the principal at the high school, on Thursday afternoon, March 7. My annual evaluation had been prepared, and, as was customary, I had been summoned for a conference, a reading, and a signing.

> **Mr. Sullivan has assumed a most difficult assignment this year—coordination of the Alternative School in its first year of existence. The excellent reputation achieved by the Alternative School in its first year gives ample evidence of Mr. Sullivan's high quality contribution. His rapport with students and staff is strong. The curriculum, the school spirit, the parent relations, and the college application endeavors all are excellent as a result of Mr. Sullivan's conscientious devotion to the Alternative School.**
>
> **For his time, his energy, his efforts, he is thanked. A genuine vote of thanks is due Mr. Sullivan.**
>
> **Mr. Sullivan is recommended for contract renewal and for salary increase and increment.**

I drove away from the high school and headed home, pleased with my evaluation and the pittance of recognition that the system bestowed upon you if you did your job and didn't rock the boat. In actuality, the evaluation meant shit. I had tenure in the district, and aside from the narrative comments, I could be rated **S** for satisfactory, **N** for needs improvement, or **U** for unsatisfactory. There was an **S** in the rating space at the top of the yellow copy I had been given, and that was it.

What was *really* on my mind as I drove home that afternoon was a question that wasn't going to be resolved with the ease of a conference, a reading, and a signing: What was I going to do about Ann?

I didn't have to analyze the situation, and I didn't have to wonder. Everything was crystal clear. It wasn't a time for rationalizing. It wasn't a time for moralizing. It was a time for decision making. The question had nothing to do with counseling. It had nothing to do with Ann's well-being, or mine, for that matter. It wasn't something I could discuss with anyone, including her, and it wasn't something I could decide with anyone, especially her. It was a matter of hard-nose reality, not soap opera fantasy.

I took the note I had found in my mailbox that morning out of my jacket pocket. I had read it at least a half-dozen times during the day, but now I held it above the steering wheel and read it again as I kept one eye on the ass-end of the Buick in front of me on Route 4, west. She had copied the words of a song, "With You," and had addressed it "To My Prophet." The lyrics she quoted on a piece of her Kahlil Gibran stationery spoke first of sharing her days, then her nights, and finally her life with me.

Well, what was it gonna be, Charlie-nut?

I folded the note and quickly stuck it back into my pocket, a symbolic but fruitless effort to put the matter aside—out of sight, out of mind. How the hell did I get into this mess? Now I knew how Boggie felt in *Casablanca*:

"Of all the gin joints, in all the towns, in all the world, she walks into mine."

I had backed off every hint, every suggestive comment, every tease, every wink, every flirting word, every whisper—that *blouse*—every gleam in her eye, every turn of that cute little ass tucked into those tight jeans that curved around her buttocks and up into that no-man's land between. To someone else, the game might well have been an erotic diversion from a tedious job, a melodious symphony that overwhelmed the discordant sounds of everyday life. It might have been amusing or invigorating, even piquant. To me, it was torture. It was an axe over my head. It wasn't a dream about which I didn't want to hear. It was a nightmare. *She* wasn't asking for any decision; I was asking *myself*, for the sake of my own sanity. She wasn't asking for anything, but I knew she'd take whatever she got. I knew she wanted it. I knew she'd take it. I knew she'd love it. And I bet she'd do it good. I bet she'd wrap those long, lean legs, lock her ankles together, dig her heels into the small of my back, and press me right up and—

God, it was killing me! And there were still three months before she'd graduate. Enough of this shit. I had to decide, now, once and for all. Either I was going to keep backing off, keep turning away, or as sure as hell we were going to end up in bed.

Good grief! Even the thought of it was crazy. There was no way *that* was going to happen. No way. It wasn't being married, it wasn't my job, it wasn't the risk, it wasn't the fact that I was a teacher and she was a student, it wasn't the morality, it wasn't *anything*. It just wasn't me. It was absurd. No way was I gonna touch this kid, cute little blouse and cute little titties, or not. It didn't make any difference. Even if she wanted it. It was nice to think about, but no way.

So, at least, at last, I knew. At least, at last, I could relax. I could go back to school in the morning and I could enjoy Ann for another day as I had been enjoying her, and then I could look forward to having a nice weekend.

I breathed a deep sigh of relief as I pulled into my driveway. My hands were sweaty on the steering wheel, but the pains I had been feeling in my chest for the past week had disappeared. I didn't know how I had made it home. I was supposed to stop for gas, but— I didn't remember turning off Route 4 or driving up Forest Avenue past the park entrance and the children's zoo or making the right turn onto Ackerman Avenue. I didn't remember stopping for any lights. I didn't remember anything. I didn't want to. But I knew where I was now—home—and I was happy to be there.

CHAPTER 10

The next week was hell; the place was in turmoil. And I was on the receiving end of that accusing finger, trying to defend myself, and struggling to find the words to tell Ann what was happening.....

A nice weekend, huh? Yes, it was. I had a particularly pleasant weekend with Pam and the kids, with not much thought about the A-School for a change, and not much else to do but relax. It was a good thing I had it when I did. The next week at school was hell.

I spent three afternoons working with Ann on her application to the American Academy of Dramatic Arts on Madison Avenue in New York. It was like pulling teeth, first deciding *whether* to apply and then deciding *where* to apply. I had to get her to admit that she really wanted to go, and she had to muster the confidence to follow through with the application process and steel herself against the possibility of being rejected. I helped her complete the application and write her personal statement. She put together a resume of her theatrical credits, and I did the work on her transcript. We put the package together and typed the envelope. I gave her a stamp. I held her hand throughout. By the time we got the job done, she was excited and proud, happy to have a direction, pleased to be college-bound like most of her friends, and tickled to be pursuing her interest in theatre, voice, and dance.

The next day she came to school in tears, brokenhearted and demoralized. She told me her father said it wasn't worth sending her to college. He wouldn't give her a check for the application fee.

Earlier that same week, someone had tacked an article from the newspaper on the bulletin board:

JUDGE OVERTURNS VARIANCE ALLOWING ALTERNATIVE SCHOOL

In short, the article said a District Court Judge had ruled we had to be out of our Church basement home by April 15. We didn't even know the issue was still in court.

The place was in turmoil, everyone upset, confused, and on edge about the court decision as well as about a host of other things.

We were right in the middle of ending the second trimester and beginning the third, and there seemed to be some scheduling problems that were causing concern. The Steering Committee was dragging its feet on important school matters and rule changes that begged for decision. Some of the guys weren't happy with the draw for the ping-pong tournament. Marilyn had a bug up her ass about who knows what. If the kids weren't bitching about something, they were bitching over whether they had the right to bitch. The March weather was stuck in reverse, getting worse instead of better. And I was on the receiving end of that accusing finger.

Fran had pulled me into our makeshift darkroom and, in the eerie glow of the red light bulb on the wall, had blasted me with the accusation.

"I know what's been going on with the two of you, and for a long time," she had hissed.

It was clear to Fran that my motivation in spending a lot of time with Ann was so I could get into her pants, that I had, and that Ann and I were playing around together. She wasn't accusing me of an insidious plan in the making. She was accusing me of a plot that already had been accomplished, and she was accusing the both of us of a conspiracy that was continuing. When I flew into a rage, she had reduced the charges: "Are you after her body?"

The bitch's cute little words rang in my ear as I sat behind my desk. I wished I had stayed cool long enough to clarify the charges. Was it "intent to fuck," "conspiracy to fuck," or just plain "fuck"? I shook my head in disbelief. The bitch had a lot of guts. She had more balls than brains, that's for sure. She couldn't prove a plot that didn't exist; even if it did exist, she couldn't prove it. What the hell evidence did she have to support the charge of a conspiracy or an act that never happened? Man, she was off her fucking rocker.

I went home that night, furious. Pam sat on the couch and listened, stunned. She knew almost everything there was to know about Ann. She knew how much I was invested, and she knew how seriously I took my counseling. She knew of Ann's fondness for me, an outgrowth of my intensive work with her, and she knew that on several occasions I had backed off from Ann's flirting hints of affection. She may not have realized how *many* times I had backed away, and I'm sure she didn't know how tempting it was to *not* back away. But she *knew* I would.

She listened to my anger and fury as I paced back and forth across the living room, wringing my hands in utter frustration. Despite our marital malaise, Pam was a decent person and a compassionate woman. She knew how much I hurt, and she soothed my upset as best she could. It was embarrassing. She was doing everything she could to comfort me, unaware that other things that were happening in my life—serious things, unrelated to Ann, to the A-School, or to our marriage—would, in a matter of a few days, have me telling her I wanted a divorce. Nevertheless, having support at home was comforting, but I needed it at school.

The next morning I called an emergency meeting of the A-School staff. I don't know what I expected their reaction to be. For the most part, they didn't react. Janis, Ann's Seminar teacher, didn't say anything. Neither did Ben. Fran had already said enough, too much. She didn't argue or find fault when I quoted her comments. She didn't elaborate on anything. She just sat and said nothing. Marilyn, Fran's best friend, said nothing. Lisa appeared upset, but said nothing. It was obvious that some, if not all, had discussed the matter beforehand, among themselves.

I moved to acquit myself, giving an account of my actions and behavior as they related to Ann since September. I explained the motivations for my actions and behavior as far as possible without breaking Ann's confidence in me, and I offered to address their questions.

Most of their queries I answered. Some I wouldn't. Confidentiality was the key to the door of counseling, and I'd be damned if I were going to let them steal the key. I never told them how to teach, and they weren't going to lay down the rules for my counseling. It was a matter of principle, professional principle. Ann having been raped wasn't any of their fucking business, anyway. And neither was someone else's perception of the size of her vagina. I knew the absence of detail made my case look skimpy, but what the hell else could I do? I refused to discuss any question that would violate Ann's trust in me. They didn't like *that* at all. Instead of the accusation being the issue at hand, my adamant refusal to reveal *everything* Ann had told me seemed to become the bone of contention. *I* didn't like *that* at all. To me, it was their way of getting off the indefensible hot spot onto which they had gotten themselves. The blank faces hurt, but the lack of trust killed. I didn't know if I were more pissed than frustrated, or if it were the other way around.

"Okay," I said firmly and slowly, addressing Fran and pointing across the table at her. "You have one of two choices: either keep your fuckin' mouth shut, and I don't wanna hear one more word of this trash, or take your God damn charges to the Board of Education, and make it a public issue. *Then* we'll see who's telling the truth and who loses their job."

I got up and walked out. There wasn't anything more I could do or say. I could deny until I was blue in the face. For what, what good? It just had to be put up or shut up. So, that's what I made it be. Prove it, bitch.

That took care of the issue, but it didn't take care of me. God, I hurt! I hurt something awful. Where was all the support? "We know you wouldn't do that. We don't believe these things. It's a shame you have to go through this. It's not fair. We believe you, Charlie. We trust you. We respect your integrity." Where the hell was it? Calling me a lecher was just calling me a fucker. I could take that, as tawdry and cheap as it was, but I could take it. A fucker was a fucker. But I wasn't *dumb.* I wasn't stupid. How could they possibly think I was stupid? They were saying I was a lecher too stupid to cover his own ass. C'mon, now. Did they honestly believe that if I had been fucking around with a student for five or six months, for one month, or for even one day, I would be stupid enough to let them or anyone else see it out in the open, or see anything at any time, anywhere, that would arouse even a speck of suspicion?

Despite everything, I knew I was in a tough spot. I knew it was almost impossible to prove a negative, to prove something that didn't happen.

"Am I after her body? If I were after her body," I had shouted in the staff meeting, "you'd be the last ones in the whole fuckin' world to know, not the first to suspect. And if I were dumb enough to risk my job going after a body, it sure as hell would be a better body than that one, too."

The absence of trust was galling. Shit, they knew *me.* Where the hell were they coming from? My word was as good as gold; they knew *that,* for Christ's sake. I wasn't a playboy or a philanderer. I wasn't even a flirt. I had so much integrity, it made *me* sick. I never had cruised around looking for a piece of ass, even when I was a teenager. I didn't play games. When I said, "yes," I meant, "yes." When I said, "no," I meant, "no." And when I said something was true, it was true. No one doubted my word, ever. No one had to. Everyone trusted it was good. Everyone knew damn straight it was good.

And these assholes just sat at that table with blank stares on their fucking faces.

* * * * * * *

When I saw Ann, I didn't know what to say. I was beaten and blistered, a broken egg unceremoniously splattered into an ungreased frying pan to be seared, sizzled, and crisped brown around the edges. I was furious, but that was only on the surface. Inside, I was broken, disappointed, depressed, and disillusioned about everything.

For the benefit of the outside world, I always had compensated for my deep-rooted insecurities and the feelings of inadequacy I secreted from others by being a perfectionist and a workaholic. My self-esteem was anchored in doing well the things I could do well. I gained the respect of others through meticulous performance and unquestionable competency. The attack on me was an assault on those very underpinnings. The accusation damaged them severely. The lack of support from my professional colleagues, people I thought were my friends, caused them to collapse completely. Always a person with strong, deep feelings, I fell hard. I went down fast, like a ship with its bottom torn away. They had ripped away my mainsail, that billowing white canvas called Ann, set abaft my mainmast, fluttering in the breeze, making steady my course, and giving purpose to my job.

She was heading toward the bulletin board.

I came up behind her and looked at the ping-pong tournament match-ups over her shoulder.

"Heavy shit goin' on in there this morning, huh?" she said without looking back. "I saw you come stormin' out, but I was on my way to the portables, and I couldn't miss my ride. I've been dying all day. What happened?"

"I didn't even see you around this morning. I looked, but—"

"I was around. I saw, but then I hadda go."

"I'm glad you didn't hear," I said tentatively.

"Why? What's goin' down?"

"It all depends on who ya listen to and who ya believe," I shrugged.

I wasn't trying to toy with her. I just didn't know how the hell I was going to say it.

"So, tell me the story, and I'll tell you who to believe," she said with growing impatience.

"Oh, *you'll* know who to believe. And *I* know who to believe. It's the rest of them who don't have their fuckin' heads screwed on right."

She turned fully and stood with her weight on one leg, her hands on her hips, her stance and facial expression telling me to get on with it. I took a deep breath. How the hell—

"Ann, are we fuckin' around?" I blurted.

I knew as soon as the words came out of my mouth that they weren't the right words and that it was a stupid way to start.

"*We* fuckin' around? No, *we're* not fuckin' around, Charlie. I'm trying to find out what's goin' on, and *you're* fuckin' around."

She turned abruptly back toward the bulletin board and feigned reading the tournament results, waiting, a child held from going into the water until an hour after eating, insulted at not being treated more like a grownup. She stood there with her back to me, sulking, impatient for the minutes to pass and the promised time to arrive.

"Annie, I'm trying very hard to tell you what's going on," I explained with care, "but I'm really having a lot of trouble."

I usually called her Annie only when I was making a joke or when I was really serious, like when we talked about her pot smoking or her parents. She knew this was no joke. She turned to face me.

"Shit," she whispered, "you're serious, aren't you? You almost look like you're gonna cry."

"I just may, before this is all over. If I do, don't touch me, you hear? *Don't fuckin' touch me.*"

"Charlie? Charlie, what the hell happened in there?"

"Look—" I still didn't know how to say it. "Let's start all over again. Are we fuckin' around?"

Oh, shit, man. The same stupid words came out. I knew she didn't know what the hell I was talking about.

"Just answer me, yes or no, even if it sounds dumb. Are we fuckin' around?" I demanded roughly.

"No. I don't know what that means, but, no," she replied quickly, pointedly.

I swallowed.

"Well, they all say we are."

"They all say we are?" she repeated, carefully. Then, with surprise, "*Fucking around?* They all say we're fuckin' around? You gotta be kiddin', right?"

Silence.

"Like fucking, not like playing around or joking around. Like fucking, really fucking, you and me?" she questioned with a squint.

"You got it, kid," I choked. "They all think you and I are fucking."

Christ, I didn't think I could actually say it. I didn't think I was going to cry, either, but my face was wet. She reached out impulsively, circling her arms around my neck and holding me tightly, her head on my shoulder, talking into my ear.

"No—" I objected.

Just what I didn't want to happen. A few kids were scattered throughout the basement. A few more were on the stage. I didn't know where the teachers were. This is the last thing I had wanted anybody to see. And then, all of a sudden, I didn't care who saw. I just didn't give a crap.

"I'm sorry, Charlie. Oh, I'm *so* sorry. It's my fault. It's all my fault It's my fuckin' fault. Those assholes—those fuckin' assholes, those dumb….. Don't cry; please don't cry. Let me cry. I hurt so much for you. I'm sorry. They don't know what—It was Fran. It was Fran, wasn't it?" she hissed. "She sucks, the bitch. They all suck. They should all go fuck themselves. I love you so much, Charlie. Please don't cry."

I tried to unwrap myself from her arms. She held on.

"Yeah, it was Fran," I muttered, "but it was all of them, too."

"I knew it was Fran. That bitch. She knows I love you, so she figures we're screwin'."

"Whaddya mean, she knows you love me," I gasped.

"She's a woman. She knows. She can tell. Let's get her now. Let's get them all," she bristled angrily. "Let's tell them all the truth, so they know."

"I already told them the truth," I said, as I tried again to free myself.

"Stop it!" she demanded. "Damn it, let me hold you. I wanna hold you. I'm so, so, so, so sorry. *We* should tell them. *I* should tell them. I know the truth. You could have fucked me a hundred times. I wanted you to make love to me. You never touched me. You never put a hand on me, not a finger. I'm not afraid. I'll tell them. I'll tell them the real truth. It's all my fault, and it's not fair."

"We gotta get outta here," I wavered, my head spinning. Even with her holding me, I felt wobbly. I couldn't handle this. "Ya can't tell them anything. They're not listening. They don't want to hear it."

"That bitch, that fuckin' bitch," she huffed.

"Ya have a class comin' up?"

"Fuck the class, Charlie. I don't even remember if I have a class. I don't *care* if I have a class. Stop worrying about a fucking class, will ya," she chided, tugging at me and already heading for the front stairs. We ran up the steps together. I felt like I was running away from home. "I can't believe you're worrying about a fucking class."

"Shit, you're right," I sputtered as we reached the top.

"I know I'm right. Let them have their classes, and their school, and their fuckin' lies….." she railed as I pushed open the front door.

"…..and, if they wanna entertain themselves, they can have their fuckin' fantasies, too."

We got into her car, and she pulled out of the driveway with a squeal, a brazen effrontery to what was being left behind.

"Where to?" she asked.

"I don't care—anywhere. I don't care where. I don't care about them, I don't care about where we go, I don't care about anything. I don't care, I don't care, I don't care....Let's just go some place where we can sit and talk."

I slumped back against the seat, my body aching, my spirit crushed, my mind—a moment—that's all it took. It hit like a flash. Why the hell not? Who cares? What the fuck—

"So, what did ya dream about a coupla weeks ago? Ya gonna tell me?"

.....in a single moment.....no hesitation at all.....

"I dreamed we were in bed together, making love, fucking each other outta sight!" she burst.

"That's what I thought it was about."

"I'll tell you all about it. It was great!"

CHAPTER 11

"He tasted the ingratitude of his Republic….." Yes, they cut out my heart. The truth, my folders of personal treasures, my adamant denial, and my reputation notwithstanding, the ingrates cut out my heart…..

As a counselor, personal counseling was my strength. I was very good at college counseling, not quite as good at educational counseling, and only mediocre at career counseling. But personal counseling—ah, that was different. That was my cup of tea. It came easy for me. I enjoyed it with relish, and I was good at it.

I prided myself with the knowledge that in the regular high school, if I went into my office with a student and closed the door, in five minutes I could get the kid to tell me anything. It made no difference what the problem was. I had some kind of uncanny ability to establish quickly a receptive atmosphere in which kids would feel safe spilling the beans about being pregnant, thinking about suicide, being the victim of abuse, using dope or stronger drugs, being a kleptomaniac, being a nymphomaniac, having an incestuous relationship, popping pills, running away from home, or whatever. And then we went to work…..

Many of these situations required a significant investment of time and energy over extended periods of time, usually days, often weeks, and sometimes months. It wasn't a matter of, "Gee, kid, that's something. Well, I hope everything turns out okay, and have a nice life." It took time. When I couldn't handle a problem myself, I knew how and where to get the help I needed. I knew I was good. The kids came back, and they sent their friends. Often they came back *with* their friends. When we were done, when matters were resolved, and when they felt better, they sent me priceless notes and cards, they gave me hugs, they drew me pictures on scraps of colored paper, they wrote me letters and attached a candy Life Saver, or they wrote me poems. And then I moved on to the next one.

I had a folder at home for each year I was a counselor. I put a rubber band around the old one each June, and I started a new one each September. I saved all those cherished mementos—the notes, the poems, the letters—into which the kids had put their hearts and souls and tears. It was my ego file. It was mine, and it was private. It was the tangible evidence of what I was capable of doing, of what I had done. My annual evaluations, typed on official pink forms with yellow copies to me, meant shit, but these items, precious messages from one human being to another human being, were my personal treasures. *I never shared them with anyone.*

I wasn't any different as a counselor at the A-School. I was the same person. I didn't do anything differently, except I didn't have an office. The office at the A-School was my office, but it wasn't *my* office. It was a beehive of activity for students and staff, the location of our only telephone, the chaotic residence of Betty Boop, a social center, a meeting place for meeting whomever one wanted to meet, a Grand Central Station where chatterbox travelers awaited the barking list of scheduled stops: "McDonald's, Portables, Bowling Alley, Blimpie's, High School, Votee Park—All aboard!" It certainly wasn't any place for counseling. I counseled wherever I could. And that, of course, had been my mistake.

In the fish bowl openness of the A-School, my regular and on-going contacts with Ann had been, for the most part, in full view of all. Had she been coming as frequently to my office at the regular high school, no one would have noticed, and no one would have raised an eyebrow. The talks on the stage, the notes in the mailboxes, the trips to the back steps, the drives to the bowling alley, the ping-pong games, the lunches together—all parts of the Alternative School experience—beautifully facilitated the informal, non-threatening communication vital to the counseling process. I counseled *all* the A-School kids in those student-friendly places, not just Ann.

Witnessed by all, however, the amount of time I spent with Ann cost me dearly. The time and attention I gave Ann raised first the eyebrows, then the curiosity, and finally the ire of the other staff members. Shit, I knew the teachers were pissed because I didn't teach more classes. Fuck them. I wasn't a classroom teacher. I was a counselor and an administrator, the only one of each on site, working without a guidance office, a principal's office, assistant principals, a records clerk, an attendance officer, an athletic director—working on a shoestring. Who was going to take care of all this shit if it wasn't me? I had all I could handle—more. I wasn't cheating anybody. I wasn't neglectful. I never turned *anyone* away, ever. The place didn't fold up for lack of effort on my part. No one accused me of not doing my job. They couldn't. I did my job. I did my job, plus. But even the plus wasn't enough. They wanted *all* the extras. They wanted the extra time, *my time*, that I chose to give to Ann—my after school time, my between classes time, and my lunch time. The amount of time and attention I gave Ann also caused distress to other students whose initial lack of understanding eventually turned to jealousy-induced hostility. Yes, jealousy reared its ugly head.

Jealousy—the most insidious of all negative feelings, the one negative feeling so different from all others because it evolves as a response to a *positive* act rather than to a negative one. Jealousy—felt by those who envy the favored position of someone other than themselves, felt by those who wish themselves the beneficiary of someone else's attention. Funny how Judith didn't bitch when *she* had been the beneficiary for almost two years. But that's the nature of jealousy: the same act that is so satisfying when *you* are the recipient becomes so angering when you see someone *else* get it instead of you.

I could have placated the upset, smoothed the ruffled feathers, and silenced the wagging tongues. It would have been easy. All I had to do was withhold the time and attention I gave to Ann. That's all, nothing else—just cut it, look good, and hello, Mr. Charlie Nice Guy. Or I could have done what I did, put my *effort* where the *need* was and not care what it looked like. Shit, man, there wasn't even a choice. Which one of them in need, student or teacher, would have had me say to them, "Sorry, but to give you my time will make me look bad, and you *know* what others will say," huh? No one.

Alternative bullshit was no different than regular bullshit, except it came from alternative assholes. It still stunk.

I should have realized what was happening, but I didn't, except, perhaps, minimally. Except for the extended Sunday night discussions, I never even tried to cover my ass. Whoever heard of covering your ass so people couldn't or wouldn't see how you worked, what you did, how you made your living? I was proud of what I could do and what I did. I wasn't trying to hide it. The accusation was, at its worst, not only unfounded, but reckless. At its best, it was the charge of an ignorant fool. Either way, however, it hurt. Either way, it had the same results.

* * * * * * *

Pam and the kids were asleep. I had gone to the racetrack, returning home shortly after midnight. The track was my therapy. It was the place where I could unwind, relax, and forget everything. The race program was an end in itself, doping out the sheet and picking the winner of the next race the only thing that mattered, the lone problem to solve, the sole objective of the moment. Everything else was nothing. The noise was nothing, the crowd was nothing, and yesterday's problems were nothing. Even the previous race was nothing.

But now I was home, and it was quiet, and I was alone. I had lost a lot of money. Over the past week and a half I had lost a bundle. I mean, big time. I felt lousy. The track had put me in an unsolvable financial position. And now, the false accusation at school had fucked up my head. I went over to the closet next to the front door and pulled the packet of folders from the top shelf. I sat on the couch with the manila folios on my lap. I didn't have to open them. I knew what was inside—my treasures. I guess I sought their company to reassure myself that I was something, that I was somebody, and that there were people who liked and trusted me.

I was down and still sinking. It had been a week—maybe only two or three days—I don't know. It seemed longer. Nothing more had been said. Fran had kept her fucking mouth shut. That was one of the two choices I had given her, and I guess that's what she decided to do. But it didn't help. I had thought about going to the Board of Education myself. I had thought of getting a lawyer and suing the bitch. I wasn't going to give up. I *couldn't* give up, not without one more try.

At our next staff meeting, I tried. Over the whole stinking mess I went, again telling them what I had done and why, and telling them what I hadn't done. And in direct and precise terms, I told them exactly what I thought of them. The room was deadly silent. I spoke quietly, for me, but my voice still echoed off the cinderblock walls of the conference room where we all sat around the table.

"Every one of you—every *damn* one of you—should be ashamed of yourselves. Every one of you, either by opening your fucking mouth or by keeping your fucking mouth closed, is part of this," I impugned. "You must know—Christ, how can you *not* know—that this accusation is an outright lie. Without just cause—without *any* fuckin' cause—without any proof, facts, evidence, or any information except what you've heard from a liar, you're all chomping at the bit to jump on the bandwagon.

Well, aren't you something—just butcher me and spill the blood on my family and an innocent kid. Who cares if someone gets hurt? You're havin' a good time with this, right? If you don't feel shame, there's gotta be something very, very wrong with you. You all think you're so fuckin' smart, huh? You know everything, and you know me, too, huh? Well, you're not very smart, and you don't know me at all, none of you—maybe what you see on the outside you know, but not what's inside me. You wanna know what's inside me? Ya wanna know who I am?"

Blank faces.

My anger boiled within, a volcano bubbling on the surface, steaming with tumultuous agitation beneath, seeking vent. I was going to change those fucking emotionless, unyielding, unfeeling stares if it took everything I had. I was desperate.

"Well, I'm gonna show you what's inside me. I'm gonna give you a good look at who I am."

I reached down into my briefcase. I took out my folders, and I threw them on the table. The letters, notes, and papers spilled out the open top of the folders and slid across the laminated surface of the table. I felt like I had taken off my clothes. I felt naked.

"There's the story of all the bodies I ever went after, in their own words. Take a good fuckin' look, damn you, and when you're satisfied that you know who I am, I hope you fuckin' choke on your accusations."

American History had been my subject when I was a classroom teacher. I was great with historical quotations. I loved them. I could run them off, one after another, from memory. As I stood at the end of the table and looked at my "guts," my private guts that no one had a right to see, that no one deserved to see, I thought of my favorite quote, a statement written by William Allen White when the Senate had refused to ratify Woodrow Wilson's dream, his League of Nations.

> **He tasted the ingratitude of his Republic—this statesman's ancient cup of hemlock. No wonder, that on that high and empty altar, where the flame of his fame was quenched and the cold, dark ashes strewn, he lay helpless while the high priests of the temple cut out his heart.**

I didn't say it, I just thought it. That's what they had done. The fuckin' ingrates had cut out my heart.

I picked up my briefcase, and I left them sitting there.

"Fuckin' bastards," I muttered, as I walked out the door. I was crying, but those fucks weren't going to see it.

I don't know if any or all of them ever looked at my personal treasures. I hope they were too embarrassed to look, but I don't know. Somehow, the folders, with all of their contents, were returned to me, and I never heard another word about the accusation. It was poetic justice. When nothing was happening and everything was up-front, they stupidly climbed all over my ass. Later, when I was guilty as hell, the dumb asses never saw a thing and never said a word. And they thought *they* were smart and *I* was dumb? The fucks. They were *so* dumb I could have been fuckin' their fuckin' daughters right under their fuckin' noses, and they wouldn't have known what was happening.

Lisa was the only one who made any move. She came around a short time later, and we went for a walk together. I'll never forget it. I needed it so badly.

We didn't talk. We just walked. It seemed like I was walking in a limbic trance, on the frayed border between two mutually exclusive desires, on the razor's edge of two equally supported feelings: I had to go through everything in my head once more but, at the same time, I didn't want to give another thought to the whole thing. It was so painfully nice not to be in touch. As we walked, I shook my head often, still finding it hard to believe what was happening to me. I always had liked Lisa, but for now, I loved her. She didn't ask any questions or push for further explanations. I had to believe she trusted me. It *was* a matter of trust. Except for Ann and me, who could know the truth? It all came down to trusting me and my word, with no way to prove it, or believing Fran and her accusation, with no way to prove it.

If anyone had any shred of "evidence" more than anyone else, it was Lisa. If anyone was going to make a value judgment on everything they had seen or heard, Lisa had the one piece of information that nobody else had, and it *wasn't* in my favor.

It had happened over the Christmas vacation on one of several afternoons I had gone to school to clear up paperwork. Ann, lost for something to do and itching to get out of the house and away from her father's grumbling at her mother, had taken off for a drive in her car. She had driven past the A-school, and, seeing my car in the parking lot, had stopped and come in. I was running off things on the mimeograph machine. Thankful to have a pair of helping hands, I had Ann begin to staple the sheets together. That's when Lisa walked in. She had taken a bus from the City, where she lived, to come to a holiday party her Seminar was having that evening. Her walk from the bus stop had taken her past the Church, and, seeing lights, she had come in. Ann and I were working. That's all there was to it—nothing else, but it must have seemed odd. If Lisa had wanted to be suspicious at finding the two of us together in school, she could have.

And now, as we walked silently together, there was nothing more I could say or offer. I just had to believe, right or wrong, that she believed and trusted me.

CHAPTER 12

Adversity and threat brought us closer together, united in like purpose, common cause, and self-defense. The revelation of her x-rated dream led to the start of x-rated activity, and the contract was sealed.....

Ann and I didn't change a thing. I kept driving her to the portables along with everyone else. She piled into the car with the others when we went to the bowling alley. We continued going to lunch together, sometimes with a group and sometimes just the two of us, as we always had done. We talked in the lounge after school when I was finished my work, just as frequently and for just as long, no more and no less. Any staff member or student who might have been suspicious of our behavior before must have continued to be suspecting. What they saw now was no different than what always had been open to view and subject to scrutiny. If petty tongues wagged before, shit, I guess they still were wagging. Fuck them.

But it wasn't the same. It was crazy. Ann and I were *plotting* to do now what we always had done as a matter of course. The accusation made contrived and illicit what before had been automatic and innocent. It was unreal, a staged drama that changed the dynamics of everything. The counseling continued, but within an atmosphere of hushed whispers, passed notes, and a continual awareness of who was around. As clandestine as our behavior became, concealed and disguised in a Halloween costume of false image, masked and curtained as a child hides his trick-or-treat identity, we changed none of our activities. We soaped their windows to obstruct their view, but we changed nothing, except for a single addition.

When we left school at the end of the day, usually between four-thirty and five, after playing ping-pong—I always beat her—or talking in the lounge—she always out-talked me, except on the afternoon I told her that I had told Pam I wanted a divorce—we didn't each go home. Adversity and threat had brought us closer together, united in like purpose, common cause, and self-defense. We went back to that little park in Bergenfield where she had driven that day a week before, when I wanted to go some place where we could sit and talk, that day I told her what Fran and the others had claimed we were up to, and that day she said she'd tell me all about her dream.

It wasn't until our third or fourth trip to the park that she, emboldened by the fact that my marriage was now virtually over, actually told me.

I drove to the end of the cinder road that bordered the park, turning around in the cul-de-sac as had become routine. I pulled ahead and parked on the right-hand side under the overhanging trees, a clear view of the expansive park to our left, the open cinder road ahead. A police car had driven past to check us out on one of our previous visits, but we were just sitting and talking—no hassle.

"Gee, it's getting lighter and lighter each day. This is about the same time we've been getting here, isn't it?" she asked benignly.

I looked at my watch.

"We're a little early today, but it's about the same time," I answered.

I took off my glasses and rubbed my eyes, yawning at the same time.

"Tired, babe? Busy day, huh?"

I grunted as I looked out across the empty athletic field.

"It wasn't that bad. I just—I'm just not into it any more," I breathed with a sigh. "The same amount of work takes more energy and more time and makes me more tired than it used to—not more tired, more blah, ya know?"

She had kicked off her sneakers and rolled a joint as soon as we had pulled out of the Church lot, and now it was almost played.

"Ya coulda fooled me," she said, as if surprised. "I didn't get a chance to see you all day. Every time I looked, you were in the middle of something. Ya wanna toke before this goes out again?"

She offered the clip and what remained of the roach. I took it and drew a deep hit.

"Christ," she laughed, "wouldn't Fran have a shit fit if she saw you now!"

"Yeah," I chuckled, holding the inhale. "I bet she would."

We had joked about it several times before.

"Right on the fuckin' stage, too," she giggled, slapping her knee.

She was stoned. When she was stoned, she often interjected a lingering thought or recollection from the past into the middle of a conversation. It usually was related in some way, but sometimes I had to stop and try to figure out how. Not this time. I didn't have to figure this one out. She was making humorous reference to the time, a month ago, when she, Lois, and Julia had done a joint in the lounge at school and had tried to turn me on to grass.

It was late in the afternoon, after everybody but the four of us had gone, and one of them lit up a jay right in the middle of the stage, like it was perfectly okay, like why not? The reefer was passed around, shared in the customary and typical manner users employ to blend their common purpose into a circle of fraternal bond. When it got to me, I had a hit, too, the first time in my life—they didn't know that, but I think they suspected—that I ever had smoked grass. The joint went around three or four times until everyone was wrecked but me. I didn't feel a thing. I was too scared to get ripped. They kept asking me, "Do ya feel anything? Do ya feel anything?" and I kept saying, "No, no." They were laughing and giggling, practically rolling off the couch, and I didn't feel a thing, not even a buzz.

Since that time, Ann usually would offer me a hit when she lit up. Sometimes I had one or two. Most often, I didn't. Sometimes I'd take one and fake the second, abashed to admit my appetite for her inhaled escape from reality paled in comparison to the ravenous craving she exhibited.

"Yeah, right on the fuckin' stage," I repeated with a cackle.

We sat for a while without talking. I don't know where her head was. She snuffed out the roach and carefully dropped it into her little black film cylinder, replacing the lid with a snap and tucking the container in her flowered cosmetic pouch with the clip and the packet of rolling papers that had been on the front seat between us. For Ann, stowing a roach was a sacred ceremony, a solemn ritual that held the fervent promise of a future high.

"Ya know," she started, hesitantly, "I never really told you about my dream, did I?"

"Well, you really did, didn't you?"

"No, not really, but I would now, if you wanted me to."

I shrugged without emotion—without any showing, anyway.

"You told me it was good, right?"

"I said it was nice," she corrected with a purr.

"And nice means what?" I tickled.

"Nice means horny." She said slowly, enticingly.

"I thought so. I figured it probably was an x-rated dream. And when we squealed out of the parking lot last week, you blurted out that you dreamed—"

"I know what I said," she interrupted with a smile.

"And was that true? Was that the truth?"

"Yeah," she blushed.

"Whew. And there's more to this dream that ya wanna tell me?"

"Well, ya wanna hear the whole story and all the details, don't you?" she questioned cautiously, teasingly.

I felt the surge. It was slow, but it was steady and warm. I must be crazy, I thought. I was gonna let her tell me this? I wanted her to tell me this? I think I wanted her to tell me.

"Okay," I said with a nod.

I held my breath. I didn't know what her reaction was going to be. Shit, I didn't know what *my* reaction was going to be to all of this.

"Okay, I'll tell," I heard a little girl's voice say, as if she were responding to her mommy's question as to what she had done with all the cookies. "I'll tell you the trooth, the whole troooth, and noth….."

"…..ing but the trooooooth," we both finished in unison, as we laughed together.

She wiggled and squirmed her way across the seat until she was pressed against my side like a little girl settling next to her daddy to have a story read to her. But this was her story, not mine.

"Once upon a time—do ya wanna hear the whole thing from the beginning, or just the good parts?"

Now the surge was throbbing and growing. Damn, I was sitting the wrong way. She had to be blind not to see it.

…..I wanted you to make love to me…..but you never touched me, you never put a hand on me…..I wanted you to make love to me…..You could have fucked me a hundred times…..I love you so much…..We were fuckin' each other outta sight…..I wanted you to make love to me…..

"The good parts."

Holy crap. I couldn't believe I said it. It just came out with blinding speed, faster than a speeding bullet, more powerful than a locomotive, able to leap tall buildings in a—but I sure didn't feel like Superman. I was scared.

"Here, let me.....turn around.....and put my head down here on your leg.....and my feet up.....here." She did it as she said it, stretching out on her back across the seat, the back of her head resting on my right thigh, her knees bent, both feet flat against the far-side window.

"How's that?" she asked, looking up at me from between the steering wheel and my body, her hair swirled over my lap, covering the tell-tale bulge in my jeans. "Okay?"

"That's nice, babe."

Holy Christmas. What was I saying? Nice means horny. It *was* nice. It was perfect, perfectly nice.

I bent forward and down as she raised her head to meet mine, and we kissed. It happened automatically, spontaneously. We wanted it to happen, so it did. It was time. We kissed again, a long time, and I ran my tongue over her lips, before I sat back with a deep breath, and she let her head down on my leg, her eyes closed.

Except for the three or four times her emotional upset had made her needy of tenderness, or me needy to console, I hadn't kissed her until the past week when we had said goodbye each night, innocent pecks that took but a split second to engage, perhaps a trifle longer to release with each successive day, but who was noticing? It hadn't been anything like this. I saw in the fading half-light the peaceful expression on her face, her head cushioned in the bed of controlled spirals and twists of her long, brown hair, beautifully at rest, comfortably relaxed and dreamy. I was scared shit.

Asshole Fran, and those who were dumb enough to support her absurd accusation, thought Ann and I had been fucking each other for God knows how long, yet here we were, kissing for the first time. I knew that, at least partially because of the goading effect of Fran's accusation, this was but the beginning, a fool's fantasy now on its way to becoming reality, an impossibility soon to become possible.

"I dreamed," she began slowly, "that we were together—"

My bone pulsed involuntarily, once, and then again.

"I felt that," she swiveled in quiet surprise, looking at me. "Wow, I could feel that."

Christ, she had a lot of guts! She looked right at me and acknowledged my arousal. Should she do that? We both knew it was there, but, shit, it took guts to *say* anything about it. I had a boner on my first date when I kissed Arlene goodnight. I was twelve and in the eighth grade. But *she* didn't say anything about it. She had to feel it pushing, but she never *said* anything. Ann's directness, her blatant words that admitted her noticing, scared the hell outta me. But it heightened my awakening as well, her unafraid declaration a token sign of acceptance, a waiver of discreteness that provoked my courage and made me move to her sweater, the light gray, knit garment loosened from her jeans, her waist exposed in a narrow circle of nakedness above her belt. I reached under the ribbed edge of the sweater and pushed up to her breasts, my forearm dragging her sweater half-way up. She quivered as my hand found her breast, and my fingers rubbed against and then grasped the erectile flesh of her arousal.

Good night, she was in my hand, in the palm of my hand, alive and breathing, soft and warm. It was beautiful. I felt exhilarated—humbled, as well—that she was giving and trusting her private body to my touch.

This wasn't playing a game. This wasn't tick-tack-toe on a book cover or playing footsy under a table. This was touching Ann, feeling her. And in that captive moment as my thoughts raced wildly, it felt as if every topless woman I ever dreamed about, every *Playboy* centerfold, every bathing suit I ever tried to look down, and every naked native dancer I ever saw was exposed before me, and every tit in the world was in my hand.

I enjoyed Ann's gift and felt her heartbeat. I let my fingers ply and knead the softness, her smoothness. God, she felt good, and she was letting me, allowing, permitting.....

"Ohhhh, I wanted you to do that. God, did I want you to touch me!"

.....and she wanted me to, her body in resigned surrender, her budding efflorescence under my touch.

I flicked the protuberance sharply from the underside with my thumb and felt its full extension, holding up and back before letting go and dropping my hand quickly, pressing my palm over the entire surface, squeezing softly.

"Ohhhh," she exhaled and shivered, as she raised her head, her lips pursed and searching.

I kissed her hard, my tongue darting as I enjoyed the moisture of her lips and the warm spittle of her tongue flicking and fluttering in panicky retreat from mine. My hand slid from one breast to the other and quickly back, and she allowed her head to rest back on my lap.

"Pretty small, huh?" she said apologetically. "I haven't got that much."

"You're not small," I said. "Just right."

As I pulled up one side of the sweater, she tugged at the other side, both breasts popping simultaneously from under the released tension of the binding sweater, her nipples quivering like a taut bow string with the release of an arrow.

"You're pretty, but not small," I said, fondling her gently and becoming familiar with the rounded curves and the warm firmness of both breasts with their matching nips and silky smooth and puffy—definitely adolescent—rosettes.

"Didn't anyone ever tell you that anything more than a mouthful is just a waste?" I chortled, hoping a little lightheartedness would allay my nervousness and steady my hand.

She giggled as she straightened her legs, pushed herself away from the far window with her feet, and lifted her buttocks onto my lap so that her head was cradled in my arm against the door. I watched her breasts jiggle and swing as she made the adjustment—cute little cream puffs, so nice, so within reach now.

"That better?" she asked.

I struggled, really, to block the compelling spasms of voyeurism that twitched my thoughts, spattering vulgar images across my mind's eye. My superego buckled, overwhelmed by a fantasized carnival of bawdy side shows. I found myself mastered by irreverent thoughts unbefitting the occasion, succumbing to a panorama of passion's carnal delights, the impulses of my male id rising unchecked within me as an ocean shore boardwalk awakens with inimitable certainty in a flood of gaudy lights and hawking sounds on Memorial Day weekend. On my mind's TV screen, sun-drenched, bikini-clad bathers danced their dangling strings on a sandy beach that stretched to my imagination's horizon, and one by one I stripped them helplessly naked, touching with salacious perversion only the snow-white patches no sun had reached, probing with spiteful ritual the private parts my mind boldly had exposed to view. No primetime euphemism here—only HBO uncensored.

"Perfect, babe."

My stirring was now trapped, a spire pressed tightly upright against my body, and I knew she must be able to feel its throb and pulse against the side of her thigh. I leaned forward and suctioned her nipple, drawing it into my mouth and pushing it against the back of my teeth with my tongue.

"I love you, Charlie," she breathed into my ear. "Shit, you make my whole body hot."

I lifted my head slightly, pulling the liquored gumdrop between my lips, stretching it fully, and releasing it with a quick flip, letting it spring back.

"Aaahhhhh," she moaned in delight. "Ohhhh, nice."

She let her left leg slip off the edge of the seat onto the floor, and she lifted her right leg up onto the back of the seat.

"My crotch is so wet, it feels like I wet my pants," she exclaimed.

Jesus! Again the beast in me swelled, rising like a loaf of bread in a heated oven, fired by glowing embers within my body furnace, fueled by her talk of sweet effluents overflowing her passion's caldron, her admission sanctioning approach, her position a further invite.

"I'm soaked, too," I admitted. It was a confession, but not an apology, an admission that put us in like position, in like mind, and in like pursuit.

I drew my hand back over her bare stomach, tucking my fingers under her jeans and squeezing down over her cotton panties, far down until my finger tips rose up and over, then down and around, searching, and then finding. The length of my finger was dampened as I pressed gently against the crease to which her panties—wet all the way through—clung so loyally. As inviting as the position of her legs had been, her jeans were pulled tightly against her. There wasn't much—enough—room to move.

"Go under, underneath," she insisted, with urgency.

I pulled my hand back and again pushed it forward, this time under the elastic band of her panties. My hand's breadth was flat against her smooth abdomen, my fingers searching, my heart pounding, my head reeling, my mouth feeling like it was full of cotton—my TV on—my mind hijacked, captured and captivated, by swishy visions of a stripper's suggestive performance.....

.....her skimpy chiffon décolletage, translucent red and daring, removed with slinky intrigue and dangled with sultry finesse over her bare shoulder before being dropped behind her back to the floor,

.....her strapless, black demi-bra unhooked with a soundless snap, her hands clutching the lace-frilled half-cups to her cleaved bosom before sweeping the flimsy silk undergarment to the side and twirling it tauntingly in the air from her finger tips, her bud-tipped breasts released to swing freely in parallel circles to a legato drum roll from the orchestra pit,

.....her cheesecake strut, her sensual prance, her bump and grind routine, her gyrating hips, corkscrewed again and again, around and around, to the howling, clapping delight of her audience,

.....her appreciative response: a humping, jerking, thrusting lower torso, arms stretched above her head, upper body stiff and rigid save the springy flounce of her cherry-topped cupcakes,

.....and then, her backward bow, bent deeply from the waist, her bottom upturned, outturned, her soft, rounded moons squeezing crescents from the sides of the red-fringed G-string, her polished fingernails stroking the soft, thin cushion between the spread of the stockinged legs that rose from high-heels flat on the stage floor, her finger tips then hitching beneath the narrow, elastic band and flashing the smooth fullness of her splendidly firm rump as the lights dimmed in eerie, misty anticipation of the last unveiling, the final unsecreting.

Down, slowly but not teasingly, over the smoothness I moved my hand. I felt the baby-fine hair. Then I felt nothing. And then my finger dipped into her wet softness.

She was opening her belt and unfastening the top snap and undoing the zipper to relieve the pressure, using her thumbs to jerk her jeans down to make room, putting the spread position of her legs now to advantage.

I kissed her lips, then her breasts, then again her lips. Our tongues met between our mouths, lashing, twisting, thrashing, each to affect its own circuitous entrance, a lovingly selfish duel of desperate daggers of heat and wetness. I submitted, allowing her entry, up, over, around, and in, our saliva mingling, our teeth gnashing in an imperative drive of haste and hunger which I matched below, my finger separating, then penetrating with firm pressure, well up and in.

God, I was doing it—as far as I could reach, my finger embraced to knuckle depth, wiggling for passage, surprised by the extension of curved openness beyond its stretch. My thumb slipped across the smooth triangle of creaminess above my probe, seeking the buttoned rise of her excite—an unnecessary effort, really—all the buttons already had been pushed.

Her panting breaths came in hurried gasps as if she were running in panic from an onrushing train, the choked, agonizing wail of its whistle rising from the dryness of her throat with the shrill screech of steel on steel braking. She pulled her head back from mine and slammed it punishingly against my arm, at the same time bringing her legs tightly together, locking my finger.

"Holy shit. Fuckin' shit. I dreamed—holy God. I dreamed that you—holy fuckin' shit. Ahhh….I think I'm….."

A chorale of staccato breaths and helpless moans swelled me with prideful satisfaction, pleased she was pleased. I tried to cover her mouth and muffle her yelps and squeals, but my free hand was trapped, pinned behind her neck against the door. She raised her shoulders and quickly slammed her head back against my arm, again, and again, her breasts heaving and jouncing with each slam, her hair tangled and flying, her eyes glassy and glazed.

"Oh, man. Yes, yes—Ahh…..Yes…..Ahhhhh….."

I felt the squirts—holy, good God—one little shot after another. I never felt anything like it in my life. *She came in squirts.* I felt the spasmodic contractions, the pulsing squirts, warm and mellifluous, soaking my hand with the honeyed nectar of her release. Holy shit.

My body jerked upward. I held my breath, and—no, not yet, not now, no—it came, jolting me as the wind seizes the sail of a catamaran and drives it forward with a lurching, surging splash.

I started to laugh, embarrassed that my restraint had been so limited, my experience so useless. All my expertise notwithstanding, I had had no more staying power than this novice, this beginner who popped off with the single push of a finger. Some fucking teacher I was!

I looked at her face. There were tears in her eyes, but she was laughing, too, laughing and crying at the same time. We kissed each other's noses, cheeks, eyes, foreheads, throats, and lips. We purred like a pair of contented kittens, and I again found the slippery openness at her vertex and brushed its bud with gentle circles, butterfly touches, and feathery tickles, an unconscious action, an automatic reflex, as she jerked both legs up sharply, arched her shoulders forward, and grasped her knees, squeezing them tightly against herself, pancaking her breasts.

"Ohh—Ohhhhh, yes, yesssssssss.....I'm comin'!"

Again, I felt the releasing twitches and the dribble as my finger, freed by her hoisted position, milked her pocket of its squirting, gurgling essences with insinuating promise, deliberate portent. Damn. I would have given anything to see it.

"I love it, I love it!" she yelled, almost at the top of her lungs, rocking her head from side to side, then up and down, her forehead pressed to her knees. "God, I love it!"

The words sent a rush of pleasureful warmth throughout my body. I rubbed her back and the back of her neck, sticky and sweaty under her hair. She released the grip on her knees, letting herself fall back onto my arm, her legs straight out in front of her. She lay prone, out of breath, spent.

"I dreamed—I dreamed you made love to me, but it wasn't this good."

Her face was a rainbow of colors and creases from crying and laughing and holding her forehead against her knees. The top of her jeans had slipped to the middle of her thighs, and her panties were drenched, a crumpled clump between her legs, my hand still tucked inside. One more time? I didn't have the heart. She was exhausted. I was soaked half-way up my arm. I withdrew my hand and pulled her soggy panties up, giving her a loving pat on the mound.

"I think we both should get phys ed credit for this, don't you?" I chuckled. "Ask Fran in the morning if we can get credit."

She laughed out loud, burrowing her face into my chest. Her sweater was a tight roll around her throat. I pulled the top down on her back, and, when she drew away, down over her front.

"Good-bye, little titties," she giggled. "Charlie will see you again," she spoke caringly as she shook herself free beneath the sticky cling of the knitted material.

"That was one unbelievable come," I said in quiet reflection.

"Two," she corrected. "Do we get double credit for two?"

"Three," I said with a sheepish grin. "I'm a little sticky, too."

"Oh, yeahhhhh, that's right," she said impishly. "I felt you go."

"You must have been saving that up for months. You really let loose," I flourished.

"For months?" She looked at me with bewilderment. "That never happened before," she said softly. "I never had a climax, ever."

"Holy shit," I whistled. "It was beautiful. It was unbelievable."

"It was. It was beautiful. I can still feel it."

We embraced spontaneously and hugged each other tightly.

"You made me feel like a real woman, Charlie," she whispered in my ear. You made me a woman today, and I love you for it, very much. I love you, just for nothing, too, just because I do. Christ," she said, pulling her head back abruptly and looking into my eyes. "you can do more with one finger than a lot of people can do with a cock."

"Maybe that's because you haven't had enough cock," I teased.

"Yet," she flashed with a wink.

Geez, I couldn't believe she said that.

"Yet," I confirmed, and the contract was sealed.

CHAPTER 13

We couldn't get enough of each other. Our passions ran wild. But above and beyond the sex, something stronger was emerging, and I finally told her.....

There was a note in my mailbox the next morning. There were no more open notes. Notes now came in sealed envelopes. I tore open the envelope. Inside were three pages of sky blue stationery with white clouds above a field of tall grass. On each page Ann had written one verse of a song by Carole King, with a postscript by Ann.

I read the moving song lyrics to myself. Her choice of songs had been deliberate. She had "adopted" the beautifully revealing lyrics of "You Make Me Feel Like a Natural Woman" as her own and had used them to share with me the thrill of her first loving sexual experience. I was overwhelmed by the sincerity of her message and her admitting postscript: "You know, I can still feel that tingle down to my toes."

I was so excited, I didn't know what to do or think. I hadn't expected there to be any aftermath of regrets; her note clearly put to rest all doubts or questions about that.

We went back to the park again that afternoon to make sure the tingle lasted through the weekend.

I was almost afraid to walk into my own house when I got home at night. I loved the scent of her sex. It intoxicated me. I knew it was suicide, but I didn't want to wash my hands. The aroma seemed to be everywhere. I couldn't tell if it were on my clothes, in the car, in the house, in the school, or if it were just in my nostrils. There was no doubt about it being in my head.

Two afternoons of "playing" had infuriated my passions, drawing the most boorish improprieties to my mind's video, the bright screen of the knobbed box displaying a catharsis of mental collages, inelegant images, whimsically imagined sequences, and coarse hallucinations set to a musical fantasia of ribald sounds, a living-color porno flick of singular focus and repetitive insistence. I wanted it, I wanted it, I wanted it—my maleness, my urge, my lust dismembering the organ from the body, from the person. This was a picture I could tune in, brighten, set the horizontal, and let roll. But I didn't need my mind's TV this time.

This time my thoughts were for real. I knew, now, that undressing Ann, seeing Ann, having Ann, and loving Ann were no far-flung fantasies, no impossible dreams, and no false illusions of maybe's promise. I knew my objectives were finite quests, absolutely attainable, time only the hurdle, and I wanted them; I wanted all of them.

Damn, I wanted to see it. I wanted to take her panties off—not down, not raised in stretched restraint above my struggling hand, not lingering in an absorbent roll to absorb the excess of a plunging finger's love-labor in the darkness. I wanted the damn thing off and gone, so I could see. I *dreamed* about taking her panties off. Twice, with my hand tucked and busy in a lower place, I had seen them teasingly slip to reveal the ringlet curls of her mound's swell, but they still held pastel cover of the wreathed cavity I could see only in my imagination. And now I wanted more. I was dying to see that of which my eyes were jealous of my fingers. I wanted her panties off. It was driving me fucking crazy. It was the only thing I could think about, the only thing on my mind.

Over the weekend, I had re-lived—a dozen times, at least—our last two afternoons together, parked beneath the trees along the cinder road in the park. She must have done the same thing. We couldn't wait to see each other Monday morning. I knew she wouldn't be in until late, so I busied myself with twice as many cigarettes as usual, one eye on the clock, and a nervous flutter every time I heard the upstairs door open and close. She came in just before Seminar. I was waiting for her by the mailboxes, and I prattled for her benefit as she bounced down the stairs.

"Gee, I wonder—I wonder if I'll get any mail today?"

"No mail, babe, but I have a secret message for you from a close friend," she whispered. "Christ, I wanted to come in early today, but I knew it would look bad. I wanted to get here when you did. I love you, babe. You're the tops!"

"I'm glad you didn't come in early," I responded with an appreciative smile. "It killed me, but I'm glad you waited. What's the big secret message?"

"I wanna come." she whispered.

"Ssshhh," I cautioned with a laugh, giving her a pinch on the ass.

"Don't worry so much," she preached. "You don't see anybody around, do ya? I really wanna come. I'm desperate. I hafta feel ya; I hafta come. I'm dying for it."

"God, I couldn't stop thinking about it all weekend, either," I conceded. "I could feel you on my fingertips, and it was driving me nuts. C'mon in the office. I gotta sit."

I was lucky. There was no one in the office.

"I have to get rid of this bone before anyone comes in," I moaned, sitting behind the desk.

She leaned over the top of the desk and looked down. She spoke in the low sing-song voice of Humphrey Bogart. "I can take care of that, sweetheart, if you'll take care of me. What about lunchtime, babe—a nice, sweet, warm lunch?"

"Shit, I'll never get rid of it that way, babe," I said seriously. Then I added with a laugh, giving her a little bit of W. C. Fields: "Keep it up, babe, and maybe we'll go for an early lunch today."

I wanted the damn thing to go, and I wanted it to stay.

Marilyn and Jordan walked into the office.

It went—real fast.

"Okay, see ya later, Ann, after Seminar. You don't have a class, do ya?"

"No, no class. I'm goin' for an early lunch. Ya wanna come?"

"Yeah, I'll come."

As she left, she laughed quietly at the words we each had exchanged for our good-bye tease.

I stayed seated behind my desk for a few minutes, just to make sure things were the way they should be.

****

We left school at eleven-thirty and headed straight for Bergenfield and the park, grabbing at each other, poking and playing, and talking dirty the whole way. By the time we got there, we had worked each other so hot we were in fever, barely able to wait for the car to come to a stop. She sat across my lap again and exploded eleven times in fifty minutes. I went the third time she did. She wanted to go for an even dozen, but I told her we had to get back to school. I told her eleven times was a world's record, anyway.

That afternoon, I left school at three-thirty sharp—alone. I had something I had to do.

Tuesday morning, I gave her the news.

"I have some good news and some bad news. Which do you wanna hear first?"

"Oh! I have a choice, huh?"

"Did you forget where you are? This is an Alternative School, so ya always have choices," I said in reminder.

"Then, I choose *you.*" she giggled.

"Oh, c'mon, get serious," I prodded. "You already got me. Ya want the good news first, or the bad?"

"Gimme the good news, Charlie-nut. And it better be *good!*"

"I bought a van," I exulted with pride.

"You bought.....a van?"

"Yeah, is that good enough news for ya? Whaddya think of that! It's not new, it's used—eleven hundred and fifty bucks—a '70 Ford, green."

"How come ya bought a van?"

" 'Cause I think we outgrew the car," I whispered playfully. "Why else would I want a van? Aren't you excited?"

She was excited. It was written all over her face.

"Holy shit, Charlie. What did Pam say?"

"Nothing. I told her the truth. I told her I wanted to use it for camping this summer, and I could use it now to drive kids to bowling and to the portables. And now she can have a car for herself. I saw the van over the weekend….."

"Shit, a van!"

"…..when I was driving home from my parents' house. We went by this house in Oradell, and I saw this van with a 'For Sale' sign on the back, sitting in the driveway. So, I went back there after school yesterday, and I bought it!"

"Why didn't you tell me? I looked all over. I didn't know what happened to you. I thought you got tired of me," she pouted.

She tried to look hurt and punished, but she couldn't keep a straight face. I couldn't, either.

"Yeah, I got tired of you, so I bought a van to keep myself busy," I tantalized as I caressed and fondled my middle finger.

"Oh, Charlie, you're dirty!"

"I know. Don't ya just love it?"

"Yeahhhhhh, a van. Geez, that's gonna be neat." She was entranced, beyond words.

"But it's gonna take a coupla weeks. I have it, but I have to get it registered, get plates, and get the insurance changed. And I hafta do some work on it and get used to driving it."

"A van—that's—Wow!"

"I know, babe. Now, are you ready for the bad news?"

"I almost forgot. Yeah, that's right. You said there was some bad news, too. Okay, what *don't* I wanna hear?"

"I can't keep comin' back from lunch tryin' to hide wet spots on my jeans and smelling like a lilac tree."

"So, hold back…..and lilacs grow on bushes!" she retorted brazenly.

She knew her horticulture, but not as much about the birds and the bees of the garden as I thought she did. I already was holding back as long as I could.

"I thought I did great yesterday getting past the first two."

We went to the park at lunchtime, anyway, and I came back with beautifully fragranced fingers and slightly sticky pants, again.

But that afternoon she had a better idea. All the way back to the park—our second trip of the day—she told me how much she wanted to come, how she couldn't get enough of it.

"Do you think there's something wrong with me? I mean, I want it so much, so often."

"There's nothing wrong with you, babe," I assured her. "It's just hard to believe you never had a climax before last week. Didn't you ever, you know, didn't—didn't ya ever do it, ya know, like, do yourself?"

"Wellllll," she blushed, "I tried, but I never thought too much of my body, so I guess I just didn't try hard enough. Maybe I didn't get into it enough. That's funny, huh?" she gurgled. "I didn't get into it enough!"

"Well, there's nothing wrong with you or your bod, babe. Everything's in fine working order. It's beautiful."

"I know, at least I think I'm beginning to know, now. But when I tried—before, I mean—nothin' ever happened. I didn't know my boobies had anything to do with it. Christ, Charlie, when you pull on my titties, you know, and suck a little, the whole bottom falls out," she twittered. "Do ya know what I'm sayin'?"

When we got to the park, I was ready, a sprinter toed to the mark, awaiting the report of the starter's pistol. I knew what she was sayin'. But she didn't sit across my lap as usual. She slid over beside me and unzipped my jacket.

"This time it's your turn, hon," she said with seductive imprudence. "This time it's my treat."

Good gravy.

She gave me a quick kiss before opening my jacket and addressing herself to the pounding bulge in my jeans, covering it with the palm of her hand, squeezing gently, and massaging up and down.

"I never did this before," she said with uncertainty, almost apologetically.

I didn't say anything.

"You may have to help me," she continued. "It's warm. I can feel how warm it is."

She stroked slowly and steadily, letting her hand slide all the way down and under, squeezing lightly as I raised myself in beg of her continued pursuit. Then quickly, she slid her hand back up the underside to the top.

"I know, I can feel it, too. It really feels good."

"I didn't know it bounced around so much. I mean, I knew it got big and hard, but I didn't think it moved around."

"It's lookin' for a place to go," I laughed. "It has a mind of its own….."

She ran her fingernail from top to bottom against the stretched denim and then, pressing harder with the point of her nail, back from root to tip.

"…..and right now, you're blowin' its fuckin' mind."

"Good, oh, good!" she exclaimed excitedly, delighted with her success and the fact that I was being pleasured.

She leaned in intense watch of the pulsing, the curiosity of her virgin exploration and the uninhibited wonderment of her new discovery a prodding firebrand that sizzled me. She stroked firmly, pressing against my body as she worked her way up and down. I reached out, but she turned her shoulder to me and playfully shook my hand from her blouse.

"Uh uh," she shook her head, without a break in the relentless rhythm she had established. "No tittie for Charlie," she admonished. "No tittie—until Charlie comes."

Oh, wow, she wasn't just playin' around. She was gonna take me!

She took a firm hold through my jeans with her thumb and forefinger and pulled away from my body as far as my jeans would allow, letting go with a slam, like a screen door on a tight hinge. She did it again, and a third time, forcing the hinge further each time, then letting the door slam with a thud, before returning to the stroke.

"God, you're doin' it good. You got me goin'."

She had been turning around, facing me more and more, as she had grown bolder, more confident, and more fascinated by her own actions and my responses. Now, almost on her knees on the edge of the seat to the side of the steering column, facing me and bending to her task with enthused vigor, she used both hands in long, hard, determined ups and downs. I could feel my foreskin slip effortlessly up and over and down—again, up and over, my spermic tide ready, throttled, but committed.

"I gotcha, Charlie. I gotcha," she spoke to my cock. "Now I'm gonna take ya. Now I'm gonna take ya. No place to go, no place to hide, Charlie-cock. Not gonna wiggle away, either."

She spoke to my cock! I clenched my teeth and closed my eyes, but I still could hear her talking—stroking, rubbing, stroking—and talking to my cock.

"You're gonna give it up, you're gonna give it good. Ann's pussy, now Charlie's cock. Oh, are you gonna come! Yeah, do it. C'mon, you can come. Come to me; come to Annie," she implored in a rising voice. "Gimme a cunt full, you fuckin' cock. Wouldn't you like that? Wouldn't you just *love* to do that?" she taunted with surly arrogance.

She talked to my cock!

"Give it up! I want it."

"Not inside, not inside," I gasped, biting my lower lip, crushing my teeth tightly together.

She knew, her hands already in motion—unzipping, helping herself without hesitation, grabbing with confidence and pulling away from my shirt. She either had the natural artistry of a skilled and talented wench or she was a hunch player on an incredibly lucky run, making the right move at every turn. Maybe she had played out her fantasies in rehearsal with as much practice as I.

She gave a single upwards jerk followed by a series of short, quick, finger rolls just beneath the head, and a final, slow, hard pull downward, my foreskin stretched back almost to the rim, a crystal clear droplet—glistening—brought forth in oozing prelude.

"Come to me, Charlie-cock. Show me. Ann's ready. Le'me see it. C'mon, shoot it, shoot your fuckin' sperm!"

"Sperm" did it. I don't know why. Maybe because it was so blatant, so uncamouflaged, so unfashionably honest, so devoid of euphemistic cover—so naked, like my cock.

"Ahhhh, ahhhhh.....Ohh, ohhhh, ohhhhhhh." I moaned, twisting my face, and I shot straight up, sounding, I think, like an owl in heat, or a climber falling from the edge of a cliff, one risk too many, one mistaken step too short.

"Damn—holy fuckin' shit—yeah, yeah, yeah, keep doin' it, keep it goin'," I bugled, as she held on tightly, her hand flying in a blur, my hot release spurting, flying, and dripping over her clenched fist. "Ahhh.....yeahhhhhh, that's nice, babe."

"What a fuckin' thing! I can't believe I did it all by myself. What a thing to watch. Did I do it right? It really came—what a blast. Holy crap, my pussy's dripping. Did it feel good, honey babe?"

My breaths came in deep, heaving succession. How the hell could I talk? I reached out with my right hand and pushed between her legs, rubbing her crotch through her jeans with my fingers.

"Ummmmm," she cooed.

She squatted lower onto my outstretched hand and moved her hips in swirling circles, pressing down to make hard contact and warming friction.

"So, Charlie.....can't have.....any tittie, huh?" I teased in gasping pants, menacingly.

"Ahhh."

"So, guess what naughty, little Charlie.....is gonna have, instead. Big, bad Charlie.....is gonna take your sweet juices, right through your pants—through your fuckin' undies—and through your pants."

I freed one finger and used my nail to scratch quickly, striking an imaginary match against the rough surface beneath which I knew the blushing bud of her arousal stood amid a slippery wash of simmering fluids, glowing incandescence but a spark away.

"Dirty, little Charlie is gonna lick the sweet juices from your pretty little lips, and stick his tongue into your hot, little honey box, until....."

"Ohhhh, Charlliiieeeeee—"

".....your whole fuckin' body turns to cum. Wouldn't *you* like that? Wouldn't *you* just love me to do that?" I taunted as she had done to me.

"Ahhhhhhhhhh, yes, yesssssss.'

She heaved up, and pressed down hard, before falling forward against me.

"Oh, God, thank you. Thank you, thank you, thank you, Charlie. Thank you, thank you. Oh, you're a fucker. You're the tops, but you're a fucker, you. Thank you, thank you."

We kissed and hugged and kissed some more, loving each other with breaths and sighs, tongues and tear drops, soft touches and tender whispers, until eternal minutes made forearms tingle, fingers numb, and feet fall asleep, all parts aching in unison for a changed position and renewed circulation.

I was feeling things I hadn't felt in a long, long time. Over the past weekend I had deliberately focused my attention on the recall of our sexual activities; when I considered my emotional involvement, it scared me. It was easier to savor the sex than it was to deal with the belief that I was falling in love.

She broke from our sleepy embrace and sat upright in the descending darkness, leaning back as far as she could in the tight quarters. She stretched her arms out to either side and took a deep breath, releasing it slowly in a long sigh of contented fulfillment. She stretched here arms even further, her elbow in touch with the center of the steering column, the horn sounding a shattering blast in the evening quiet.

"Holy shit, be careful."

"I'm sorry, I'm sorry," she apologized with embarrassment.

We looked at each other and laughed. Her jeans were smirched with a wet spot the size of a saucer between her legs. There were wet spots on my pants, on my shirt, and on the car seat. There were sticky spots on her blouse, on her forehead, and in her hair. Everything we had touched was wet and sticky.

"Maybe I should blow the horn again," she said in jest. "I think we need a maid."

"Yeah," I agreed with amusement, "I think we have a little mess to deal with."

"It's the nicest mess I ever saw," she said softly, as she leaned forward and puckered her lips. I met her half-way. I closed my eyes as our lips met, and I breathed in deeply the aromatic and musty scents of every wet spot our pleasuring had made together.

"You're just so much sunshine in my life, sweet baby," I said quietly.

That's exactly what she was—sunshine in my life. I wasn't afraid any more. No more.....

"I love you, Ann."

There it was. I don't know how I had held it back for so long. I don't know why. She hadn't held her feelings back. Had my hesitancy been because I was married? I don't think so. Was it the age difference? I don't think years and numbers are a barrier to love. Was it the teacher-student thing? I'd like to say, "No," but I guess so. And now—what was different, now? And now I saw myself a man, not a teacher, and she a woman, no student—a big difference between—a man in love with a woman.

"I love you, Ann," I repeated.

"Oh, I love you so much, Charlie. I love you so much....."

CHAPTER 14

"I want to love you now, but I can wait until tonight. I mean, I can't, but I will....." I tried to look like I knew what was doing. "Room 208, yes, upstairs.....second floor, make a left.....enjoy your evening, sir....."

"You're sure you never did that before, huh?"

"No, Charlie, I never—I really—Oh, come on, you creep! You know I never did that before. Why are you teasing me like that?"

" 'Cause I'm after your body," I said, squeezing her shoulder and pulling her close with a laugh.

We were sitting in the car at the park, the previous afternoon's activities the topic of conversation.

"Want me to do it again?" she implored.

"Sure, ya gotta keep doin' it 'til ya get it right, ya know," I ribbed. "I mean, it wasn't bad, but—"

"I did good, huh? At first I was afraid, but then it seemed pretty natural."

"You did it good, babe."

She grinned, pleased and contented, assured by my lighthearted gloss that her performance had been more than satisfactory. She gazed out the window with a distant look in her eyes, her face gradually breaking into a full smile as she brought yesterday's experiences to today's reality.

"Ya know—can I tell you something?" she asked quickly.

"Sure, babe."

"Well, when I, you know, yesterday," she began hesitantly, "When I.....took you.....it looked funny—not funny, I don't mean funny. It was.....different."

I laughed with uneasy discomfort; she was embarrassed, too. Twenty-four hours ago she said "cock" with deft immodesty, called it by name, talked to it saucily, and pumped it in cadence with her fevered urgings. Today it was an "it," and it was funny!

"I know," I responded self-consciously. "I was gonna tell you before, but I never really had a chance. I'm not circumcised."

"Ohhhh," she said pensively. "I thought everybody was circumcised."

"No, not everyone. Most, but not everyone. Did it bother you?"

"No, it didn't bother me. I just.....was a little surprised, I guess. I never saw anyone who wasn't circumcised. I don't remember even seeing a nudie picture of someone who wasn't."

"Well, I come in the original, plain, brown wrapper," I said lightly. "With me, you don't get shortchanged. Ya get everything ya paid for."

"Yeah, I got everything!" she giggled. "I didn't get shortchanged."

"Sometimes it's good. Sometimes it's a pain in the ass," I continued. "I'll have to tell ya all about it sometime.

Ya hafta handle it a little differently. But you handled it just fine yesterday, I can tell you that. Whew!"

She sat quietly, obviously engrossed in thought. I looked out over the athletic field, imagining the heroics of daring base stealers and tenacious fly shaggers of seasons past. Darkness had descended quickly like a heavy blanket, the street lights in the far distance and the house lights beyond twinkling like tiny stars, winking coded messages behind wavering tree branches so far away. I had worked late in the office, and she had waited faithfully, knowing as the hour got later that our time together would be short.

"Having a van is really gonna be nice," she reflected quietly, as if thinking aloud.

The words hung suspended in what had become an extended void of silence. I let them hang, delectable little dewdrops that danced lightly in a dreamy world where we sat in sculptured quiet, holding hands, a clasped pair on my lap, two joined on her right shoulder, my arm resting around her neck, she reaching up to grasp my fingers. She had sent me such a sweet note that morning, just a few words scrawled on the back of a Fruit Stripe gum wrapper.

> **I cherish every moment that we're together.**
> **I love you.**

"Are you thinking what I'm thinking, or am I thinking all by myself?" she asked.

"No, I'm thinking the same thing, sweet, but it's gonna be a coupla weeks—maybe not that long, but a while, anyway."

She snuggled closer to me, and I gloried dizzily in the warmth of her body and the scent of her person—her signature—the scent I had come to know as distinctively hers. So little time, actually, we had been together. First, we had been friends for months—close, but not in bodily touch. Then came the fevered burst, incited by outside torment, to explore each other's anatomy and investigate the harmony of our sexuality together. And now, paused for a moment to savor love's softness and tender holding, sweet preface to the certain invite of complete intimacy we both fashioned in mental portrait, I knew what was coming.

"I don't wanna wait for the van, Charlie. I want to make love with you."

She cuddled close, her head nuzzled on my chest. It took me a long time to respond to her breathy overture, her proposal sparing me the indignity of request.

The wetness and strong firmness we both knew were beneath our clasped hands on my lap, our fingers intertwined, belied the soft and gentle feelings I felt within.

I sensed my emotions melting into an avalanche of nothingness, my body filled with an infusion of cascading warm sensations, my mind's notions spilling into a yawning fissure of openness, my very being engulfed in the ecstasy and serenity of a vast plain outstretched before a mountain that wasn't there. In a presence without end, my memory recalled no past, and my thoughts knew no future.

My body surfaces were alive with the tactile sensations of a million unknown and unseen fingertips, my eyes blurred with the illumination of a thousand stars, my nose treated delightfully to the earthy fragrances of a hundred spring rainfalls, my ears filled with the soft hushes of a dozen breaths. It was mind-blowing.

I drew close this beautiful person who now wished us together in a consummation of our kindred spirits. I held her tightly.

She separated her hand from mine and pressed it between my legs. It wasn't a move of lust. She wasn't reaching for my cock or maneuvering to entice or enflame. It wasn't a sexual advance or a wishful hint to come, or fuck, or jerk boiling sperm from within the depths of my testicles. It was a simple move of tenderness that carried no hidden message and no pretexted meaning save the search for warmth and closeness, the overt and physical expression of the wish for love, her wish to love. I enfolded her and pressed my hand on top of hers.

"I love you, my sweet sunshine. God, do I love you! But where, and how?"

"We could go some place," she offered in response.

"Sweetheart, I want to make love with you, to be inside you and feel the two of us together. I want to love you *so* much, but *some* place? That's shitty. It's not right. It's not the right way."

"We'll make it right. We'll make it the right *way,* and we'll forget about the right *place.* What choices do we have? Wait? Weeks?"

"How the heck are we gonna go to a motel?" I posed with exasperation. "I mean, that's what we're talkin' about, a crummy motel."

"We'll go to a nice motel, not a crummy one. Tell Pam you're going to the racetrack," she suggested without hesitation.

The little devil knew exactly how to handle it—the spunky little devil.

"And just when am I supposed to do that?"

"Tonight."

"*Tonight*?" I gasped in horror. "Tonight?"

"Why not? I want to love you. I want you to love me. I want to love you *now*, but I can wait until tonight. I mean, I can't, but I will."

* * * * * * *

I pulled off Route 17 and into the parking lot, drawing up between the painted lines on the pavement, a red Saab in the parking spot to my left and a Dodge station wagon, I think, on my right.

"You wanna wait here, babe?"

"Yeah, I guess."

I got out of the car and walked swiftly to the door with the red neon "Entrance" sign overhead. When the heavy, glass doors of the front lobby swung closed behind me, I found myself in somber inspection of the spacious vestibule with its vinyl, polyester, and foam rubber appointments, aluminum-framed abstracts on the wall. I tried to conceal my uneasiness and look like I knew what I was doing. I approached the young woman behind the desk and began to tip-toe through the totally unfamiliar motions with the clumsy ignorance of a welfare recipient in the plush ante-room of a Wall Street brokerage house.

".....just fill out this card, please.....is that a Jersey plate number?.....two of you.....twenty-three, ten.....here's your change—ninety cents makes twenty-four, and..... one is five.....and here's your key.....208, yes—upstairs. Go out and around to the back—you can park there, and you'll see the door. Go up, second floor, make a left….. you're very welcome…..enjoy your evening, sir."

She was used to it. She knew exactly what the story was, knew I was scared stiff, and knew I didn't know what the fuck I was doing. She didn't ask any stupid questions about me having any luggage. She handled it like a professional. I wasn't a pro. I felt like a klutz. I turned quickly and went out through the glass doors and back to the car to get Ann.

I followed her directions to the letter and we found Room 208 precisely where she said it would be. I was scared stiff, but I didn't get lost, so I guess I was making progress.

"I'm *so* nervous," Ann said as I unlocked the door to the room and pushed it open.

"Ya shoulda been at the desk. I wanted to use a phony name, but I couldn't even think of one. You can call me anything ya want tonight, babe—Ralph, Edward, Raymond. I don't know what the hell I ended up using."

I closed the door and locked it behind us before walking to the dresser and switching on the table lamp.

"How safe do you think it is?" she questioned. "I mean, ya don't think anyone saw us, do ya?" she queried again with uncharacteristic nervousness.

"I didn't see anybody. It's safe. It sure would be one helluva sweet mess tryin' to explain, wouldn't it?"

Explain? How in the world could a teacher explain what he and a student were doing together in a motel? And who would be dumb enough to ask for an explanation?

"I just want everything to be nice for us," she said, holding back a section of the floor-length drapes and peering out the window.

"I know, babe. It will be. It's warm, it's cozy, it's comfortable, and it's ours—for now, anyway. And we're together. That's the important thing. Everything is gonna be fine. We even have our choice of beds! Now, that's alternative, isn't it?"

"You're sure you never did this before?" she laughed, throwing my words of this morning back to me.

She let the drapes fall back in place, lingering a moment before turning from the window toward the bed.

"Very funny, very funny. I'm shitting in my pants, and you wanna know if I ever did it before. Well," I continued the playful hoax as I walked to the side of the bed opposite her, "to tell ya the truth, I never did it before on a weekday night with a senior—weekends, sure, with sophomores and juniors," I quipped with amusement, "but never during the week, I swear."

"I'll bet. Is that a 'his' bed, and this a 'hers'?" she asked coyly.

We had bantered just enough to find ease in our new surroundings and space in which to pause and breathe so that heart poundings didn't echo. It surely hadn't been a romantic tumble. It hadn't been the orgasmic happening of which novels are made. It had been the bashful search of two timid souls, each acting alone yet in harmony, to secure themselves in neutral positions—close, but not too close. Now we stood face to face on either side of the bed, the stillness to be reckoned with, the final distance to be traversed.

"No, they're both the same, but this one is 'ours,' " I said, pointing to the one in front of me that separated us. "Let's pull this down," I suggested, motioning toward the top of the bedspread that covered the two pillows.

We each pulled a side together—symbolic, I thought—stripping back the green spread, the thin, striped blanket, and the top percale sheet, all at the same time, letting them rest in loose folds at the foot of the bed.

"They're too crispy and crunchy," she said, hitting both pillows and the bottom sheet with her hands to loosen and soften them. "Too much starch."

"All the comforts of home," I sighed, kicking off my shoes. I switched on the small reading lamp at the top of the maple headboard, and I turned the roll-back lamp cover to reflect the illumination upward toward the ceiling.

"That's a lot better. I like it like that. It makes the room so much cozier," she said approvingly.

We both had the same impulse at the same time. She unbuttoned her blouse and let it drop off her shoulder behind her as I took off my shirt and tossed it on the bed behind me where we had put our jackets. We were following a joint script, unrehearsed but not unenlightened.

My thoughts came in disoriented flurries. I knew I was clean, but I hadn't taken a shower. No one takes a shower to go to the filthy track. Damn, I should have bought a pack of condoms. What the hell was the matter with me? It all had happened so fast. I didn't have an erection, but I should have, shouldn't I? I was too scared. Was she going to think the idea of going to bed with her didn't turn me on? How the hell could she be so calm? She didn't seem to be nervous at all. Holy shit, nice titties. I really loved those titties! Gee, I had fantasized about undressing her, but it wasn't happening that way.

By the time I had pulled my undershirt over my head and threw it back on the bed, she had unsnapped her jeans and let them fall to the floor around her feet. She stepped out of them with amazing ease and stood there in her bikini panties, sheer nylon with white daisy appliqués.

It wasn't as easy for me. My jeans were new and stiff. When I unhitched my belt, my jeans didn't just slide down and fall in a neat pile. They crumbled below my knees, and I had to bend over and push them down and hop around, first on one foot and then on the other, to free myself. I stood up, uneasy it had taken me so long to undress and uncomfortable I wasn't hard. But she hadn't been watching. She probably was too embarrassed to see a grown man struggle with his pants. She had removed her wrist watch and had walked over to set it down, and now she was looking at herself in the large mirror above the dresser. She turned around and leaned back, her two hands on the dresser top supporting her. She crossed her legs and looked at me with a smile, a model striking an "on stage" pose as if she were in the middle of a Streisand song—relaxed, cool, and confident, totally in control. I turned to her, naked, my jeans in my hand. I wasn't relaxed, I wasn't cool, I wasn't confident, and I couldn't even control my own dick, which I desperately wanted to go up. I looked at her in amazement, letting my jeans drop to the carpet. She looked stunning.

"You are beautiful….." I said slowly. I tried not to gasp. "…..just beautiful."

She was. It was incredible—a love goddess right in front of me. I unashamedly looked her over from top to bottom, from her straight, dark brown hair that flowed down her back almost to her waistline, to her long, slim legs, smooth and firm with their lean-muscled calves; from her small, young breasts, upright and pointed, the dresser lamp highlighting one gleaming, brown-violet rosette and the indirect light creating a mystery of hazy darkness around the other, to her slender waist, richly golden in the light's glow; from her tiny, centered navel, to the full, rounded hips that framed the prominent mound between her legs; from the elastic band of her bikini panties that clung low on her hips, to the puckered daisy appliqués that partially filled the inverted triangle below; from the sheer nylon mesh that only attempted to secret the baby-fine hair beneath, to the bottom point of the triangle where my fingertips so often had played in the concealed darkness and so frequently had been blessed with the rich spending of her fulfilled pleasure.

I took a long time. She let me take a long time, not interrupting my attentive study by moving or speaking. I wasn't nervous any more. My member stirred.

"This is the body you're not happy with, huh? Too small, not enough, and all that?" I mocked.

"Well, I *wasn't* happy with it. But you made it happy, so now I'm happy with it."

"You should be—"

"You wanna see my sultry look?" she murmured coquettishly.

"No, I'm not kidding," I started, not wanting her to make a joke of it. "I don't think—"

She wasn't listening. She shook her head quickly several times, letting her hair swish from side to side, finally grabbing the long, shiny bundle of turbulence in one hand, pulling it over her shoulder in front of her, and letting her hair fall over one breast, its ripened raisin peeking from among the parted strands. She dropped her chin on her chest, pursed her lips, and looked up through narrowed eyes that fired ablaze, set and still. She wasn't making a joke.

My member began its ascent to fullness. Rising, rising—I had been embarrassed when it hung limp. Now I was embarrassed that it was pointing at her, rigid and straight.

"I thought you'd never notice. Yes, it is *so* charmingly nice to see you, too," she spoke with urbane eloquence. "Do come in," she invited, reaching out as to "shake hands" with my erection as a lady of nobility would greet a chivalrous gentleman caller.

I took a small step forward and bowed gracefully.

"Thank you so kindly, my fair lady."

"Allow me to consider what I might have to comfort and relax you," she said thoughtfully. "Perhaps something to eat?"

"I would be much in your debt, my lady, but only if it were not to cause you trouble or inconvenience."

"No inconvenience," she assuaged. "Suck my tits, Charlie."

The stage voice was gone. The short play had ended.

She squeezed both breasts tightly, one in each hand, and pushed the choice of excited nipples to me. I obediently kissed first one and then the other. My tongue flicked across the breadth of her chest, first in one direction and then in the other, uncertain where to settle, frustrated by the deliciously equal choice. My mouth was eager for both swollen extremities with like fervor, jealous to leave one unsuckled while the other received its anointment of warm wetness and its full measure of moist tongue-spanking, kindly nibbles, and stiff stretching. I lapped, licked, sucked, tugged, fingered, and pulled. I knew she liked it hard. Her moans avowed she loved it hard—low prolonged moans, rising and falling as the wind through bare trees on the side of a mountain; deep-throated guttural sounds of a sweaty construction worker, overloaded and overburdened; mournful articulations of a grieving mother in painful lament at the loss of her infant child; pleasure-pain expressions of satisfied oh's and ah's that beseeched continuance, again, and more.

She reached to the steepled organ that pressed against the white appliqués, now dampened, moving the rigidness to a warm and snug imprisonment between her legs, our heated parts now separated by the barest of fabrics, much too thin to shield the pulsing of both, one from the other—only one thin piece of material away from the touch of togetherness, the forward move to unity, and the push to entry and consummation. The removal of one last piece of thin material would leave us as one, genital to genital, hardness to softness, no distance between.

I placed my hands on her shoulders and slowly turned her around, moving her backwards to the foot of the bed, our lips sealed in kiss, my stiffness still immured between her thighs. We fell together on the bed, becoming undone and unattached as we wiggled and squirmed like two excited inch-worms to the pillows at the top of the bed.

"I love you, I love you, I love you."

"I love you, I love you, I love you, I love you, I love you."

"I love you, I love you….."

We each spoke the same words—together, separately, over again, together, slowly, softly, quickly.

We kissed, long, hard, and deeply. I raised myself and knelt at her side, leaning across her body to slip her panties around the lower part of her hips and over her thighs, the crotch of the thin undergarment catching momentarily between her legs—a last, reluctant grasp—before giving way as I continued to further slide the delicate, nylon covering piece over her knees, down her closed legs, around her ankles, and under her heels—*off.* It was supposed to be one, smooth, erotic movement, like in the movies, but it turned out to be a herky-jerky effort, and I hoped my intense focus and concentration made up for my nervous display of awkwardness. I had looked at nothing, my eyes focused on her panties for the full time I had attended to their removal, except at the very beginning—a shooting glance—when the stretched ribbon of elastic had rolled below the softness of her freshly exposed nest of silken hairs.

I tried to conceal my shaking hand. I wasn't supposed to be nervous. I reached behind me and dropped the moist roll of panties to the floor at the foot of the bed. Now my eyes fixed determinedly on the finely entwined, light brown patch of growth that covered the rising mound above. I wasn't supposed to be nervous, huh? Right. I was scared to death!

She lay motionless, her head back on the pillow, her eyes closed. I was *so* thankful her eyes were closed and her legs still tight together. I wasn't sure I could handle my nervousness, my uncertainty, and my excitement all at the same time.

I stretched out on my stomach alongside her and put my arm around her waist, snuggling as close as I could, her body hot against me, both of us seeking the reassurance of warmth and nearness, both of us apprehensive and stalling.

"How are ya, babe?" I asked as I kissed her cheek softly.

"Okay, babe," she said quietly without moving, without opening her eyes, without emotion.

Scared, she was. As scared as I—petrified.

"You okay, hon?" I queried in absentminded repeat.

"Yeah, I'm okay," she whispered. "Just a little nervous, I guess."

"Me, too," I confessed. "But I love ya, babe, ya know that, don't ya?"

She smiled, just a little smile that would have made me feel better if I hadn't felt the rest of her body still tight, tense, and stiff against me.

"Yes, I know that, hon."

I slid my arm up from around her waist and cupped her breast in my hand, a popover gathered in a muffin holder, still warm, but dried from my previous suck and lick ministering, its purplish-brown and puffy plum giving rise to a fully textured and erect nip, exaggeratedly bulbous from my under sided squeeze. I played, flicking lightly with my finger, watching its rubbery stretch and its resilient pop, back to its upright position. I loved it. I loved to watch that—like a toy I had when I was a kid, a thingamajig of some kind on a flexible stick or rod. When you knocked it down, it jumped back up, quivering its delighted return—a tease, just to show you that you weren't so hot stuff, after all.

I raised myself on my elbow, turning toward her side, leaning to kiss and suckle her other nipple. I felt her tremble and her leg move against mine. She sighed softly, and I trembled, too. My nervousness at removing her panties and stripping her of those last protective daisies had caused me to go soft. It was embarrassing. But now I felt the return of warmth, her peaceful sigh of surrender and the movement of her leg against me triggering a rising swell against the outside of her thigh.

"Ahhhh," she sighed again. "That's good. Oh, that's nice, Charlie."

The stirring against her leg? The flicking of my finger? Or the swirl of my tongue as I licked quick circles around the budding of her other breast and gave it pleasure nibbles with my lips? There was no way to know, but her body was alive again, and my confidence was retrieved. I pressed my cupped hand up and over, my palm grazing lightly, deliberately, on the extremity, before slipping down her side, across her abdomen, and into the grassy hillock below. For some reason, I expected her to part her thighs so I could continue my obvious approach unimpeded, but her legs remained rigid and closed. I glanced up, curious and uncertain, as I let my fingers wind endless circles in the curly tousle. Her eyes still were closed, her face emotionless, but she was breathing heavily, and I watched the undulating of her bosom, my firmness now rock hard, fully enlarged, and pulsing as my finger wound around and around, barely an inch away, only a touch away.

Still scared shit. Both of us. I wondered why we were so afraid, fear never having been a part of our previous togetherness activities when we were parked on the cinder road in Bergenfield.

I pressed my hand gently between her legs, daring not let hesitancy betray by fright, separating her thighs. She responded, parting her legs with a low, croaking moan, and my finger slipped down, out of her nest and into the warm slipperiness below. My member throbbed, jolting against her side, a pounding reaction to her frog-like position—flat on her back, thighs spread, knees bent outward, legs bent in, the flats of her feet in patty-cake position—a giant, horned toad—my television on—a hump frog, spread on its back, tailless, wet and slippery, croaking, horny.

"That's beautiful, that's beautiful, Ann," I murmured as I leaned, still propped on my elbow, to kiss her lips.

Her tongue met mine, and I felt her hand on the back of my neck, pressing my mouth to hers, a sense of urgency in her grasp. She turned her body to me, and we shifted, moving our hands, elbows, and arms in an awkward search for new positions of comfort before I nuzzled my face in her hair, my cheek near hers, my mouth close to her ear.

"I love you," I whispered. "I love you so much."

I felt her breasts rub against my chest.

"I love you, too, hon," she answered softly into my ear, kissing my cheek.

My face was burrowed in the darkness of her hair, my own breath warming my face close to hers. I could smell her hair and feel its clean softness, and the Ivory soap freshness of her cheek and neck. How the hell did she have time to take a bath? I could smell the single drop of perfumed fragrance she had dabbed on her ear lobe and the aromatic scent of her body—a person's body—the distinctively wined bouquet of a person, unadulterated with over-sweetened essences of spice, herbs, musk, or tropical flowers.

I raised my head, propping myself again, taking a reluctant but needed breath of cool, fresh air. She withdrew slightly and rested back comfortably, stretching her arms over her head, and, with a deep sigh, lifting her torso and pushing her legs straight and stiff in front of her, pointing her toes. Quickly, then, she let her body go limp and drew her legs back and her knees up. Now a woman—no frog—a woman.

I watched her movements with designed attentiveness. My finger had become dislodged from its tuck, but my hand never had left its nest, my palm still covering the rise between her raised and parted knees, my fingers curved downward with unobstructed access. I looked at her face to see if there might be a confirming favor, a sign for me to heed the message the position of her body now offered, but her head was back, her eyes once again closed.

I turned my attention back to the open vulnerability between her legs, her knees in breezy sway above the picnic spread my fingers were set to pillage like so many busy ants, my hand taking full advantage of the access afforded by her raised loins, my middle digit running the full length of her cockled, puckered cleft, from top to bottom, then delicately and meticulously up the shaft to the spread umbrella, then down again, daintily, to the tablecloth, the wet folds separating in wavy unwrap like the loosening of the paper label of a pickle jar submerged too long in water. When I felt the soft lips affectionately close around my finger and embrace its probe, I pressed well up within her depths.

She groaned, long and pleasurably, as she pushed forward, insuring the fullest extent of insertion, countering the involuntary squirm that had accompanied my entrance.

"God, God, good God," I exulted in strange thanksgiving. I love to feel you. I love to feel you move."

"I *live* for you to feel me," she exclaimed. "I just live for it, sweet man."

My mouth roamed in oral hunger, in frantic outreach, finally finding hers and crushing her lips to mine, the cartilage of my nose feeling the unyielding squash of hers, her nails digging the side of my neck, squeezing in rhythm to my organ's pulse, my finger sliding, stretched and searching, the suction of each withdrawal drawing me back into the pliant orifice that gurgled her moisture.

"God, I wanna be inside you." I murmured. "I love you so much, Ann. I want to love you with my whole body."

"Please, yes….. Charlie. Please, Charlie."

I heard my name from far away, a forlorn and tragic call from behind the pines. I heard the prolonged, hungry whine of a wild, wandering coyote, snowbound, howling in the cold and starless night, starving, lost, and urgently hunting survival.

The quickening rush of my finger, in and out, slipping easily now, with no resistance, no clinging, and no suction, brought forth her appeal, her pleading. "Take me, Charlie. Take me, please. Do me."

I responded instinctively, my thumb in tender caress of passion's queenly gem in showy, solitaire rise—a stem of gleaming quick-silver its posted setting, a spilth flow of honeyed nectar its lustered band—first on every advance to the royal chamber, then continually, regally, 'round and 'round the castle's jewel-tipped turret, lady's lips folded back, spread asunder, in majestic oversee. The rural province between offered no fortification to the kingdom's most guarded and treasured store of priceless, flowing fluids.

"Take—"

Her body trembled and then stiffened. Her breasts heaved, her open-mouth scream nothing but a contorted grimace of silence, the bolting rise of her buttocks signaling the spending of her climax in my hand.

"Holy shit! Holy shit! Holy fuckin' shit," she cried out, the cute little gushes and squirts—uniquely hers, excitedly mine—dousing my hand and soaking the sheet beneath her legs.

"Charlie! Ohh….. ahhhhhhh, I love—ahhhh….."

Jesus Christ! If I ever got caught now, I was dead!

I raised myself on my knees, my organ swinging from side to side, and I positioned myself between her legs. I looked down at the wet patch of matted hair, and, beneath it—for the first time—holy shit—I saw, below the moist ringlets, the glistening shell-pink opening that dripped her scented fluids.

It was beautiful—cute, puckered, and small—little hint of the capacious cavity my finger had left wanting. My mind's TV screen had served my fantasies well, but never had it pictured the beauty of the blushing pink rose crease of soft, moist folds that now awaited my entry.

I leaned forward to couple myself with her, admit myself to her coral entrance, the entrée of my fantasy's appetite, as I looked at her face.

Now her eyes were open—open wide, bulging, her face frozen in shocked horror, ashen and vacant. She drew a deep breath and held it, completely motionless, suspended, and terrorized. Her arms were stiff by her sides, her fists clenched, her knuckles white, her lips tight, her frightened body warped, burled, and cringing, tied in a cataleptic knot.

I stared back at her, afraid to move a muscle, afraid to speak, afraid and shocked myself at what I saw, afraid to breathe, hurting terribly, feeling her hurt.

I melted. My entire body drooped limp as if someone had pulled the plug and every drop of blood had drained from my veins. I looked down on that poor, exposed, naked, frightened creature who lay prone before me. I felt sick to my stomach. The sexual excitement that had been, and the anticipated pleasures to come, were no longer important, no longer compelling.

I moved instinctively from between her legs to her side. I took her in my arms and held her quivering body close, wrapping my arms and legs around her and cradling her head under my chin, against my body. I wanted *her* to be inside of *me*—inside and safe. I couldn't hold her close enough. I felt her tears trickle down my chest, and I saw my own droplets fall into her hair and on her forehead.

"I'm sorry, Charlie. I just—"

"Ssshhhhhh," I interrupted. "Ssshhhhhh, sweet."

I rocked her back and forth in my arms.

"My sweet little Sunshine. I love you so much, babe," I whispered, my eyes wet and blurred.

"I wanted you inside me, so much, Charlie. I wanted it to be so good for you. I'm just no good. I'm just not—"

"Ssshhhhhh," I cut her off again, and she wept quietly, our sniffles the only sound in the room for a long time, our gentle rocking back and forth the only movement. There were no sounds, no noises, inside or out. Christ, this was a fuckin' quiet motel. No children? No TV's? No clocks ticking, doors slamming, toilets flushing? No footsteps on the stairs, coins in the soda machine, the ice machine quiet? We were in a world of silence, everything and everybody, it seemed, in anxious, breathless wait to see if everything was going to be all right.

When she finally raised her head very slowly and looked up at me, there were tear streaks down her face, her lips were dry and cracked, and strands of soggy hair matted against her temples, the loose ends straggling in disarray alongside her cheek. Her face was puffy, and her eyes were red and swollen. She was a mess, shivering and sniffling.

I loved that shivering, sniffling mess *so* much. I put my hand under her chin and raised her lips to mine and kissed the softness turned to sandpaper. I pecked small, quick kisses over her face, tasting the salt in almost every location. I kissed her lips, again—wet them for her—and my tongue unconsciously searched for hers, our mouths pressing together with firmness, our tongues darting and circling together. We wrapped around each other and hugged tightly, each in fear the other somehow would slip away. I was surprised and embarrassed that my member, long since soft and forgotten in the upheaval of emotions in which we both had been caught, had become sympathetically engaged, sharing the heated intensity of my feelings, and now once again was upright and sturdy. I enjoyed its concerned warmth but let it be, my attention magneted to the young body that clung to me, the embracing grip I hoped never would be released.

"I'm sorry," she started.

"I'm sorry, hon," I broke in almost simultaneously. "I didn't mean to hurt you."

"You didn't hurt me," she responded with shy embarrassment. "I just got scared. Good heavens, it was nothing you did. It's happened before. I keep seein' pictures in my head. I can't get rid of them, and I get scared."

"I know, babe," I said sympathetically.

"It didn't have anything to do with you. I want you so much….." her voice trailed.

The fuckin' rape, I thought. That fuckin' rape. It was scaring the shit out of her. Bad enough it had made her feel like shit when it happened, but now it was making her feel like shit all over again.

"We'll do it, and it'll be nice for you, and you won't be afraid," I promised. "You'll see. Are you with me?"

"I know, I know, I know it," she said, emphasizing her words with quick, tight hugs. "I'm with ya. I'll always be with ya. I know we'll do it good! Ya know, I'm not really afraid until you're ready to go in. Everything feels so good, and then, as soon as I start to think about it, I get scared, and I panic."

There was a pause, and I could see tears welling in her eyes again.

"That fuckin' asshole," she said angrily.

She knew. Her thoughts were the same as mine. Of course she knew.

"That fuckin' asshole," I repeated slowly.

"He hurt me so much, Charlie."

Again there was silence for a long time.

"Are you okay?" she asked softly.

Our individual thoughts had gone their separate ways, had come full circle, and now met again.

"Sure, I'm okay, sweetheart. I just love you so much I don't know what to say. I don't know what to do."

I leaned forward and kissed her on the cheek. She reached up with both hands, one on either side of my face, and pulled me down to her lips and kissed me.

"Let's get the fuck outta here," she said with a soft smile. "We can come back again."

"Yeah, let's get outta here."

We dressed quickly, leaving the bed an untidy heap of soiled and rumpled linens about which the morning maid could draw her own irreverent—and erroneous—conclusions.

"Let us take leave, my Lord," she said laughing, as we picked up our jackets, "for the hour draws late, and surely a rapid departure will augur a swift return and affirm an early resumption."

"You got it, bitch."

I pinched her ass, and she jumped through the doorway into the quiet hall.

"Did you call me a bitch?" she countered, turning abruptly.

"No," I responded, tongue in cheek. "I said, 'I still have that itch.' "

"Yeah, me too. I'll scratch yours, if you'll scratch mine."

I took her by the arm, and we went back into the room and closed the door. We didn't get undressed or go over to the bed. We didn't even bother to lie down on the brown, tweed carpeting. We stood in the small, dark hallway by the closet and the bathroom door, and we wildly groped, fingered, and stroked each other's horny crotches—rubbing, twisting, squirming, and squeezing against each other's bodies in frantic, extorting agitation until we both popped off together in a laughing burst of indistinct, slurred and very, very naughty exclamations. We had been there to have a *good fucking* time; we left after having just a *good* time. But no one was complaining, not even a little bit.

****

Thursday morning I put a note, a quotation from Kahlil Gibran, in Ann's mailbox.

> **"Love that is cleansed by tears will remain eternally pure and beautiful."**
> **I love you, Sunshine**

By noon she had responded on a scrap of yellow composition paper.

> **Your handwriting showed through the envelope. Wasn't that observant of me?**
> **I miss you loads, honey. See you soon.**
> **XXXOOO**

It wasn't until three-thirty that we finally saw each other. It had been a strange day for me. My attention to the work I was trying to complete was diverted continually by mellow recollections and brief images of the night before, cameo silhouettes and striking vignettes my mind stretched to grasp and then butter-finger into memory's hall to be recalled and replayed again and again, complete with saucy movements and naughty words. And those other words, not from the night before, but from barely more than two weeks before, those other words I couldn't believe I had said: "*.....And if I were dumb enough to risk* *my job going after a body, it sure as hell would be a better body than that one."*

I laughed to myself every time I thought of it—"*.....a better body than that one."* Who would have known? Not me! I hadn't thought Ann was anything special, as far as looks were concerned—not much different than any of the other girls at the A-School. She was nice looking—maybe not as pretty as one or two of the others—but certainly attractive and cute with tasteful feminine lines, smooth skin, and a fluidity of movement that was appealing and inviting.

It was a strange day. Every girl I happened to look at by chance, I *looked* at, really looked at. Then, no longer content to leave matters to chance, I started making a deliberate effort. I went out to the stage. I sat in the lounge and looked. I looked at everybody. I looked at *every body.* I looked from the front. I got up, feigning leave, and walked around to look from the side and from the back. I looked at everything. I looked at faces, legs, tits, hair, asses, waists, chins, and crotches. "*.....a better body than that one"*—like whose?

.....too big.....too small.....too short.....pretty, but chunky.....all bones.....no hips.....bad teeth.....much too heavy.....mousy looking.....okay, but nothing special..... top heavy.....kiss her?.....flat as a pancake.....cute ass, but straggly hair.....walks like a truck driver.....everything perfect, from the neck down.....could use a shave..... sorry, not on a bet.....

"*.....a better body"*—like whose? Nice kids—I loved them all, but—

I looked at enough crotches and watched enough asses bent over to pick up a book, a pen, a ping-pong ball, a shirt, or a dime to give me a boner for a week. I never got a rise.

When Ann walked into the office later that afternoon, I tried to give her the same scrutinizing examination. I couldn't. When I looked at her ass, I wanted to run my hands over the taut smoothness of her rounded buttocks and let my fingers stray into the splendid crack of her young rear. When I looked at her breasts, I saw the bulging nipples she so deliberately had held out to my mouth, and I heard her saying, "Suck my tits, Charlie." When I looked between her legs, I saw white appliqués and pink softness. Her face shone like sunshine. Her eyes danced. Her hair flowed. Her lips, her cheeks, her stance, her waist, her legs, her scent—When I looked at Ann, I saw a woman. If I were going to risk my job—why the hell not? It would be worth it.

"You came in here just to give me a hard-on, didn't you?"

"Ssshhhhh, Charlie. Lisa and Janis are right outside the door."

"Ooops, sorry 'bout that. You came in here because you had an itch you wanted me to scratch."

"Char—lie!"

"I love you, pumpkin," I whispered. "I love all of you, every inch of you. Are pumpkins male or female? Do they have pussies, or do they just stand in doorways and rub their stems?"

"You're fuckin' crazy, Charlie," she laughed aloud, holding her hands to the sides of her head. "You sound like a horny toad. Where did all this come from?"

It had been a strange day.

CHAPTER 15

We tried again and again and again, the painful memories of the violation of her body and mind preventing consummation. But there were other things to learn and do.....

The ping-pong tournament droned on. It had become more of a marathon than a tournament, with delays, squabbles, arguments, and more delays. Ann and I had been eliminated early, so we didn't give a shit about it, anyway. It wasn't sour grapes or being poor sports. We just didn't give a shit about anything that had to do with school. We didn't even give a shit that a judge had ruled we *didn't* have to vacate our Church basement by April 15. We could stay and finish the year, but we couldn't come back again next year. So, who the hell gave a shit about next year? There were only two things I gave a shit about: When was I going to tell Pam I was going to "the track" again, and when was Ann going to get back to doing some homework so she'd pass here courses and graduate?

The first question was quickly decided.

"Why don't you tell Pam you're goin' to the track this Saturday?"

"Okay."

The second question wasn't resolved as quickly or as easily.

"Fuck, Ann, you *gotta* find the time," I chastised.

"Fuck, Charlie, like when? You think there are more hours in the day for me than there are for you?"

We had talked about it yesterday. I had told her at a quarter past three I'd help her catch up with some of her work when I finished mine, but at ten after four she was nowhere to be found. This morning her note was in my mailbox.

Charlie,

I started getting real bad cramps around 3:30 and when Sally offered me a ride home, I couldn't refuse. I meant to leave you a note that I'd be back, but she rushed me so much I didn't get to it. When I got home, I was informed by my father that he had three emergency deliveries for me to take—one in Teaneck, one in Fort Lee, and the other in River Edge. When I completed that mission, I had to take Mom to Packard's and wait in the car until she accumulated five bags of groceries. By this time, not only couldn't I do some work, I didn't have time to lie down, I didn't have time to get back to school, and it was too late to even call you. I did manage to get down some supper and be 20 minutes late for my first rehearsal, and I took the

> **liberty of crying to my pillow. Probably I'll tear up this letter before I finish this page, but if I don't—oh, I don't even remember what I was gonna say. I love you, darling. Please be patient. I know that I'm being unfair to you, but things will change soon, I promise. You are my strength.**

She was right. She was in rehearsal for two shows, she was making deliveries for her father's drug store where she had been working less frequently than usual over the last few weeks because of all the "nookie" time we had been enjoying together, and she was with me. I certainly wasn't about to complain about that.

"But at least ya gotta do enough to keep them off your ass, ya know?" I reasoned, firmly but sympathetically.

"I will, Charlie, honest, this weekend, but not tomorrow night."

"You gonna be okay for tomorrow night? What about your cramps?"

"I shouldn't get it for another day or two, maybe more. Who knows? But I'll be okay for tomorrow."

She was so irregular—sometimes days early, often weeks late. I didn't know how she could be so sure about tomorrow. She had told me that sometimes she'd even skip a month. The little sweetie was going to scare the shit out of me.

She was okay for Saturday, and we went back to the same motel, the same desk clerk. I tried my damnedest to remember the same name.

We went again the following Wednesday and again on Friday. Each time the poor baby ended up in tears, unable to accept penetration, embarrassed, frustrated, and apologizing. Each time we got a little bit closer.

"Thank you for being so patient with me; thank you for being so gentle," she told me again and again.

How could anyone be anything but patient and gentle? The poor kid was going through a hell of torment and torture, reliving painful memories of the violation of her body and her mind. "Getting in" became unimportant. We laughed and played a lot, never leaving the room until we had had a good time together. We never talked about our tears. We never mentioned anything about disappointments. There *weren't* any disappointments. We knew we were going through something that we just had to go through, and we weren't unaware that a pot of gold was at the end of the rainbow. We kidded and joked and laughed. We talked about the good things and the good times. And we had a good time, every time. We learned how to share our bodies. We found out what tickled, what was pleasureful, what hurt, what was fun, how to hold, how to touch, how to excite, what to do, what not to do, and how to talk, how to communicate, physically and verbally, in the arousing and lubricious language of sex. She learned how to be licked—for the first time—and I learned how to lick, to use my tongue in ways that would produce maximum excitement and mutual enjoyment. To say that I had gagged my way through fifteen years of marriage would be an exaggeration, a slight exaggeration. To say that I was a reluctant and hesitant licker wouldn't be. But I learned. Ann taught me. And I loved it.

She talked to her pussy like she talked to her titties, like she talked to my cock. Her uninhibited lewdness turned on my x-rated television. She made me a slave to the box. And then she showed me, live and in colors more vivid than N.B.C.'s peacock, scenes that even made my TV blush.

She talked to her pussy.

"Okay, now, let's see what's goin' on down there. Pussy? Pussy, are you there?" she cajoled without mercy. "Oh, there you are, and you *are* awake. Oh, are you awake, you cute little rascal, you. Oh, yes you are. You're a rascal! I think you're all closed up and takin' a nap or something, and when I put my finger down there, you're open and wet, with your little clitty pushin' up to peek out the top. Now, *that's* bein' a rascal."

Did she know how to play with my antenna?

"Let's take a look. That's it, that's it, open, that's it. Now, Charlie is gonna be comin' down to see you. Charlie's a very special guy, ya know, so I want you to treat him right, you hear? C'mon, c'mon, Charlie. Look at this. Look what little Annie has down here for you."

I hoped I wasn't dreaming.

"That's it, Charlie, that's it," she encouraged as I positioned myself on my stomach between the spread of her legs and her hoisted knees. "You just get down there and make yourself comfortable so you and Pussy can get to know each other. Okay, Puss, let's show Charlie," she cooed. "Let's show him his favorite color—pink."

Her nimble dip of two fingertips part way into her genital opening was followed—oh, so deliberately—by a hard pull upward, the slick lower portion of the cleft unsealing with a moist ripple, the lurid wetness of her entrance revealed, as she moaned in self-induced ecstasy.

"Tongue it, Charlie, tongue it."

Ann didn't know how to play things cool. When she was hot, she was hot. She wasn't afraid to say she was hot, and she wasn't embarrassed to say what she wanted—exactly what she wanted.

"Deep, hard, deeper, in and out, that's it, hard in, hold it there, hold it. Ahh, ahhhhhhh, hold.....ahhhhh, ohh, ohh, oh—don't, don't take it out..... ohh.....don't you dare take that fuckin' tongue out.....yeahhhhh, take me, take it, yeah, take it, right on the tip of your tongue. Fuckin' shit. Give it, Pussy, give it to him, give it up, you fuckin' puss. Lick it, Charlie, lick it, babe. Ohh, ohh, ohh, ohhhh—don't. Easy, easy—take it all nice, lick it up, lap it up, puppy baby, my puppy baby, and my pussy."

I did everything she wanted me to do and everything she told me to do in the blatant, bold, and brash language of a pornographic dictionary, the pages of which seemed to be turned with each flick of my tongue.

"Okay, cunny," she spoke roughly. "Now we show the fucker what he really wants to see. Now we show him fuckin' everything."

How the hell did I get into an eager-beaver heaven like this?

She pulled hard on her two fingers again and slid them slowly, tantalizingly upward, the lips folding closed over the pool of her spilled fluids and my tongued saliva at the bottom, separating and spreading further up, closing below and separating higher up, one folding pleat blending into the other as she stretched its length before my eyes in a brooklet of endless ripples. Then, as she reached the summit, her apex, from between her straining fingers emerged the tip of her love-button, lucent red and shimmering in all of its tropical splendor and engorged majesty, peeking from beneath its canopied shelter.

I came. Lickety-split. She showed it to me, I looked at it, I saw it, and I was gone—I couldn't hold back. Then and there I became a slave before Queen Lady's throne.

"Therrrrrrre," she purred in melodious relief, her pinnacled ornament freed from the steady pressure she had fixed to it. "There it is, all for my man, all for my sweet man. Easy on this, babe. Nice and easy. Soft and gentle at the top, soft like butterfly wings. Then do your thing at the bottom. Ahhhhh, ahhhh, ahhhhh. That's it, that's it.....Go get it, babe, make me wiggle, fight me, drive me crazy, make me run away, chase it, lick it, kiss my soul. Ohh, ohhhh, God, ohh, my cum is comin'. Easy, easy, easy—oh, oh, oh, oh, ahhhh. You fuckin' cock, you. Nibble it, nibble, nibble it, quick—easy, you fuckin' prick, you cunt-hungry bastard—squeeze my ass, squeeze my ass, harder, harder! Charlie! Charlie! Charlie! Charl.....comin' again.....Char—Charlliiieeeeeeee. Easy, easy, man. Mannnnnn.....my mannnn, and my pussy, pussy, pussy, pussy.....my comin' pussy."

I came the whole time she chummed me with her narcotic burble of explicit words and enticing demands, my ball's fury ejected on the bed sheet in a thin ribbon of egg-white that reached my waist and trickled into my navel, the lower trunk of my body squishing in the run of sticky discharge while I picked daisies with the tip of my tongue and tasted the sweetness of her excitement.

She said words I *never* heard a woman say. Never. She said things I only had seen scrawled on john doors in gas stations and diners. I always wanted to call one of those 781-33whatever numbers to see if Alice M. *really* wanted me to eat "the world's juiciest pussy." On the opposite wall, Jolean D. offered the same irresistible treat—that's what Frank T. promised in honest-to-goodness magic marker. I always wondered why, if it were so damn good, someone would want to share.

She said words *she* never would have said in the normal course of events, from one day to the next. But when her sexual fuse was lit, she was no sparkler or two-bit firecracker; she became fissionable material, a bomb that exploded every-which-way—physically, emotionally, mentally, and verbally.

She showed me things—shit, she wasn't afraid, she wasn't intimidated, she wasn't embarrassed. She just let it all hang out, spicing every movement with a salty barrage of breathtaking and arousing language—no inhibitions, no forty-year old hang-ups, no false modesty, no holding back, no polite society etiquette, no bland presentation, and no veiled censor to shroud the honesty of her feelings or the mandate of her needs. There was no searching for the "right" words so that things sounded "okay," either. She ordered me around, demanded I hurt her, pushed my pace, and pushed my face. She insulted me and called me names that made me mad, licking mad. I loved it. I wish *I* could have been so open, so free, so honest, so vocal, and so verbal.

She shoved my head away and pushed her hand between her twitching thighs, rolling over on her side, clutching herself. She pulled her knees up to her breasts and heaved a long exhale of satisfaction.

"Christ, I don't know how many fuckin' times I came. Did you count? God, I love it, Charlie. You did me good.

I think I love it too much. I love my body as much as I love your tongue,"

She giggled, then chuckled, then laughed uproariously, her body almost in convulsions. She rocked in hysterical laughter, trying to talk.

"I hope.....when you get into me.....that you have... ..a tongue.....between your legs," she choked between laughs.

I kissed her rounded ass and tumbled on top of her, my hand gripping her crotch from behind, hers gripping from the front, and we laughed and laughed and laughed and laughed.

She taught me how to lick. She made my tongue her slave. She sucked it right in and made it obey her commands, heed her wishes, fire her desires, and service her needs, an obedient and faithful servant at her disposal.

"Anything else you want me to do?"

God, I loved it as much as she did! Green used to be my favorite color, but now, man, she was right—show me the pink!

CHAPTER 16

"Finally!" I triumphed. "Finally, finally," she cried..... Passion's door opened, we fucked ourselves silly.....Spring was in the air and the scent of our sex was everywhere.....

"Maybe we should use the van instead of going to the motel this time," she had entreated. "Now that we have it, I hate to see you wasting all that money."

"You think it's a waste of money?" I zinged.

"No," she demurred, "Not a penny."

"Then we'll go to the motel."

We did. That was Friday, my fourth sign-in, our fourth try.

Now it was the following Wednesday, down the hallway from where we had started. We played for half an hour. We played leap-frog in the buff, goosed each other, and tongue-fucked each other's ears. We chased each other around the room. We chased each other around the bed, over the bed, and around the room again. We fell, exhausted and expired, panting and laughing, into each other's arms. I rolled her over and licked her to climax. She kissed the tip of my erect penis, once, lightly.

"I really can't—" she started, apologetically.

"I know, babe."

"I want to do so much more for you, but I—"

"Lie back, sweet. I want to be inside you. Just spread those beautiful legs. That's all you have to do for me."

"Come to me, Charlie. I want my sweet man inside my body."

I went into her quivering and yielding body with a single stroke, all the way through heaven's gate. I felt my balls slap against the crack of her ass, and I exploded. She already was a captive of her own tingling spasms, the twitching contractions of her competent passage bedewing her sacred julep upon the pulsing organ that extended within her depths. She spent the essences of her sweet surrender in sugar-frosted plentitude, each tiny squirt a joyful release from frustration's anguish, each luxurious droplet a tear never again to be shed, each heave of her loins a jolt from bondage, her body, mind, and spirit set free at last.

"Finally!" I triumphed.

"Finally, finally," she cried.

"Thank God, for your sake, babe," I breathed heavily.

"Oh, thank God for *your* sake," she gasped. "Thank God, thank God. I can feel you inside me! Ohh….. God, I'm still comin'."

"I love you, sweet Sunshine. I wanna be inside you forever."

I had been supporting my weight from her torso, but now I let myself down onto her, holding her body to mine in copulative embrace, *no distance between.*

"I can't believe you're inside me. Holy shit. I can't fuckin' believe it. Hold me tight, hold me. Oh, I love you,

I love you. Hold me; don't let go. You're in me, Charlie. Your body is inside my body! Holy geez. Le'me see," she implored, raising her shoulders. "I wanna see."

I leaned back as she up righted herself partially, straining to see our connection. I withdrew from her slightly, and she reached down, feeling the base of my organ and her own clinging wrapper, slippery, stretched, and gripping.

"I can feel where we come together, and the rest of you is inside me! Damn. I'm not too small at all, am I?"

Now I had to wonder if *I* were too small!

"Wow, that's pretty. That's a pretty sight," I avouched. "I could look at that all day. God, loving is beautiful, man," I exclaimed, dazzled by my own view of thin pinkness in a tightly wrapped circle around my shaft—the cute, rounded mouth of an infant clinging to a mother's provident breast.

I had come so quickly, I was still rigid. I responded to the instinctive impulse, the innate and instilled drive to seek her depths again. I shoved to the hilt, her hands squeezed away as I entered her fully, the swift admission invigorating me further, and I gave her the full throttle of my humping buttocks with resolute determination that we both should share the blessings of another of her climactic offerings.

"You're not too small, sweet baby. You're just cock-size. Cock-ready and cock-size."

"Oh, Charlie, fuck me good. Fuck me. Fuck the hell out of me. So long.....so long.....Fuckin', fuckin', fuck....."

She was crying like a baby, her emotions, too long caged and trapped, now free to run, a babbling brook submerging her, helpless, out of control. She wept.

I heard her squeal in exultant delight. I heard her beseech me not to quit her yearning insides, not to abandon her need, not to stop. I felt her explode again and again, but it was all a blur. Tears streamed down my face. My body responded instinctively to her imperative cries, her relentless conjure, the urgency of her writhing frame, and the heightened passion of our love-making. My mind careened and swerved like a driverless car on a rain-slick freeway, I, too, out of control.

I think I came again as I collapsed on top of her and rolled to the side, she rolling with me, drained but still attached. We didn't say another word; we couldn't talk. We wept and sobbed softly together, petting each other, soothing each other, holding each other, touching, hugging, and caressing each other, until it was too much effort to lift a hand, too much effort to move. Mercifully, tenderly, we fell asleep entwined in each other's loving arms, our bodies in complected interweave.

****

Ah, Spring! How I love to pack up my heavy coats, gloves, boots, and scarves and squirrel them away for another year! A week later, I may regret not having left at least one woolen sweater handy as the fickle weather of the vernal equinox plays havoc with the thermometer, brings on colds and runny noses, and embarrasses the full bloom of forsythia bushes and the long, flowing, apple-green strands of budding weeping willow branches.

Spring—and a young man's fancy turns to potholes, each one a threat to the front-end wheel alignment of his car, each road work-crew a detour or a standing wait in backed up traffic.

Spring—the lamb that follows the windy, lion days of March.

Spring—when you *finally* take the car to the car wash and have the grit, salt, and grimy residue of sanded and salted winter roads washed away by mechanical brushes, and—surprise! Look at all those rust spots and paint chips you never knew were there. Dings everywhere!

Spring—and Easter vacation. The schools call it "spring break," "spring recess," or "spring vacation" so the non-Christians don't get upset, but everyone knows it's really Good Friday and Easter vacation. Ten days with no school—ten fuckin' days. Ten days fucking.

I saw Ann every day. One way or another, I got out of the house every day or night, sometimes day *and* night, using every excuse I could contrive. I went to school "to do some typing." I went to "the track." I went "shopping." I went out for "a ride." I went to "get some rocks for the garden." When I ran out of new extenuations, I played the old ones over again.

I went to see Ann. I always picked her up at the same spot, on the corner near the hospital, two blocks from her house. She always was there on time. She stood there and waited in the rain, soaked to the skin. She stood there and waited when I got caught in traffic on Route 4 and was late. She stood there and waited when I had to stop and sit on a gas line for half an hour. She stood there and waited—like she wasn't waiting—when someone she knew walked by or waved from a passing car.

When I picked her up, she'd climb into the back of the van or sit scrunched down in the front seat until we got to the highway. We thrilled—absolutely thrilled—in seeing each other, but we likewise suffered the torment that came with the secret liaison we shared, the forbidden tie we had knotted, not able to kiss or fondle each other until we were away to a safe place. She'd roll her joint, and I'd head up Route 17 to one of a number of hideaways we had adopted, one at a time, as "ours."

Passion's door opened, we fucked ourselves silly. At night we'd go to the drive-in theatre or we'd park in the bowling alley lot or at the diner. They were close, but they were safe. We didn't care what movie was showing—we were the skin flick stars of our own film festival. We didn't bring our bowling balls—we balled each other. We weren't hungry—well, maybe we were hungry. In the daytime, we'd go further north to Wild Duck Park in Ridgewood or to the small, wooded spot off Hilltop Road near the Mahwah-Ramsey border where we'd picnic and fool around in the grass by the stream in the woods. Sometimes she'd bring lunch, and sometimes we'd stop along the way to pick up munchies.

"I thought you were gonna bring a picnic today, babe," I said as she wiggled her ass onto the front seat.

"I did, hon."

"Where?"

"You're lookin' at it. What you see is what you get."

Whoopee, box lunch! Who needs lunch when you can eat the box? What a scrumptious picnic. We didn't leave a crumb, just several fragrantly intoxicating moist spots in the matted grass to drive the grasshoppers insanely out of their fucking minds.

We went back there a few times, never failing to leave behind a pleasantly scented memento of a daisy being planted there.

After Easter vacation, "the track" became such a frequent alibi for leave that Pam must have believed I was a prime candidate for Gamblers Anonymous. It was easy to use because I *did* go to the track often, generally in spurts for a few weeks at a time, then not at all—always alone. When I did go—when I *really* went—I usually brought home a program or an admission token for my next trip. I'd come home and empty my pockets on the stereo in the living room, and it was common practice for me to leave the folded track program there as well. When I said I was going, but didn't go, I was stuck. I began the deceptive practice of folding back the dated cover of a previous night's program and leaving that under my wallet. Sometimes Ann and I would make the long drive to the track and make love in the faraway parking lot, picking up a discarded program before we left for home.

It was game time, and we learned how to play the game. What *I* didn't think of, *she* did. We both did a lot of thinking. Every thought was an excuse. Every excuse was time together. And every time together was a nibble, a tickling flick, an aroused adventure in a fairyland of enchantment, a sacred communion of bodies and souls in splendid conjunction, a gush, a flow, a circling, spiraling, dizzying, creamy, dreamy amalgam of rubbed noses, tongue-licked eyelashes, and butterfly-kissed cheeks, and, finally, a tumbling collapse into outstretched arms, forget-me-not pleadings, and forever promises.

We sure had good times! The van became our love house on the other side of the rainbow. A parking lot—

any parking lot—became our pot of gold. Our bodies became the toys of our amusement, our love-making the sustenance of our lives, and the school—oh, yeah, the school—our ball and chain, the thing we had to do, the place we had to go, the price we had to pay.

* * * * * * *

In the time that had elapsed since Fran's accusation, my interest in the A-School had shallowed, my performance bottomed. My working relationship with the staff gradually had been restored, but it was nothing more than a working relationship. An undercurrent of tension, stiffness, and awkwardness prevailed. I must admit, also, that an undercurrent of unforgiveness on my part didn't help. I continued with my own administrative responsibilities, but they were now tasks, chores performed in a perfunctory manner without enthusiasm. As far as school was concerned, I wanted the year to end. As far as next year was concerned, I couldn't have cared less.

"This isn't easy, Charlie, but I'm going to bring you back to the high school next year."

He sat behind his cluttered desk in the principal's office. Partially bald, short in stature, a little stocky for the lifeless, brown suit he seemed to wear without change, he always had a harried, worried look about him. Every time I saw him, I wanted to hang a long, yellow, cloth tape measure around his neck—the perfect Jewish tailor! Even the dignity of the principal's office of a large, well-known high school wasn't enough to make him look important.

"That's okay with me," I nodded acceptingly.

"I can either transfer you myself, or you can resign if you want."

It was all so perfectly clear—not surprising, but clear. Nothing more had been said to me directly; the issue had rested. But somehow, someone had leaked it to him—just enough. "They" had their ways, and I *knew* the bitch Fran was behind it.

But I was ready for it. I had *my* ways, too. Tipped by a friend at the high school that this was coming, I had had plenty of time to think about it. As I sat in front of the principal's desk, Ann waited outside in the back of the van, already knowing how I was going to handle it.

"I'll resign," I said without hesitation. "Thank you for giving me the option. I appreciate it."

A few days later, on April 24, I returned to his office with my one sentence letter. He looked as if he'd been sitting there in shock since the time I left. There hadn't been any reasons, explanations, excuses, or discussion. I hadn't asked him any questions.

"Don't you have.....anything to say? I mean—" he fumbled, scratching his head.

He knew this wasn't like me. He knew I was a scrapper who went for the jugular. We had gone toe to toe before, several times on different issues. But I think he knew, as well, his own weakness. Everybody in the school knew that when you went to see this principal about anything, you wanted to be the *last* person to get his ear. On any matter requiring his decision, he was known to be swayed by the last voice he heard, and I had learned as acting director of guidance the previous year, and as a counselor before, that I *always* got my way unless a *next* person, arguing the same issue, wanted a different decision. Then, *he* won. *The first shall be last, and the last, first.*

"Isn't there anything you want to say about this, or talk about?"

He almost expected an argument. Maybe he wanted one.

"No," I said with a vacuous shrug. "You're the principal. If you want me up here next year, that's where I'll be."

"Have you—did you say anything to the others, the other teachers, yet?"

"We had a meeting this afternoon. I told them I was resigning and I had asked for reassignment to the regular high school for next year."

That was it.

The decision didn't hurt. It was a relief. But my pride hurt; my ego hurt. I had no interest in going back to the A-School next year. Ann would be gone. The Church basement would be gone. My favorite kids, the seniors, would be gone. But I had wanted to drop the last shoe myself. I hadn't wanted it to be a forced resignation. It was a bitter pill to swallow. Even though the whole situation had changed since the original accusation, nobody knew anything provable, and I knew I still could fight it. But it just wasn't the same. It just wasn't worth the fight. The best I could do was end up winning, and that would be losing, because I didn't want to be at the A-School next year. The energy for a fight wasn't there, and neither was the incentive. It was natural to mount a defense in a defensible position, when right and wrong were the issues, when truth and justice were on my side. But to go through the whole thing again, with the deck reshuffled and someone else holding the joker? It was easier to swallow the pill and tell myself it was candy in disguise.

****

It was easier to sit in a gas line and play with each other's crotches, too. We were right in the middle of the gas crunch created by the mid-east oil embargo. For the kids who drove cars, having an odd or even numbered license plate became more important than playing ping-pong, attending Town Meetings, sitting in the lounge, heading down to the tennis courts, or doing homework. The kids, like everyone else, got gas when they could. It was to their advantage that the flexible scheduling at the A-School often meant blocks of free time when they could sit at a gas station for an hour to get filled up or to get the maximum allowed. They read books, knitted, cat-napped, or did crossword puzzles to pass the time as they waited on lines to get to a pump. Ann and I played, too. We played with each other. Sometimes I'd get pumped; sometimes she'd get filled up. We took the wildest chances imaginable, but we employed the highest level of calculated strategy to achieve the lowest degree of calculated risk. It wasn't that difficult. We played gas line frustration in reverse, something like playing tick-tack-toe to lose. We looked for a station with a long line and few pumps. That meant a lot of time between the stop and go advance of cars, and that meant we could actually screw our way to the station island! It was sick. We knew it was sick, but it was funny—and fun. It was fun sex with the added appeal of fucking "the system."

She'd strip and wait in the back of the van. I'd hop back and forth between her and the driver's seat. If the line moved too quickly, she didn't wait. She'd work herself to heat, and I'd just hop back to pop her off.

"Ya like this game I invented, huh?" she'd coo with the delight of a Milton or a Bradley. "Better than crossword puzzles, right?"

"Yeah, I get a big bang out of it," I'd respond with a waggish twinkle, and we'd tickle each other playfully until we were both in stitches.

One afternoon—I think it was a Wednesday—I laughed my ass off all the way to the pump. Every time I hopped in the back, she'd hit me with a new name for our crazy game—duck and fuck, slip and dip, fall and ball, jump and pump, hop and pop.....

Everybody moaned when they started to run low on gasoline and had to face the dismal prospect of finding a filling station with a green flag. Then they had to reckon with the hour or more wait on line that followed. I didn't mind at all. I actually looked forward to the gauge needle approaching "E" so we could play our game. We didn't do it every time. It was too sick. Besides, some days I'd come too quickly and fuck up the whole game. But I'm positive we set a world's record for climax action on a gas line—sixteen at the Exxon station on Route 17 on a Friday afternoon with everyone waiting to fill up for the weekend. She went off three times by hand, six times on the tip of my tongue, and twice with the pilot in the cockpit. Four times she got so excited she took herself before I could make the hop. The final blast was mine. She did me with but two cars left in front of us, and I got my pants zipped up just in time. When I rolled the window down and told the attendant, "Fill her up," Ann looked at me with hurt.

"That's my line, creep," she snapped.

Then we'd whip back to school and play there. We put the Alternative School to alternative use. It was "easy play" there—nothing heavy—a suggestive wink, a quick grab, a flashed tit, a teasing look, maybe a little feel, until lunchtime.

We made sure we didn't develop a pattern. Sometimes we'd leave for lunch together, and sometimes we didn't. Sometimes we went for lunch at eleven-thirty, and sometimes we went at twelve or a quarter past. Sometimes we'd go in a group with other kids, and sometimes we went alone. Sometimes we'd picnic together in the park down the street from the school in full view of everyone, and sometimes we'd park in the maze of cars at a shopping mall, and she'd peel the clothes from her body like the skin from a tangerine and spread-eagle herself on the soft, green, shag carpeting in the back of the van, and we'd fuck our bodies dry and our minds into oblivion.

We lived on the brink of orgasm, slipping from one climax to another, forever hungry for each other's body, each seeking for ourselves the sublime relief of spilling the juices of our own passion, each thrilling in the benevolence of moving the other to a joyous spending of love's magic potions.

Then we'd high-tail it back to the Church. After Ann's afternoon classes, we continued our deliberately deceptive and pattern less efforts. Sometimes she'd leave, and I'd stay. Sometimes it was the other way around. Sometimes we'd both go, and sometimes we'd both stay. It made no difference to us. A rendezvous always was planned in advance, time and place previously established, agenda subject only to imagination and inclination, for either later that afternoon or that night.

Again there were no patterns. Sometimes she made deliveries for her father in the afternoon, sometimes she had show rehearsals at night, and sometimes I had things at home that kept me from getting out. We worked around the obstacles, whatever they were, and then we went to park at the bowling alley, the diner, the drive-in, or the mall. On particularly nice evenings, we went to one of the nearby parks. We got to know where all the safe ones were.

We made love whenever and wherever it was possible, and in some places where it was damn near impossible—on slatted park benches carved with initial-filled hearts, a wad of bubble gum stuck to the seat; in a wooded thicket with bare floors that straightened our backs and powder-dusted our writhing rumps; in a brambled bush hollowed out for cops and robbers kid's play and abandoned for our equally climactic gun-shooting pursuits; at any parking spot on either side of Route 4 or Route 17 where the tell-tale back and forth rock of the van was likely to go unnoticed; under a viaduct where the echoed sounds of our loving gave booming effect to the bigger-than-life, spray painted genitalia on the concrete walls; at the track where the toil of the day was laid to rest sometime after the fourth or fifth race.

"You've got the keys to the Church. Let's do it at school," she often teased. I never knew if she were kidding or not.

"You do it in the school, cumquat. I'm crazy, but I'm not fuckin' insane."

One night we drove up the Palisades Interstate Parkway, parked at one of the lookouts above the Hudson River, and ran hand-in-hand across the northbound lane into the narrow, wooded dividing island, enjoying each other there on a giant slab of flat slate. Cars zoomed past in opposite directions on either side, no one ever suspecting that, in the harbored vestige of Nature's bosom, between the trafficked lanes of highway macadam, we deciduously had shed our clothes as trees their autumn leaves. No one ever saw the love-struck urgency on our faces as we gazed into each other's eyes at the very moment our genitals dispersed their bountiful wash of succulent fluids upon each other. No one ever heard the climactic pleasure shrieks of the two naked bodies who loved in primeval fashion among the buddings of spring, surrounded by the fresh smell of cool, clean earth. No one ever knew that the consummating embrace of a teacher and a student was taking place fifty yards from two parked police cars, their uniformed assignees judiciously going from car to car through the lookout parking area, knocking on breath-steamed windows and scaring the shit out of teenage couples trying to get a little feel.

CHAPTER 17

Risky business.....four cops, two police cars, spotlights, a bullhorn, red and blue flashing lights....."You're in a helluva lotta trouble, mac....."

Love knows no fear. There may be risks and you may piss in your pants, but love knows no fear.

Some risks were obvious to both of us; others were matters of speculation.

I was risking my job. If anyone at school ever found out, I was gone. There could be no explanations, no excuses, and no simple transfers to appease the alarm and outrage of complaining tongues. I was out. But at no time did I *fear* losing my job. If I lost it, I lost it, and I'd have to go on from there.

I was risking my divorce. If Pam ever found out, it wouldn't have been nice. For all practical purposes, the marriage was over, but we were in the process of working out a divorce settlement and I didn't want things to get messy. But at no time did I *fear* Pam finding out. If she found out, she found out, and my hopes for an amicable agreement might not be as amicable as I wanted it to be.

I guess I was risking jail or some kind of legal prosecution and punishment. She wasn't a minor, or "jail bait" as they call it, but I was a teacher and she was a student, and I really didn't know how I stood with respect to the judicial process if we got caught and someone chose to press the matter. But at no time did I *fear* legal reprisal. If it happened, it happened, and there didn't seem to be much I could do about it.

We risked her parents finding out. If they ever found out, it was all over. I don't know what they would have done or could have done to her or to me. Neither one of us wanted to find out. It certainly would have been all over. But at no time did we *fear* them finding out. If they did, they did, and we'd have to live with it—or without it!

I guess she risked being thrown out of school in her senior year. Who the hell knows what happens to a student who gets caught fucking around with a teacher? Knowing how screwed up the system is, I suppose she would have been suspended, placed on home instruction, and required to have a psychiatric evaluation, the wisdom of the establishment, I am sure, determining that she was E.D., emotionally disturbed. But at no time did she fear being thrown out of school. If she got bounced, she got bounced, and she'd get an equivalency diploma and go on with her life.

We both were risking pregnancy. I should have been using a contraceptive every time we made love. She knew it, and I knew it. Sometimes I did, and sometimes I didn't. But at no time did we *fear* her getting pregnant. If she did, she'd be tickled, and I'd be up the creek. We talked about it a lot. She didn't care if I used a prophylactic or not, but she promised not to talk me out of it at the last minute as she had been doing.

We did what we could to reduce the risks. We were careful about where we went, when we went, how we went, where we parked, whose car we took, what time it was, how we dressed, who we might see, and who might see us. But there was a limit, and at times we were foolish, times when we went to Van Saun Park—much too close to school—and backed into a parking space so we could enjoy the late afternoon sun and look out at the geese on Walden Pond or watch squirrels in the picnic area dart from tree to tree and scratch for last fall's stored acorns. We sat and talked and smoked, happy to be together, bikers, joggers, and cruising vans and convertibles passing in front of us. Sometimes we'd even chance a stroll around the lake in the twilight. On days when it was overcast or drizzling, when the area was deserted, we'd climb in the back—very risky.

At other times, it wasn't a matter of risk, and we weren't being foolish. We were downright stupid.

I headed north on Valley Road through Upper Montclair. We had gone to see *The Sting* at the Bellevue Theatre, and now we were on the way back, talking about the intriguing plot of the film, glad it had been showing at a theatre where we knew we'd be safe. Our conversation gradually drifted to other things.

"Do you still go to bed with Pam? I mean, I know you still sleep with her, but do you make love?"

"Well," I shrugged, "Yeah, we go to bed. We make love sometimes."

It was a logical question. Ann knew that the marriage was over. It was understandable that she should wonder about the marriage bed.

My sex life at home had followed the course of our other activities, down the interminable path of routine lifelessness, bordering on drudgery. Once every two weeks, then three weeks, then four weeks was the characteristic movement, and then only to keep peace in the house, to maintain some semblance of normalcy, and to make it easier to get out with increasing frequency. Recently, however, there had been a change. I walked around horny all the time. Ann's body had inflamed mine, my mind and body experiencing a rekindling, a rebirth of innate desires from the long-smoldering ashes, a flame from among the embers. Pam had become the unwitting and unknowing recipient and beneficiary of a body Ann was opening to fresh and torrid delights. Pam mentioned it once, acknowledging the demise of our marriage but noting the apparent improvement, in quantity and quality, of our sexual activities, obviously puzzled by the discrepancy, unaware that the "hots" came from an outside source.

"Do you like it with her?" Ann pursued.

God, I didn't want to lie. I didn't want to make up a story. I never had lied to her about anything. I didn't want to hurt her, either. And I didn't want her to think I was a bastard. I tried to answer truthfully, but avoidingly.

"It's very, uh—" I stuttered. "I mean, I'm married, ya know. We've been married a long time."

"But is it—do you *like* it?"

She wasn't going to settle for diversion, and I wasn't going to lie. I told her the best way I could.

"It's a physical thing, a physical relief. I'm not gonna tell you I don't *like* it. It's just not very emotional. It's not very romantic, not very fulfilling or exciting. It's physical. If I had to tell you, 'Yes, I like it,' or, 'No, I don't like it,' I'd have to admit I like it. Physically, it makes me feel good rather than bad, even if the act itself is pretty bland, ya know what I mean?"

Please, know what I mean.

"Yeah, I know," she said somberly.

She didn't know. She didn't have the slightest idea. I mean, I didn't *hate* Pam; I didn't even *not like* her. Our problems were more directional than personal. We got along in bed. It wasn't the catapulting kind of sling-shot sex, unstymied by conservative and traditional mores, that Ann found to be so natural, normal, and comfortable, but it wasn't chopped liver, either.

"It bothers you, hon, doesn't it?" I said, acknowledging the obvious.

How could it *not* bother her? It bothered me.

"A little. I guess it bothers me a little. I mean, I understand, and I guess I knew, but I'm glad you told me the truth."

"It makes you feel hurt, huh?"

She didn't answer.

I made the right-hand turn off Valley Road and up the ramp onto Route 46. I looked over to her, half expecting a delayed reply.

She had her jeans down around her ankles, and she was wiggling to pull her panties down.

"What the hell are you doing?" I squawked in surprise.

"It hurts a little, yes," she said, struggling. "But I'm not really jealous. She can get hers. That doesn't bother me, as long as I get mine."

Holy Moses.

"I'm gonna get mine….." she continued, pushing her panties down over her knees, "…..even if I have to do it myself."

I looked around, quickly. I made a sharp right, into the Bowlero parking lot. The enormous bowling complex, with its adjacent shops and stores, was a safe place to park.

"Oh, you're gonna get yours, babe. You don't have to worry about that," I said lustfully. "You'll get yours."

"Oh, it'll probably be just a physical relief kinda thing," she toyed. "Nothing exciting, just a little keep-the-family-together physical thing."

"Yeah, I probably won't feel any emotion at all," I jested as I mischievously stroked the upright bulge in my jeans with one hand and whipped the wheel with the other, turning into an empty spot.

"No, me either," she drawled. "I'll probably hafta finger-fuck myself to get off," she sighed with forlorn dullness as she licked provocative circles around her middle and index fingers and slipped the wetted digits between the spread of her legs.

"Get outta there, you hot little cumquat. I'll take care of that," I erupted, switching off the key and turning off the headlights. "C'mon."

I grabbed her arm, half pulling and half shoving her between the seats into the back of the van. She tripped and stumbled, one foot out of her jeans, the other still inside, the pants leg trailing behind. She sprawled headlong, laughing, onto the carpeting in the back, flat on her stomach, her light blue panties around her calves, her sweater half-way up her back, her bare rump, with its rounded half-moons, jiggling with her laughter. I fell on my knees between her legs, my manhood pulsing with the long-fantasized anticipation of entering her from behind.

But it wasn't going to be from the rear—not now, not yet. She wiggled forward on her bare belly toward the back corner of the van and turned over on her back as I struggled with my belt, my fly, my pants, a towel from the dresser drawer.....

"Up, lift your ass."

.....a rubber—fuckin' little packet that won't tear open—the hell with it. I threw her a pillow. Shirt off.....

"Why do you call me a cumquat? I don't even know what a cumquat is. Why don't you call me your donut?"

"My *donut?"*

"Yeah, a powdery little thing with a hole in the middle."

.....a sneaker, a sock, another sneaker.

She pulled her sweater over her head and flung it to the side, propping herself, spreading—oh, man.

"Hurry up, cunt man," she urged in a seductive whisper, "The cunt lady is here. Wanna taste my fingers?"

"No, I want that pussy," I demanded, crawling between her legs on my hands and knees.

"Say, 'please.' Say 'please,' " she cooed with delight as she clasped her hands, one on top of the other, over her furry cache.

"Please."

"Say, 'Please, can I have a little licky-lick.' "

"Please, please, can I have—please, fuckin' please," I rejoined with tormented eagerness.

"No, say 'Please can I have a—' "

I pulled her hands away roughly, exposing the folds of her entrance, and I pressed my tongue deep within, my mouth enwrapping, my lips working to deliver the plumed cockade she had attempted to hold for ransom.

"Ahhhhh, say, 'please, please, please, please, pleasssssssse.'.....Ahhh, ahhh, ahhhhhhh," she gushed in climax, a victim of her own incensed torture. "Holy shit, you didn't—you didn't say fuckin' 'please.' Oh, you're a bastard, you. You cheated!"

I pulled back from her.

"Fuck me, Charlie, fuck me," she screamed in urgent anguish. "Fuck me."

"Say, 'please,' " I panted.

"Please! Please!"

"Say, 'Please fuck me,' " I demanded with feigned insistence.

"Oh, Charlie, please fuck me."

I held my organ in my hand and moved toward her raised and parted legs as she strained to lift her buttocks and meet my advance.

"Gonna tease me, huh?"

"No, I'm sorry."

I held myself before her, a staff of tooled Ceylon hardwood, an Aztec bell tower on the side of a mountain in spired oversee of the sacked pair of Mexican jumping beans below, a spiraling yucca emerging from a thatched crown of spreading leaves on the flat of perspiring Arizona. Tease me, huh? The sweet, pretty little pussy. She should have known better. She could exact her tease when she was withholding what I sought, but not when I was holding what she wanted, my banana-shaped rise of Honduran origin, the American pole she wanted to climb and enwrap with her flag of surrender.

I grabbed the shaft of my phallic arrow with the triumphant flourish of a skilled bowman, his quiver carefully culled of its swiftest, surest weapon, and, with silent, dead-centered fix, targeted the circled bulls eye ahead, showing the strength of the pointed missile with which I intended to halve her unprotected sanctuary.

"Ya want it, huh?" I menaced with jocular cunning.

"God, I want it! Yes!"

I touched the stiffness to the claret cirque and slipped slowly upward to the moisture and warmth at the top of the puckered cleft, throne of love's queen lady, and then back down.

"Say, 'Please fuck me, Charlie, and I promise not to finger-fuck myself unless you're there to watch and lick it all up'."

"Please fuck me, Char—," she started.

"Ya better hurry. "I'm gonna change my mind," I threatened.

"PleasefuckmeCharlieandIpromise.....I promisenotto—I'll fuckin' promise anything you want!" she screamed. "Anything! Please!"

She strained, stretching with every ounce of energy she had, practically sitting on the base of her spine, her feet almost touching the roof of the van. Then, with an expending thrust and grunt, she jolted upward, a final surge, and I let go the bow string, my arrowhead piercing. I went in so far I thought I hit a light switch.

The inside of the van lit up like a Hollywood movie set. Illumination filled every corner, the glaring brightness finding us looking into each other's eyes with startled and squinting expressions of bewilderment. I turned my head toward the front and the blinding glare through the windshield. I turned back quickly, the disarray of scattered clothing in flicking kinetograph—a 16mm movie film jumping its sprocket—as my eyes scanned the interior of our exposed love house.

"Get outta there. C'mon, *out!*"

The commanding voice cut like a razor, a gelding razor.

"Holy shit. Get your clothes on; get your clothes on, quick." I said frantically, withdrawing from her. "Quick, hon, put your clothes on. Fuckin' shit."

"Oh, my God," she gasped.

"C'mon, babe," I pleaded.

We both grabbed what we could and put it on in an awkward scramble of arms, legs, and elbows, bumping into each other, stepping on our own feet, tripping over a loose sneaker, never for a moment able to be free from the piercing glare—helpless, with no place to hide. We were caught in a relentless bath of intense and uncovering illumination, the privacy of our parts and our act violated by the peering, bulging, lecherous eyes we knew gleamed behind the merciless lights.

"C'mon, get the hell outta there."

"Oh, shut the fuck up," Ann muttered under her breath.

"Don't tell 'em anything. Don't say a word," I whispered as we pushed ourselves to the front.

"What the fuck am I gonna do now? Holy crap."

"I'm not tellin' 'em shit," she said, too loudly.

"Shhhhh. Christ."

They grabbed us as soon as we opened the door and stepped out. There were three or four cops, two police cars, a man not in uniform, spotlights, a bullhorn, and more lights, red and blue flashing lights.

"Ya don't hafta grab," I heard Ann's captious objection as they took her to one side. Two stayed with me.

I was shaking like a leaf, physically shaking in tremors. I stood there in my unbuckled jeans and my socks—no shirt or sneakers—shivering. It was early May, and the days had begun to show the signs of summer's promise, but at eleven o'clock at night the pronounced chill of the evening, combined with the consternation of the moment, penetrated to my bones. My teeth chattered as I tried to answer the barrage of questions being hurled at me, and I strained to hear what was happening to Ann off to my left.

"What the hell do you think you're doin'?.....This your van?.....You have the registration?.....Where's your license?..... Ya know, buddy, you're in a mess. You married?.....Got kids?.....Is this your address?.....You work?.....You're a *teacher?*..... Where do ya teach?....."

He read me my rights. It went something like, "You're in a helluva lotta trouble, mac." That was it. The fuck!

".....Ya know this chick? Nice piece, huh? She go down on ya, give ya good head.....?"

Now I knew why the kids called them "pigs."

".....You payin' her?—Tell me the truth. How much?..... She married?.....You're a teacher, and *she's a student?* In the same school? Holy shit. Ya know what can happen to you?

Well, I don't wanna tell ya, 'cause I don't want ya to shit in your pants, fella."

"Yes, sir.....No, sir.....I'm sorry, officer.....Yes....." I sputtered, shivering. "She's eighteen."

I told him the truth about everything. It was humiliating and embarrassing.

I couldn't hear what they were asking Ann, but I could hear some of her answers.

"Nothing. He's not paying me nothin'! I'm not a whore.....You saw what we were doin'. Why do you keep askin' me?"

Shit, Ann, be nice. Don't give him a hard time, will you.

"Bullshit, you did. I don't go down on nobody. You didn't see nothin' like that. You just wish you had..... Yeah, I have a license—here."

"So, you're....."

"Eighteen, nineteen next week. No, this isn't my fuckin' birthday party.....Yeah, didn't it look like I was havin' a good time? That's none of your fuckin' business, anyway."

Christ, she was gonna get us locked up!

It went on for an hour, a whole fucking hour—questioning me, questioning her, switching off and questioning each of us again, and then talking among themselves while we stood shivering. Another police car came on the scene with a screeching halt near the others, with more cops, more flashing lights, more spinning red lights, and more questions. I was freezing. I felt sorry for her, but I couldn't even get close to her.

The last fifteen minutes were a game. I tried to play it, but I didn't know the rules. I knew something was up when they hadn't whisked us away to the station house at the very beginning. I knew I had the head honcho, obviously the one in charge. He had sent the others off. First one car left, then the other two. His buddy was with Ann, and now the big gun planted himself squarely in front of me.

"I hate to see you in such a helluva lotta trouble like this, fella."

I knew what the commiserating bastard wanted. I had figured it out. I had sensed the easing up in the questioning. I had heard him tell he others that he was going to "take care of things." I had seen him leave himself behind, only his partner remaining with Ann. I still was afraid. I didn't know how to make the offer.

"Ya know, I'd give ya a break if it was just me, but there are all the others, ya know? I don't know how I can cover this up for you."

"I'd appreciate anything you could do," I started, timidly, but encouraging further dialogue.

For crap sake, if you can't say it, give me a hint. What the fuck am I supposed to say?

"Is there anything I can do?" I questioned, pleadingly. "I mean, I've got a lot at stake, and if there's anything, uh—"

Shit, help me out! Can't you see I'm trying?

"Well, it's gonna be tough. I won't know until I get back to headquarters. Then, there's a lotta papers to get together. It's a lotta work. I'm not even sure I can do anything for ya."

The negotiations continued for another five minutes, a painfully prolonged five minutes—the unspoken words, the understandings worked out, the details settled, confirmed, repeated back, and confirmed again. The deal was struck.

Ann and I climbed back into the van, together for the first time in an hour, shivering, consoling, and scrounging around for the last pieces of our clothing, seeing the remnants of the time we had spent together before the glow of our dream had been overwhelmed in the gaudy glare of an unholy, flashing nightmare.

"I'm sorry, babe. I feel so sorry for you, hon."

"The fuckin' bastards," she yelled. "They were pissed because I wasn't a prostitute. They wanted me to be a hooker. The fuckers wanted a piece of the action, can you beat that! Not *my* puss, they're not gettin'. Are they letting us go?"

"There's a deal. I think we're okay. Shit, my feet are so friggin' cold, I can't stop shakin'."

"What's the deal, sweet?" she pressed.

"It's gonna cost. I don't know how much," I responded. "I knew what the fucker wanted, but he was real cagey. I thought he was gonna take all night. He had me by the balls. I couldn't offer him anything. He coulda busted my ass for tryin' to bribe an officer."

"So, what do we do?"

I looked out the window as the patrol car hesitated before wheeling out onto the highway. The bastards! She wasn't a minor, and she wasn't a prostitute. We weren't doing anything in public, and we weren't causing a disturbance—no public lewdness, no public nuisance. We weren't perverts hanging out a car window and enticing seven-year olds with candy and balloons, then flashing our genitals. So, what did they have besides two consenting adults screwing around in the privacy of their own van?

Big deal. Not the most appropriate place for love-making, granted, but—three police cars and half a dozen cops, for an hour? Under aged drunk kids stumbled out of the bowling alley lounge and weaved their tipsy way through the parked cars, a trail of up-chucked beer and pretzels behind them, hell-bent to take to the roads in a stupored fog, and these bastards could spend an hour hassling *us?*"

It was stupid, almost as ludicrous as the ridiculous sign in McDonald's parking lot in River Edge: *No eating permitted in parked vehicles.* A town ordinance. I used to sit there in my van and munch my lunchtime quarter-pounder with cheese, rehearsing in fantasy my test of that absurdity in court: "Yes, your Honor, and what about picking one's nose? Can I pick my nose, or fart, in my own car? Yeah, what about a fart? Or is there an ordinance that prohibits—I'm sorry, your Honor—Yes, you're right, I was being facetious. I apologize, honest. But, begging the Court's indulgence, shouldn't there be a law or ordinance that says a fuckin' cop can't bust your balls for fooling around in the back of your own van and then blackmail you for a payoff to keep his fuckin' mouth shut?"

"We go home. He'll call me in a few days if he can squash all the papers and do a lot of hard work," I added with a mix of adopted complacency and borrowed cavort. "He knows I'll be very grateful, and he'll tell me when and where I can drop a grateful envelope just to show my grateful appreciation. Isn't that real fuckin' grateful, now? And, I shouldn't forget, too—this is just for all his *extra, off-duty, unofficial* hard work."

"Fuck him," she hissed. "Don't give him a fuckin' penny. How much does he want?"

"Whatever I think it's worth to me," I said mockingly.

"It's not worth shit. He got his thrill for the night. How many pussies does he get to see in a day? If I had let him dip his dick, we woulda been outta here in three minutes. That's all the bastard wanted. He probably wouldn't have lasted more than a minute, anyway."

I ignored her anger and her advice to "fuck him." I got his call a few days later, and I made a special trip back to Clifton after school. I followed his instructions and gave the envelope to the woman behind the counter at the pizza parlor in the Bowlero complex.

"This is for—"

"I know," she stopped me.

I said goodbye to my fifty bucks, and I hoped it was enough. I didn't want any more calls. If he called back for more, I was going to turn the bastard in, deny everything he said, and take my chances. I never heard from him again.

****

"I made the drop after school yesterday."

"Oh, hon, I would've gone with you, baby."

"I know. I just wanted to go and be done with it. I didn't think you'd appreciate goin' back there, ya know?"

"What assholes we are, huh?"

"Yeah, I guess we're not as smart as we think we are. That was a close call. We're so careful about everything. Then we almost blow the whole thing. Ya can't let up for a friggin' minute or someone's on your ass. We can't take any more chances like that in the van, babe. We're gonna hafta get a curtain or something. I think I can hang a curtain across the front."

I tried to visualize the inside of the van. There was nothing to hang anything on, or from. Maybe, if I had a metal drill I could do something, or maybe I could just punch a hole through.....Yeah, I could do something. I had to.

I did. I strung two panels of heavy, patterned material behind the front seats on a combination of curtain rods attached to each side of the interior, with a center hook in the roof to support the rods. Pam helped me with the material, sewing a wide hem on the bottom, a pocket in which to store things. I cut out cardboard pieces and carefully taped them over each of the two back windows. The back of the van was now private, safe, and secure. I should have done it when I first got the van.

The next afternoon I checked my mailbox—for the third time. No note. Where the hell was she? I knew she had been in her afternoon classes, but then she was gone. I went out and sat in the lounge. I'd wait. I chatted for a time with Jordan, Yvonne, and Marlene, trying to drum up some interest in the horseback riding group I was attempting to put together as a physical education activity for credit. The notice had been on the bulletin board for a few days, but nobody had signed up.

"I thought a lot of people would really go for it," I said.

"Just too many other things goin' on," Marlene responded. "Everybody's up to their ears with all the yearbook stuff and the tennis."

"And the teachers are really piling on the work, too," added Yvonne. "I think they're tryin' to get as much out of us as they can, before kids start slackin' off with the good weather and all."

"Yeah," Jordan agreed. "This isn't alternative. This is old fashioned homework," he exclaimed with a dispirited look, tapping the three or four books he held on his lap. "Look at the weather outside. It's beautiful. And I hafta go home and read all this bull. I don't have time for horseback riding any afternoon."

"Me either," said Marlene. "I don't have the time, and I don't have the money. I'd *love* to go riding. God, that would be great, but—"

Where the hell was Ann? Damn it! It was frustrating. No Ann, no note, and no nookie. Had she told me something, and I forgot?

I walked back to the office.

Try to remember, Charlie. No, she hadn't said anything. We hadn't made any arrangements. Well, she sure as hell wasn't here.

I grabbed my briefcase and went out to the parking lot. I sat in the van with my arms crossed on the steering wheel. She hadn't said anything, had she?

I didn't know where to go or where to look.

"What took you so long?" I heard the soft voice from behind me.

I turned with a start and pulled back the curtain panel.

"Holy shit. What the fuck are you doing here?" I asked in shocked surprise.

The little jerk was curled up in a blanket on the floor. She was curled up in a round, little ball, her head sticking out one end of the bright yellow blanket, her toes wiggling at the other end. She looked like a fuckin' canary!

"What the hell are you doing?"

I was shocked and surprised, but I was happy and relieved. I was happy every time I saw the little air-head. I turned to push the button down on the door. Then I turned back again and slipped between the seats into the back on my knees, closing the curtain behind me.

"You're fuckin' crazy. You're a crazy woman," I whispered.

I knew she didn't have any clothes on.

"I'm trying out the curtain," she said, bashfully.

I tried not to laugh.

"You're trying out the curtain?"

"Yeah, you wanna try me out? I love ya, sweet man."

She was stoned.

I looked down at the silly grin on the funny-looking face that protruded without a neck from the blanket. She was a canary in heat, and I wasn't far behind.

"I've already tried you out quite a few times, babe."

"I know. Why don't you try me out again to see if I'm still good?" she asked in a demurred and suggestive tone.

"You're good, you little cock-teaser," I said as I capitulated, my hand slipping under the blanket, my fingers running up the inside of her warm thighs.

"No, wait—would you say I was a fair lay, a good lay, or a great lay?"

"Let me feel that pussy fuzz," I prodded, pressing my hand to her mound and then to the moist fissure below. "You're the best lay anyone could ever want. And right now, I want it."

We did it right there in the parking lot, my hands clasped over her mouth every time she yelped and moaned, every time her buttocks lurched alive with the squirtings from her honeyed groove. She reached up and pressed the blanket over my mouth when my balls tightened, and I withdrew quickly, spilling hot cream in spurting shots from her hair patch to her rose-nippled breasts.

We were fucking crazy.

CHAPTER 18

Happy birthday, happy anniversary—
and a surprise gift.....

"Almost a year—can you believe it?" she posed as she looked up into the wavering tree branches and munched the last of her apple. "We've known each other almost a year."

The brilliant rays of pre-summer sun, mid-May's benevolent gift to the last of Spring's daffodils and tulips, was a satisfying substitute for the lunch we had decided to forego as we stretched out on our backs in the grass behind the portables.

"Do you mean it seems like only yesterday, or it seems like forever?"

"Both," she responded. "It seems like I've known you forever, and it seems like only yesterday, in the hall at the high school. Remember? Wow, a lot has happened since then, huh?"

"Yeah, that was the day after your birthday. You remember what I said? 'We'll probably be celebrating your birthday in the A-School next year.' "

"I remember. That's why I brought it up," she said with roguish cunning.

"And do you remember what you said at the picnic? 'Don't forget, we have a date.' I thought I was gonna die."

"C'mon, you loved it," she sparred.

"Bullcrap, I loved it. I was shittin' in my pants. I couldn't believe you had the balls to say, 'We have a date.' You were really pretty cocky, weren't you?" I teased.

"Oh, you wanted me to say it. I bet you jerked off thinking about it that night!"

"Yeah, sure, like I jerk off every time I think about Fran."

"So, do we have a date for my birthday or not? It's Monday, ya know."

She was as excited about her upcoming birthday as a flea in a kennel. This was the third time she had mentioned it in the past few days, the first two times with stealthy finesse, this time with blatancy and a trace of impatience at my seeming lack of enthusiasm.

"Monday's your birthday, huh? Geez—"

"Cut it out, will ya."

"I don't know; I may be busy. I'll hafta check my social calendar and let ya know. I can get back to ya, can't I?"

"I don't want you to *get back to me*. I wanna *back up to you*," she tittered. "That's what you really want, isn't it? If we have a date, I'll wear my birthday suit, if you want me to," she tantalized, holding the apple core between her teeth and flashing her eyes.

The vision—it came and went with the flick of a channel.....her bare-assed naked body.....standing.....

decorated with bows.....draped in ribbons.....the cherry-topped cupcakes of my mind's favorite burlesque stripper dancing in front of my eyes.....a Valentine heart tattooed on her thigh.....a Fourth of July firecracker in her navel, a sparkler in the raised hand of the Statue of Liberty.....a basket of Easter eggs on her arm, Little Red Riding Hood on the way to visit the three bears, poppa bear, mamma bear, and Little Black Sambo bear, who had fucked the three little pigs while grandmother gave the big, bad wolf a blow-job in Mr. McGregor's pot garden—Achoo!—and good luck to you, Popeye the sailor man, in bed with Goldilocks.....a hand, clasped between her legs, dangling a sign written in lipstick: "Do not open 'til Xmas—but if ya just can't wait, you can open me up for my birthday,"..... the run-amuck perversion of a nursery rhyme ditty: "Little Jack Horny, sat in the corny, eating his sister—"

Shit, she could scramble my brain before the egg was out of the shell. She could fuck my mind as fast as a flasher.

"Your birthday suit, huh? I bet you will."

* * * * * * *

Monday was a day I'll never forget.

She bounded down the steps and met me in front of the mailboxes. It was early, and nobody was in view. I could hear voices coming from the lounge, but I felt safe giving her a quick peck on the forehead.

"Good God, you're pretty, babe. Your hair is just beautiful. Happy birthday, sweet."

"Oh, thank you, Charlie. I'm so excited. I don't know why. I know it's my birthday and all, but I'm just so excited and so happy. Do you think I look nineteen?"

She stood there, motionless, begging examination. It wasn't her birthday suit, but she looked as pretty as a picture, cute and spunky and radiantly happy.

"When I look at you, I don't see numbers."

"Whaddya see, hon? Oh, tell me what you see."

I shook my head from side to side. How could I tell her I was so happy for her, happy to see her so happy, proud of her—just unspeakably happy and proud?

"I see sunshine, pure sunshine."

"You still think I'm sunshine, huh?" she questioned with a doubting look. "After all this time? I love you, Charlie-nut. You're *my* sunshine."

"I love you, too, babe, a whole bunch. I really hope you have a nice day," I said, kissing her on the cheek. "I'll see you for lunch, okay?"

"Yeah, let's go somewhere special. I really don't give a crap about goin' to *class,* ya know. Oh, I hope everybody remembers!"

"Get to class," I pushed, and she hustled off, bouncing with joy, bubbling and sparkling like a freshly uncorked bottle of pink champagne.

Today was Ann's day. I guess everybody remembered. She was still flying high with effervescent exuberance when we went to Liboniti's for veal parmigian and spaghetti at lunchtime.

She had seen me bring the package, slightly larger than a shoebox, into the restaurant and put it on the seat next to me in the booth. It must have taken the ultimate effort for her to reserve mention of it until we had finished eating. With the final bit of rich sauce mopped up from both our plates, however, she could contain herself no longer.

"Is that for me, Charlie?" she asked, trying to hold her enthusiasm in check.

I thought she'd never ask. It was *my* restraint that had been taxed! I handed her the wrapped box with the white ribbon and bow.

"Yup, it's for you, babe. Happy birthday from Charlie-nut."

"Yeah….." she smiled, "from Charlie-nut."

She tore away the wrapping and took from under the lid two furry, stuffed animals packed in pink and blue tissue paper, a snow-white, fluffy kitten with a pink nose and a pink ribbon around its neck, and a fuzzy, brown and black striped raccoon with ringed markings on its tail.

"Charlie," she squealed. "Oh, they're *so* cute and cuddly! They're just darling. Do they have names?"

"No, babe, that's *your* job!" I laughed. "I just hope you like 'em."

"Oh, I do, I do," she said excitedly. "Look at that raccoon. He's just like the one that sneaks into my cabin up at camp. And look at this cute little kitten. Oh, she's sooooo soft. I'm gonna call her 'Pussy' for me, and this guy 'Cocktail' for you," she giggled impishly, dangling the raccoon by the tail over the table.

"I knew you'd pick out names like that. How did I know that?"

"Thank you, Charlie. I really like them a lot. I love them. I'm gonna sleep with them….." she gurgled, holding both of them close, under her chin, "…..all night long."

Jealous? She made me so fucking jealous I thought I was going to turn as green as a kid's wrist dangling junk jewelry. "…..all night long…..," the treat of treats we couldn't share.

She reached over into her pocketbook on the seat beside her and took out a flat box.

"I got you a gift, too, hon," she purred.

"For me?" I exclaimed in surprise. "It's not *my* birthday. It's yours, not mine!"

"I know, but it's not a birthday gift. Go ahead, open it," she encouraged as she pushed the box toward me between the shaker of grated cheese and the ashtray on the table.

It wasn't wrapped. It was a stationery box. I recognized it as the box from the Kahlil Gibran stationery she often had used to write me notes. I raised the cover and lifted a top layer of cotton. Arranged in a circle in little pockets in the cotton matting below were twelve beautiful seashells, each different, each unique, each with its distinctive sea-worn smoothness and soft pastel coloring.

"Oh, my God, they're beautiful, babe. Where did you get these?"

"I've been saving them for quite a while. Every time I go to the shore I look for one or two that are really unusual," she said with obvious pride.

"Oh, they *are* unusual—so different, every one of them. They're precious."

"I call them the Crown Jewels. They *are* precious. There's one for every month we've known each other."

"Oh, honey—"

"It's an anniversary present."

"Oh, babe, that's *so* nice. God, I love you," I said, overwhelmed, as I leaned across the table.

She met me halfway and we kissed, tasting each other's lips, sharing our garlic breath.

"Happy birthday and happy anniversary, babe," I whispered. "And I have an anniversary gift for you, too."

She jumped back in surprise.

"You're kidding!"

"Well, it's sorta a combination birthday and anniversary present," I said, reaching into my pocket.

I took out a small box and put it into her hand. She held it tightly, almost afraid to move.

"Go ahead, look inside. Don't get yourself all excited. It's not a ring or anything like that. It's nothing much, really. Go ahead. It won't bite."

"I can't believe this. It rattles."

"Go on—"

Ebullience was jumping inside me, a tumbling floor exercise of springing cartwheels and tucked somersaults, a forward roll to a hand stand, and a backward flip into a twisting dismount. I thought I was going to piss in my pants. She removed the cover carefully and looked inside.

"Charlie! What's this?"

"It's a key."

"I know it's a key, silly. Is this the key to your heart? You're fuckin' crazy! And where'd you get this chair? I can't believe it. This is *my* chair, my red chair, in miniature!"

"It wasn't red when I bought it, babe. It was brown. Don't get caught with it out in the rain," I laughed. "I had to give it a little paint job of my own. I got it in a doll furniture store. I hafta have the key back, by the way. It's just a symbolic gift."

She looked closely at the brass colored key with "ST. PAUL" stamped into the metal.

"Charlie? Is this the key to the church, the school?"

She looked at me questioningly as I smiled back at her and watched her puzzled frown slowly ease into a hesitant grin mixed with uncertainty and astonishment.

"What's this all about? Charlie? Are we—? Holy shit. We're gonna do it in the school, aren't we?" she whispered, leaning forward on her arms. "We're gonna fuck in the fuckin' school! Holy shit, what a scene—right in my own red chair. Holy fuckin' ass!"

I sat there grinning, thrilled first by her dawning awareness and then by the flourish of her excitement.

"Well, you're always bustin' me about doin' it in school."

"Oh, God," she said quietly. "If there's one place in the whole world—just one place—where I really want to make love with you, it's in that poor, beat-up, dilapidated—beautiful, lovely chair!"

"I know, babe. I feel the same way."

"Can we, really?"

"Happy birthday and happy anniversary, babe," I whispered as I leaned across the table and held her hand.

"Holy geez—tonight? Tonight? What about—what about tonight?"

"Tonight," I confirmed. "It's your birthday, right?"

"Holy good night. I'm gonna have a fuckin' birthday!"

* * * * * * *

It was dark. After we got halfway down the stairs and lost the little trace of light from the front door window, it was pitch black. We felt our way, groping for familiar landmarks, past the office, past the mailboxes, and out to the stage. We didn't say a word. We had parked three blocks away from the Church and had walked to the school quickly and in silence. Now we held hands with tense anxiety, trying to step carefully, the blind leading the blind through the intrigue of a familiar place lost to sight.

"I got it! I'm gonna turn it on and see how much light there is. Ya ready?"

I switched on the small table lamp. The shock of brightness made the room appear as if a searching flare had been ignited. I turned it off quickly.

"Damn, it's like a fuckin' flood light!"

"Wait," she said in a hushed tone. "I think I saw, over here—here it is. I think it's somebody's sweatshirt. What about hanging it over the lampshade?"

"Good idea. Where is—okay, good, good. I mean, we gotta have *some* light. I can't see a thing. There—there, okay, I'm gonna turn it on again, okay?"

I flipped the switch.

"Well, it's not bad. It's a little brighter than I thought it was gonna be, but—see if you can find something else. If we had another sweatshirt, or a towel, or something—yeah, let me have that," I said, as she held up another shirt that someone had left on the back of the couch.

I draped the second shirt over the top of the lampshade with the "COLUMBIA" sweatshirt, letting them both hang down over the sides, blocking out as much of the light as possible.

"Perfect!" she exuded. "Just enough light for us to see, but not enough for anyone else to see. That's perfect!"

"Well, maybe not perfect, but it's the best we're gonna be able to do."

"It's gonna be perfect. Look," she said, pushing the big, red chair across the polished hardwood surface of the stage to the warm glow of the covered lamp on the bookcase. "How's that?"

"Now, that *is* perfect," I agreed enthusiastically.

"Not yet, not quite, but it will be in just a minute," she replied.

She unhitched her belt buckle and let her jeans drop to the floor. She was naked from the waist down.

"Not yet—"

"You had this all planned, didn't you?" I said, nodding wily acknowledgment to the absence of her panties.

"Of course. You *never* wear any underwear, so I'm just following your lead, teach," she quipped with a flippant laugh as she climbed into her red chair with an extended sigh and settled herself contentedly.

Undershirts, yes, from time to time. Briefs or boxers, never. I hate them.

She sat there as I had seen her sit so often before, slouched down slightly, comfortably nestled between the two, wide, upholstered arms, her heels up on the edge of the seat cushion, her knees up in front of her. Unlike past times, however, now there was no tightly stretched denim around the curves of her pretty rump, no dark blue seam between her thighs. The soft glow of the draped lamp illuminated the milk-white skin of her rounded buttocks and the light brown nest between. I marveled at the agreeably tasteful contrast as I kicked off my sneakers and removed my jeans, my member responding appropriately to the attractiveness of the view she naughtily presented for my mindful inspection. She moved a hand between her parted legs and let her fingers play softly in her hair, stroking herself lightly and separating the strands gently, brushing them to the sides with an enticing circular motion until her fingertips found the bowered cleavage.

"*Now* everything's perfect. Do me nice, tonight, sweet man," she implored in a quiet whisper.

Slowly, I let myself down in front of her, my eyes fixed on the peacefulness of her face, the consonant expressiveness of her eyes, then down to the dainty separation between her hoisted thighs.

"I'll do you nice," I breathed with emotion. "I'm gonna let my body melt into yours. I'm just gonna melt right into you….."

…..an ice pop in the sun…..plastic in a flame….. honey on toast…..snow in spring…..the wax of a burning candle…..butter on an ear of corn…..maple syrup on a waffle…..hot fudge on a sundae…..

"…..so that every motion, every movement, every feeling, and every thought says, 'I love you.' "

"I've wanted this so long, hon," she said. "It's like a dream come true, a fantasy that's almost too good to really happen. It's still hard to believe I'm *here* with my red chair—everybody thinks it's just a piece of junk—and my sweet man, my strength. Oh, I love you, sweet."

I licked softly between the hair she had so neatly parted, savoring the first dewdrops of her sweetness and the first exquisite scents of her humid entrance. I dipped the tip of my nose between the velvet-like folds and slid upward, separating the smoothness, allowing the flat surface of my tongue to follow in a broadening sweep, moving from side to side, then quickly up, approaching the summit and seeking the cochleated pin knot I knew awaited the agitated entertainment I was eager to bestow upon it. I treated it to the royal licking it deserved, coaxing the rounded swelling from its cloistering sheath with gentle suction, pampering its tip, peppering its pillar with ruffling tongue flicks, until it ceded the heated, pulsating cascade I sought with unspoken eagerness and keyed delight.

"Ohhhh, ahhhhhhh—hold it, hold—Oh, God, God, God—ahhhhhhh."

Her head tossed wildly, the red chair vibrating and creaking its approval, an equal partner in the victorious sounds of a crowning achievement and a happy accomplishment. I watched as she clasped her hands to her mound and closed her legs as if to secure the pleasure of her spending, her fingertips too coarse a sieve, her jubilant wash too bountiful, her spillway flooded, her need triumphant over her will. She submitted, unable to stem the tide or stay the flow, grasping her head now with both hands, moaning in unabashed transport, and allowing her loins to relax, her knees fall apart, and her body to release.

"Ahhhh, fuckkkkkkkk, fuckkk—no rubber, no rubber. Fuck me, fuck me out—no rubber."

"No rubber," I acceded to her frenzied pleadings.

I raised myself and leaned, my hands on the arms of the chair, and I pressed myself to her center, entering fully and firmly, catching her in mid-climax, applying enough pressure to prolong and perpetuate the spasms of her convulsing orgasm and its rich rush of splendid fluids. It was like taking a bath, immersing my firmness within the slippery and luxurious offerings of her body's sacred oils. I slipped effortlessly into a chasm of gurgling fragrances and bubbly softness as deliberately and delicately as a woman of elegance would step into a steaming tub and prepare to bathe, eyes closed and mind afloat, senses peaked and nerve endings tingling, enjoying in ecstasy the heavenly relaxation of a body cleansed of its worldly cares, my organ pleased and warmly pleasured in the clinging wrap of the softest towel.

"Oh, nice, ohhhh."

I cupped my hands under the mounds of her buttocks, raising her bottom from the cushion of the chair to effect a straight, firm, forward entry, stroking slowly—melting—enjoying the slip and slide, insisting on a full measure of extension, forcing the surrendering moan of satisfaction that signaled the deepest implantation and full conjuncture, before initiating the slow exit that spread her in a perfect circle of grasping pleasure around my retreating member.

"Look at this, babe. Look at this," I implored.

"Oh, I love you," she murmured, intently following each inward stroke and its subsequent withdrawal. "In….. and out, in…..and out, in, in, in, ohhhh…..and out. Oh, I love it!"

I maintained the slow but steady rhythm, her body responding with effectively measured and spaced countermoves as we both witnessed the calculated mating of our bodies, our genitals in perfect harmony, one stretching the other to its full length and depth, the other dearly clinging, clasping, hugging, and gripping—sweet coalescence—reluctantly releasing only enough to allow the eventual backstroke amid an ebb and flow of slick lubricants.

I repeated the sequence—the straight and firm reentry into the warm, soft, quicksand pull, her pouted outer lips almost sucked inside with the final forward moves that combined our hairs between the urgent press of our bodies.

"You're fucking me into heaven," she gasped. "I must be in heaven."

We watched with enthralled rapture as we each played the movements over and over again to the entranced audience of the other. Both of us strained to hold back the imperative and incessant urge to increase the tempo and quicken the pace into a spiraling crescendo of spasmodic seizure, holding back, drawing it out, forestalling, as long as possible, as long as humanly possible, the inevitable twitching and shooting eruption that would heave us both into a delirium of unabated senselessness.

Even with my body partially blocking the dim light of the table lamp, we could see, and we watched our loving, our togetherness, race to its not-to-be-denied conclusion.

"No, no—don't, please don't. Not yet, not—wait….." she begged solicitously, pressing her clenched fists against my shoulders and holding, holding me back. But it was too late, too late.

"Oh, Christ. That's it, that's it. Oh, you can fuck. Oh, Goddddd, you can fuck. That's it—"

I threw my head back as I felt her twitch, and I shot as we groaned in unison, the clonic throbs of our organs splashing and squirting the extravagance of their boiling cordials in confluent accord to each other, her rutting wail inciting a flurry of final collisions.

When at last I withdrew from her, I looked down at the wetness on her thighs and the drenched and soggy tangle of auburn hairs that framed the medley of colors at her entrance—agitated flame red, a cockscomb at the summit, simmering hot pink at the center, and shell-whorl coral at the bottom.

"You're not going to be able to walk tomorrow," I offered sympathetically.

"I'm not gonna be able to walk for a week," she said gravely as she looked down. "It looks so bad, I don't know how it felt so good! How do *you* feel, hon?" she queried as she picked up her jeans and began to dress.

"A little sore. I was really ramming at the end. Damn, where did my pants go?"

"It was great, hon. What a screwing! What a party!"

"Everything was great, everything," I agreed.

I moved toward her, leaned over, and we kissed deeply as I fondled her breasts under her crumbled blouse.

"You forgot all about my little titties tonight, didn't you?" she pouted in fun.

Me? Forget her sweet muffins, fresh from the pantry, toasted marshmallows with raspberry toppings, delicate swells of sugar-coated confection, delectable sweetmeat morsels? Never! Their soft swings of collusion, their jelly-roll bounce, their cruller-like twists, and their sponge cake lightness had been an all-night treat, a fancied tour through a French bakery of custard-filled éclairs, cream-filled puffs, and fruit-filled turnovers—seen, sensed, and enjoyed without ever being unwrapped.

"I didn't forget 'em, babe. I sorta had my hands full with other things," I wheedled. "You never took off your top, so I figured you were saving them for someone else."

She gave me a playful poke as we stepped across the darkened stage to sit side by side on the couch.

"Yeah, you had your hands full," she laughed. Then, tossing her head, pulling her hair over her face like a mask, and peeking through the strands, she giggled with obvious glee. "Not bad for someone with a cunt that's too small, huh?" she asked bashfully.

"Wellll—"

"Oh, you fuckin' creep," she bristled, feigning annoyance. "You never had anybody with a shaved little beaver like mine. How many have you seen as pretty as mine?"

"It's not shaved," I countered.

"Well....." she fought back, "it's not shaved, but I trimmed it real nice for you, didn't I? Did ya notice? Ya know, maybe I *should* shave it," she contemplated cloudily.

She was either giving the thought very serious consideration, or she was deliberately taking me on a hair-raising, heart-pounding trip through my TV's barber shop. A shaved beaver—I could almost see it, its pinnacled tuft crew cut of its silky pompadour, its curved roundness stripped of its moss undergrowth, and its front yard mowed. Clipping the ringlet bangs of her Venus mound and tonsuring its frizzy Vandyke would leave her puffed quarters bare and naked, as nude and hairless as a nine-year old, ready to be sponge washed, lemon scented, cream polished, spit shined, and licked clean.

"How many have you seen as pretty as mine? C'mon. Two? Three?"

"Happy birthday, Sunshine," I acceded in surrender.

"The answer is 'None,' " she triumphed. "Happy anniversary to you, sweet man. Thank you for everything. You're the tops."

How could I answer her question? I mean, I didn't have a backlog of vaginal sightings that I could reference. I had seen two before hers, my wife's and that of my first serious girlfriend in college. Both looked pretty good to me. The difference was, neither one of those women seemed to really appreciate what they had or how to use it to their advantage. Ann did. She knew what she had, and she sure as hell knew how to use it. She loved it. She loved to touch herself and to explore herself. She always told me when she did; she often showed me when she did. When she wasn't enjoying it herself, she offered it to me, for my enjoyment as well as for hers. I played with it endlessly. I played, but it was no plaything, no toy. I viewed it with complete reverence and genuine appreciation as the sacred centerpiece of the temple that was her body, and I was continually humbled at the altar of her soul. Often its sexual identity was lost, even when it was dancing on my fingertips, surrendering to my tongue, or welcoming my entrance, as my thoughts focused in thanksgiving on the meaning of the act rather than on the act itself. When I thought about it and when I talked about it—and even now as I write about it—I find it difficult to refer to it with an appropriate and acceptable name, although from the beginning of time, I suspect, it has been tagged with every imaginable label to either deify it and make it sound clean and attractive, or degrade it and make it sound dirty and disgusting. To me it was always a gift. Ann presented it to me that way, and I always was grateful accepting it that way—as a gift to take but not to have, a gift she loved to share with me, not give me. She knew what she had. And it was she who taught me to treat it with respect and veneration as her most personal and private possession. I never did anything less.

We laughed and rolled together, a stinging ache accompanying the swelling that was returning between my legs.

"We better not push our luck. We gotta get the hell outta here," I said with concern as I remembered where we were. "We've got a mess to clean up here, too. You're not all that neat when you come, ya know?"

"How come I take the rap for the mess? It's not all mine, ya know," she impeached. "And ya didn't even use a rubber to protect me," she pouted with pretended dejection as we began to pull the furniture around in place.

"Yeah, you sure took care of *that,* didn't you? And if you hadn't twitched," I chastised, "I wouldn't have come, and we wouldn't have anything to worry about or clean up. We'd probably still be screwin'."

"Bullcrap. I knew you couldn't hold it any longer, anyway. You think you're fuckin' Superman?"

She stood in front of me and stepped close, gyrating her crotch against me, her arms wound around my neck. Then, with a quick jump, she wrapped her legs around my thighs and hung suspended against me, her hands clasped behind my head, as I instinctively threw my arms around her. I reeled with the sudden and unexpected impact, and we stumbled together in a heap on the couch.

"I only twitched it once. I wanted your cream," she gurgled saucily.

I rolled over on top of her, cradled in her crotch, her legs still entwined about me in a clamant vice.

"So, you got just what you wanted, and now we hafta clean up," I pressed.

"Yeah, but now I'm so sore I won't be able to walk until I'm twenty," she countered. "Holy geez, twenty sounds so ancient."

"Oh, goody. Can we do it again when you're twenty?" I begged with boyish enthusiasm.

"Maybe, if you treat me right. Maybe I'll let you. It may not be as much fun, though. We may be married by then."

I think Fran could have heard me gulp, all the way to her house a mile away.

"C'mon, up!" I snapped, grasping her arm and giving a tug. "Enough of this chatter. *This,* fair damsel, is a school and should be thusly treated. 'Tis not a frolicking playground," I admonished tersely. "It ain't even a great place for a birthday party, so let us be about the business of attending to its composure and proper setting lest tomorrow's pupils sniff out all the places you squirted and ask their knowledgeable teacher what he makes of it."

"Well, aren't we just witty," she lamented, throwing her arms in the air. "To think that barely a moment ago I thought you to be the princely stoker of the fires that rage betwixt my wanton loins only to find that, in the twitch of a cunt's hair, I'm nothing more than your Monday harlot, and you're a simple, fuckin' teacher!"

We laughed uproariously, stomping about the stage like two drunken players.

"Not bad, not bad, good lines," I clucked in humorous compliment. "Maybe you can use those lines in an audition someday, huh?" I roared, probably too loudly for our situation.

"You weren't too bad, yourself. You might have *some* stage potential," she boosted with a modest degree of admiration. "Some—but I don't think you're quite ready to take it out on the road. Try it at your next staff meeting and see if it flies," she heckled with a mocking laugh.

She had dropped to her hands and knees in front of the chair and was trying to wipe up the drips of wetness with a tissue from her pocketbook. I bounded over to her before she had a chance to look up, and I took her in my arms and held her tightly against my chest.

"Is this because I'm cleaning up the mess or because I said you might have some stage potential?" she chuckled in response to my springing leap to her side.

"Nope, neither," I said as I squeezed her close. "It's because I love you so damn much I don't know what to say or do. I mean, I can't—I just—" I sputtered, the right words failing the call of my feelings. "I love you so much, babe," I said with genuine tenderness. "There isn't anything I wouldn't buy you, there isn't anything I wouldn't give you, and there isn't anything I wouldn't do for you."

"And if I should have your baby?" she braved cantingly as if to confute my extravagant benevolence. "How cool are you with that?"

I thought for a moment. I felt the warmth of her body close to mine. I felt her heartbeat.

"Well," I started with a sigh, "we wouldn't have any more secrets, would we? The whole world would know….."

I felt her snuggle her head under my chin.

"…..but nobody would ever know, or could even imagine, how much feeling, respect, and caring went into our loving," I concluded.

She withdrew from me, just enough to look up at me with tears in her eyes.

"Is that the truth?" she begged.

"That's the truth," I affirmed.

"And a baby?"

"I'd be cool with that," I acknowledged. "I'd be in a mess of trouble, but I could deal with it."

"Thank you so much, you sweet man, my sweet man. I love you too much, but not nearly enough," she exulted.

"You love me, and I love you, perfectly."

"Oh, I do, Charlie, I do."

"I do, too, you little cumquat. Douse the light."

"I'm a donut. Turn it out yourself."

****

Her young body showed a remarkable degree of resiliency. Not only was she able to walk comfortably the next day, but she was panting for more. I confess, I was, too. We obliged each other that night with feverishly hot recollections of her birthday celebration and our first-year anniversary party, retelling the feelings and thoughts, reliving the memories, restating our "vows," recapturing the tenderness, rekindling the fires, reviving the passion, and once again relinquishing the sultry, boiling gushes of love's naturally sweet confections to each other in the breathless, gripping, and loving conjuncture to which we each had become addicted.

Two days later we were horseback riding together, none the worse for wear!

CHAPTER 19

Aside from making love together, we spent our most enjoyable and intimate times horseback riding at a family-owned stable in Allendale. "Ya think there are other people like us—like a teacher and a student?"

Nobody signed up for the horseback riding. The notice gathered dust on the bulletin board, neither attracting much attention nor arousing much enthusiasm, except for Ann and I who decided it was an opportunity too good to miss.

The school year was drawing to a close, and nobody at school seemed to be paying much attention to anything except putting the yearbook together, and most of that work already had been completed. People paid so little attention to Ann and I that when she left her "message" to me on the Tuesday after her birthday—a large square of glossy, black paper cut from a magazine advertisement showing the words "Love is always original" in bold white lettering, *not* in an envelope—I let it stay in my mailbox for the entire day just so it might confound anyone who wished to be confounded. Fuck them.

There was no way we could turn the horseback riding into a class for credit or do it on school time. We decided to do the next best thing. We decided to go riding together once or twice a week on our own time, after school, for our own enjoyment.

We headed up Route 17 in the direction of our usual "safety zones," spending several delightful afternoons visiting stables in Ramsey, Upper Saddle River, and Franklin Lakes. It was on the third or fourth of these late afternoon excursions that we found the ideal situation, a family-owned riding stable on a beautiful piece of wooded land, a surviving vestige of farm and country living nestled in the quiet of residential Allendale. It was just enough off the beaten track so that when we drove up the driveway and pulled behind the blue, corner house, the welcome sight of the riding ring, the barn, and the backwoods bridle paths made it easy to forget that sprawling suburbia was only a block away, an Erie Railroad trestle was around the corner, and a bustling super-highway was less than a mile distant. Aside from making love together, Ann and I spent our most enjoyable and intimate times once or twice a week at the tranquil setting we affectionately called "Nine Miles to Heaven"—eight miles north of Route 4 on Route 17 and one mile west.

We looked forward to our riding ventures with eager anticipation of time to relax, to be with each other, and to be outdoors through what remained of the budding month of May and into the lazy days of June. Best of all, Ann's parents and Pam knew exactly where we were and what we were doing. They just thought it was a school activity and we were doing it as part of a group. It was easy, therefore, to dress for riding in the morning, come home smelling of horses and hay, and relate our happy riding experiences with only the minor embellishment of adding a few imaginary members to our "group."

Taking the Allendale exit off Route 17 and making the subsequent turns onto Franklin Turnpike, followed by a right on West Orchard Street, down under the trestle, past the low stone fence on the left, and around the corner onto Allen Street always brought song from Ann. Her chatter of camp stories, told for the seventy-third time, complete with elaborate descriptions of cabin interiors, the waterfront dock, and burlesque caricatures of campers and counselors—stirred to remembrance by the joint she had started on Route 4—gave way to the songs of Judy Collins, Linda Ronstadt, and, of course, Barbra Streisand, as we neared our heaven of fresh straw, horse trailers, white fencing, horseshoe tracks in the powdered dirt, and the whinnying of the chestnut mare she always rode.

It was the kind of place that was easy to love—neat grounds, clean barns, and friendly people whose interest was in their horses, not in who we were or what we were doing together or why. We were accepted as everyone else, as people who loved the place and loved to ride. Despite the obvious difference in our ages, never were we asked any questions, and never did we feel uncomfortable being seen walking together, holding hands, hugging, or showing affection.

It was a family-owned stable, a do-it-yourself operation. We picked our own saddles from the rack, saddled the horses ourselves, adjusted the stirrups for each other, and walked the friendly animals to the ringed enclosure. When we were done for the day, we watered them, brushed them down, and picked their shoes. Then we'd stick our heads inside the kitchen screen door at the back of the house, call the woman owner, and pay her for the time. She'd always give us more than a fair break.

Ann was a much more accomplished rider than I. Each visit we spent some time in the riding ring together so I could learn to post and trot and canter without ending up with a sore fanny. Then we'd take the horses out to the road, around the corner and under the trestle, down Elmwood Avenue to the dead end, and into the woods.

I'd sing softly the beautiful words of John Denver's "Sunshine On My Shoulders," perfectly suited to the occasion as we guided our horses from canopied shadow to open sunlight, then back again into the deep mystery of dark green cover, aware that at any moment we might be treated to a wildlife display of grazing deer or the fitful scurrying of a rafter of wild turkeys.

We'd usually ride for an hour or more along the bridle paths that wound through the birches and elms, across the stream, up the gentle rise to a grassy meadow, and down the other side into the maples.

The fragrances, sights, and sounds of the woods were delectable—the fresh smell of moist earth, the pollywogs in the stream, the sharp snapping of last year's dry twigs under hoof, the heavy snorting of the horses after a quick run, and the afternoon's golden rays that streamed through trees partially dressed in their early season's fine attire.

The sunlight glistened in Ann's long, flowing hair as she rode ahead of me along the path bordered by the lush undergrowth of broad-leafed ferns and tiny, white, star-shaped flowers.

I'd watch her ass bounce in the saddle in front of me, and it was difficult not to give meditative thought to the many times I had set that same pretty ass in similar rhythmic motion, but aside from such fleeting titillations, of all the times we went riding together in the woods, we never gave a thought to stopping and making love. The entire exercise was a love-making and a love-sharing in itself, a fulfilling communion between the two of us within Nature's breast, experienced from atop a pair of four-legged beasts that we cared for and loved as much as if they were our very own children.

Ann rode a brood mare in foal, pampering her with tender care, gentle whispers, soft songs, and an occasional carrot or a "forbidden" cube of sugar, as eager for the mare's time to come as an impatient midwife. Nonetheless, her eagerness turned to disappointment when the animal's time finally approached and she had to be stabled. Ann reluctantly picked a replacement which she rode for weeks. Before we left for home after each visit, however, we always made a special stop by the stall where "her" mare stood in waiting. Ann always offered a word of encouragement, a pat on the belly, and the promise to be there when she foaled. But as the days passed and the mare went far beyond her time, the owners became concerned and eventually had to call a veterinarian to induce labor. We missed the birthing event by a day.

"Damn, I wanted to see it," Ann grumbled with annoyance and disappointment as we headed quickly to the barn.

"I guess they couldn't chance waiting any longer," I consoled. "I wanted to watch, too. Geez, that would be something to see, huh?"

We raced to the stall like two little kids bounding down the stairs on Christmas morning to see what Santa had left. We peered over the slatted door of the stall.

"Holy shit, look at that. Oh, what a cutie, what a beauty. Oh, look at that, Charlie. Oh, what a honey. Look at him nurse."

The spindle-legged colt, sleek and reddish brown, wobbled aside the mare, his thin neck tucked beneath her underside, his head upturned at an angle, his mouth tugging.

"Suck it, baby, suck it good, ya little fucker," she squealed in delighted exuberance. "Oh, God, she had a beauty, didn't she?"

She did. I was speechless. The whole thing was beautiful. I put my arm around Ann as she stood up on one of the lower slats and tried to reach over to touch.

"Damn, I wish I could get in there," she declared with obvious frustration.

The mare turned her head slowly and nudged the rear of the colt, his frail knees buckling as he fell clumsily onto the straw-covered floor of the stall.

"I guess it's not supposed to be feeding time," I offered. "Christ, he's cute. He's bigger than I thought he'd be. Look how long his legs are. They're skinny, but look how long."

"I wish I could.....just.....reach him," she strained, stepping one slat higher and stretching out as she gripped the top of the stall with her other hand.

"C'mon down, babe, before you fall in on your head," I cautioned. "You're not gonna be able to reach."

She hopped down reluctantly, and we held each other closely.

"It's a miracle. It's a God damn miracle, isn't it? They talk about the miracle of birth, and it really is, isn't it?" she exclaimed quietly in awe, looking at me for confirmation.

"Yeah, man, it is. It's really hard to believe."

"I wanna have a baby, too," she said in a foggy trance as she squeezed me to her and looked into my eyes.

"Hey, hold off a little," I begged pleadingly. "You think I'm really ready for miracles?"

"What about one? What about one miracle, by mistake?"

I hoped she was just teasing, but I knew she wasn't.

"I think I'm more into planned miracles, not mistakes. Christ, we take enough chances on a mistake as it is."

"Oh, c'mon, hon."

The subject of a baby wasn't new. It had come up several times before, but no serious discussion had ever ensued beyond the first mention. It wasn't going to be discussed now, either, but as we shuffled out of the barn together and meandered hand in hand across the dusty expanse toward the riding ring, aimlessly kicking pebbles and small stones ahead of us, we both suspected that a time would come when the matter would not be so easily dismissed. We stopped and leaned side by side, each with our arms crossed on top of the white fence railing, staring blankly straight ahead into the empty ring, sharing together the silence of our private thoughts.

"Ya think there are other people like us, Charlie?"

"Like us—ya mean who love each other like we do?" I asked in surprise, uncertain of her question.

"No, like us. You know, like a teacher and a student?"

A teacher and a student? I almost had forgotten.....

"Gee, I really don't know," I responded thoughtfully but perplexed. "I really don't know, hon."

I had to think about that for a long time. I was still thinking about it long after we had kissed good-bye for the afternoon, and I was heading home.

Whew, a teacher and a student.....

CHAPTER 20

The Eleventh Commandment: Never hit a student, and never "hit on" a student.....

"Never hit a student—ever!"

That's what I was told when I did my teacher training work in college. That's what all of us were told. "Don't hit a kid. Don't touch 'em—not in New Jersey—you'll lose your job."

Now, the idea of a teacher becoming *sexually involved* with a student—well, that was such a preposterous thought it simply wasn't utterable. I mean, if you can't hit a student, it's pretty obvious you can't "hit on" a student. "Don't get emotionally involved." That's as close as they ever got to saying it. "Never hit a student" was the verbalized directive. "Thou shalt not fuck a student" was the unspoken—not even whispered, not even breathed—Eleventh Commandment. For God's sake, no teacher was so dumb they had to be told *that.* Even hitting a student—you'd have to have your fucking head examined.

The idealism that was part and parcel of the indoctrinating education classes to which I, as every would-be teacher, was exposed while completing my college preparation was short-lived. I wasn't even a teacher, yet. I was a junior in college when a good portion of it went down the drain. A three-week period of junior year observation was a prerequisite for the twelve weeks of student teaching scheduled for the following year.

For my observation, I chose to return to the high school from which I had been graduated. It was close to home, familiar, and otherwise convenient. Besides, Pam, whom I was dating at the time and whom I later would marry, was a high school senior there.

A requirement of my junior observation included getting a list of questions answered and forms completed. Late one afternoon toward the end of the three weeks, I found myself in the area beneath the gymnasium, winding my way through the subterranean bowels of the school where the athletic department's locker rooms, shower rooms, equipment rooms, and coaches' offices were located. It was there, as I stood in the stale, dank air of the boys' locker room and hastily scribbled the answers the Director of Athletics had provided to my innocuous questions, that I, still a year and a half away from professional certification and still very much wet behind the ears, got my first behind-the-scenes glimpse into the real, hard-nose world of being a teacher.

I don't know what the problem was. I don't know who he was or what had happened. Maybe he was a student athlete who had broken training rules or a wise guy who had been messing around in somebody's classroom. I don't know, but he was there, brought into the locker room by two teachers, both coaches. The three of them stood talking intently between the long rows of green lockers. The kid, trapped between the two strapping men, turned first to one and then to the other. As their verbal exchange became increasingly heated, one of the coaches grabbed the boy by the shirt and shoved him forcefully, the kid stumbling backward over the wooden bench that ran in front of the lockers. With a resounding clatter, he smashed against the metal cubicles, careening into the arms of the second coach who pushed him back, this time against the line of lockers on the opposite side. The boy voiced helpless objection as he vainly attempted to maintain his balance and stay on his feet. They threw him back and forth four or five times—a human volleyball—each time ricocheting the kid off the lockers, his knees, elbows, head, and shoulders taking brutal punishment. I thought they were going to crack his skull. I thought they were going to kill him. I stood there, just out of sight, my eyes bulging in disbelief and my heart pounding in fright.

"…..and if we hafta bring ya down here again, buddy, ya won't have two legs to walk out on."

He wasn't kidding, either.

I was scared shit. I never said a word about it. I never said a fucking word to anybody. I just turned in my list of asshole questions with their proper answers when I got back to college and kept my mouth shut.

"Never hit a student—ever!" Holy shit.

****

As far as the "hit on" section of the Eleventh Commandment was concerned, I was naïve, and I remained naïve for a long time.

School wouldn't be school without the petty nonsense of students having "crushes" on teachers and teachers having their "pets," particularly in the early years of high school. I, like most young teachers, had to learn how to deal with them, starting with Patty. Patty sat in the front row of my second period civics class, my first year on the job at the ripe old age of twenty-one in the newly opened Northern Valley Regional High School in Demarest, New Jersey. Patty sat and rolled her big, brown, flirting eyes at me all period long. I loved it! She wrote me "secret" love notes without signing her name and handed them to me on the way out of class as if she were an innocent messenger. She would tell me on Friday that she was going bike riding over the weekend and, sure enough, I'd see her riding back and forth in front of my house on Saturday afternoon. I lived with my parents in a neighboring town a good ten miles from where Patty lived, but the distance didn't deter her. One weekend during the fall, she left an apple and a note on the front seat of my 1950, light blue, Ford convertible parked under the trees in front of the house. The little kid had guts, and my ego ate it up!

The telephone rang at the house on Sunday afternoon a week or two later.

"Hello, can I talk to Mr. Sullivan, please?"

"Yeah, hold on, just a minute," I replied.

"Hey, Dad, it's for you," I called to the kitchen as I rested the receiver on the hall table and returned to the television set in the living room. The New York Giants were—

"It's not for me. It's for you," he called back to me a few seconds later.

It was Patty. Shit, I was still such a greenhorn, I hadn't become accustomed to the fact that *my* name, too, was Mr. Sullivan. The only place I ever was called "Mr. Sullivan" was in my classroom! Naïve? The Eleventh

Commandment was never so safe! I didn't even know my own friggin' name.

The year after Patty there was Jill, then Sally, then Maryanne, and Lorraine—I think that's what her name was; she wasn't in school that long…..she was pregnant before Spring vacation—all with their innocent "crushes" that lasted for days or weeks or months or until they just faded naturally, forgotten and harmless, a muted backdrop to the close-up concerns upon which teachers have to focus every day in the classroom.

Twelve years later, I was in my first year at Teaneck High School, thirty-three years old, married, second daughter just arrived, now a counselor rather than a classroom teacher, hair thinning, well beyond the "crush" age, but not yet ready for the Ice Age.

I loved tennis. I played every chance I could, indoors in the winter and outdoors during the summer. I followed the big-name players and tournaments in the newspapers. I had been the tennis coach at my previous school, and I had spent the past summer as the tennis instructor and coach at a day camp. I gave private tennis lessons on the side.

Along came Debbie—bright, articulate, attractive, and athletic—a senior applying to colleges and first-court singles player on the girls' varsity tennis team. Debbie and I spent a lot of time discussing colleges and working on her applications and her personal statement. We talked about her S.A.T. scores and the pros and cons of Early Decision, and we talked about tennis. She was a frequent visitor to my office. She always stopped by after a match to tell me how she had done, what she was doing well, and what strokes were giving her trouble. Her parents had me to their home for dinner so we could have an extended conversation about Debbie's college choices and to talk tennis.

Debbie was in the middle of a great season. I wasn't the least surprised when, happy with her success and pleased by my interest in her game, she asked me if I'd like to watch her next match. *Her next match!* Wow! Nothing could have been more perfect—an "away" match at Northern Valley Regional High School in Demarest where I had begun my teaching career, on courts I knew like the back of my hand, against a coach who had been a teaching colleague, a friend, and a coaching counterpart within the district. Of course, I'd go!

Three days after the match, Debbie came to my office in tears.

"Debbie, what's the matter? What happened?"

"My coach just told me.....I better....."

"Better what? Here, here's a tissue. Better what, Deb?"

"Better.....be careful—" she sniffled.

"Careful?"

An awkward silence followed my query.

"Careful of you," she said hesitantly.

"Huh?"

"My coach.....said I better.....be care—" she began to repeat haltingly as the tears streamed down her cheeks.

"Go to class, Deb," I interrupted. I had heard enough. I didn't need to hear it again. "Go to the girls' room and clean yourself up before you go to class. If you want, come here instead. If you're too upset to go to class, come back here to my office, okay? I'll talk with you later, honey. It's gonna be all right. I'll take care of that bitch."

I took the steps two at a time, downstairs to the girls' gym. Josephine Reilly, the Girls' Director of Athletics, was in the physical education office. She wasn't the one I wanted. I wanted Jessica, the tennis coach. The fucking bitch—

"When ya see Jessica, would ya tell her I'd like to see her in my office as soon as she can come up?"

I tried to say it calmly and with ease, not like I felt like slugging somebody. I wanted neither my voice to betray the anger and urgency I felt within nor my breathlessness to reveal that I had run all the way from the second floor.

"Sure, Charlie," Josephine said, looking up from her cluttered desk. "Anything I can help you with?"

"No, thanks, I just need to talk with Jessica for a few minutes."

"Okay. She should be coming in just before the period ends, in about ten minutes or so."

"Thanks, Jo."

I retraced my steps back upstairs to my office. Deb wasn't there. I closed the door and sat in the swivel chair behind my desk, my elbow on my knee, my hand to my chin, tapping the fingers of my other hand on the blue desk blotter, waiting, seething.

Jessica came to my office fifteen minutes later. I don't think she knew too much about me. Maybe she didn't know anything about me, but I wasn't in any mood to be accommodative with introductions. I lit into her savagely, venting my anger without restraint.

"Did you tell Debbie she better be careful of me?" I blustered.

"Well, I said—"

"Let me tell ya something, sweetheart. *You're* the one who'd better be careful of me. You've got a big problem with your fuckin' mouth….."

Five minutes later she knew everything she had to know about me, and she had heard more than a few words I was sure she wasn't going to write in her diary.

It was two days before she came back.

"I don't know what to say. I'm just so very sorry I said what I did, Charlie. You're sorta the 'new guy on the block,' and I didn't know then what I know now. I know now that you're a very unusual and very sincere man. I'm really sorry. I already apologized to Debbie."

"Forget it."

She came back. I had to hand it to her. I didn't think she'd ever want to face me again. I knew she didn't want to, but she did. She came back and apologized. It couldn't have been easy to come back and say "I'm sorry" to someone who had raked her ass over the coals. Her capitulation, unequivocally offered and totally accepted, fostered a mutual respect that lasted for years, allowing us to work together with student athletes who needed scholarship aid for college and allowing us to be partners on the tennis courts and play together in a faculty mixed-doubles tournament. Jessica was okay.

It was just about this time, three years before the opening of the Alternative School, that I first became aware of assaults on the Eleventh Commandment—not by me, by others.

The first incident actually occurred some time before. It was just a simple matter of Sal, one of the math teachers at Northern Valley, marrying a popular female pupil, the student president of the Girls' Athletic Association, almost immediately after she had graduated from school. It didn't even create a stir. Who the hell wanted to stir *that* pot? If anything had been going on between the two of them while she was still in school—and who was going to be foolish enough to suggest that nothing had been going on—no one wanted to know anything about it. *No one* wanted to know *anything.*

The second incident—well, that was no simple matter. That was a pip!

The Wednesday night poker game in which I had played for years with half a dozen teachers from the new Northern Valley Regional High School in Old Tappan—to which I had moved after four years in the Demarest building—continued even after I had left the district for another job. The location of the game rotated from house to house each week, and the cast of characters changed from time to time, but I was still right in the middle of it. The game endured with the "old-timers"—Bill, Tim, Donnie, Lou, Ricky, and myself—persisting with undaunted regularity. It was a good game with good relaxation, good talk, and good clean fun with nobody getting badly burned, although the stakes—a quarter and a half, three raises maximum—built up some handsome pots.

The poker game was my contact with my former school and my old friends, a lifeline to my past. It also was the place where I was to find out, gradually and shockingly, amid the shuffling of cards, the jingling of change, and the puffs of cigarette smoke, about Ed and Susan.

"Ed Richards?.....No!.....With one of his students?..... You gotta be kiddin'..... Pregnant?.....C'mon.....What about his wife?.....You're pullin' my leg, right?.....He's *living* with the girl?.....in Hackensack?.....Susan who?..... Holy shit, her sister was one of my counselees.....This is Ed, Ed Richards, right?.....Hollllllly Christmas!"

Ed Richards.

If someone had taken a poll to determine the faculty member at either of the regional high schools *least* likely to become involved with a student, it would have been a unanimous win for Ed Richards. And if the same poll had been taken *before I had left* the regional high school district, it would have ended in a flat-footed tie—Ed Richards and me!

* * * * * * *

"Richards.....R-i-c-h-a.....Richards, Edwn P.—That's the one!.....154 Beechwood Av Wstwd—Westwood? I thought he lived in Hackensack.....must've moved, 'cause that's him, I'm sure.....666-3772.....Holy shit, he lives right around the corner in the next town!.....6-6-6-3-7-7-2.....C'mon, c'mon.....somebody, some—.....Ed?..... Ed Richards?.....You're never gonna believe who this is, Ed.....This is Charlie Sullivan.....yeah, right!.....yeah, I know—a long time.....almost eight years.....I know it doesn't, but it has been.....yeah.....uh, listen.....I've got something I'd like to talk to you about.....yeah, well, not really a problem.....I can't talk now, but.....yeah, if I could meet you.....yeah, I know where that is.....maybe tomorrow?.....tomorrow afternoon.....I'll see you there..... right. Okay.....thanks, Ed."

He was just the same as I remembered him—short, medium build, dark and wavy hair, glasses, smiling, and cordial. His open sport shirt, light windbreaker jacket, and dark brown slacks gave him a straight, conservative appearance that belied the fact that he was a teacher who had ditched his wife three years before to marry a student pregnant with his child.

People who whisked by the two of us as we stood in the middle of the Valley Fair discount store in Park Ridge, exchanging handshakes and pleasantries and remembering when we taught together at the same regional high school, could hardly have known by the outward appearance of either of us that the rakish tales we were about to exchange were those that high school principals and members of boards of education live in dreaded fear of ever hearing.

"How the hell did you get away with it?" I questioned with intense curiosity.

"Well, nobody really knew, until it was all over."

Ed—man of few words, but if I got him started—

"Didn't anyone suspect?" I prodded.

"No, not really, except maybe Larry. You remember Larry, the science teacher?"

"Larry?" I exclaimed with mild astonishment. "Jesus, of all people. I remember Larry. He suspected?"

"Oh, I don't know if he actually suspected, but one day—it was late in Susan's senior year—he grabbed me in the hall after school. You know, Larry always hung around a lot after school like an orphan without a home, and, of course, I was always there late, and Susan would stay and give me a hand in the Audio-Visual Aids office, so Larry was in a good position to see us together a lot."

"What the hell are ya doin' in the A.V.A. office?" I interrupted with alarm. "I thought you were teachin' Latin.

"I had been—I was—I am, but there aren't enough classes. Nobody takes Latin anymore," he said with a disappointed shake of his head. "In fact, I even had some Spanish classes. Then the powers-that-be substituted work in the A.V.A. office for a couple of classes to fill my schedule. Well, anyway, Larry grabs me in the hall and tries to give me his fatherly advice—'people are gonna talk,' you know, because Susan and I are spendin' so much time together."

"I can't believe he had the guts to say anything. I remember him as more timid than that, not even the kind of person who would notice, much less say anything. Here, let's move over here, outta the way."

"Yeah, he said something. I was furious," Ed continued as we stepped aside, out of the traffic of afternoon bargain hunters. "I told him he'd get a fist in the face if he didn't mind his own business. I figured if I could scare him into keepin' his mouth shut, everything would be okay, and it was. But that was the only time I worried about bein' found out."

"What about later? How can ya scare someone into forgetting there's a baby?"

"Well—"

Ed unfolded his story to me over the next few weeks. We saw each other several times for lunch, and I was tickled and thankful to have someone with whom to talk about my own situation with Ann, someone who could fully understand what I was going through, because he already had gone through it himself.

CHAPTER 21

The two teachers least likely to become involved with a student share their respective stories. The saga of Ed and Susan answers Ann's question: Yes, there were others like us.....

What began between Ed and Susan at the end of her sophomore year at Northern Valley Regional High School in Old Tappan actually had its unlikely origins fourteen years earlier in the rolling hills and rich farmland valleys of western North Carolina. It was there, at the Greyton County High School west of Charlotte, that Ed's appetite was whetted.

Ed sat in a booth at the local greasy spoon, a small but congenial hangout suited to the needs of neighborhood folk looking for a quick bite or a steaming cup of fresh coffee. For a young teacher, just out of college, on the job only three weeks, alone in a new place, short on friends and long on time, it was a comfortable haven to wile away a late afternoon in September. Ed didn't know the woman who turned from the counter where she was sitting and leaned in his direction.

"You're Ed Richards, aren't you?"

"Yes," Ed said, looking up.

"Hi, I'm Doris Williamson, Carolyn's mother. She's in your Latin class."

The chatty conversation that followed was the beginning of a relationship with the Williamson family that saw Ed a frequent and welcome visitor to the upstairs apartment, a few doors down the block, of Doris and George Williamson, as friend of the family and Carolyn's Latin tutor. Ed maintained close contact with the Williamsons over a lengthy period of time, often tutoring Carolyn alone, her father out getting drunk while her mother was in town keeping company with the deputy sheriff.

It was on one of these occasions in early February that Ed found himself with the beautiful and fully developed, fifteen-year old body of Carolyn Williamson, invitingly clad in a nylon nightgown and a satin housecoat, lying across his lap on the couch, eagerly awaiting his "tutoring." It wasn't a complete surprise—delightful, but no surprise. Carolyn's stealthy moves, in more subtle form, had been played on previous occasions, before Ed's December marriage to his wife, Jenny, as well as after.

Looking back on the sequence of events that had brought him to this awkward, post-marriage position in which he found himself, his hand aching to move to the softness of the rising young nipples that hardened beneath the lingerie on his lap, Ed recalled, "If the wedding had been scheduled for a year later, there wouldn't have been one."

But, alas, moved by strong feelings of insecurity and the fear that no other woman would have him, Ed had become the innocent and unwitting victim of the first serious involvement and extended relationship of his life and had been hustled down the primrose path of matrimony. The marriage was two months past, not a year hence. So, despite the ache in his hand and the pulsing in his body, he succumbed to the fear in his heart. The urge was controlled, the passion squelched.

Nothing happened. Nothing physical. But the appetite—the innate human propensity to satisfy a sexual craving—was whetted. As far as Ed was concerned, the knowledge of what was possible and what *could* happen had been tantalizingly dangled as a carrot before a hungry rabbit, albeit a scared one at the time. Had Ed's nature been as aggressive as his appetite and his desires, the Eleventh Commandment would not have remained unbroken for fourteen years, but his cautious manner and general reserve imprisoned every future thought of pursuing a situation similar to "the one that got away."

"In my mind, I screwed every good-looking female student I had from that time on, and Susan was bedded down long before it ever really happened," Ed told me.

****

The pattern had been established by the end of Susan's sophomore year—the late afternoons together at school, the long talks, the sharing, the laughs, the friendship, and the chivalrous offer of a lift home because it was "on the way." And then came the seed—his instigating comment. Or was it her instigating movement? Or was it the situation, the isolated seclusion of the classroom; the deserted hallways as the afternoon wore on, only a custodian or a straggling student remaining; the togetherness of being alone; the eerie quiet of an almost empty building that seemed to compel whispers out of respect for that which should be still? Had Ed's comment come out of the blue, or had it been an outgrowth of something Susan had said or done, accidentally or on purpose? Who knows? Provoked or not, the instigating comment was Ed's, and it was a lie: "I'd sure hate to be in this school all alone with you."

It was the kind of lie that told the truth. And Susan knew the truth. Did the comment start her thinking, or had she been thinking all long and the comment merely serve to signal the time for movement, the call to action? It made paltry difference. From that point on, Susan became the eager engineer of her own seduction, as surely and steadily as a railroad locomotive hurtles in straightforward fashion along an unbroken stretch of track, reaching across a plain, curving low and small in the distance, before being snared and swallowed in the yawning gulp of the inevitable horizon. Susan threw the turntable switch which placed the innocence of verbal dialogue onto the track headed for physical connection. All aboard!

The destination was as set as rails spiked to a track bed. There were no turns, switches, or sidings, the fire of the engine stoked to its fullest heat and the course established with a skilled engineer at the throttle. Ed went along for the ride. Hell, he had waited fourteen years with nothing but the thought, "I think I can, I think I can." Now he was in the sure hands of *The Little Engine That Could*.

Even an incident as innocent and innocuous as losing a set of keys became another tie between the rails.

It was the last day of school for teachers. The last day for students had been Wednesday, but teachers returned on Thursday to clean their rooms, store supplies for the summer, clear bulletin boards, put their desks in order, and pick up their last paycheck until September. Susan came in to give Ed a hand with his close-up chores.

When the time came to lock things up and leave for the day, Ed couldn't find his keys. High and low the two of them hunted for the set of missing keys, all on a single ring with a leather strap. He had them. He *knew* he had them. He *had* to have them. He had driven to school and used his car key. Now they were gone—the keys to the school building, his room key, his desk key, the car keys, and his house key—all of them, gone.

"Think, Ed, where the hell….? What was I doing this morning? Where was…..? Doug! Doug Gratolla…..Doug Gratolla borrowed them…..right!.....early this morning….. He needed the school keys…..that's right!.....I gave them to him, damn it…..Where was he?.....Oh, Christ. He was leavin' for Florida…..for the summer! Damn, I saw him go; I saw him leave after lunch…..*Damn!* Now what the hell am I—Retrace his steps.....We gotta retrace his steps…..We gotta…..C'mon….."

Ed and Susan headed quickly for the English office. It was a long shot, but what other shots were there? They turned the place upside down, trying to surmise what Doug, the chairman of the English Department, could have done with the keys, where he would have left them—if he did leave them.

It was Susan who spied the tip of the leather strap, barely visible, protruding over the edge of a shelf high against the wall where Doug obviously had climbed to either take some books down or stack some away. He had rested the key ring on the edge of the shelf and had climbed down without it, and he had left for Florida!

They stood by the desk in the office, enjoying together the breathless calm of relief, allowing it to gradually replace the racing anxiety of the previous half hour's frantic search. Happy, relieved, and speechless, but still feeling the contradiction of hot flush and cold sweat, Ed kissed Susan appreciatively. The genuine "thank you" peck was as much an expression of jubilance as it was a fitting prelude for the revelation of deeper feelings of more significant import. It was their fist kiss. It wouldn't be their last, and it was nothing like their second.

The end of school and the start of vacation saw Susan begin a summer job as a copy-reader in the New York City office of Richard Gold's law firm, a job she was fortunate enough to secure through the connections of her brother-in-law's father. Ed continued at the high school as a summer school teacher, working six mornings a week, teaching two hours of Latin and putting in two hours of library duty a day. It was a soft job. Who the hell goes to the library during summer school? It was a joke.

Six days a week in the summer would have been a back-breaker for most people, but not for Ed. He loved it. Susan didn't work on Saturdays. Instead, she'd go over to the high school every Saturday morning. When Ed was finished with his Latin class, the two of them would sit and spend the next couple of hours together in the glassed enclosure of the librarian's office off the main floor of the infrequently used library. It was a continuation of the afternoon talk time they had spent together before the closing of school. Now, however, warm summer mornings brought Susan to school in light, provocative dresses or low-cut blouses which revealed significant cleavage and just enough exposure to make Saturday the best day of

Ed's week. She knew exactly what she was doing. She had plenty to show, and she showed him plenty. She drove the poor guy crazy, using the two hours of library duty to rack his shelves with pin-up magazines hot off her own press—her own stack—delivered in person, with centerfolds he could drool over and dream about for a week. She drove her train right through the newsstand of his railroad station without even a whistle of warning.

The second kiss was no light, gratuitous peck of small consequence. It came as part of the emotionally charged drama of saying good-bye on the last Saturday of summer school. It came with passionate intensity that unmistakably defined the nature of what the relationship had become. It came with unspoken words of fond farewell, regretful separation, and hopeful reunion. It came with the sobering awareness that Ed was headed for Cape Cod with his wife, Jenny, and their eleven-year old daughter, Cori, and that there would be no more Saturday morning rendezvous and no more teasing exposure of Susan's generously developed womanhood. It came with Ed's hand boldly and fully squeezing against the top of her dress, his palm covering her breast, his fingertips barely stretching to the cleavage and the softness of her smooth skin. It was followed by three weeks of obsessive thought and anxious waiting, three weeks of wondering what her reaction would be to his first overt move, three weeks before the end of summer vacation and the reopening of school. Three long weeks—

Susan waited, too. God, everybody who goes to school counts the days before the *start* of vacation, but when a teacher and a student begin counting the days until vacation *ends* and school *opens,* you know things are really fucked up!

Of course, Ed's concern for Susan's reaction was for naught. How far did he think his hand could have reached if the engineer at the throttle had decided to flash the stop signal? He didn't understand that he had no control over this train and that he was nothing more than a sightseeing passenger. He could have gotten away with nothing except by her leave. She could have derailed him anytime she wanted, if she wanted. She didn't.

Ed's return to school in September found him in the new position of part-time teacher and part-time Audio-Visual Aids Coordinator. He had three foreign language classes plus his own small office on the second floor where he oversaw the maintenance and distribution of audio-visual supplies, materials, and equipment for teachers in all academic departments. He found himself, as well, in the new position of leading a clandestine life of intrigue and subterfuge, a move, a word, a whisper, a breath away from losing his job.

Late one afternoon that fall, he found himself shitting in his pants. He was in that small, audio-visual aids office, but he wasn't involved with the maintenance and distribution of audio-visual equipment and materials. He was heavily involved, instead, with the exploration and stimulation of Susan's yielding body. While the experience was certainly educational for both of them, it most assuredly did not involve equipment or materials to be used for the purposes of classroom instruction, at least not in any school. The lights were out, the door locked, and the room secured as if Ed had left for the day. Suddenly interrupted by the unquiet rattling of a key in the door, the two bodies bolted upright in shocked surprise. Ed lunged for the door.

"Who is it?" he called out, trying to steady his voice.

"Ricky, it's Ricky. I need an overhead projector for tomorrow."

Ed had to think fast.

"I got a mess on my hands in here, Ric," Ed responded. "I'm developing some film. Where do you want the projector? I'll send it down to you in the morning."

Geez, that was close.

Fear? Love knows no fear. Love is blind to consequences.

Risk? Christ, yes! What could be more risky than a teacher and a student locked in a school office together with the lights out? It was almost as risky as a teacher and a student together in a motel on Route 17.

****

With August's passionate kiss leading to September's touchy-feely explorations and to October's heavy petting and finger dipping, Ed also found himself quite often parked with Susan on an isolated, dead end, rural street on the Saddle River-Allendale border. Ironically, their after school excursions to secluded hideaways took them north on Route 17, the same route Ann and I would travel less than five years later.

"That's where I learned to tell the truth about where I was," he said. "We had one 'close call' because I wasn't where I was supposed to be. That was enough."

"You almost got caught?"

"Yeah, almost," he blushed before continuing with enthusiasm. "Susan was supposed to be at a dance at the high school, and I was supposed to be doing an inventory—this was at night—up on the second floor in the A.V.A. office at school. Well, Jenny, at home, couldn't find her wallet, so she gets the bright idea that maybe she left it on the front seat of the car. Of course, I have the car at school, or at least she *thinks* that's where I have the car. So, she calls Ruth, Susan's mother."

"Your wife calls Susan's mother?" I interrupted. "How come she calls *her?*"

"Well," he continued, "it sounds strange, but it isn't. Jenny is stuck at home, she can't go anywhere, there's no way for her to contact me at school at night, and she has gotten to know Ruth—a little, at least. They had met at the Bi-State Shopping Plaza a few times, and Jenny knew that Susan was helping me out in the A.V.A. office from time to time. Anyway, Jenny calls Ruth because she lives close to the school and has her go over to look for me."

"And you weren't there."

"Hell, no. I'm up in Allendale sitting with Susan with my hand tucked in her panties," Ed laughed. "While Ruth is looking all over the school for me, I've got my finger halfway up her daughter's crotch."

"Nice. But you were just playing doctor and taking her temperature from the inside, right?" I joked.

"Yeah," Ed laughed, "and you're right—it was nice. Anyway, when Ruth can't find me, she goes home and calls Jenny. Of course, there's no way Susan and I can know what's goin' on, so we leave Allendale, and I drive her home and drop her off two blocks away so she can walk to her house as if she was coming home from the dance, and I go home."

"You're both up the creek, right?"

"Well, I am, but as far as her mother knows, Susan was at the dance. When Ruth went looking for me at school, she walked right past the door to the gym where the dance was and where Susan was supposed to be. She knew I wouldn't be at the dance, and she was so intent on finding *me* that she never bothered to look for Susan. She just assumed she was there."

I drew a deep breath and shook my head in disbelief that someone could be so lucky. Ed smiled.

"So when Susan walks into the house," he resumed, "her mother doesn't ask where *she* was; she asks, 'Where is Mr. Richards?' Susan just plays dumb and says, 'How am I supposed to know?' And, you know what her mother says? She says, 'He's probably out playing around.' "

"Holy shit."

"Yeah, but she has no idea it's *her daughter* I'm playing around with. I get home, and I get greeted with, 'Where were you?' I knew from the tone of Jenny's voice, she damn well knew I wasn't at school working in the A.V.A. office!"

"Yeah, it's sort of a give-away question. What did you tell her?"

"I don't even remember. I concocted some story—nothing too complex. Jenny is pretty dumb, ya know. She's not really very smart."

"But, shit, man, wasn't she smart enough to know that *something* might have been going on, if not with Susan, then maybe with someone else?"

Ed looked at me with a helplessly forlorn, almost sympathetic, stare.

"Look," he said with the patience of a teacher preparing to explain a verb conjugation to a student for the third time. "Wait 'til ya hear this. *Then* you'll understand how really stupid she is. This is January, right. By January, Susan and I are really into it. I mean, I haven't gotten into it yet, but I'm trying hard. We've gone through all the preliminaries. There's nothing we haven't done but go to bed. Well, Jenny meets Ruth up at the shopping plaza. They get to talking, you know—how are things? What's going on? How's this? How's that? And Ruth mentions that Susan's married sister, up in Connecticut with her in-laws, is gonna have her first baby, and she'd like to be there when the baby is born, but she can't go because she can't leave Susan alone."

"Oh, no, don't tell me—"

"Yup, before you know it, that jerk is inviting Ruth to have Susan stay at our house for a week or so!"

"Unbelievable! How the hell can you get so lucky?"

"Now, you tell me—when have you ever heard of anything so dumb?" Ed erupted, his words reflecting his lack of tolerance for utter stupidity, even though it had served his own purposes so well. "I mean, she doesn't have a God damn brain in her head."

"When Jenny volunteered bed and board, she didn't know she was offering *bed* and board, did she?" I chuckled.

"No," he replied with a laugh. "But we usually used the floor of the den, anyway. But wait, wait—let me….."

He paused for a sip of his Coke. We were having one of our lunch meetings at the Paramus Park mall food court.

"…..le'me tell you what happened. Three or four days after Susan is staying at the house—I think it was January 17—we do it for the first time. Jenny was out with Cori at the ice skating rink, and we knew they'd be back between eight and eight-fifteen, so it's a quickie. When we're done, I flush the prophy in the toilet, and we get dressed. Later in the evening, the three of us—Susan, Jenny, and I—are sitting around talking in the living room, and Cori, bless her soul, comes in and announces there's a 'rubber finger' in the toilet!"

"Oh, my God. It didn't go down, huh?"

"No, it didn't go down. The rubber is floating in the toilet, Susan and I are sitting there afraid to take a breath, and Jenny is shoo-shooing Cori away."

"And?"

"And, nothing."

"Nothing?"

"Nothing. We sit there talking for an hour or more, and she says nothing."

I leaned back. Ed's lengthy story had kept me on the edge of my seat, and as I leaned forward with intense ear, I had all but climbed onto the table where my forgotten fries were now cold and unappetizingly soggy in their paper dish. My half-eaten corned beef sandwich looked like it had come down a playground slide.

"You win, Ed," I sighed, as I reshuffled the sliced meat between the two pieces of rye bread. "You're absolutely right. She's dumb. Her brains would rattle in a thimble."

"Well, she was dumb to have Susan stay at the house. But I don't think she was dumb about the rubber," he said with consideration. "I think she knew, but I think she was too stunned to believe it. I think she just couldn't handle it, so she dismissed it as something that never happened. She asked me about it later that night, but by that time I had pulled myself together. I told her it was an old one that I had been carrying around in my wallet for years, and I just threw it in the toilet to get rid of it. And that was the end of it."

That was the end of it. It could have been the end of Susan and Ed, but it wasn't. It was just the beginning. The express was about to roll. It whistled through the end of the first semester and into March.

The excitement that Spring brings to most high school juniors—the picking of class rings, the election of Student Council and class officers for the following year, the final choosing of senior year courses—was child's play to Susan and Ed. Their attention was directed toward picking, electing, and choosing other things, particularly places—places to be alone, places to be together, places to love each other, places that were safe, places where they could take off their clothes without being screwed, places where they could screw without taking off their clothes. They found all the places they needed, even in France! They missed out in Italy, but not in France.

Susan was among the group of excited foreign language students from the high school that Ed accompanied to Europe during the spring vacation of her junior year. The trip was a challenge for Susan and Ed, a continual struggle to be together as much as possible without arousing the suspicions of the other students or of the travel group's tour leader and guide. In the end, it was the guide—a good-natured, young, Mormon fellow—who became aware of the unusual degree of closeness and contact between Susan and Ed—together on the sightseeing walking tours during the day, together at the same table in the restaurant at dinner, together on the bus, together a lot.

When the group left Italy, where each evening Ed had been assigned a shared room which made any kind of night contact with Susan impossible, Ed found himself befriended by the tour guide and fortunately, and maybe not entirely by accident, blessed each night in France with the luxury and privacy of his own room. It was a surprisingly benevolent gesture on the part of the guide whose accommodating action removed a troublesome obstacle from the path of evening rendezvous. It was a path along which Susan, in the wee hours of the morning in the hotel at Avignon on the Rhone River in the southeast of France, quietly but boldly tip-toed in her bare feet, meeting Ed in conjunctive intrigue while the rest of the student group, including her unsuspecting roommate, slept soundly through the still April night.

It wasn't long after the group's return from Europe that Susan came down with mononucleosis. Things looked as if they were headed for the railway repair yard. When she was forced to withdraw from school for the balance of the year in May because of her illness, things looked worse. It appeared that the train, at least temporarily, had run out of track.

Just as necessity is often the mother of invention, however, the relentless clackety-clack of an engine moving at top speed over steel rails can become a compelling and hypnotizing force which brings forth sufficient determination and resolve to make the most of time and circumstances. Susan and Ed made the most of time and circumstances. They turned her home-bound condition to their advantage. Ed became Susan's tutor. From May until the end of the school year and continuing through the summer, they gloried in what became the perfect arrangement.

Susan was at home. Both her parents worked. Ed had legitimate and regular access to her house, no longer having to sneak out the side door buckling his pants and zipping his fly in the dark as her parents came in the back door from the movies. No longer did the two of them have to concern themselves with how they would be able to continue their liaison through the summer months, an effort which otherwise would have been awkward and cumbersome to arrange. No longer did they have to look for a place to "do it." They could do it right in her own bed, or, when Susan's dad drove her to Ed's house and dropped her off for her tutoring, they could do it there. They did, in both places, often, and all within the apparently proper framework of a teacher-student relationship, all with the unwitting blessing of her unsuspecting parents and his hapless wife, and all in the name of education and academic enlightenment. Ed donated his services as Susan's tutor. It's too bad, he told me, it wasn't a formalized home instruction service paid for by the Board of Education. There would have been poetic justice in a situation which would have placed the Board, often positioned in the role of fucking teachers, in the unknowing and unbecoming posture of paying a teacher to fuck a student.

"Well, you can't have everything," Ed sighed in resignation. "I can't complain. I was duly rewarded, *quid pro quo.*"

Ed explained to me, in tongue-in-cheek fashion, that his tutoring of Susan seemed to pump new life into her. She was ready to return to school for her senior year in September, and that's when the countdown began. The countdown was literal. It wasn't figurative. It was a real honest-to-goodness countdown, dutifully recorded in a small, pocket-sized, Hallmark calendar booklet that Susan carried with her.

At some point during the summer's extensive "tutoring," the relationship between Susan and Ed had undergone a significant transformation. It had become serious, shedding its frivolous and pastime recreational characteristics and beginning to incorporate the dimensions of a true-to-life human drama, with meaning and ramifications that extended far beyond the next time they would go to bed together. The move to a new and higher plane brought the relationship into sharper focus for both of them. Fantasy yielded first to wondering, then to tentative speculation, and finally to overt planning, each progression extending the longevity potential of the relationship. The only consideration left to explore was the partnership of permanent togetherness.

Susan wanted more than sexual entertainment; she wanted marriage. Ed wanted less of his wife; he wanted a divorce. They both wanted a continuation of what they had begun; they wanted each other.

The Hallmark calendar booklet became the history of the past and the plan for the future, a diary of accomplishments and countdowns. It was a register of how many days remained until graduation. It was a countdown to the exact target date, June 28, when Ed would move out of his house, Susan would leave her parents' home, and the two of them would move together to an apartment in Hackensack. It was a reminder of when she had had her last period and when the next one was due. It was a running tally of penciled circles around each date, a record meticulously maintained by Susan of the 197 times they had made love between the hair-raising "floating finger" first time consummation of their union in January of her junior year until her high school graduation ceremony in June of her senior year.

They did it wherever they could—her house, his house, his mother's house, and at school. They knew the night custodian's schedule. They knew when it was safe. They'd spread their coats out on the floor to fashion a comfortable "bed" for themselves, and they'd strip naked and play with each other's bodies between the stacks in the library annex room. The Board may not have paid for her home tutoring, but it became their benevolent benefactor in another way, providing the space for their in-school adventures, the sheltering cover for their "extra-curricular" activities. At least half a dozen circled calendar dates came with the compliments of the Board of Education.

If they did it twice or three times on the same day, she circled the date on the calendar twice or three times. This was no fly-by-night operation. This was no shoddy undertaking. This was no kid's choo-choo. This was a real railroad, and it was run by a real engineer. This railroad did things right.

* * * * * * *

Of all the graduates who received a diploma in June, who could have offered better credentials for the successful completion of a prescribed course of study than Susan? If her cumulative record of 197 coitus episodes—including at least half a dozen on the library floor between dust laden volumes of Milton and Butler, one abroad, and one the very morning of graduation day in the Foreign Language Office—didn't put her at the top of her class, it put her in a class by herself.

The satisfactory completion of all of her homework assignments under the carefully supervised tutelage of her Latin teacher and mentor, her scholarly attention to detailed record keeping, and her eager participation in a variety of stimulating extra-curricular and physical education activities from the high school A.V.A. office to a quiet cul-de-sac in Allendale, demonstrated that she was an erudite pupil of energetic commitment, diligence, and tenacity. If anyone doubted her ability to pursue established goals and objectives with conscientious dedication and industrious resolve, she had ample proof. She was pregnant.

It was no accident; it was deliberate. Ed knew he never would be able to wheedle a divorce from Jenny. He knew he could have floated "rubber fingers" in the toilet for years, but she never would have budged. Forcing the issue was the only way.

The scholarship Susan had received at the Senior Awards Assembly a few days prior to graduation had come with no strings. The money would be available for any purpose of her choosing. Her father had taken the day off from work to sit in the audience with his wife and await with pride the scholarship presentation to their daughter. Susan waited, too. This was to be her big day. This was the day she would receive a scholarship and a day she would receive the test results from her doctor. Both presentations came through as expected. The scholarship money would be a welcome assist in paying the maternity bills when the baby arrived in late January or early February.

Now it was Graduation Day, the ceremony over. As everyone else, Susan and Ed became enveloped in the excitement and happiness that traditionally follows the formalities of a graduation exercise. The post-ceremony celebration, with the happy graduate encircled by a milling group of relatives and friends eager to share in the joy of the occasion, became a tumultuous tangle of enthusiastic hand shakes and congratulatory greetings, kisses, and hugs. No one knew, except Susan and Ed, that the smiling graduate carried within her womb the unborn child of the union two months previous between her teacher and herself. No one knew that the unlikely couple already had rented an apartment on Clinton Place in Hackensack.

Ed's exuberant response to Susan and his uninhibited participation in the happy festivities was eyed with some uneasiness by more than one member of the family group that clustered on the lawn of the school. Susan's married sister, Jill, noted it with silent disapproval. Her father-in-law noted it, too, as they all piled into cars and headed for a family party at Susan's house.

"They look more like boyfriend and girlfriend than teacher and student," he ruffled to Jill at the party.

Damned if they didn't, even with their conscious effort at restraint and their calculated attempt to withhold the beaming pleasure of their company together. Susan made the proper introductions, and Ed handled the uneasy situation with as much gracious attentiveness as he could muster, meeting distant relatives and engaging in the lively conversations. But never was he more than a few steps from Susan's side, and their "quickie" glances, "secret" smiles, and "hidden" comments gave rise to further speculation among those who already had curious doubts about the nature of this unusual link between this teacher and his pupil, this teacher who was in attendance without his wife. Jill didn't respond to her father-in-law's stabbing comment, but she mentioned it to her parents later that evening.

"I don't think you should see Mr. Richards any more," Susan's father commented to Susan the next day. It was more than a friendly suggestion.

With the target date close at hand, the countdown almost completed, and the train approaching its last stop, Susan knew it was no time to question, quarrel, or dispute her father's directive. This wasn't the time to make a fuss. She accepted the dictate without controversy.

A few days later, with her grandmother looking on, Susan packed her bags. Grandma may have had suspicions of her own about what was taking place, but she had, as well, the wisdom of years not to interfere with the ways of fate or to dispute the strong-willed determination of her granddaughter.

Ed packed, too, working fast, using the time between six and eight o'clock in the evening when his wife went with Cori to the ice skating rink for her lessons. He shoved his belongings into whatever was available, drove them to school, and temporarily stashed the bags and cartons in the equipment room adjacent to the auditorium. There wasn't time to worry about being caught or how he might explain why he was transporting all of his worldly possessions to school, of all places. It was just a job that *had* to be done, so he did it, as hastily as possible, but not without difficulty. He wasn't driving the roomy, $6,000 Buick Electra with which he was familiar. It had been sold two days before at Susan's insistence, a dissolution of assets she had urged to prevent a claim for it by Ed's wife under New Jersey's community property and separation laws. Instead, he struggled with a small, second-hand Opal he had bought on short notice from the parent of a student for $1,100, a stick-shift flivver that wouldn't start in the rain or on damp days and often had to be pushed.

June 28. Last stop. Everybody out, literally.

Ed told Jenny, "I'm moving out."

Susan told her parents, "I'm moving out. I'm pregnant, and I'm moving out."

It was almost anticlimactic for Ed and Susan—not so for his wife or her parents.

The train, hurtling through time for a year and a half, stopping for no obstacle, slowing for no person, and yielding at no crossing, had reached the end of the line. Through the fading dusk of late afternoons and the secretive darkness of copulative nights in Allendale, within the eerie silence and the deserted quiet of an empty library after school, and during the long hours and many days of seductive bedside tutoring, the engine had persevered in its arduous, uphill struggle against discovery. The timetable had been followed with assiduous and meticulous care, right down to the punching of the engineer's ticket!

Her parents weren't too happy about *that.* They thought it might be a good idea to have her ticket transferred or rerouted, or, better yet, cancelled. They pressed for her to spend some time with relatives in California.

"Suppose he doesn't get a divorce.....Maybe he won't stay with you.....Do you know what you're *doing*?.....What are people going to think?.....You could end up alone—with an infant.....Do you *know* what you're doing?.....

What are people going to *say? What the hell* are people going to say?"

Susan remained firm in her determination to be with Ed and have their baby. They moved into their rented apartment on Thursday, July 1, after spending a few nights together in a local motel waiting for their apartment to become available.

Did she know what she was doing? Her parents' question made her chuckle, but she felt sorry for their shock, their embarrassment, their fears, and their anxiety. She recognized their concern as being that of caring parents trying to protect a teen-age daughter who had "gotten into trouble." But how could she tell them that it wasn't like that? She wasn't in trouble; everything was perfect. How could she tell them that after 197 times she sure as hell knew what she was doing? She was a fucking expert! How could she tell them anything?

****

"And when the school found out?" I asked inquiringly.

Ed loved telling his story. Every time we met and he added another sequence or episode, his eyes sparkled through his glasses and his face shone. I knew the feeling. I understood. It was a love story, the kind of story one *enjoys* telling. But it wasn't a story that had been told to very many people. It wasn't a story that *could* be told to very many people.

"Well," he reflected, "It wasn't as bad as I thought it was gonna be. Actually, by the time the Board found out, it was all over. She had graduated."

"Yeah, but they could have had your ass if they wanted it."

"I guess, I guess so," he admitted. "I guess I was lucky the president of the Board was a shrewd character," he laughed. "He was a lawyer and he kept the lid on things when the situation came up for discussion at a closed work session of the Board. It never got out in public, not officially, anyway. The president made sure of that. 'Is he doing his job? Yes. Is it affecting his work performance? No. So, forget it. It's his personal business, not ours. He's doing what we pay him to do, the girl is graduated, and she's no longer on the school rolls. It's not the Board's concern. If someone wants to make something out of it, let them do their own dirty work.' Christ, he didn't want any headlines. You remember what was goin' on around that time?"

I struggled to recall the time frame. I shook my head.

"No, I don't think so," I said hesitantly. "Should I?"

"William Thomson, Valley High School? Mean anything to you?"

The name sounded familiar, but I couldn't remember the story.

"He got involved with a student. He actually dated her pretty much out in the open. They went to all the school dances and activities together, and they ended up getting married. It caused the Board all kinds of grief," Ed continued. "The girl's parents raised hell. *They* were the ones who pressed the issue, not the school."

"I think I remember. He lost his job, though, didn't he?" I questioned with a frown.

"Well, yes and no. They transferred him within the district, from one school to another, and I think into an office job, at least temporarily. It made big headlines for quite a while—raised one helluva stink."

Despite Ed's attempts to tickle my memory, I had nothing but a hazy recollection. Maybe I had seen the headlines and quickly skimmed the story on the way to the sports section of the newspaper. It probably wasn't true, anyway, I'm sure I must have thought at the time.

"Too early for something like that to hit home with me, I guess. I bet it made *you* shit in your pants, though," I offered with a knowing wink.

"Damn straight!" he roared. "*I* didn't wanna be in the headlines. Susan and I were right in the middle of things—no pun intended," he chuckled in an aside. "We were doin' everything we could do to keep things cool, not make news."

"So, everything sorta slid by for the two of you, huh?"

"Yeah, except I got warned," he laughed. "You remember Donaldson and Fisher, right?"

I smiled and nodded at his reference to the principal and superintendent of schools for whom I once had worked. Ed continued with his recollection of how the principal had called him into his office and told him that the superintendent was in the building and wanted to talk to him about "his situation."

"Next thing I know, Fisher comes through the door and takes me into the next office. He tells me how he had stood up for me at the Board meeting," Ed said. " 'But there are still some Board members out to get you, so you'd better walk the straight and narrow, or else,' " he quoted with a grin.

Six months before, the threat would have scared the pants off Ed, but not then. He was home free. No one was complaining. Hapless Jenny, his wife, was sitting on her hands, probably in shock. Susan's parents were tolerating the situation, the Board didn't want headlines, Susan was out of school, and not many teachers or students even knew the story. The baby was born in February, Ed's divorce came through in the spring, and Susan and Ed were quietly married in November. The next spring, they moved from their Hackensack apartment to a house in Westwood, and in early June of the following year—the year of the A-School for me, and the June of horseback riding with Ann—I found Ed's listing in the telephone book and our contact was renewed with the sharing of our respective stories.

How much of my story was lost in Ed's reverie, I don't know. But *his* accounting fell on eager ears, ears in which Ann's pensive question still echoed: "Ya think there are other people like us, Charlie.....like a teacher and a student?"

I sure as hell knew the answer to that.

CHAPTER 22

"I knew it, I knew it, I knew there were others….."
Yes, there were others, but not all of them were love relationships. Many weren't very nice at all…..

Ann almost died when I first mentioned it to her.

It was Monday of the last full week of school. The place was so empty it just as easily could have been the last week of July. Deserted by three-thirty, the church basement was but a vacant, hollow shell in which the staccato of my hunt and peck typing reverberated in monotonous tattoo from one wall to another.

Bored and tired of my chore, I pushed the work aside and sat in quiet survey of the tiny office, my back bent forward, my arms crossed on top of the typewriter, my eyes in stoic witness of what a year's use had done to walls once clean and bright and to a room once neatly kept. No abuse, mind you, save maybe the careless scrabble of feared to be forgotten numbers jotted in haste on the wall beside the phone—just the normal wear and tear of taped triangles remaining where once a poster bid its viewers "Smile," darkened patches where "urgent" notices had hung in the sunlight far beyond their urgency, and an abundance of chrome-topped thumb tacks from which had dangled colorful announcements of activities and events now long past and forgotten.

"TURN IN ALL BOOKS" a sign implored with screaming boldness by the light switch near the door. As if in defiant response, the floor beneath was strewn with an untidy assortment of tossed texts, battered three-ring binders, flimsy notebooks, and a dog-eared telephone directory that bulged its listings beyond the frayed edges of its cover. The counter shelf on the far side of the room was crammed with the gathered findings of the night custodian who was unflagging in his effort to consolidate the appropriations of his broad-broom sweep of the stage, basement, stairwells, and foyers. The metal file cabinet in the opposite corner draped a still unclaimed "COLUMBIA" sweatshirt, its continued presence an enduring titillation to Ann and me. We often had shared a wink with the joint recollection of having seen the long-sleeve shirt worn so well by a lamp shade.

Lured by the extended silence of the typewriter and the notion that I probably was finished for the day, Ann meandered to the office from the stage where she had been reading in her chair. Her quiet appearance in the doorway snapped the spell of drifting daydreams and fluid observations that had put me in a state of cloudy transfixion.

"You know, I used to teach with this fellow, Ed Richards," I began with slow, musing deliberation.

"He's the guy you've had lunch with a few times recently, right?"

I had held back as long as I could, resisting the strong temptation to tell her what I knew until I had seen Ed enough times to pull together the story parts that he had been disclosing in piecemeal fashion over the past few weeks. How or why it happened to be now that I chose to let it go, I had not the foggiest idea, but as Ann moved to the desk, hopped up on the edge, and sat in aberrant silence, her legs dangling loosely over the side, I spread the story before her.

"I knew it, I knew it. I knew it, but I can't believe it!" she gushed with repeated slaps of her knee before even the sketch of the story was out of my mouth. "I knew there were others. I just *knew* it, but now I don't know if I wanna believe it."

I had sympathy for her mixed sentiments, for I, too, felt ambivalent, happy and perhaps in part relieved to find us not alone in the kind of adventurous involvement that had become our destiny, yet somewhat cheated to find the uniqueness of our togetherness diminished by the prior experiences of others.

For the sake of our mental well-being, we coveted the small measure of conformity which Ed's story now acknowledged of our own comportment. We weren't *totally* crazy. If we were, we weren't alone. But the element of exclusivity which we had enjoyed in blind ignorance before learning of Ed and Susan was now gone. It was a balanced trade-off that left us neither jubilant nor disappointed. In return for a degree of sanction, we had to surrender the notion of unprecedented singularity.

"Some story, huh?" I chortled as I released the hold on the typewriter roller and adjusted another permanent record card in the carriage, the saga of Susan and Ed told to completion.

"Yeah, shit, two of them, Ed Richards and Thomas—Wilson, Williamson—whatever his name was. I wonder if there are more?" she questioned, a little subdued by the length of the tale to which she had just listened with dumbfounded fascination.

"Don't forget Sal, the math teacher. I mentioned him to you, didn't I—the one who married a student right out of high school? Now, you *know* something was goin' on there. And, wait—wait 'til ya hear this."

Ann looked up abruptly from the perch she had maintained on the corner of the desk.

"Ed told me about two other teachers."

"Two more!" she blurted in unbelieving surprise. "Holy crap, it's an epidemic! With students?"

I nodded.

"Not like us, though—a little different."

"Like?"

"Well," I began, tentatively, "one of the teachers is on the make, always lookin' for it."

No response.

"I mean, if ya look long enough, in the right way, in the right place—" I outlined.

"Like in a school, with a lot of girls around….." she said with steely coldness, "…..where, if ya just kinda play it cool, ya might get lucky and get yourself a little snatch, huh? Jesus."

"Something like that," I admitted with twisting uneasiness. "Maybe not quite that heartless."

"No, ya may hafta butter her up to get her to drop her pants. But the name of the game is 'gettin' it,' right? It's got nothing to do with love or feelings, does it? What about the other smuck?"

I wished I had kept my mouth shut. What had seemed like a hot story when Ed was telling *me* now was proving to be an uncomfortable embarrassment.

"He tells his female students to come back for 'a visit' after they graduate," I said quickly, without looking up. "If they take him up on the invitation, he takes them out for as many drinks as he can get into them, gets them tipsy, and goes for the score. If they screw, fine; if they don't, he's not interested in seeing them again. Ed says it's so widely known, the guy's marriage is on the rocks—his second marriage. His first wife found out what he was up to."

"That's pretty sick, if you ask me," she responded after a quiet time of absorption. "You believe it? You think it's true?"

"Are you kidding?" I snapped. "Six months ago, I would've believed it without batting an eye. I mean, it's not altogether *un*believable, is it? I *know* the guys he's talking about and, believe me, they're both capable of it."

I paused briefly before completing my case.

"Ed's a reliable source. He's no bullshitter. So, why wouldn't I believe it? Why shouldn't I? But now? Today? Despite everything I know, despite all—I don't believe nothin'," I said with disgust. "Do you?"

She sat engrossed in thought, desperately trying to figure where the hell I was coming from.

"Hell," I continued, with no wait for her reply, "You don't know any more about it than I do, or than Ed knows, for that matter. Someone tells Ed, Ed tells me, I tell you. Shit, man, a few months ago, it was you and I being passed down a gossip chain like that, babe. *You* and

I, remember? With everyone pointing their grubby fingers? I don't believe nothin'," I raged angrily as I slammed my hand on the typewriter, seven or eight keys leaping in an almost simultaneous race toward the roller. How little it took to revive the pain and hostility still attached to those recollections.

She jumped, startled by my outburst, but she didn't say anything.

"You know, Ann, there were teachers in this school, there were students here, there were people up at the high school, friends of yours, friends of mine—people we *thought* were our friends, anyway—they were all part of the chain. They soaked it up like dry sponges and squeezed it out all over the place. You were puttin' out, and I was fuckin' it. It was hot stuff, man, hot stuff. It wasn't true, but who the fuck cared about *that*. Did *they* believe it? You bet your fuckin' ass they believed it. No proof, no nothin'. They just ate it up. They ate up every fuckin' crumb, and then they scrounged around looking for more. Hot stuff."

I reached up and released the piggy-backed wedge of keys clumped at the ribbon frame, letting each letter fall back into its proper place, one at a time. Ann sat quietly. I muttered a curse at the black smudge on the permanent record card.

"So, you don't think it's true, then," she plied softly.

I twisted uneasily in the chair as I pushed my fingers up under my glasses and rubbed my eyes.

"Of course, I think it's true," I said with a sigh of bitter resignation. "Ya think I'm any different or any better than anyone else? I'm not gonna say I *believe* it—not without some evidence, some proof, something. But, deep down, yeah, I think it's true. Fuck. I don't *believe* it, but I think it's true. That make any sense?"

Like a little puppy that had piddled on the kitchen floor and now anticipated having its nose rubbed in it, I raised a squinting glance to Ann and held my breath.

"What can I say, hon? You know the people involved and I don't."

"Yeah, I know them," I replied with a morose smirk. "I know 'em both. They'd do it in a minute if they had the chance. Then they'd brag about it—pussy-chasing opportunists, after anything in a skirt, anybody they can *use.* Put a skirt on a fire hydrant and they'd try to make it."

Ann had as much difficulty dealing with it as I did.

"Ya know," she started haltingly, "I know this is gonna sound crazy, but it really bothers me when I hear something like that—really. I mean, a teacher, shit." She shook her head, obviously distressed. "It's pretty sick. It's not right for a teacher to hit on a student, you know."

I knew what she meant, and I understood the troubling paradox that caused her words to come in tripping spurts.

"What about a *student* who goes after a *teacher*?" I smiled in a bid to lighten the moment.

There was little lightness in her firm response as she nodded her head up and down expressively, repeatedly.

"Just as bad. Sick—yup. I know, I know, you don't have to tell me," she defended as if expecting a pointed reminder of self-incrimination. "But, somehow I don't see *us* the same way, ya know?"

"Maybe age is catching up with you. The eyes are the first to go."

"No, c'mon—I don't see us that way. How come I don't think of *us* as a teacher and a student? And you know I didn't go after you *that* way. I'll admit I *did* go after you, but I did because I loved you—and I still do," she winked. "That's the difference, and it's a *big* difference. I don't understand—I can't even *imagine*—a student going after a teacher just for sex. I mean, if someone needs to get fucked that badly, what the hell. But it's really sick. It really sucks. It's not for me, that's for sure," she said with an emphatic wrinkle of her nose.

"I know, I know what you mean. I don't see us as a teacher and a student, either. And I can't explain it any better than you can. But I know *me.* I couldn't screw around just for the hell of it, either. There's gotta be something more to it, more than just a quick lay."

"Oh, wait a minute. I don't know about *that,*" she retorted snappily, surprising me for a moment. "We've had some pretty nice quickies," she giggled.

Our serious discussion was over.

"I'll give you a quickie, you cumquat, you."

Arms outstretched, I lunged toward her with a lurch that sent my chair toppling backwards as the pile of manila folders and alphabetized permanent record cards slithered across the slippery desk top and onto the floor. She twisted away with a shriek, eluding my reach as she took flight for the door with me in pursuit.

"C'mon, chase the pussy!" she roared baitingly, as she scooted around the corner and out toward the stage.

"You—" I screamed after her.

Had I not kicked off my shoes minutes earlier as I sat behind the desk typing, I would have been right on her heels instead of sliding and skidding on the tiled floor with the frustration of a driver spinning his wheels on a patch of ice.

"C'mon, I'm a fire hydrant. Make me," she taunted laughingly over her shoulder.

"Damn you," I sputtered. "Wait 'til I get my hands on you."

"Promises, promises, always promises—"

It was a mismatch, the swift, graceful movements of a gazelle outmatching the slippery scurry of a duck out of water, a man with no shoes, a scampering fool who wished to be on her heels, chasing someone who for certain wanted him to be on her tail.

She bounded across the stage, hopped off the edge, and hop scotched her way over the checkerboard pattern of basement floor tiles. Easily she could have escaped up the back stairway, but, instead, when she reached the door to the foyer she turned abruptly, back to the door, arms outstretched, and waited as I completed a lengthy slide which brought me to a flattening crush against her body. I punished her with unrelenting tickles as we sank to the floor, my fingers poking and itching her sides.

"No, no, stop. Oh, no, please—" she begged between laughs.

"I told you I'd get you," I chastised without heed to her pleas.

"No, don't—don't, no. Please—"

"You sorry?"

"Oh, Charlie."

"You want more?"

"No, Charlie, please. Let me love you, hon. C'mon, be nice," she purred.

I stopped. The little rascal got me every time.

"I love you, sweet man. Be my sweetie. Don't tickle me. You don't wanna do that, do ya?" she asked in a whisper as she pressed herself to me.

Our impromptu chase had left our hearts thumping, and I felt the intermingle of rapid beats followed by the hard, deliberate rub she effected against my body to raise herself and cozy my head beneath her chin.

"Don't tickle me. Be my baby."

No, she didn't have the nerve, I thought.

"Ann, I don't—" I launched as I felt a ripple of fear. "Miguel is gonna be here in just—"

Her leg enwrapped mine, and our groins meshed in molded fit as she leaned back from the waist and, with a single sweep of obvious purpose, finger-popped the top buttons of her plaid blouse.

"Shit, woman, you're nuts! We can't—"

She urged my head to the warm softness of her exposed breast, her volunteered bosom a pillow that at least for a brief interlude between wish and wisdom, smothered my apprehension and comforted my panic.

"That's it, thaaaaaaat's it. Be my baby love. That's it, baby."

"We can't, Ann," I recovered. "Miguel is gonna be here any minute," I exclaimed, pulling back.

"Shhhh," she hushed, nuzzling me to a resumption of contented suck at her surrendered chest. "I love you so much, need you so much—So, so much—Oh, do it, do me, do your little Annie, do your donut—"

"We can't," I protested weakly as my hand slid inside her jeans, the sweaty moisture of my palm warmed by the smooth flatness of her abdomen. "If he ever came in and—"

I didn't finish my statement; I didn't need to. The unmistakable clunk of the front door—that clunk like no other door has—echoed down the front stairway and through the basement like a thunderbolt rumbling its woeful threat across an open, gray expanse.

"Holy shit! It's Miguel. I told you. Quick, button up!"

We untangled hurriedly and scrambled to our feet, the quiet we desperately attempted to preserve broken only slightly by our muffled grunts and the frenzied rustle of clothing as we hastened to restore the appearance of normalcy to our persons.

For Miguel, the custodian, to find the two of us together late in the afternoon was not uncommon. He was as familiar with our after school routine as we were of his. With the predictability of the coming and going of the seasons, Miguel would arrive daily at four-thirty, tend to his chores, and depart at four-fifty, a stuffed plastic bag of rubbish trailing his shuffled steps. His punctual entrance would be highlighted by a broad smile on his ruddy face and an enthusiastic greeting that showcased his Latin American heritage.

"Hey, Cha-lee!" the short, stocky man in his fifties beamed.

Miguel spoke only to me, never addressing Ann, never acknowledging her presence, his silence a display of bonded allegiance, a testimony of trust that pledged loyal withhold of whatever he might see, hear, or think. If he ever stole a glance at Ann and wondered if I were playing with her toys, I never saw it. There was never an exchange of knowing glances or man-to-man winks between us, no "mi amigo" bullshit. Miguel attended to his own business with no diverted attention to matters not within the purview of his assigned responsibility.

"How ya doin', Miguel?" I returned, as Ann and I strolled toward him in the direction of the stage.

"Fine, fine. How you, Cha-lee?"

Okay, okay. We're all locked up in back. Everything's tight. We're on our way out, Miguel."

"Hoo-kay, Cha-lee. I be seeing you."

"Take it easy," I said as he headed toward the storage closet. "Have a good night."

Ann and I hopped the few steps without pause and continued on to the office in silence. I nudged her ahead of me, and we returned to the brightness of overhead neon, too strong for the size of the room, and the reality of scattered folders, dispersed permanent record cards, and the overturned chair we had left in our wake.

"Well," she sighed with a grin, "as far as quickies go, that was pretty quick."

I moved behind the desk and stretched my leg under to snare my shoes with my toes.

"Yeah, fastest fuck in the east. Watch—see? Told ya I was fast. Wanna see it again?" I quipped.

"Crap, I hardly felt a thing," she said with a dismissing wave.

"It was nothing."

We looked at each other and laughed.

"I know," she said flatly.

"You got nothing to bitch about," I returned. "I didn't even get a wet finger out of it."

"You didn't even get a wet finger *in* it."

"That's good, that's good," I credited enthusiastically. "That's good."

"So, let's hear it for Annie. A little hand clapping, if you will. Where's the applause?"

"I did, I did. I gave you half a clap. Didn't you hear it?"

"Very funny, very funny. You wanna hear something else funny? Your *fly* is open, dummy!"

I felt a hot flush of panic overtake me before I even had time to look down. Miguel! Had he seen? Oh, geez! Then, too late to recover and save myself from being taken in by her fooling prank, I heard the hilarious howl of her gloating amusement as she ran from the room and headed up the stairs.

"Meeoooooow, chase the pussy, Charlie," her voice echoed down the stairwell.

Holt Shit. I cringed, my face twisted in a distorted, breath-holding grimace. How could she be such a fucking asshole? I stood motionless, both hands to my head, waiting for the world to crash down around me. I hoped Miguel was as loyal as I thought he was. I hoped his knowledge of English slang expressions was limited. I hoped he was fucking deaf.

CHAPTER 23

Waiting out the rain.....buzzed.....“telling my favorite stories and gettin’ dicked at the same time.....” Naughty, very naughty she was......

It was raining like hell.

“Damn!” Ann yelled in exasperation.

“Lousy luck,” I said, as much in recognition of her dismay as an expression of my own.

“Lousy luck? *No* luck! Listen to the fuckin’ thunder. Why tonight? Why does it have to rain tonight?” she lamented angrily. “Why tonight? Just tell me.”

I didn’t have an answer. Even if I could’ve come up with one, I had all I could do to keep my eyes on the road. The rain was coming down in sheets, faster than the splashing swish of my wipers could clear the windshield, the watery streaks refracting the headlights of oncoming cars in blurred distortion. I needed new wiper blades, but I never remembered them until it was raining.

“No sense goin’ into the City now, babe,” I commented unnecessarily.

It was obvious that the street fair to which we were heading was going to be a washout, and we both hurt at seeing our plans for a leisurely stroll up and down a crowded avenue, sampling the scrumptious foods and delectable pastries while appreciating the colorful activities and joyful music, go down the drain, literally.

"I know," she said with dejection, her resignation heavy with bitterness. "Two hours ago, the fuckin' sun was shining," she sulked.

"The radio said it was comin'. What time ya got now?"

"Seven twenty-five," she said with a glance at her wrist. "Almost half past."

"I think I'm gonna turn back, babe," I said as I eased the van into the right hand lane and slowed to take the Jones Road exit off Route 4.

"No, keep goin'," she urged. "Let's decide what we're gonna do, first."

"We gotta decide fast. I don't wanna end up goin' over the bridge," I countered, piqued at her balky opposition. "This is treacherous. I wanna get off the highway."

"Well, pull in here, park in the lot, and let's see if it lets up."

I pumped the brakes and turned into the half-filled parking lot of the sprawling motel next to the Gulf gas station. I leaned back, relaxing my shoulders, gratefully freed from driving hunched over the wheel and squinting into the blinding glare that had tired my eyes.

"Shit, you're an optimist," I said as I shook my head doubtfully and pulled into an empty parking space. "This is gonna go on all night."

We climbed into the back of the van, pulled the curtain, and propped ourselves comfortably against the rear door to smoke some grass and lazy away the time in hopeful wait for a turn in the weather. Good pot it was, too, fresh and green. With the skill and experienced gauge of a bank teller separating mixed coins, she methodically culled the seeds and stems aside and rolled a pair of thin jays with bulging centers of pure, crushed leaves.

The relentless downpour that pelted on the roof of our hideaway on wheels influenced our early conversation as first we considered and then dismissed the idea of going bowling or to the movies. When the weed hit, the patter of rain became a rousing applause, the claps of thunder a standing ovation, to a tickling and goosing session which saw us frolic and roll together in a tumble of giddy laughter until our sides were splitting in pain. We fell apart, exhausted. Stoned dizzy, I pulled myself back to a sitting position and listened in stupored silence to the tap dance of rain on metal and Ann's one maundering monologue after another. I tried to stay tuned-in to the chatter of her unfinished statements, rhetorical questions, and disjointed thoughts.

The high we each experienced from smoking the same pot was remarkably different. The weed loosened her tongue in constant wag while tying mine in a knot of speechlessness. My mind wandered in a maze of psychological and physiological contemplations mixed with the intermittent warmth of unexplainable sexual stirrings that found me reaching for her and cuddling her close. She persevered in an unbroken string of repeated camp stories. As many times as I had heard her tales of Camp Kearsarge, I somehow always found an entertaining aspect in their retelling and in the dramatic enthusiasm with which she delivered fresh insight and new detail about the annual summer work adventure in New Hampshire she loved so much. I knew the people, the places, the daily routine, and the special activities as if I had experienced them myself, right down to the intruding raccoon and the last mosquito bite.

The buzz of inhaled intoxicants which continued to prod florid recollections and memories from her now swirled my head with racy images and heated impulses that moved my hands in rambling caress of her body. She continued undaunted, oblivious to my struggle with her zipper, neither assisting nor resisting my tug on her jeans, disregarding the pressure of my wiggling finger as I wedged the damp cotton of her panties up within her.

"…..a chance to go waterskiing because the seniors had gone on a three-day overnight to Maine," I heard her say as I rolled her over on her stomach and stripped the panties down between her legs.

"…..went to the laundromat again, my second home. Even on my day off, I had to go into town—"

I put my hands on her hips and lifted her bottom into the air.

"…..wanted to take a sailfish out to Blueberry Island and have a picnic with Margie," she continued in a muffled voice, her head now in a swirl of hair, her face flat on the green carpeting, her tail in uphill sweep.

I flopped clumsily against her behind and had to clear the jumble of my stoned head to back away and unfasten my belt.

"…..color war was almost over, and the Blue Team had a fifteen-point lead—only fifteen points—can you believe it, after all that time—"

I pressed myself forward, my hands yawning on her backside, my fingers fanned and pushing sideways, my thumbs straining, pulling, and separating. I had a choice. I sought my favorite entrance, the one I couldn't get enough of, and again and again and again, in quickening succession of slams that vibrated her backside and shuffled her story into a frenzied hodge-podge of incoherent uttering and gurgled words, I intruded her moist entrance until her knees buckled under my weight, her heightened end sank, and I sprawled in orgasmic heave on top of her collapsed body. I didn't know if she was aware that she was getting fucked. When it was all over, I wondered if she knew she *had been* fucked. I was so stoned, man—I was so fuckin' ripped—I thought that maybe I had *dreamed* the whole thing. Even with my eyes closed and my head reeling, however, I could feel the involuntary twitches of her flattened behind, and I could hear the breathy gasps from the sweaty torso below that told me I hadn't been dreaming.

"Earth to Ann, Earth to Ann. Are you there? Come in, please. Do you read me?" I whispered in her ear.

"I'm here," she choked between pants. "I can still feel you."

"You okay?"

"Yeah, fine, except for a mouthful of hair and this damn green fuzz from the rug," she sputtered as she made a raspberry spit to clear her mouth.

She lifted her head, and I raised myself quickly to permit her room to adjust her position and turn on her back.

"Stay," she objected. "Don't move," and I rested back down, my chin in the tangle of her hair alongside her neck. We lay in silence for a few minutes before she again spoke.

"That was great."

"Jesus," I responded, "I thought I might be dreamin'."

I *still* wasn't completely sure.

"I didn't wanna fuck," she said quietly. "I mean, I wanted to *get* fucked, but I didn't wanna fuck. I know that sounds stupid. Ya know what I mean?"

"I know. It's not stupid," I assured.

"I just wanted to get fucked, you know?" she persisted in clarification. "I didn't wanna hafta *do* anything. I didn't even care if I came or not."

I raised a sudden finger to my lips in hushing signal, and our conversation hung suspended as, with cocked heads and engrossed lean, we gave ear to the noise outside the van—the slosh of quick footsteps on the wet macadam, the scratch of an umbrella on the side of the van, a pause, then the slam of a car door as a person—a second slam—no, a couple, were getting into the car next to us. As safe as we were inside the locked van, the sounds of people outside always were distracting, and we remained mute and motionless until we heard the car back out and pull away.

"I didn't think you even knew what was happening," I said in resumption.

"You didn't seem to need any help from me," she twittered. "You helped yourself and got to the bush okay without my help."

"You just kept talkin' about camp. I thought you were stoned out of your senses."

"I was. I still am, but that doesn't mean I didn't know what was goin' on. It was nice—telling my favorite stories and gettin' dicked at the same time," she giggled as she twisted out from under me. "You think with my tush two feet in the air and spread like *that*, I didn't know what was happening? I came early and just kept comin' to the end. I knew what was happening. I knew I was gonna get it. I just didn't know where," she said sheepishly. "I thought maybe I was gonna, you know—I thought you might try to pop my little assy."

Oh, sweet Annie, it wasn't that I hadn't thought of it, or hadn't been thinking of it for the past month. The fantasy had been a constant glow in the shadowy darkness of my mind, a smoldering ember awaiting opportunity's fan, a flame of quivering incalescence that torched my desires and fired my appetite. With the refinement of an unhurried epicurean and the skill of a midnight arsonist, she had nurtured the ember and nourished the flame with subtle and oblique nuances. She offered herself, perhaps a mite too frequently to maintain a balance of variety, in bottoms-up submission, fingering with delicate lightness the bloom of her back alley as an *objet d'art* which begged recognition beyond that of novel curiosity. At other times, flat on her back, with me nestled in tasting tuck between her drawn knees, she made certain that the teasing upturn she proffered included an incendiary exposure of her rear dimple. I had become increasingly aware that my exorability was being tested, tempted with discretely placed dabs of perfumed fragrance. The baby powder she customarily had applied to the front of her freshly bathed body before our dates had broadened its coverage to include a liberal dusting of the opening she lovingly groomed in anticipation of what she referred to as the "pop."

"You're really into that, aren't you?" I quizzed jokingly.

"Yeah, I am," she admitted with a blush as she reached for her panties and slipped her feet through. "I'm curious. I wanna see what it's like, what it feels like, don't you?"

She was a pisser. She knew damn well I wanted her ass. It turned me on just to see her tug her panties up around the fullness of her rounded half-moons.

"Sure," I said with appropriate reserve.

"I want it for you, too," she continued.

"Ya want it, what?"

"For you," she wavered. "I'm sorta sorry, I guess, that I wasn't, you know—I wish I had been a virgin for you, that you had been the first."

"Don't be ridiculous," I started with surprised embarrassment.

"No, really, I've always felt crummy about that."

She pulled her jeans up and fastened the snap.

"Really? That's silly."

"But my ass is cherry," she interrupted with prideful swell, "and that's for you, sweet man."

My release of but a short time before notwithstanding, I felt the quick pulse and the warm rise below, incited and excited by the thought of my fantasy, and her curiosity, being thrustfully satisfied. Her painstaking preparation—the powder dusting, the perfumed anointment, the fingertip caresses, the high-rise exposure—repeatedly had attested it was mine for the taking. Now, her peacocky confirmation raised my antenna and flashed mental images across my TV screen, a news caption flickering right to left across the bottom:

.....19-year old yields to teacher's probe; cherry taken as Ann gets her pop.....

"It may not be all that easy, babe."

"You don't think you'd like a little piece of my tail?"

"I didn't say I wouldn't like it," I snapped. "I said, 'It might not be all that easy.' "

"Why, what's the problem?" she queried with a rutted brow.

"Well," I began, a little skittishly, "I'm not circumcised, you know."

"So?"

"So, it's a lot tighter goin' in the back door than it is goin' in the front, you know?"

A little surprised I was to hear the trace of impatience and agitation that had stolen into my responses. Perhaps one of the most comfortable and refreshing components of our relationship was the facility and veracity with which we had come to master the skills of communication, particularly with regard to our sexual activity and our sexuality. At home, Pam and I went to bed, and we *did* it. We didn't look at it or talk about it, before, during, or after. We just *did* it.

Ann's naïve inquisitiveness, however, had created an expressive and uninhibited openness as well as a verbal and visual illumination that revealed stark reality, genuine feelings, and honest disclosures to be beautiful in their own right. Our lovemaking didn't flow from a writer's imagination—no fancied embellishment or concocted scenes of sensual arouse from the easy chair of a novelist to make housewives pant and schoolgirls faint and no make-believe swaddle of dreamy passages and gripping prelude painted over eighteen pages with barely three lines of dialogue breaking the patrician fabric of creative allure.

We grunted, groaned, and talked our way through arousal, copulation, and climax in spontaneous departure from society's etiquette, inciting by pet and tease, fucking lustily, and announcing the pleasure of our coming with no false reserve or assumed pretext. We heeded no author's euphony or prescribed tempo, followed no mapped route or charted pathway, and patronized no curiosity save our own. We found beauty in our togetherness, in our kindred spirit, in simple companionship, and in honest, open, blunt—and what others might label vulgar or disgusting—communication. Fuck the others. We found beauty in caring for each other and about each other. There were no others who had to be appeased.

Certainly, there was no beauty in the cramped confines of the back of the van we so frequently were forced to use. We did what we had to do, what we wanted to do, where we had to do it, and where we could do it. When the evening was done, the beauty shared, and the lovemaking concluded in darkness and seclusion, our world succumbed to the gaudy glare of reality, neither pretty nor beautiful, the crass camouflage of our secret sin exposed.

The towel we used beneath her butt to protect the carpeting from wetness was rolled and stashed in the far corner of the middle drawer of the storage dresser attached to the inside wall of the van. She plugged herself with a wad of tissues to keep from dripping on her living room floor when she got home. We opened the windows wide, regardless of the weather or the temperature, so that the rush of air on the ride back would sweep away the lingering, poignant smell of our sex. Out the window and onto the highway pavement I chucked the used condom, hoping its milky contents didn't splat against the side of the van. I spit into my hands and used my own saliva to wash the scent of pussy from the skimpy scruff of goatee I had sported for the past year or so. To be sure, there was nothing pretty or beautiful in the ritualistic clean-up that had become a routine but necessary part of our continuing subterfuge. Only the memories were permitted to linger, later to be savored with relish and discussed in full.

A single sexual experience could last for days with reminisced words, thoughts, feelings, and fears leading to questions, ideas, and fantasies that often overflowed from one physical encounter to the next.....

"God, that felt so good.....a little bit higher—there, that's the spot.....Yeah, we gotta do it that way, again..... Easy, easy, nice and easy.....I wasn't sure if you wanted me to stop or keep going.....Can you make it that way?.....Try lifting up a little.....Of course it was uncomfortable, but I loved it.....You got me so fuckin' hot, I couldn't hold it.....Did you like that? Tell me, tell me.....I thought I was gonna die—what a fuckin' way to die!....Tell me what you see—give me the mirror; I wanna see, too.....Don't stop; oh, don't stop, please.....It was like a flood, like I was floating on an ocean tide.....Do it, man, do it hard.....I felt so giving, so at your mercy.....Oh, I love you.....Let me lick your finger and see what I taste like.....You make me feel so good.....I trust you with all of me; you trust me, don't you?.....I thought I was gonna laugh—Would you have felt badly if I had laughed?.....You like it better that way?.....Oh, thank you, thank you.....You shot it all over me.....I have no way of knowing, so you have to tell me.....Oh, sweet baby, my sweet baby.....Hold me, hold me. I need you.....Don't even ask; do me anytime you have the urge.....That was so fast—too fast.....Oh, my sweet man.....Let me show you, silly.....What a fuck!....."

Ignorantly free and unencumbered, Ann said what she meant, asked what she wanted, and did as she pleased. She didn't say "go to bed" if she meant she wanted cock. Like a child with a re-discovered Christmas toy from three years past, she examined, explored, and played with her body parts, talking to herself out loud about what she found and how she felt about her discoveries, unmindful of either my notice or presence. Simply and undisguisedly, she did and said whatever she had a mind to, with no attempt to expurgate, cleanse, censor, purify, or conceal. There was nothing done for the purpose of turning me on, encouraging me to participate, pushing me to perform, or having me respond—although at times I did. She didn't know any other way. How could she be ladylike or unladylike if she didn't know the difference?

I taught her everything I knew. And with each of her seeking questions, it was *I who learned.* I learned about the naked woman, as seen though Ann's eyes, unfurled from the wrap of dainty euphemisms. She didn't talk about "grassy mounds." It was a place where cunt hairs grew. She didn't speak of her need for a "sturdy shaft" when she wanted a six-inch cock lodged within her. There was no flimsy pretense that the rise of her "firm young breasts" was something other than proudly nippled tits. She never wanted "intercourse." She wanted to get fucked—often, hard, and with emotion. There was no false blush of propriety that turned cracks, holes, and slits into more acceptable "crotches." She told it like it was. She didn't "reach her climax." She squirt her cum juices on my fuckin' tongue with ohhhhh's and ahhhhh's of delight. One day I teased her about it, painting myself as the drowned victim instead of the benevolent benefactor of her release. "And if ya didn't get it, you'd probably cry like a baby," she counter attacked. She was naughty. She taught me every naughty thing I knew.

For a student, she was one helluva teacher—helping me, positioning me, and correcting my mistakes—a lot of mistakes. She was eager to illustrate and to demonstrate. She encouraged me to try, to try again, and to try harder. She applauded my successes, and, with schoolmarm patience, tolerated my floundering. If I flubbed, she'd let me try again; sometimes I flubbed on purpose just to earn a second or third opportunity. She gave me instruction and counseling—how, when, where, why, and how much. There was a time for work and a time for play, time to let things slide and push ahead, and time to shoot the works. She gave me as much support and encouragement when I was rising to unheard of heights as when I was plunging to new depths. She answered all my questions, no issue too sticky or too hot to handle. When things got particularly hard or I found myself in a tight spot, she'd let me beat around the bush before getting down to it.

A teacher's teacher, she always made certain I got my licks and enjoyed the sweet taste of success. I always got extra credit for extra work. In clear, concise terms, in words I could understand, she outlined and explained everything I needed to know. She called a spade a spade, a prick a prick, and "protection" a rubber. The difference between a snow man and a snow woman was snow balls. Naughty this schoolmistress was—hot, sultry, sexy, and naughty. Very naughty. Straightforward naughty. Maybe it was because she grew up in a house with two older brothers. Maybe it was because she didn't know *how* to be anything but straightforward and forthright. Whatever—so honest, so revealing of her true feelings, and so openly expressive she was, that sometimes it scared the hell out of me.

And here I was, unable to match her candor, squirming like a worm at the end of a hook.

"So, explain. I don't see what the trouble is with tight," she pursued. "I thought tight was good."

I groped for the words, the honesty, and the courage—mostly the courage.

"In a tight spot like that, my foreskin will be pushed back so far it'll kill me before I even get in," I said with as little hesitation as possible. "It only goes back so far."

For me to admit to any kind of sexual inadequacy or inability was humiliating. I knew the embarrassment showed. I felt like a teacher who had walked into a classroom of honor students without a lesson plan, unsure, unsteady, lacking the confidence to continue, and insecure about my capacity to function and to do what was expected of me.

"So, you'll use a rubber. What's the diff? Use a lubricated rubber. My dad's got all kinds of them in the store. You last longer with a rubber, anyway. And you won't get dirty, either," she assuaged with plucky confidence. "I just want you in my ass."

CHAPTER 24

Still waiting out the rain.....a daily double.....“This time it’s gonna be different.....I’m gonna like being the boss.....”

A half hour later we still were waiting for the rain to let up, more stoned than when we started, but still waiting.

“Ya want any more of this?” she asked, extending the clip with the small stub of what was left of her second—maybe her third—joint of the hour.

“Christ, no,” I groaned. “I’m fuckin’ wrecked.”

We sat together, the deluge outside showing no sign of abating, she still talking a blue streak, me still drifting from exaggerated attention to melancholy disinterest, my mouth open, my eyes fixed in glassy stare, my stoned mind dwelling on a disoriented comment she had made five minutes before, my senses dulled to talk. Christ, I was in no condition to carry on a conversation. My emotions floated in sentimental transport, my hand groping halfway down inside her jeans, and then I couldn’t remember what the hell I was reaching for. I snapped back as if emerging from a trance, a silly grin stretched broadly across my face. But nothing she was saying or doing, or had said or had done, was the least bit funny or amusing! Damn, the stuff really got to me.

"No more for me, babe."

"You *know* I just love camp, don't you? I mean, sure, sometimes the kids in my bunk get to me, and I have to lay on the discipline, especially when they get rambunctious late at night, but….."

She snuffed the roach in the ashtray and set it aside, done for the moment with the weed, not quite as finished yet with her continuing saga of last summer's camp experience.

"…..I'm not very good at playing the heavy. You can picture me laying down the law, right?" she laughed.

"Yeah, yeah—"

"Are you with me, babe?" she implored, questioning my attentiveness.

"Yeah, man. I'm really fogged, but I think it's startin' ta lift."

"It's not gonna be long, ya know."

"Yeah, I know," I replied automatically, before I realized I didn't know what the hell she was talking about. "Long for what?"

"Before I leave for camp," she said quietly.

"Oh, I thought you meant long before graduation."

"Well, that, too. Are you gonna come?"

"Am I gonna come? Or, am I gonna go? I came a half hour ago. So did you."

"C'mon, Charlie, I'm serious."

"I'm serious, too. I'm serious. I'm bein' serious. I'm tryin'—I'm just havin' trouble pulling everything together. How much of that God-awful stuff did we smoke?"

"You're gonna go to graduation, aren't you?" she asked, her question pushing mine aside.

"I don't know."

The silence seemed to magnify the sound of the rain, its intensity deafening in the void that neither one of us moved very quickly to fill.

"I don't know if I can handle it, babe," I finally said. "It's really heavy shit. I don't know—"

"You feeling bad about not going back next year?"

"Hell, no, that's the last thing," I responded with a dismissing shrug. "I have trouble handling any graduation. The emotions really get to me when I see all the kids I've come to know and really like are leavin'. But *this* one—this one's gonna be a ball buster. I'm feelin' bad, I don't know, I guess about you leavin' and then goin' to camp, havin' the year come to an end, saying good-bye—everything."

"I love you, sweet man," she said softly, resting her head on my chest. "I'm not leavin' ya. I'm graduating, and I'm goin' to camp, but I'm not leavin' ya. I'm never gonna leave ya."

I shook my head from side to side as I took off my glasses and rubbed my eyes.

"Don't ya get it, hon?" she pleaded quietly but with emotion. Don't ya get it?" she repeated. I love you more than anything in the world. Ya think I'm gonna love ya less if ya don't go to graduation? I'm not. You think I'm gonna love ya more if you go? No way; I can't. That just isn't possible. So, be at peace with whatever ya decide, sweet. I'm gonna love ya always, no matter what. I'm stuck on ya, babe, and you're stuck with me. Ya love me?"

"I love you so much," I said with a choke as I dried my eyes with my hand and leaned to kiss her forehead. "I don't know what I'm gonna do, babe. I'd like to go to graduation, but, shit, man, it would tear me apart, just tear my guts out. I wanna be there with you, but, Christ, it would just rip me up."

"I know, hon."

"Ya think I don't wanna be there when you graduate, when you get your diploma?"

"I know you do. Whatever you decide is okay with me," she said as she looked up and brushed the wetness from my cheek.

I squeezed her *so* hard—too hard. I thought I'd crack her ribs. I needed her close to me. I needed *her*, the only thing I had left from the Alternative School. Not going back next year was an easy matter. It was a joke. That wasn't the problem. The end of *this* year was killing me. I wasn't blaming anybody. I had no one to blame but myself. I was just getting what I deserved, but it was killing me just the same.

From the time I had announced that I wasn't coming back next year, it had been all down hill. I did my job, but that was it. I did the fucking job right down to the last evaluation, the last phone call, and the last entry on the last transcript. But, that's all, nothing more. At three-thirty, I was gone. It wasn't my *job* to stay late so the kids could stay late and use the building. It wasn't my *job* to be the last one out every night, to turn the lights out, and to lock up. It wasn't my *job* to squirm under the couch on my belly to retrieve the last ping-pong ball that wasn't cracked. It wasn't my *job* to clean out the refrigerator every Friday afternoon so the person who opened it on Monday wouldn't be bowled over by the stench of soured milk that had been sitting there since Wednesday. I had done it before, but no more, thank you.

I retreated, and they made me pay for every backward step I took. They didn't have to talk to me about next year, so they didn't. They could handle the year-end arrangements without me, so they did. Judith, still smarting from the dissolution of our once flourishing relationship, paid me back in kind, excluding and ignoring me in fulfilling her role as editor of the A-School yearbook. Two years before, after being in the high school for only two years, the Senior Class had dedicated their yearbook to me:

> **.....We respected only those who earned respect, and we confided in those who cared. That is why we so often turned to a man who was eager to express his deep and sincere concern; a man of warmth and action. In our years here he exhibited faith in people and was an inspiration to us all. It is with great admiration, love, and respect that we dedicate.....**

Now, today? I would have been hard pressed to have anyone from the Alternative School show up at my funeral.

"Discovery!" was nothing but a memory. Bowling was over. Town Meetings were empty and useless with only a handful of kids bothering to go. Everyone was waiting for the last day. The teachers were tired, and the students were treading water, a deadly combination which reduced serious academic pursuits to little more than an anemic effort to keep the school a school. There was nothing left. Everybody was just hanging on. I hung on to the only thing I had left—Ann.

"I'll tell everyone I'm goin' to graduation, but I probably won't go. Or, maybe I will, and just stand in the back and slip out quickly when it's all over. I don't know—and then, in a few days, I guess you'll be leavin' for camp, huh?"

It was a perfunctory question. I knew she was leaving.

"Yes," she said quietly.

She wasn't going to change her mind, either. I wasn't going to be dumb enough to ask.

"You gonna write?" she questioned.

"Sure," I answered. "You gonna?"

"Of course," she replied, then added with ridicule, " 'Dear Charlie and Pam. Having a great time. Wish you were here.' Shit."

"That's okay, that's good. You can write that. It's perfect."

"Sure," she said sarcastically. "Sure it is."

"It is, really. Then, when you're gonna write to *me*, you mail it to Ed Richards' address."

She looked at me, puzzled at first, the remaining wooziness of her head a barrier to swift comprehension.

"Ed Richards' address?"

"It's all arranged. I asked him a few days ago. We're gonna use his house as a mail drop for your letters from camp," I explained with cocky assurance. "He lives so close, I can stop by every day or two and see if there's any mail from you."

"Oh, geez, that's neat! What a great idea," she exclaimed, her eyes brightening. "I can write to you all summer! Neat-o! Can you come up with a way to visit me, too? Then *everything* would be perfect."

"I'm working on it, babe. I'm working on it."

"Really? Charlie, think of something. You can think of *something*. Ya gotta. I'm gonna miss you *so* much. Two months—" her voice trailed.

"It's not gonna be two months, babe, not if I can help it. I'll find some way to get up there. I don't know how, but somehow."

How the hell was I going to get to New Hampshire?

"Oh, that would be great," she gushed.

"I miss you already, and you haven't even left yet," I said with cotton-mouth dryness. "Shit, I wish I had a can of soda or somethin' to drink. My mouth is as dry as a sand trap."

"Go up front and stick your head out the window," she jested.

"I don't wanna move. I don't think I *can* move."

"You still zonked?"

I considered the question. I had smoked enough weed to be blitzed for a week, but I seemed to have my wits about me. I sure as hell wasn't going to try to stand up, but as long as I was lying back comfortably, I was okay.

"No, just tired—and thirsty. Damn."

"Want me to run in and see if there's a soda machine in the lobby?"

How the hell was I going to get up to New Hampshire? I thought I was a genius for setting up a mail drop. Now she wanted me to make a three hundred mile trip for a visit. It was a great idea, exciting even to think about it, but not so easy to pull off. How the *hell* was I going to get to New Hampshire?

"I don't know if I can, babe," I said foggily.

"No, me. I'll go for you."

We exchanged questioning frowns.

"I don't think we're talking about the same thing," I said with a squint.

"Me either. What are—I said I'd go and see if I could get you a soda, maybe something for me, too. I got the munchies."

"Oh, shit, I was talkin' about getting up to New Hampshire this summer," I said, chagrined that my thoughts had found their way into our chatter. "No, no thanks, babe. You'll get drenched. It's not worth the soaking. Fucking rain. I *told* you it wasn't gonna stop. Just wait and see."

"I'm waitin', I'm waitin'. I'm tired of fuckin' waitin'. Maybe we should stop waitin' and start doin'."

"Doin'?"

I threw an unknowing look in her direction. There wasn't much to do, not much we could do. We already had given uninspired consideration to several possibilities, discarding each one in turn, no idea able to arouse sufficient enthusiasm to get the necessary two votes.

"What bright ideas you got that we haven't already thought of?"

"What about the obvious?" she winked. "We're not gonna have that much time together before I go," she said. "And after I go, it'll be a long time. Maybe we should just be cozy together and see what happens."

She was talking about a daily double! I wondered if I could get up for a second one.

"I'm afraid we're gonna have even less *obvious* time than you think," I said soberly. "I think it's almost time for a friend to visit you."

Her eyes blazed wide in disbelief.

"Oh, for Christ's sake," she exploded with annoyance. "Again? Already? Oh, for Christ's sake."

"Listen, be thankful for small favors," I consoled. "I know that opinion doesn't necessarily reflect the views of the management, but try to be thankful, anyway."

"Small favors, yeah, just what I need. Jesus, you keep track of that?"

"Somebody has to."

"Shit, I spend half my life with the plug in. I never get a break. I get cramps two weeks before, and I still have cramps two weeks after. The only time I'm not doubled over is when I'm bleedin', and then I'm a mess. Shit, when am I due?"

"You really don't want me to tell ya, do you?"

She looked at me with icy coldness, the etch of pain ragged in her features.

"Oh, shit. Between graduation and when I leave for camp, right? Right? Fuckin' shit! I *knew* it."

I nodded the correctness of her worst fears and put my arm around her slumped shoulders.

"Relax, you're too hard on yourself. It's not that bad."

"I know," she conceded grudgingly. "Maybe I should go on the pill. It would regulate my period, ya know? It wouldn't be so heavy, either, and we wouldn't have to sweat every month. God, my mother would shit a brick! I didn't want to get my period *now.* I wanted us to spend a lotta time together before camp. I'm really gonna miss you."

"We *will* spend a lotta time together."

"But I wanted us to spend a lotta lovin' time together."

"We will," I assured. "You could even end up being late, as usual, and everything will work out fine."

"Or I could be early, and that's the end of that, huh?"

I shrugged at the dismal prospect.

"Now, c'mon, be honest. It didn't bother us that much last month. We worked around it okay, didn't we?"

"Yeah," she blushed. "I remember. We worked around it."

"So, relax," I encouraged with a kiss.

"So, you vant I should relax, yet?" she toyed, the heavily exaggerated Yiddish accent signaling the passage of her dismay.

"Yes, already. I vant you should relax."

"So, give me another kiss," she said as she pushed a pucker to me. "Mmmmm, ah, as good as chicken zoup. I vould relax, and you vould vork around it, huh? You vould vork it around?"

"I'll vork it around."

"So, already, ve now should do it. Ve should practice, no?"

"Ve should practice, yes," I laughed in agreement.

We stripped quickly in the tight quarters, and I marveled at how, over past weeks, we each had established a pattern of physical movements to accomplish the task of undressing so that our bodily extensions, twists, and turns made maximum use of the limited area available, neither she nor I competing for the same space in conflict, the timing of our moves in harmonious compliment, our naked conclusion reached separately but simultaneously.

She talked quietly throughout. To herself? To me?

"Nobody's gonna sneak up on me from behind this time. You didn't think I knew what was happening, huh? You'll know what's happening, that's for sure. Lie down, lay back. C'mon, lay back, lay back, let me—lay back, will ya. Let *me* do this."

She pushed me on my back and hovered my midsection, straddling, looking down with flushed excitement, her body moves and facial expressions confirming her eagerness for control, her delight for a new twist. I don't know why I worried about getting it up again. It was already on the move.

"This time it's gonna be different," she murmured cloudily.

She wiggled her hips provocatively, her soft hairs grazing lightly, her eyes twinkling as she wet her lips with her tongue and playfully raised and lowered her eyebrows in Groucho Marx fashion.

"I think I'm gonna like being the boss," she grinned. "Say the secret word—"

Funny, I never thought of myself as "the boss," the person in the controlling position. To me, the tease, not the position, was the prominent factor in a sexual union, with Ann's teasing, even when it came from a submissive position, dictating what she wanted and how she wanted it. I rather preferred the role of the obligor to that of the controller. Now, however, I realized the difference was of little consequence. I thrilled with equal arousal as the little nymph, who already had stirred my blood alive, readied herself in the overt position of dominance that would make her master of her own contentment. I was going to like her being the boss, too.

She centered herself above my rise in misty illusion of New Year's Eve, a minute before midnight, all eyes fixed on the top of the pole as the slow, sliding descent began, the final downward pitch in frenzied anticipation of the last stroke of old times past, the first stroke of new beginnings. I almost could hear the cork pop, see the lights light, feel the exploding celebration of fireworks and firecrackers as the angelic cherub, as naked as the New Year, came to seated rest, almost too snugly.

"Just move, just lean—that's it, a little bit forward."

She leaned toward me slightly, adjusting, and I felt the tightness folding away, yielding its final resistance, engulfing as quicksand.

"God, I'm stuffed—so good," she reveled.

"Nice," I said in compliment.

"That's the secret word, my sweet man—'Nice!' Now, watch, watch me. I'm gonna sit still and feel my man—sit still forever.....or ride. I can't decide what I wanna do," her voice trailed as she stirred ever so slightly in unhurried contemplation of her preference.

"Whatever you want, sweet," I offered, the choice not as magnanimous as it sounded.

In a position of control she was, but in no position to choose her pleasure. Her ever so slight stir had sealed her fate. With that small mistake, she had forfeited her choice. Nature now would have Her way, with no heed to Ann's wishes, desires, or choices. She now was as helpless as a tree trying to hold its leaves beyond the snap of autumn's chill, as choice less as a flowing mountain stream rushing downhill.

The young body that sat astride me, her weight supported by her flat-footed squatting stance, was entrapped, unaware that her wish to sit still forever was as futile as a moth's yearning to flutter unsigned in the magnetic heat of a candle's flame. She would ride.

She moaned with compunction as she rose slowly.

"Don't come off, babe," I pleaded with caution.

"I'm not comin' off. I'm comin' on, sweet man. I'm not gonna come off—comin' on and gettin' off," she gurgled with delight as she returned herself in scintillating slide to a sitting, fully engaged position.

"Feel it good, babe; feel it good," I inspirited as she again moved, this time with less reserve and reluctance, more commitment, her rise and fall accompanied by the infuriating jiggle and jounce of those exclusively female fleshes. Small but firm, erotic in motion, smooth and white, at first jiggling like jello and then bouncing wildly like the headlights of a jeep racing across a rocky terrain, they had the power to reduce a grown man to a groveling, bleating, hungry, little boy.

Up, then the downward pitch. Up and down, and again, quickening, my senses in plethoric burst, flooded, the smell of sex, the sound of exertion, the feel of gripping union, the taste of my own tongue breathed parched and arid, and the sight—the entreating, enslaving, enraging sight—of those fucking tits, now bouncing in rhythm, their rosettes dancing like purplish-pink flowers placed for decoration on vibrating mounds of soft, vanilla pudding.

Twitching and pounding below I felt, as the warm massage and relentless stroke continued and increased. Above, the jiggle and swing now had expanded to a lusty flop—as much as the firmness of young breasts with their raised bulls eyes would permit—disobedient, out of sequence with her body's thrust, annealed tips bouncing wildly out of control, unable to follow the rapid changes of route, unsure themselves in what factitious direction they might next be flung, their chaotic frenzy like the scramble of a broken-field runner scampering through a disorganized backfield for a fifty-yard gain.

Then, down, I looked, between her thighs, and I watched the contrasting control with which she employed the piston-like rise and fall of her bottom, the control and discipline of a beautifully matched, neatly fitted, and perfectly synchronized performance of a world champion figure skating pair, almost monotonous in the repetitive precision of their performance together in concert.

Wildness above, serenity below—

My mind was bombarded with audio absorptions, every sound—the tiniest noise—snared at its point of origin, assimilated and amplified to grotesque caricature. My ear caught the orchestration of body movements—the crack of knuckles and hip joints, the ball and socket roll of kneecaps, the straining pull of leg muscles and tightly curled toes, the rhythmic beat and cadence of body impacts and, in vocal accompaniment, the inimical squeaks of the floor and sides of the van as it attempted to counter the motion, resist the peppering attack on its frame, and disperse the swaying pitch and roll of its chassis.

My head spun with perfumed sensations, each scent—the faintest whiff—captured at its peak of flavor, the heated aroma of naked bodies, the naked aroma of heated bodies, inhaled and savored with intoxicating delight.

It was what I saw, however, rather than what I heard or smelled, that nudged me beyond the bounds of civil restraint and made me wonder whether my sanity had somehow slipped away in a wash of perverted and depraved thoughts.

She knew—she must have known—that the jack-hammer ride atop me set her mother's milk swells in a vibrating frolic that goaded and taunted my senses with more arousal than even the direct stimulation of her driving axis. Those fucking tits were an enraging flaunt of her womanhood. Genital parts we each had—different, naturally, but equally employable, equally enjoyable, in ways appropriate to their respective forms. But tits—shit, I didn't have tits. I barely had the beginnings of hair on my chest! In the final, hazy snare of weed's distorting influence, I saw myself in overwhelmed submission, dominated not only by the physical position of a schoolgirl who rode my loins with frightening shamelessness, but as well by the ostentatious blazonry and indelicate display of her female maturity, her bosom's full-flowered scoff at my manhood's lacking.

The sights and sounds were driving me crazy. I heard the steam whistle of a calliope, the wavy shout of the circus ringmaster, and the call of the midway barker:

"Ladies.....and.....gentlemen.....children of all ages.....step right up.....the greatest show on Earth.....the daring bare-back rider.....the lion tamer.....the bearded lady.....popcorn and jelly apples.....the juggling and jiggling act of the side show clown.....the queen of the flying trapeze....."

My television—was my TV on?

She clasped her hands behind her head, her elbows extended outward from either side. She rode me with the sultry bravado of a daredevil cowgirl astride a bucking bronco in a rodeo show, her hair flying, her eyes fixed in a vitreous stare, her torso rocking back and forth with almost as much vigor as it hoisted and plummeted. Her breasts now were pancaked across her chest, her springy nips—bulging and stretched taut by the raised position of her arms—struggled to bounce free.

I reached out spontaneously, instinctively, with both hands and grabbed the pair of swollen extremities that were tormenting and inflaming my passions. I pulled and tugged at them until her seemingly inexhaustible and insatiable compulsion to ride up and down with zealous ardor shook them from reach.

A sudden heave. A collapsing tent. A flailing lunge with a wail, as if struck by lightening in the midst of a high-wire act. She fell forward on her hands and knees above me with the exigency of an injured acrobat, crawling, dazed, and seeking the help of relief, of release.

She pressed, nuzzled in the dampened tangle of cotton candy between us, her forward lean wedging me, stretching her, in tight conjunction. With rapt, almost raffish, urgency, she strained for release, the roller coaster assault of her hips spinning the rest of her body into a Ferris wheel of involuntary responses. I stretched my hands behind her and dug my fingernails, pressing her to the center ring. Her hair, head, and breasts swung freely like dangling pieces of severed rigging, lashing, grazing, and flouncing my chest, arms, face, and forehead, at times almost blanketing me and smothering me. My body was peppered with heated panting, sweaty moistures, intrepid movements, humid exhales, guttural sounds, and the disorderly swaying, bobbing, tossing, bouncing, thrashing, and flailing of those God-damn, mother-fucking, little—

"I'm gonna come," she gasped as she squeezed her buttocks tightly and threw her head back, arching her body backward. "Oh, you got me, babe. Holy shit. Nice, I love it, I love it, I love it. I'm comin' yeah, yeah, yeahhhh, beautiful."

I felt the squish between our clamped bodies—the trickle—I but a moment away myself. There was nothing I could do to hold back, nothing I wanted to do.

"Beautiful come," she reiterated with contented exhaustion. "Nice, super nice. Now *you*, fucker, now you. Quick, now, your turn," she gushed saucily. "I fucked myself, now *you* fuck me!"

She hastily reverted to her original squatting position over me and lifted slightly. I took advantage of the freedom to jerk upward, rising in direct ascent to the concealed warmth which lingered barely a twitch above.

"Go, baby. Fuck the pussy. Gimme it."

I withdrew partially. She hung in suspension above me, summoning re-entry with an impatient squirm.

"C'mon."

I lurched upward a second time, a third, a fourth.

"Hard, you prick," she railed. Fuck it, hard. Fuck me."

An embarrassing grunt accompanied my lifting shoves as I rammed in rapid succession with full force, jolting her entire body as she met each violent thrust with calculated resistance.

"Are you gonna fuck your Annie or are you just gonna play games with me, you prick," she admonished. She tucked her fingertips beneath her bottom, opening herself and inviting a resumption of assault.

I couldn't see. There was ample light, but her shadow fell across me and obscured my view. My head was back too far, anyway. But I knew what she was doing, and a sweeping fantasy put my eyes in piercing gaze beneath the imagined spread of her entrance. With vivid recollections of the page I had sneakily torn from a biology book at age eleven, my mind examined the detail, tracing from memory the labeled diagram of the female organ, recalling the arrows that identified each exotic and mysterious part. Little understanding I had then of the clinical words, but I fell in love with the drawing—I knew what the damn thing was—and with the fevered reaction the very thought of it had on my own genitals.

"I want your cum." It was almost a hiss that went beyond petulance. "Hurt me, damn you, hurt me. Slam it to me, ram it in. All or nothing—give it to me or get it the fuck outta there."

Infuriated by her impertinent taunting, I fucked her wildly.

"You bitch!"

Oh! Oh! Oh! Oh! Oh, my God!" she extolled with exculpatory emotion after each blistering penetration. I think I'm….."

I returned her insolence by whip-fucking her with savage vengeance, invading her, splitting the whorled spiral of that pink, turreted shell, catapulting her high above me and.....

".....gonna come, Charlie. I'm gonna—"

.....riding my pulsing organ to the fullest depth of that sweet commodious opening she taunted me to fill, before she literally was thrown off as I shot and spurted in mid-air.

".....comin' to ya. Holy shit," she caterwauled impulsively.

"Oh, comin', comin', comin' to ya," I panted. "Ahh, fuckin' nice. Great fuckin' cunt, you buster, you."

I laughed and groaned as we both watched the ooze and splash of my excited release. She stood in her squatting position, now high above me, almost to the roof of the van, leaning forward and looking down between her bowed legs, her palms on her knees, and we watched together the final tiny squirts and drippings of her relief, tiny puddles accumulating in the hair of my pubic region, across my abdomen.

"Holy shit, I can't believe *I* came again," she marveled in genuine surprise. "God, you fucked the hell outta me! Look at me dripping."

I was still heaving, breathing with exerted effort, gasping for controlled breaths, my supper bolting in my gullet, a viscid backwash of curdled macaroni and cheese in distasteful misdirection, but I was watching. I watched the gurgling trickle of juices that my punishment had set free, the sweet-perfumed secretions that hung in resplendent droplets from her tenderness, then dribbled onto my steamy body, forming tiny rills and rivulets of roving anointment as my body heaved its final exhaustive swells. It was as fucking wet inside the van as it was outside.

"Every drip says, 'I love you,' sweet man," she cooed.

I looked up at her, overwhelmed by the sensitive declaration that came in the wake of the cunning guile she had just used to induce brutal assail of her innards and to appease my debauched fantasies and free my inhibitions.

"You're a pisser, ya know that?" I said in acclamation.

"I liked riding on top of you, sweet man. I got myself so fuckin' hot I had to push my button before I burned up. I was steaming. My whole body was on fire. That's why I fell down on you and rubbed myself in your hair and came. And then you screwed me just the way I love it. Hard and harder," she laughed. "God, you fucked me out! It still feels like you're inside me," she reminisced.

"Give me a few minutes, and we can do it again, if you want—go for a triple instead of a double—"

"Oh, yeah? 'Say the secret word and divide a hundred dollars,'" she quoted Groucho Marx again. "And I'll bet my fifty you can't get it up in a few minutes."

"You're right," I confessed. "And I'll bet my half, my fifty, you couldn't take another fucking like that in a few minutes, either," I said, returning the challenge.

"You're right. It even hurts to think about it. Now, maybe in a few *hours*....."

"I love you, Ann, very much."

"I know you do, Charlie. I love you, too. Whaddya think of my boobs? You think my tits are okay?"

Oh, man—if she ever knew; like she didn't know, right? Yeah, sure.....

CHAPTER 25

Ann graduated, but not without a last minute flurry of activity..... she went to camp, and I went to pieces.....But a plan had been formulated for a rendezvous in New Hampshire.....

I went to Ann's graduation. It wasn't easy, but I went. I stayed to the end, standing alone in the back, high on the stadium steps overlooking the athletic field where portable bleachers had been erected and the graduates-to-be sat proudly on display before an equally proud assemblage of parents and friends.

A number of A-School seniors distinguished themselves by emblazoning their mortarboards with large, taped A's, the white adhesive tape standing out boldly against the dark blue caps. Others—a large majority, in truth—in a rare demonstration of restraint and self-denial, distinguished themselves by enduring the lengthy ceremony without reefer. A few of their less distinguished classmates were unable to resist the temptation to vent thin curls of gray smoke into the early evening sky as the body of four hundred restless graduating seniors listened to guest speakers and invited dignitaries offer candied words of congratulation and stern messages of responsibility in extolling the youth of today as the promise of tomorrow.

Ann distinguished herself by being there. She came close to not making it. Checking her permanent record card back in early May—I don't remember why, but for whatever reason—I was ill prepared for what I found—more properly, what I *didn't* find. One trimester of American History, a course she needed to satisfy the State requirements for a high school diploma, was missing. I could have strangled Janis. The Seminar teachers had been carefully reminded that it was their responsibility to review the card and schedule of each of their seniors to make certain that all credit and course requirements had been met or were scheduled. Janis either hadn't checked or had fucked it up. Either way, Ann was screwed.

It didn't make any sense to go after Janis. There was nothing she could do, so I went after Ann. She was furious when I told her what I had to do, but I had little choice. I established an independent study course, "Theodore Roosevelt and the Happy Years," and I tutored her. She bitched and moaned for the full three weeks I made her read books, write reports, take tests, do homework, and keep a notebook, learning more history in three weeks, I believe, than she had learned in the previous three years. At first she begged for relief.

"C'mon, Charlie, gimme a break, will ya?"

"Ya wanna graduate?"

"Yeah, but—"

"So, read the next twenty-five pages for tomorrow, and don't give me a hard time. I'll give you a quiz at lunchtime."

"You know what I have to do tonight?"

"Yeah, read twenty-five pages."

"Fuck!"

"Not before the quiz."

After a week, she knew I was serious, but her effort to convince me to back off and let things slide lingered half-heartedly.

"Hey, I know this one," she erupted in the middle of a test late one afternoon in the lounge. " 'Speak softly and carry a big stick,' right?" she beamed.

"Right. That was an easy one. I hope that's not the only answer you know."

"You gotta big stick for me?" she whispered. "Let's sneak into the bathroom, and I'll show ya where to stick your stick."

"You drop your pants around here," I threatened with false malice, "and I'll pull out every hair, one by one."

"I was sorta hoping you'd put me over your knee."

"Finish the test, asshole."

"Would you really fail me?" she questioned a week later on our way home from horseback riding. "I mean, if I bomb the final, you wouldn't really *fail* me, would you?"

She had me by the balls, and she knew it.

"Try me," I challenged.

"You would fail me?"

No answer.

A few days later, I gave her the news.

"Ninety-four."

"Ninety-four!" she screamed with a jump of delight. "Wow! I *knew* I could do it. I knew the shit backward and forward!"

"Thank you, babe," I said quietly, my reserved comment in sharp contrast to her joyful burst.

"You're welcome, Mr. Sullivan," she replied with sincerity. "I knew you couldn't fail me. I knew you wouldn't, no matter what I got. That's why I wanted to do well. I knew your back would be against the wall if I failed. Oh, I'm so happy! I'm gonna graduate! Oh, thank you. Shit, I'm gonna pee in my pants."

"I'm *really* proud of you. You did some job on that exam, even the essay. Unfortunately, now you'll never know, will ya?"

"Never know what?"

"Whether I would have failed you or not."

"Oh, c'mon, how could you fail your favorite pussy? That would be like failing your mother. You wouldn't fail your mother, would you?"

"Ya never know, ya never know," I said with a wink.

Maybe it was best she'd never know. Maybe it was best *I* didn't have to know. My mother? I would have failed her without batting an eye.

From the back of the stadium the graduates all looked the same, the boys in blue gowns and the girls in white. I was able to find Ann among the sea of faces, and I never took my eyes away from her. The invocation, the speakers, the choir, and then, one row at a time, one student at a time—it took forever—the graduates paraded in single file to the area in front of the bleachers where they received their diplomas as their names were announced into the microphone.

".....Ann Jordan....."

Thank God *that* was over.

****

I knew it was coming. It had to come. I think I handled it reasonably well—no, pretty damn well—until she was gone. Then I went to pieces.

Ann went to camp, and I went to pieces.

For ten months we had been daily companions—for the last few, lovers. Our lives and spirits inexorably entwined, we had moved in smooth connection like the mesh of two interlocked cogwheels. We had existed as two adjacent pieces of patchwork quilt with a common side stitched in close attachment, our destiny sewn together in zigzag bind. Now I was alone and frayed, my complement ripped from my side, loose threads dangling from the torn edge.

The first year of the Alternative School had come to an end. I had traversed the brown and tan tile squares of the basement floor for an emotion-filled final time. I had closed the door to our "Discovery!" classroom on the last day of school and walked to the front, pausing near the stage. I knew that when I turned away, I never would see the red chair again. Oh, the stories that battered chair could have told! With tears in my eyes, I had stood in the empty basement, choked by the hiatus of familiar blare. I had stood and cried, then smiled in sweet recollection, a composite indulgence of private feelings I had reserved for myself before snapping my briefcase and heading up the stairs. I had paused again at the top of the stairs, caught in nostalgic introspection, then had let the door swing shut and bolt in resounding punctuation to my final exit, the A-School behind me and past. Ann had made her farewell tour earlier and was waiting in the van.

But now, Ann, too, was gone, and I felt drained, leeched of my life's sap by distance and a far away camp

I knew only through adulated stories. Our labored plans to stay in touch, formulated before her departure, had added spice to our diminishing time together and had made bearable the approach of her time for leaving. Now, however, her absence a reality, I realized, on the one hand, how hollow and insignificant our plotting efforts had been and, on the other hand, how valuable and cherished each plan for contact was. Franks and beans are a big letdown from steak and potatoes. In the face of starvation, however, franks and beans become prized morsels. Our morsels, the flimsy lifeline of nourishment that was called upon to maintain our atrophied contact enough to keep the wolves at bay and the vultures away, consisted of a mailbox at Ed Richards' house and a pay phone on the corner of Washington Avenue and Pascack Road in Washington Township. It was a meager subsistence, to be sure. I hungered for steak—to see her, be with her, hold her, touch her, feel her, and taste her. And, I had the plan.

A play in three acts:

Act I, Scene I—The previous winter, Pam and Charlie sit on the floor in the living room of their house in Emerson, a map of New England spread between them. They plan a college visitation trip for the summer, picking colleges which offer overnight accommodations to visiting counselors and their families. Ironically, their focus is on scenic New Hampshire with its tranquil and beautiful lakes and mountains.

Act I, Scene II—Approximately four months later, Charlie is at his desk at school. The disintegration of his marriage has cast serious doubts on any vacation travel with Pam. Uncertain, but still hopeful, Charlie continues to pursue plans without Pam's knowledge, mailing reservation confirmations to the colleges, submitting a proposal of anticipated college visits to the Director of Guidance, and typing a request for compensation for travel expenses for Board of Education approval.

Act II, Scene I—Two months later, the night before Ann is to leave for camp, Ann and Charlie sit at a table at Jerry's, their favorite pizza place, in Fort Lee. As they sit drinking Cokes while waiting for their pie, they reflect in sublimely buzzed and sexually fulfilled contentment on their good fortune that Ann hadn't gotten her period before leaving. Charlie gets an idea, and in hushed tones they discuss the details.

Act II, Scene II—Two weeks later, Ann sits in her bunk at camp. She takes a folded piece of composition paper from her pocketbook. It is a letter in Charlie's handwriting, addressed to Charlie. On a clean sheet of stationery, Ann copies the letter, word for word, in her own hand. It tells the story of Ann, a frightened girl at camp who has missed her period, fears she's pregnant, is scared to tell "her boyfriend," and hints at suicide. She folds the letter, slips it into an envelope, and addresses it. This letter doesn't go to Ed Richards' house. It goes to Charlie's address. This one is for Pam's benefit.

Act II, Scene III—A few days later, Pam and Charlie stand in the kitchen of their house in Emerson as Charlie shares the frantic letter of Ann's fake distress. It works. Pam's concern is sufficient for Charlie to feel safe to say, "I better go up there before she does something stupid."

Act III, Scene I—Two days later, Charlie's van heads up the New England Thruway, New Hampshire bound in compassionate mission, the ploy successful, the timing perfect. Ann has arranged to meet him on the main road into Elkins, to be out of her bunk for the night, and to be off duty the next day. It is Pam's belief that previous plans for a college visitation trip had been scrapped or were never concluded. But approval had been granted by the school, a reserved overnight accommodation now waits at Nathaniel Hawthorne College in Antrim, New Hampshire, less than an hour from Ann's camp. Ann will be making a guest star appearance as Mrs. Sullivan, wife of a visiting counselor from New Jersey, and the Board of Education will be picking up the tab for mileage and tolls.

As the curtain rises for the final scene, two girls on the right side of the road wave wildly at the approaching vehicle.

"Oh, geez, I thought you'd *never* get here," Ann screamed as she jumped into the van even before it came to a complete stop.

"Hey, whaddya mean? I'm right on time, Sunshine," I screamed back happily, reaching for her with both hands.

"I know, I know, but I thought you'd *never* get here."

She squirmed into the space between the two front seats, and our mouths crushed, my lower lip caught between our teeth in a pinch of pleasure pain. Moments before, careless in excited anticipation, I had hit the brake pedal too sharply as I rounded a curve. My brown valise had come sliding forward on its side from the back of the van. Now, Ann used the suitcase as a low perch, sitting on its edge, resting her head on my lap, wrapping her arms around my legs.

"I thought I'd never get here, babe," I said as I rubbed my hands over her back, then under her armpits and around to her front, cupping her breasts, feeling the softness ripen beneath her yellow T-shirt.

"God, I can't believe it. You're here! Any trouble with the directions? What time did you leave? Do ya wanna see—Oh, geez, I'm sorry, Dede. I'm sorry. Hop in—c'mon," she beckoned to the girl in shorts and a halter who had stood and watched in silent observation of our excited reunion.

The girl blushed shyly as she stepped up and moved onto the seat.

"Charlie, this is my best friend, Dede. She knows all about us. I guess that's pretty obvious. Dede, this is Charlie."

I smiled a welcome. An accompanying friend hadn't been part of the rendezvous Ann and I had planned. I wondered how much Dede knew.

"Hi, Charlie. Ann didn't wanna wait alone," the darkly tanned girl said apologetically.

"No, that's fine." I assured.

With Ann making little attempt to hide the fact that her hand had slipped high between my legs, I assumed there was little Dede didn't know.

"I've been *dying* without you, babe," Ann gushed, drawing my head down to hers. Our tongues flicked, her saliva and warm breath a reviving treat which pulled from memory a melting recall of her warm insides—the oral cavity she offered with a hungry upturn of her face, and the outline of her lower entrance, puffed against her thin shorts, spared immediate touch and firm massage by Dede's presence. Her knees parted as I rubbed my palm up and down her legs—smooth, shaved this morning in the shower, I bet—richly tanned and so smooth. How come everybody else tans so nicely, and I burn with blistered, peeling skin? Fuck it. I didn't give a damn. Up to the crease I stroked, pressing to its center, feeling the heat and her pliant acquiescence.

"Ohhhh," she gurgled. "God damn, I've missed you. Feel me."

Ann's verbal acknowledgment of what I had tried to conceal from Dede's view brought an embarrassing redness to my face as I stammered an apology to the guest who found herself in the ironical position of being an outsider in the middle.

"Don't—" Dede interrupted. "It's all right. I'm sorry I'm here. I shouldn't—"

"No, it's okay," Ann interjected with a turn. Then, back to me, "She knows I've been going crazy."

"Me, too," I confessed, releasing her reluctantly to light a cigarette. I had to restrain myself and take things one at a time. "The only stop I made on the way up was for gas—no rest, no lunch, just one stop for gas. I couldn't wait to get here. You gotta go back to camp, or what?"

"No, I'm free!" she said with a burst. "My bag's been packed for a week. I didn't think I'd be able to get out 'til tonight, but I'm free now. We just have to drop Dede at camp, and we can go anywhere we want. Isn't that wild? I don't hafta be back until late tomorrow night! Ya wanna get somethin' to eat? Ya hungry?"

"Nah, I'm not really hungry. I'm too excited to eat anything now. I think I wanna get over to the college and check us in before it gets too late. Ya ready for that?"

She had gone along with the plan, but I knew she had some reservations.

"I guess I'm as ready as I'll ever be," she winked. "Here, slide, Dede. Let me out. Le'me get my bag and my guitar, and we'll drive past camp and drop you off, okay?"

CHAPTER 26

A dormitory all to ourselves!

"Shit, that was a breeze, a fuckin' breeze!"

"Of course it was," I chuckled smugly, flipping the keys into the air. "What did ya think it was gonna be? I told you there was nothing to worry about."

"I didn't think it was gonna be *that* easy."

"Why? You make a great Mrs. Sullivan," I said with a hug. "Besides, she was too busy apologizing about the room not bein' ready. Something musta gotten fucked up. She didn't know I was comin', I'm sure of it. I'm glad I had their confirmation letter. Usually they roll out the red carpet when a counselor comes to visit."

We walked briskly along the concrete sidewalk that cut the broad green in half and led to Peabody Hall, the ranging, two-story, brick building to which we had been directed. The sun, past its peak but still richly warm and blinding in the cloudless sky, hung in satisfying fulfillment of the typical summer day promised in New England travel brochures.

"Can you believe we have the whole place to ourselves, a whole dormitory?"

"Can you believe we're gonna spend a night together?" I said in topping fashion.

"I never spent a night with a man. I can't believe any of this."

"We'll take a peek at the room," I said as we approached the colonial front entrance with its freshly painted, white, French doors. "We can walk back to the van and get our things later. I'm so happy ya brought your guitar. Ya gonna sing?"

" '*Oh, my man, I love him so.....*' "

"Yeah, and—"

"John Denver?"

"Yeah."

" '*Sunshine..... on my.....*' "

"No, you know, the other—the chimes, the bells will chime?"

"Oh, I can sing that one—I know the words and how it goes. It's beautiful. But I don't think the title has anything to do with chimes. Doesn't it have an odd title like "For Baby," or something like that?"

"That's it. I love it!" I said as I turned the key in the door. "I wanna take your picture here by the door. Remind me tomorrow morning, will ya, babe? Wear that same shirt, okay?"

"Not in my new nightgown?" she asked with a giggle as she adjusted the strap on the leather handbag slung over her shoulder.

"Nightgown?" I exclaimed with alarm. "Nightgowns are for old ladies!"

"Oh, no, they're not. You'll see."

Closed to sunlight, the interior of the dormitory was dim and cool with a hollow, still emptiness that averred its temporary idle state. Long hallways extended in austere, narrowing silence left and right of the center entrance, the darkness of the corridors broken at regularly spaced intervals by open doors.

"I don't know why the hell she gave us room keys. All the rooms are open," I whispered as we took a few uncertain steps to the right.

"It ain't The Ritz, is it?" she said stuffily, peering through the doorway of a room as I looked over her shoulder.

The Ritz? It wasn't even a second rate motel.

"Take your pick," I said looking into the room across the hallway. "Not much to choose. They're all the same."

Stripped to the bare metal of a bed frame, the rooms were embarrassingly naked, closet doors pushed aside in vacant exposure of leftover hangers on otherwise empty clothes rods, small desk and dresser areas cleared of accessories, blue and gray striped canvas mattresses pulled from the beds to the floor.

"Maybe we'll use all of them!"

"Not a bad idea," I said. "I got a better one, though. C'm'ere, gimme a hand. We'll just use one room, but, sure as hell, we're gonna make it comfortable."

Ten minutes later we surveyed our makeshift quarters, a single room into which we had pulled a dozen mattresses. We had lined them side by side and end to end in spongy cover of the entire floor, a giant bed onto which we now flopped in playful bounce, our bodies readied, the anticipation built as we had fashioned, one tugged mattress at a time, our bedchamber with the only accouterment necessary for the present.

We hurriedly discarded our clothing, and I was up and inside her with swift move, little effort, my body a covering blanket of her yawning spread, our bucking movements screaming the agony of absence, pressing the mattress beneath us into a crush of thinness on the floor, until we rolled contentedly from the wet spot and held each other in embrace.

"That's one—" she heaved. "God, a long time comin', but it was a *good* one. It was worth the wait."

"Nice, yeah," I breathed heavily. "They're all good. How many ya got planned?"

"How many ya got in ya?"

"I don't know, but who's counting? God, I've missed you so much."

I traced my fingertips over and around the protrusions of her breasts, black-eyed peas mounted on swollen—very adolescent—plums springing from the rise of scooped pudding dips.

"Oh, it's so good to have the real thing," she said clutching between her thighs. "I've played with myself so much, I'm surprised it hasn't fallen off. I've shoved so many things. Everybody walks around with the hornies. It's a girls' camp, ya know. There're not that many guys around. The other night I couldn't take my eyes off one of the dishwashers. I hadda run from the dining hall to the shower so I could get off."

"The shower?" I questioned with a tucked chin.

"Where else can ya get off in a cabin full of girls? There's always someone around—no privacy at all—and how can ya do it quietly? I mean, we're all doin' the same thing. Shit, we should all do it at the same time."

She rolled toward me with a howl. "Can you imagine what *that* would sound like?" she laughed. "Ahhhh, ahhhh."

I parted the silkiness of her thighs with my hand, letting it rest in the warmth and wetness.

"Jesus, I have so much to tell ya," she continued. "Let's smoke. Gotta show ya how I get off in the shower, too," she said as she rolled back to the adjoining mattress and reached for her leather bag. "And the pictures—ya get 'em back yet? And my last letter—did ya get a letter just before ya left? Oh, there's so much to talk about. Let's have a joint."

Nonstop we had talked for the duration of our excited drive to the campus. Still, it seemed, we barely had scratched the surface. There *was* so much to catch up on, to do, to say—to remember.

"Relax, relax."

"I can't. I'm hyper," she said, sitting. "Oh, I needed that screwin'. I needed you a whole lot, sweet man. Look, I already have one rolled."

"Good," I said. "Let me bring you up to date before I get so zonked I can't talk. Yes, I got the pictures, the photos. Yes, I got your letter. I got another letter, too. I'll tell ya about that later. Yes, I could use a smoke. And, yes, yes, yes, I needed you, too. God, I needed to be inside you."

She snuggled close to me, and we fell back together, kissing and fondling.

"This is gonna be *some* weekend," she sighed. "I know it's not a *weekend*, but it feels like one. I've been looking forward to this for a long time."

"Me, too. We don't even have to do anything special tomorrow. Just being together—" I said dreamily.

"I know, but we're gonna do a lot. There's so much I wanna do and tell ya about and show ya."

"I know. Ya can show me everything. We'll do it all. Time for weed," I prodded.

She lit the joint with a deep inhale, and I wondered how her lungs withstood the constant punishing attack of breathed irritants. I hadn't smoked grass since she had left for camp a month ago.

"Okay if we have a party tonight?" she asked softly.

"A party?" I responded with surprise.

"Yeah, just a little party," she said, holding the hit.

"I don't know what ya mean," I said pulling back and scanning her face. "What kind of party?"

"A few kids from camp," she said in abbreviated explanation, half announcing, half inquiring.

I squeezed my eyes shut tightly. It wasn't what I wanted, but I knew from her approach that it was set.

"Just two or three girls who have the night off and a couple of guys from the kitchen. They have guitars. We can sing, smoke some grass, drink a little beer, and have some munchies—they're gonna bring everything. Ya want a drag on this?"

She made it sound as attractive as possible.

"They're not staying, are they?"

"No, no, they'll go. And then we'll have the whole place to ourselves for the night."

"As long as they're not gonna stay," I cautioned pointedly as I returned the reefer to her. "Here, it's almost played out. Give it another match. I don't wanna get in trouble here, really. A gang of kids here isn't—and, shit, I don't *want* anybody else around. I want us to be together, alone."

"Me, too. They'll go. They know they can't stay. But we can have a good time, and then we can spend the night together, alone, okay?"

"Wellll," I surrendered with a sigh, my reluctance yielding to my wish to please her.

"Oh, that's great. Thanks. We'll have a ball!"

"We'll have a good time, and then we'll ball," I corrected with tongue-in-cheek devilry, as she directed a hefty puff of smoke in my face.

****

Before departing the campus in search of a bite to eat, we took a walk in the fading sunlight to fetch our things from the van and bring them to our dorm room. We must have looked as if we were moving in for a week. She was weighed down with a suitcase in one hand, her guitar in the other, and a pillow tucked under each arm. I was lugging a valise, a box into which we had tossed blankets and linens, and a bag of toiletries and miscellaneous essentials scavenged from the van dresser.

"We need all this stuff, right?" she grumbled, perturbed at the amount of time I had taken to rummage through the dresser drawers.

"Look, you don't wanna hafta run out here in the middle of the night, do you?"

"For a ruler?" she asked, incredulously, "or a deck of cards?"

"Wellll—"

We went for a quick dinner at a small local restaurant. It wasn't a very attractive looking place, but it was close.

As soon as we were seated and the elderly waitress had taken our order, I showed Ann the pictures about which she had asked.

"Yeah, I picked them up a few days ago. They're not bad. Some are pretty good. Here's the first batch, the ones we took in my back yard before we went to play tennis," I said, handing her a half dozen photographs.

"And before we screwed in the parking lot," she added, completing the remembered account of our afternoon's activities. "The van was like a friggin' oven."

"Yeah, you remember how—"

"Shit, Charlie," she burst. "They're awful—you *gotta* keep the sun off my nose! Look! It looks like I have a beak, for Christ's sake. Oh, Charlie, I *gotta* get a nose job. Now, see, this one's all right, and this one."

"They're the ones I like, too. It's not easy taking pictures there. There are too many trees. Not enough sun gets through."

"Except on my nose," she huffed. "Where are the ones we took by the reservoir?"

I handed her a second group of photos, and she laughed as she flipped through them.

"Shit, I was really stoned, wasn't I?"

We had driven the back roads of Woodcliff Lake to the reservoir, seeking an open gate or a hole in the imposing fence that ringed the picturesque watershed. We found our entry, a scooped hollow through which we could squirm under the fence to a cleared but secluded area in the trees near the water, a great spot for some finely planned pictures I wanted to take before she left for camp.

"Oh, this one's really nice. I bet—"

"Hey, whaddya doin'?" I complained with alarm. "How come ya took that off the bottom?"

" 'Cause I knew that's where you'd put the best one, silly. I bet it's your favorite, right?" she chuckled. "There must have been a chill in the air. My nips are hard."

She handed me the photo. It *was* my favorite, taken from a squatted position, she standing in front of me, smiling down as she held both sides of her denim shirt open to the sun, the arousal of her breasts sufficient to cast a shadow.

"Almost good enough to lick," I chortled.

"Suck," she corrected. "You don't lick my tits, you *suck* my tits. You *lick* my pussy. Now pay attention," she lectured with a smile. "Suck tits, lick pussy, got it?"

"Shhhh," I hushed with embarrassment. "You want to give that guy a hard-on?" I whispered with a glancing nod toward the table to my right. "Jesus, you're dirty."

"I was doing him a favor," she whispered back in response. Then, with a jerk of her head in the direction of the gentleman's homely companion, "He's never gonna get a boner with *her*."

"Damn, you're awful."

The waitress came with our sodas and our order of burgers and fries. I asked for some ketchup, and our conversation resumed.

"I know. I'm so horny, my own pictures are turning me on. This one isn't bad—a little bleached out, but cute titties. You should have had me take off my jeans, and taken some *good* shots. God, this one makes me look like I'm twelve years old. I'm not *that* small, am I?"

"Well—"

My hesitancy was calculated to provoke her. It did. I had to get even with her for giving me a hard-on when I couldn't use it.

"You bastard," she retorted. "I'm *not* that small."

"Eat your fries, will ya. Don't get grease on the pictures."

She shoved the pile of photos toward me.

"Someday I'll be a 42-Double D and you'll be sorry. You'll either get smothered or you'll choke to death. Then you'll wish for the good old days when you had Annie's cute little cupcakes to play with. What about this 'other letter' you said you got?"

"Oh, yes. Ya know….." I said as I made a valiant attempt to swallow the mouthful of what New Hampshire called a hamburger. "This thing is fuckin' awful…..your six-month probation was up at the beginning of the month. I didn't hear a word, so I wrote to the Court for a case transcript so I could find out what the hell was goin' on…..That's when they must've cooked this hamburger—six months ago……anyway, this is what I got back."

I took the folded envelope from my pocket and reached it across the table to her. She took it with hedging demurral.

"Am I gonna like this, or is this gonna be *my* too-tough-to-swallow New Hampshire burger?" she squinted.

"Read it. It's okay," I assured.

She removed the typed document from the envelope and read the letter from the Criminal Court of the City of New York to herself while I attempted to drown the taste of my burger with an additional application of ketchup.

Ms. Ann Jordan
c/o Sullivan
125 Ackerman Avenue
Emerson, New Jersey 07630

Re: Docket No. 400559/74

Dear Ms. Jordan:

This will acknowledge receipt of your letter dated July 8, on the above captioned case.

Our records show that this case was "Adjourned in Contemplation of Dismissal" under section 170.56 of the Criminal Procedure Law of the State of New York and was Dismissed on July 5, in Part 3 of our Court.

Accordingly, the records are sealed and there is no official record of this arrest. Copies of the sealing order are sent to the Division of Criminal Justice Services in Albany advising that this case has been sealed and ordering that department to expunge their records on this particular arrest.

As a result, you revert back to the status which you previously held before this arrest. In other words, if you had no prior arrest record before this arrest, with the sealing of this case your status reverts back to one of no previous record and if you are asked by law enforcement agencies or personnel

departments, you can state that you have never been arrested.

However, if you should be arrested in the future on a violation of the drug laws, a revealing order, signed by a judge, can be sent to Albany, and the sealed case can be opened up on that order, setting aside the sealing order.

Therefore, since this case in point has been sealed and there is no official record of this arrest, we cannot issue a transcript record on this case.

In view of this, we are returning your one dollar fee which is enclosed herein.

Very truly yours,

John D.Luby
Asst. Court Clerk

"Oh, that's great. I'm free!" she exuded, her reading concluded. "But where are my mug shots and my fingerprints? I was supposed to get them back when the case was dismissed."

"I'll write them again and ask, if ya want."

"Geez, can ya beat that. I'm free. You're not even my guardian any more." She leaned across her empty plate with a wink. "You realize you've been screwin' your guardianship? Is that what I am, what I was? Is that what you call it, a guardianship? Shame on you."

"I've been screwin' around with a high school student, sweetie, and I think that would get me into more trouble than screwin' around with a guardian. Come to think of it, maybe not. I don't know."

"But now, ya have nothing to worry about. You're not my guardian any more, and you're not my teacher any more."

"Right, right, nothing to worry about. I'm just shacked up in New Hampshire with a teenager impersonating Mrs. Sullivan in a dormitory at a college I'm supposed to be visiting at Board of Education expense while my wife and two kids are home in New Jersey. There's nothing to worry about."

"It sounds serious when ya put it that way. Is it?"

"That's not the worst of it."

"What else?" she pressed, caught momentarily in the grip of the situation I had outlined so grimly.

"We're gonna miss our own party if we don't get the hell outta here!"

"Ohhhhh, you're always bustin' my ass."

"Well, I'm still thinkin' about that, too."

CHAPTER 27

A party.....a nightgown.....beauty and the beast....."I wanna be your woman and your lover, but I wanna be your baby, too...," a night together.....and a yucky surprise.....

Six of them—nice kids they were, too—came down from camp, Ann and I hosting them in our humble dwelling, the bold "carpeting" of our boudoir prompting risqué remarks of assignation and wall-to-wall carnality. They knew. Who wouldn't, even if they didn't notice the remaining wetness on the third mattress in the second row?

The eight of us pranced like spring-legged children on a backyard trampoline. We finally settled in a corner, sitting Indian-style with our backs against the wall. We smoked, laughed, and sang Peter, Paul, and Mary songs to the mellow strings of two guitars, simultaneously polishing off a case of Miller High Life, two half-gallons of wine, and a mountain of pretzels, potato chips, and M & M's. We all had a good time.

They left before midnight, slipping out in the darkness like Bedouins on the roam. As high as they were on alcohol and grass, they departed with remarkable decorum, the case of empties and a box of crumpled bags and drained bottles in hand. The slam of the front door behind them echoed down the hallway, proving departure, leaving silence, and signaling to both of us the begin of our awaited night together.

"I'm glad they came, but I'm glad they're gone," she said with the lunge of an uncaged lioness at my belt, pushing me backward.

"I hope they get back all right," I said as I flopped back groggily onto the mattress.

"They will. Sheila's driving. She didn't have much. Don't worry. I wanna feel your tongue."

"It's not in *there*, you cumquat," I said with a laugh as she started to unzip my pants.

"I know, I know, I'm not that ripped. I want *that*, too. C'mon, gimme," she implored.

"I wanna lick, too," I beseeched with equal fervor.

I obliged her requests and she mine, half on one mattress—her stroking massage accompanied by a whispered chant of welcoming return to her hand and promised pledges of release and relief—and half on the other, my purred murmur within the inverted scissor-lock of her legs repeated with each licking. I went right to the button, then to the surrounding softness, and then greedily but gently back to the kinked knot, urging and demanding its display.

Too much we enjoyed our separate delights—too much to bring them together. Too fast her clenched hand whipped—too determined, too fevered, and too good. Too coaxing and ruffling my tongue flicked—too swift, too heated, too feathery, and too good. Too late it was to mate our pleasured organs.

"Squirt, you cock. Give it up, damn you!"

"Squirt, bitch!"

No enigma was there in the urgency of our mutually expressed demands of the other's manipulated parts, no mum result. The entangled tumble of our inflamed entities was a sonorous address that rumbled down the empty corridors with tattling disclosure, a telegraphed announcement of celebrated release, a sally of passion frozen too long, now thawed in splashing, flowing, three-dimensional harmony.

"Oh, ohhhh," we blended in unison, twisting and wresting with wont, contented but not consumed, our respective stems still alive and electric.

"Jesus.....Christ. How'd I go without this for so long?" I panted. "Oh, nice."

"What.....a.....blast," she exhaled. "Did I drown you down there?"

"Damn, damn, too good. Damn, I wanted to be inside you."

"Next time, baby. Oh, what a—"

"Here, come up here. Let me hold you," I pleaded as she wiggled free of our upside down intertwine.

"I think we shot two mattresses at the same time," she quipped. "Let's roll over one to the left."

We clung to each other as I pushed with my foot, and we rolled to the left like a gnarled log in a sluice, me on top of her, then she on top of me, to a final uncoupling sprawl that left us side by side on our backs, roaring with laughter.

"Ya wanna get the blankets?" I choked.

"No, you," she sputtered. "I can't stop laugh—Oh, Christ, I gotta pee. Where do ya pee around here?"

"*Not* around here. Down the hall."

"Okay, be right back."

"Oh, sweet sleep. What a fuckin' day," I moaned as she fumbled through her suitcase and shoulder bag. "I'm exhausted. Shit, five hours of drivin'."

"When I get back you can hold me, and we can go to sleep together," she entreated as she crawled over the mattresses on her hands and knees, her bare ass a full moon in the dim light.

Reluctant as I was to have her take leave of her nestle in my arms, I knew I had to fashion the linens and blankets into some semblance of a bed. I raised myself on my elbows and finally to my feet as I heard her scamper to the bathroom. Unsteady in the soft mattress, I moved ploddingly to arrange a sleeping spot near the window. My slow-motioned and inexperienced effort would have pained any chambermaid worth her salt but, hell, her skill, too, would be put to test had she been stoned, spent, and called upon to balance herself on a sponge cake surface and hop like an Indian with a hotfoot between the sunken dips of mattress buttons.

Christ, how long did it take her to pee? I had a whole bed made.

I patted the pillows in place, looking back to the doorway only as I sensed her presence. She stood silently at the entrance, her hair now freed from its tieback and brushed to a shining luster—still slightly frizzy from static—the lace, ruffled neckline of her white negligee plunging deeply between her soft swells, the nightgown's flowing pleats falling from midriff to ankles.

"Can I come in?" she inquired softly. "I know I'm an old lady in a nightgown, but I'd like to spend the night with you, just the same—if it's okay."

Beauty and the beast. An unholy sight I was in contrast. In the sag of a naked mattress, I stood nude, as limp as a dead fish, the glare of a camp lantern highlighting the embarrassment on my face and every imperfection of my body, the careless arrangement of sheets too large and blankets too small at my feet.

"And who might you be?" I queried in hollow joke, caught off guard and entrapped by my own ignorant remark about nightgowns and old ladies.

"I'm your cunt, stupid," she ridiculed, lifting the length of her negligee to her waist with the two-handed hoist a construction worker would use to empty a bag of sand into a wheelbarrow. "See, recognize me?"

"I'm sorry, sweet," I repented. "Sometimes I'm just a mental midget. You look beautiful. C'mon, c'mon in."

With dainty steps she tiptoed over the mattresses in her bare feet, and I met her with outstretched arms to steady her.

"You're not a mental midget," she said as she put her arms around my neck. "But, sometimes you don't give me a chance to be all I wanna be for you. I wanna be your woman and your lover, but I wanna be your baby, too. Like tonight, I wanna curl up close and go to sleep in your arms like a baby."

"Of all times to wanna be a baby. Ya look more like a woman tonight than ever," I said in compliment.

"But this makes me *feel* like a baby," she explained with patience as she stepped back and ran her hands down over the front of the negligee. "It's pretty and soft and covering and cozy and cuddly, like a baby in wraps. So, let me be your baby. C'mon, turn out the lantern and let me snuggle close with your arms around me under the blanket. C'mon, come and hold me."

Twice her age I was but less than half as smart. *Still* she was teaching me how to love her. I turned out the lantern.

"I love you, sweet baby," I whispered as we slipped under the crudely arranged blankets.

I found her lips and kissed her tenderly before nuzzling her head to my chest, enfolding her in my arms and wrapping my leg over hers.

"And I love you, my sweet man. Let's sleep together, forever."

"Good night, my love," I said, kissing the top of her head and squeezing her close.

"Good night, my love."

****

I found out what New England travel brochures *don't* tell you about New England nights. You can freeze you ass off, even in the middle of the summer.

I must have gone out like a light, and I don't believe I had the energy to move a muscle thereafter.

When I awoke before daybreak—it must have been about four in the morning, still pitch black—it came with a shivering tremble and an awareness that the corner of the blanket I clutched over my shoulder was the only corner which still covered me. Ann was, wouldn't you know it, sleeping like a baby, like the baby she so longed to be tonight, under a pile of blankets, lying on her side, her back pressed against me, knees drawn up, the roundness of her rear snugly fitted into the contoured shallow of my midsection, my thigh a curved shelf around the bottom of her butt—spoons arranged tandem.

Pleased I was that she had sought my body for her warmth and comfort—staunch and steady protection from the night chill—some recompense, at least, for the fact that her tuck against me and her pull of *my* share of the blankets had left my hindquarters inelegantly exposed in frigid uncover. I considered how I might correct the inequity without disturbing her slumber, my first inept attempt at pulling not a very successful effort except in provoking a groan of annoyance and an unconscious toss of her arm. Stuck. Barely could I move any part of my body without disrupting our points of contact, an almost unbroken chain of touches stretching from my chest to my legs—warm contacts, wanted contacts, contacts I appraised one by one, my attention diverted from external shiver to a focus on a growing internal warmth. Upward pressure applied to her bottom by lifting my thigh produced a stir, and I felt the matted patch, the grassy lawned entrance to a fine estate.

Where was her nightgown? Long and flowing it had been when she had stood in the dim light of the doorway. Now, in the darkness, the blackness of night, only my mind found it, its pleated length slipped high to her hips, the gathered folds of white satin and lace a snowcapped mountain rising in billowed drifts above a flat plateau. Further below, the fertile valley, the palmed sanctuary of a tropical oasis, awaited.

I wrapped my arm around her, my hand grazing the tipped fullness that lolled in lazy float over the lace-trimmed plunge of her negligee. I continued to the lower swell which nested within the clutch of clinging, pocketed satin. She moved with dexterous mission, unwinding herself as a stream flowing down a mountainside, rolling, wandering, twisting, yawning, stretching, spreading, yielding the delta, the blankets kicked aside, her svelte legs in triangle.

"Oh, my love," she murmured in the spell of half-wake.

"My baby," I breathed, reaching for her crux.

"Oh, God, I want you," she whispered.

"My little Snow White in a nightgown—I love you."

"Please love me. Love your baby. Hold me, hold—Oh, ohhhh."

My finger plied her tenderness, soft as doeskin, wet with dribble.

"Be in me. My nightgown—come to me. Oh, yes, please. My nightgown—"

Her nightgown? I didn't understand. Did she want her nightgown off? I could barely see it, obscured in the darkness but indisputably present, a gather of softness around her waist, ineffectual in its cover, but indispensable in its illusion. Blindly, I gripped two handfuls of the silky material at her sides as I twisted my kneel within her lie, my thighs cradling her buttocks, raising her hotness.

"I love you, I love you, I love you, sweet man. Inside me," she cried.

"I'm there, my sweet. Into my baby, in.....all my love," I babbled as I tugged at the crumble of nightgown, lifting as a sling, pulling her to the press of my loins.

"Oh, yes. Oh, yes. Oh, yes, yes," she sobbed.

I clamped my mouth to hers, interrupting her exhilarated yelps. I felt her hands beneath me, squeezing the puffs of her chest, roughing their appendages, pulling and tugging, as I rocked in and out, corkscrewing and rotating.

"Come with me, come together with me, with me, baby, now."

"Now, my man, with me, now."

"Now. Now."

"Now—NOW."

"Nowwwwwwwww.....Yes!"

****

"Oh, shit! Fuckin' shit! Charlie!" she screamed. "Damn! God damn mother-fucker!"

I bolted upright in the brightness, shocked awake by her bloodcurdling outburst.

"What's the matter, what's the matter? What happened?"

"Damn it. God damn it!"

"What's wrong, what's—" I sputtered, groping for my glasses and turning to where she sat at the foot of our makeshift bed.

"You're not gonna fuckin' believe this," she cried.

"What the hell happened, hon?"

"Ugh," she shrieked with disgust. "Oh, what a fuckin' mess."

"What happened," I questioned again as I tried to rub my eyes open and awake.

"I got—Oh, shit, Charlie. Oh, Christ, it's on you, too," she said, stretching toward me. "Oh, I'm sorry, honey. I got my fuckin' period. Oh, it's all *over* you. I'm sorry, babe. I guess last night, before we—what a mess, what a fuckin' mess."

I looked down at the brownish smear on my leg as she leaned with the corner of a tissue and tried to erase the dried stain. On my hand, too, it was, my middle finger showing a faint crusted circle above the last knuckle.

"It's okay, it's okay, hon."

"It's in your hair, too," she motioned with a downward point.

The rust-colored residue matted in the hair above my slack member attested to a penetration of extent within the blood flow of her menses during our nocturnal escapade. A super fuck it was, achieved in a blood bath of mucosal discharge into which we had simultaneously expended our climatic juices. God, it was great. We had slipped so effortlessly and slid so freely in the warm anointment of our creamy fluids and the slippery paste of other oily lubricants unknown to us at the time.

"Don't worry about it. Clean yourself up," I consoled.

"It really did a job on the mattress, right through the sheet. I'm sorry, hon."

"I love you, sweet, very much, you know?"

"How the hell could I get my period?" she started in disbelief. "It's so fuckin' late, I thought I was gonna skip one."

"Well, ya got it, that's for sure. You got it, I got it, the mattress got it….." I listed with lightness, "…..my finger got it, the sheet got it—"

"Your cock got it," she added with an embarrassed laugh. "It's a good thing you didn't go down for a lick—ugh, messy, messy."

"I probably wouldn't have known the difference," I shrugged.

"Until it was too late," she chuckled. "What the hell time is it, anyway?" she asked, still trying to swab encrusted smudges from my legs and hers. "Oh, look at my poor nightgown. It's a mess, too."

I had wedged my watch with my cigarettes and lighter between two mattresses to the left of my pillow, and now I reached for it.

"Ten after.....eight," I replied. "Oh, wow. Good morning, love. How are ya, this bright and sunny morning? Gimme a kiss. Sleep good last night?"

"Yuck, don't kiss me. I'm a mess. But, yeah, like a baby. I slept like a baby—just beautiful. What about you?"

"Like a bug in a rug. Warm and cozy....."

CHAPTER 28

We said goodbye to our dormitory room and headed out to follow the plans Ann had made for a glorious day in New Hampshire.....

"I've had a glorious day here in New England!"

F.D.R. said it first, in the midst of his presidential campaign against Wendell Willkie in 1940. I echoed the sentiments with just as much gusto—to slightly less applause—on the evening after our dormitory stay.

It hadn't been as much fun dragging a dozen mattresses back to their respective rooms as it had been assembling them for our one-night stand. And the crumpled wad of soiled sheets we stuffed into a paper bag and carried out to the van the following morning somehow lacked the freshly starched, folded neatness with which they had crunched the night before. Our total effort, in fact, at cleaning up and moving out would have been a depressing and tedious chore had its conclusion not been known to herald the start of a day that Ann had planned with exciting activities—too many, of course—for us to enjoy and share in the New Hampshire countryside she knew so well and loved so much.

I took her picture as she stood by the front door of the dorm, her hand on the latch, in the yellow T-shirt she reluctantly had worn after a sniff test of its underarm areas—not the best, but acceptable. There were no jokes this time about taking her picture in her nightgown. There was no talk about the nightgown at all.

"Christ, you'd think I was cherry," she had bristled with dismay before stuffing the soiled peignoir with its harsh reminders into the bag with the sheets.

We drove from the campus, heading north, the van bouncing along the tree-lined country road as if in happy sync with our spirits, lighthearted and free of care.

"Geez, there are so many things I wanna show ya, so many things I wanna do," she bubbled.

"Well, it's a perfect day to do them," I exclaimed. "God, it's so crystal clear."

"It's always like that up here. Every day it's clear and clean—no smog, no smoke, no polluted stink—fresh and invigorating. Usually it's crisp in the morning but nice after the sun is up a little. I just love it."

"Fuckin' cold at night," I reminded. "It's as cold as a cue ball in an ice bucket, as cold as a witch's tit."

"Ya get used to it."

I gave mental question to her response. I wondered to myself how long it might take someone to "get used to it," and whether it wasn't more a matter of tolerance or endurance than of acclimation, but I held my reservations within, content to listen to her excited outlining of the day's planned events.

"We can stop and get things for a picnic. Keep your eyes open for a store, okay? I don't know this area that well. And then we can go to Sunapee State Park and take the gondola ride to the top of Mount Sunapee, or to King Ridge—that's the ski center—facing Mount Kearsage. Then maybe we can rent some horses at Bit of Heaven Stables and go riding over by Little Sunapee Lake or go back to Elkins Beach—ya know, where Dede and I met you yesterday. That's on the eastern end of Pleasant Lake; camp is on the north shore. I'm gonna get rid of this stinkin' shirt, okay? I brought my purple pull over," she said as she skinned the yellow T-shirt over her head. "You like that one, right?"

"Be my guest."

"And I wanna show ya the Barn Playhouse in New London. Someday….." she mused, as I tried to divide my attention between the curves of the winding road and the sun-kissed curves of her upper torso, ".....someday, I'm gonna be on that stage. And, oh, maybe we can go over to Otter Pond," she said without a break as I watched her cute titties disappear too soon beneath the pulled down cover of her purple top. "Then we can have dinner at Sunapee Harbor. There's a great place to eat there, right on the water, and the food is to die for. I don't know if we're gonna have time for everything. Damn, I wish I could bring ya into camp and show ya my bunk. Well, at least we can drive by and you can look from the road. I'd *really* like to take a sunfish out on the lake and go sailing with you."

"Maybe we can leave that for next time," I said, cutting short her list, sure her agenda already had extended beyond the time we had available. I mean, we couldn't do everything.

But we did. We managed to do it all, or almost all—the horseback riding, Elkins Beach, the Playhouse,

Otter Pond, the drive past camp, the ski center, our picnic lunch, dinner at Sunapee Harbor, and the gondola ride—6,800 feet to the top of Mount Sunapee in an enclosed aluminum and glass, four-passenger car strung on a cable. Stoned and scared. She was stoned, and I was both. I'm *terrified* of heights—always have been. Can't stand going up and looking down. I hate airplanes, the Empire State Building, trams, lifts, and gondolas. But, there I was, sitting across from her in that dangling box, gripping the varnished wooden, slat seat under me and trying not to look out at the passing treetops—shit. I took her picture, more to divert my attention from the steep incline we were traveling than to record the event.

"Wait 'til we get to the top. You're gonna die….."

"Please don't say that!" I gasped.

I thought I was gonna die *gettin' to* the top.

"…..You're not gonna believe the view," she gushed excitedly.

I thought we'd *never* get to the top. I thought I might throw up on the way. Holy, good night—I *knew* it either was the end of the world or the end of the line when the damn thing came to a clanking, jolting, rocking stop and my stomach flipped.

"Christ," I gasped a few moments later, my feet firmly planted on God's good, green earth. "Wow!"

It *was* a spectacular view, and *so* thankful I was to be out of that fucking cage, too.

Spread below was an unending stretch of rolling green in all directions, blue splotches of lake painted in the distance, a sun-drenched panorama of hills and valleys canopied by azure so expansive it took my breath away. When we later strolled around the bushes and grass at the top, our picnic treats consumed and the relax of a sunbath completed, there didn't seem to be a good place where we could lie together unseen, although there couldn't have been another human being for miles. And, crap, she had her period, anyway.

We made the return trip to the bottom—an eternity—back to the van on shaky legs and away to the next of our adventures, tripping along through happy hours, playing out the day, filling it with togetherness, the time flying in too fast approach of the inevitable.

Our waters edge dinner was as delicious as she had promised it would be, but it ended too quickly. Our walk by the water after dessert went too quickly, as well.

Despite the day's busy schedule, we had enjoyed an unhurried, leisurely pace, moving from one entertainment to another without rush, enjoying the sun, relaxing with deep breaths, holding hands, touching each other's bare skin with gentle brushes, remembering, trying to remember—tender touches—not to forget, never to forget.

But now, everything was going too quickly. The night was advancing with too much speed. Too soon the time was coming to return, her to camp and me to the murderous ache of a lonely road home with still too many things left to say. Everything was happening too fast, ending too soon, and hurting too much.

"Did ya have a good time, today, sweetheart?" she asked, her face pressed against my chest, her voice barely audible.

We stood in the darkness, leaning against the side of the van, the lake's edge a few steps in front of us, the water still and sleek, an outspread of black velvet that reflected a snaky ribbon of moonlight through the overhanging trees along the shore and disappeared in the black wrap of distance. I knew I was going to fall apart.

" 'I've had a glorious day here in New England!' " I exuded with feigned exuberance, a robust effort to put lightness in a moment weighted with heavy charge. But it wasn't light enough, not good enough. The tears streamed down my face, and I felt her tremble, heard her soft sobs, felt her shiver in my arms as I squeezed, imaging her strained through my skin and absorbed, consumed within my body, her being one with mine, us as one….. *no distance between…..*

"I love you so much, sweet man. I don't want ya to go."

"I know," I choked. "Me, either. I don't wanna go."

Our kiss was instinctive and spontaneous, sliding and skidding. Our cheeks were slippery surfaces, warm in their press together, cool in their exposure to the evening chill. Our eyelashes glistened the moisture of our heartache. Our mouths tasted salty droplets on tongues too wounded to fight. Our lips were cracked and dry in the midst of a summer night's shower. We stood, bare tree trunks within a lush tropical rain forest, shells of our former splendor, reduced, despite the majestic blaze of the day's fire, to smoldering remains, ashes being extinguished in a nighttime downpour of emotions, our hearts heavy with the unpreventable parting that loomed before us.

"Look, hon," I begged pleadingly, "when I drive you back to camp, ya know, I'm just gonna stop and let you out. I'm not—I can't—" I stammered. "Jesus Christ."

"I know, babe. I can't handle it, either. I don't wanna say goodbye. Just drop me off. I'll go."

That's how it happened. I slowed as we rounded the bend and let the van coast to its inevitable stop. I stared straight ahead—never turned—as she picked up her shoulder bag, her suitcase, the guitar, the paper bag, the two pillows. She got out, her hands full—used her behind to slam the door shut—and left, the glare of the van's headlights in inconsiderate strip of her dignity, her tear-streaked face and the slumped shoulders of her dispirited body revealed in haloed profile as she crossed the road with quick paces and disappeared into the shadows. I'll never forget it. It was a pathetic picture. Overburdened physically and emotionally spent, she did what she had to do while I sat motionless and did what I had to do, sit—fucking sit—helpless, empty, brokenhearted, and crying—and let her go, happy, beyond tears, for a glorious day spent in New England.

CHAPTER 29

Our telephone lifeline.....and Ann's news of another attack on the Eleventh Commandment, this one including some real surprises.....

"Hello? What took ya so long?"

"Oh, I'm so glad you're still there," I heard her voice crackle.

"Hi, babe. I'm still here. I didn't give up on ya."

"There's only one phone in the office here. I know I said I'd call at twelve-thirty, but there was a line. I was afraid you'd think I forgot. I thought you might leave. I guess twelve-thirty isn't a very good time."

Sweltering in the August heat, I stood at the familiar pay phone at the busy intersection near the Hillsdale-Washington Township border. The thought of leaving really hadn't crossed my mind. I had filled my wait of a quarter of an hour with the idle clocking of the traffic light to see how many seconds it stayed red in each direction and how many cars could make it through before the change. Earlier, the itch of impatience had prompted me to dial the camp number several times, the repetitive buzz of a busy signal the only response. I surmised the problem and settled into a monotonous stroll up and down the sidewalk in front of the Fin and Claw Restaurant, the phone only steps away. I had wanted to cross the street to the service station on the opposite corner and get a soda from their machine, but I couldn't take the chance of missing her ring.

"We can change the time. We can go back to what it was before. Eleven-thirty was better for you, anyway. But it's good to hear ya, babe. How ya doin'?" I asked.

"I really miss you, hon. Ya get my letter?"

"Yeah, the day before yesterday. What's the big deal, Sunshine?"

"No big deal. It's wild, though. You're gonna die! I didn't wanna take the time to write it. I wanted to *tell* ya. You ready for a shocker? I mean, a really unbelievable shock?"

I didn't know what to expect. "Something incredible to tell you" was all her letter had said. Sometimes her degree of shock depended on how much weed she had inhaled.

"Go ahead."

"There's this girl up here. Her name is Sarah. I've known her for a couple of years."

"Yeah?" I responded, the receiver sticky against my ear.

"She goes out with one of her teachers."

She must have been smokin' a hell of a lot.

"Surprise! What else is new?"

"No, listen. She's got pictures….."

"Pictures?"

"…..of the two of them together, makin' love together—photos, photographs."

I mopped the perspiration from my forehead and stuffed the damp handkerchief into my pocket. It was hotter than hell—a great day to pick blackberries along the Parkway. That was my plan for the afternoon—pick some juicy ones, take my shirt off, catch some rays, get some color. Now, what the hell was this photos stuff all about?

"These are real photos?" I finally responded. "Are you sure?"

"Of course, I'm sure," she ruffled with annoyance at my doubting question. "I'm positive. I saw them with my own eyes. I saw his picture in the yearbook, and I saw him with her. I don't mean one or two pictures. I'm talkin' about a whole stack, maybe twenty-five or thirty—more."

"Holy cow! Makin' love?"

"Fucking, fucking. And, wait—with another girl, too," she whispered.

"Another girl? With her? Hold on. Whaddya mean? Another girl with her or another girl with him?"

"Her friend—Sarah's friend—Freida. Sarah's got pictures of her—herself—with him, and she's got pictures of Freida with him," she explained laboriously. "You should see them."

"Jesus, what the hell did they do, take turns?" I asked, covering my exposed ear as a Tanis cement truck idled noisily at the light, its center ring rotating with the slow rumble of an overloaded stomach. Now, I didn't want to miss a word.

"Uh huh."

"Holy shit. Is there anybody around? Can anybody hear ya up there?"

"No, everybody's gone. I can talk. Sometimes people come in, though—"

"They took turns fuckin', and they took turns takin' pictures?"

"Yeah, fuckin', suckin', everything—ass fucking, playing with themselves, jerking him off—close-ups."

"I can't believe it! And she's up there showin' these pictures around? Jesus," I exclaimed in amazement.

"I'd *never* believe it, but I *saw* them. Rachel and I both saw them. She showed 'em to the both of us. You should see them."

I wondered how they'd compare with the visual images my imagination already had conjured.

"I wouldn't mind."

"It's really weird. I mean, it's somebody I know. It's a real person, sittin' right there next to us in my bunk. There wasn't a dry seat in the place," she laughed.

"Wow."

"She showed us these pictures of her getting layed….."

"God damn," I gulped.

"…..and then Feida's gettin' it and Sarah's takin' the pictures. And then he's comin' all over Freida's tits—"

"And I thought we were bad!"

"Charlie! We're not bad. We're not like *that*. Don't even say that. Don't even joke about it!"

"Whose idea was it to take pictures?"

"I don't know. We were so shocked we didn't ask anything or say anything. Can you imagine her showin' us, showin' anybody? I never said anything about us. She just volunteered, just showed us outta the blue. Ya can see everything," she expressed with hushed astonishment.

"How can ya get pictures like that developed? Isn't it illegal or something? They weren't Polaroids. They were bigger."

"He didn't send them to Kodak, that's for sure. Ya don't think Dede mighta said somethin', ya know, about us?"

"No, no way. I'm sure," she ruffled.

"They color or black and white?"

"Geez," she hesitated. "I don't remember. No, they're not color. They're black and white."

"That's what I thought. He probably had a friend develop and print. Anybody who has a darkroom can do it. Maybe he did it himself," I offered in explanation. "Where are they from, Sarah and Freida? Are they from up there or around here?"

"Long Island, somewhere. I'm not sure where, but I know they're from Long Island. And I know Sarah's a junior. I think Freida is, too. I think they both graduate next year."

"Jesus. Any chance—"

"What?"

I hesitated.

"What, babe," she repeated.

"Any chance you could get your hands on the pictures?"

"Char-lie! Don't be an idiot! How can I get my hands on them—and for what?"

"Just curious."

"God, you'd die. They're unbelievable. Babe, I gotta go. I'm on duty at the waterfront."

"Okay, I love ya, sweet."

"Love ya, too."

We concluded our conversation hastily, and I put the receiver back on the hook. I checked the coin return. I always check a pay phone, doesn't everybody? I'm always hopeful that the final click of a completed call will trigger a slot machine windfall of dispensed silver. No luck this time. I turned to the sidewalk, empty handed.

Engrossed in thought, a little wobbly in the knees, I walked to the parked van, off the road a few yards from the corner. Shit, the Eleventh Commandment sure was taking a pounding. And the fuckin' asshole had another kid taking his picture! It boggled my mind.

It was hard to believe that I once thought Ann and I were unique. Unique? We were babes in the woods!

Geez, my handkerchief wasn't the only damp bulge in my jeans.

CHAPTER 30

With Ann back from camp and I back at the regular high school, our loving resumed.....Ann's talk of trying some coke with her friend, Terri, sparks a flashback to Ann's outrageous suggestion that I engage in a very questionable ceremony.....

Most people hate to see summer go. Not me. Not this summer. It couldn't happen fast enough to please me.

Despite my preference for warm weather—the warmer the better—and despite my love of vacation time—the longer the better—I was tired of summer. I was tired and bored. I had the time—the time to relax, to enjoy, and to be happy—but I didn't have the person. I had a stack of letters. Ann wrote with true regularity, her letters a diary-like chronicle of her daily activities, thoughts, and feelings. I had a pay phone, its distinctive ring able to make my heart flutter, its hungry money slot capable of eating up my rolls of quarters on alternate occasions when I called her. And I had beautiful memories of a trip to New Hampshire. I had re-run the mental tapes of that delightful experience with the fanatic ardor of an Elvis fan spinning treasured platters until the point of near melt. But, damn, I didn't have the one thing I really wanted.

The last days of August dragged, their virtue appreciated only in their passing, the time of Ann's return more imminent with each penciled cross within the consecutively numbered squares of a calendar sheet. Plans for me to make a second trip to New Hampshire never materialized. Our sunfish sail on Pleasant Lake would have to wait until next year when, surely, Ann again would return to be a Kearsarge bunk counselor and water ski instructor. As summer closed, our final exchange of letters and telephone calls planned her arrival, our reunion, and, at long last, a resumption of our loving.

We celebrated her return appropriately and then gradually settled into routines and settings both new and old to the both of us.

The tag days of summer which preceded autumn saw Ann, now out of school, working full time for her father behind the counter at the drug store or behind the wheel making deliveries and hustling tips, with time off for trips to the City for an audition or a tryout, an ounce of good stuff, or a copy of *The Village Voice* as soon as it hit the streets on Wednesdays.

Ann's weekly voice lessons in Tenafly and drama classes in New York kept her tuned for performances with a number of community theatre groups, each week of the fall and winter season sprinkled with tryouts, rehearsals, and show dates.

Me? I was back in the regular high school, back to the old office, the old desk, the old thing, but with new students—some sophomores and some seniors—who could see me as often as they wished and for as long as they wanted without raising eyebrows, suspicion, or hell, and without anyone thinking I was after their bodies.

I hadn't thought I'd miss the A-School, and I didn't. It opened on schedule, the portables becoming the home base rather than the annex, the district judge's order still standing, the church basement no longer available. A summer's search for another suitable location had proven fruitless. I still drove kids home after school. I still—not as frequently as in the A-School, but often enough—went to lunch with a student. I still stuffed my briefcase every Friday afternoon with left-over paperwork for the weekend. Although I don't think the administrators at the high school approved, I still wore jeans. And, thankfully, I didn't have the nonsense of the A-School with which to contend—no handyman chores, nobody telling me to "fuck off," fuck myself, or fuck their asses, no demands for taxi service, no Town Meeting hassles, no Fran, and nobody on my ass for physical education credit for shoveling horse shit and cleaning stalls at a stable. I forget who had asked for that, but someone had.

The best part of the A-School—*that* I had, only a telephone call away. When the pay phone rang at the store, she knew it was Charlie-nut. Who else called a public pay phone in a drug store? If she wasn't there, Florence would answer. A part-time cosmetologist, Florence didn't know my identity, but she knew I was calling for Ann. She knew the game, and she was a safe person with whom I could leave a message. In an ironical twist of fate, Florence's son later became my counselee at the high school and, on Parent Conference Night, Florence sat in my office discussing her son's behavior and academic status, me face-to-face for the first time with the person from the other end of the line, she unaware of the numerous times in the past she had spoken to me, Ann's secret lover, on the telephone.

Ann made the high school a frequent stop on her delivery route. Up Elizabeth Avenue she'd whip in the white, compact, delivery car. She'd park at the curb, reach out the window and peel the "Hometown Pharmacy" stick-on sign from the car door, chuck the plastic sign in the back seat, check her hair in the mirror, hop out, bop up the central outside stairs to the second floor entrance, and burst through the Guidance Office doorway with a flourish. Routine arrival. Without fail, she'd stop at Joan Bermingham's desk and chat for a moment with my secretary before heading for my office. If I wasn't in, sometimes she'd wait and sometimes she'd go, leaving a note behind on my desk, usually something silly signed, "Me." If I happened to be busy with a student, she'd sit outside my office door and flip through college catalogs until I was free. If she found me alone, she'd bounce in, close the door, and throw her arms around my neck. One day in late September she came in with her customary hug just before lunchtime.

"Wait," she said excitedly before even releasing her grip. "I'll be back in a sec. Wait," and she was out the door as quickly as she had come in.

"What the hell was that all about?" I quizzed upon her return a few minutes later.

"I went to the girls' room," she whispered sheepishly. "I wanted to take off my undies. C'mon, let's go to lunch. I have the dessert."

We went to the deli at the Plaza for sandwiches. We parked on the street in broad daylight, had lunch, and then enjoyed dessert in the back of the van.

"You coulda taken your undies off here, ya know. You didn't hafta go to the girls' room."

"I know," she said with a devilish smile. "Just wanted to give ya somethin' to think about. Didn't want ya spending too much time with your tuna fish."

My return to the high school was not without its surprises. As aware as I had been that A-School kids were viewed by students and teachers at the regular high school as "different," "oddballs who carried their books in knapsacks on their backs," "long-haired hippies," and "flower children," I was shocked at the extent and depth of negative feelings categorically directed toward A-Schoolers. The more frequently pinned labels to A-School kids were "fuckin' weirdoes," "freaks," and "druggies," although most A-Schoolers were talented and creative college-bound students who were no more into the drug scene than their regular school counterparts.

Neither had the A-School teachers been spared the unkindness of labeled generalities—"coddlers," "bleeding-heart liberals," and "elitists"—this despite the respected status we each had enjoyed within our respective departments as well as within the overall school community before we had made the move to the A-School. The labels were grossly unfair. As much as I hated Fran, she was no coddler. She and Marilyn had more the characteristics of task masters, pushing kids to perform and produce and having little tolerance for slackers or goof-offs. Lisa and Ben were reserved, unpretentious, and down-to-earth, hardly elitists. Janis was so straight it must have pained her to sit down, and I took shit from nobody.

Imagine my surprise at finding myself welcomed back by some professional colleagues as a hero of sorts who had "seen the light" and returned to the tried, true, and tested educational pathways. But, that wasn't the case at all.

I continued to espouse alternative education concepts. I continued to resist the assembly line process of the traditionalists who regarded kids as molded automobile parts to be hammered into place and rolled out onto the streets as uniform models with few, if any, factory-installed options. I continued to believe that the realization of each student's promise and potential as an academic being and as a person required a fluid and unencumbering environment in which individual strengths and talents were provided the time, space, and encouragement needed to develop, grow, and thrive. I continued to believe that the Alternative School, while it certainly wasn't for everyone, fulfilled the unique needs of unique people who otherwise would have languished, uninspired and unchallenged.

Despite my departure from the Alternative School, I had no compunction about discussing the A-School with my counselees and encouraging them to visit the portables and see for themselves the interesting opportunities the A-School had to offer. I became the Guidance Office advocate of the A-School and helped Lisa and her committee as much as I could with their annual recruitment efforts.

****

"No mug shots and no fingerprints," I told Ann when she stopped at the school to visit on a blustery day in late October.

"Ya heard from them, huh?"

"Yeah, I heard. They say there's nothing to release. Everything is sealed up."

I handed her the letter from the Police Department, City of New York, F.P. Identification Section. She read the carelessly typed memo with its incorrect grammatical structure:

> **SUPREME COURT RULING**
>
> **NO FINGERPRINTS RETURNED IF RECORD IS SEALED; YOUR RECORD HAS BEEN SEALED BY COURT ORDER DUE TO THE CHARGE YOU WERE ARRESTED FORANDCANONLYBEREOPENED BY COURT ORDER**

"C'est la vie," she shrugged. "It really doesn't make any difference, anyway, does it?"

"Nah, I don't think so, unless you're dumb enough to get busted again. Then they'll unseal everything and reopen your case."

"If I get busted again, it's not gonna be for weed."

I had trouble reading the funny expression on her face, but there was little doubt that her words implied a threat of doings that didn't thrill me in the least.

"Oh, no?"

"I got some coke in the City, yesterday," she waivered with a blush.

"Coke? Yesterday?"

"Yeah."

"Jesus Christ! How come ya didn't say anything about that last night?"

"I know," she confessed. "I was afraid."

"Bullshit!"

"I was! I was afraid you'd be mad, and we were havin' such a good time, and it got so fuckin' late."

Shit, it *was* late. She was right about *that*. We had gone to the drive-in on Route 17 for a movie she had wanted to see. Geez, it was awful—I mean, it was *really* bad. I hadn't had much interest in it in the first place, and, after watching fifteen minutes of incoherent dribble and enough violence to start World War III, she had seen enough, too.

I turned off the sound box I had pulled through from the outside post and hung on the front side window, and we retired to the rear of the van, pulling a heap of blankets completely over us in fun, undressing and connecting in the pitch blackness of our shifting tent, playing the game of not exposing any part of our naked bodies, not even our heads, to the outside chill. Sight was not essential to the fulfillment of our act or to the collapsed sleep into which we each fell in contented aftermath, enwrapped in each other's arms, entangled in removed clothing.

Who stirred first, I don't know—maybe our waking was simultaneous—but when we both pushed our heads out from under the blankets and peered through the front curtain, we responded with equal shock. The movie screen was dark, only a half-dozen scattered cars remained in the lot, and the concession stand to our left, although still lit, was empty except for a small clean-up crew attending to close-up duties. A quick glance at my watch, her panties dangling from my wrist—sweet touch—confirmed my worst fears: the time I usually came home from the track already had passed, and it would be at least another hour before I could get out of the drive-in, take her home, and get my ass back to Emerson.

"Yeah, it was late, but you coulda told me if ya wanted. You should have, you know. Christ, it *was* late, wasn't it?" I exclaimed in temporary leave of the issue at hand. "I don't even wanna tell ya what excuse I came up with. It was so complicated I didn't understand it myself, but she bought it," I heaved with a sigh.

"I knew I shoulda told you right away, damn it," she said, angry with herself. "What an ass."

We always told each other the truth about anything and everything, and without the juvenile delay of waiting "for the right time."

"Forget it. I do the same fuckin' thing sometimes, and it pisses me off, too. So, we just keep tryin', right?"

"Ya wanna do the coke over the weekend?" she asked, pressing past the embarrassment of her delayed admission.

"Not me, man. I don't wanna touch the fuckin' stuff. You're crazy. You're fuckin' crazy."

"Ya don't think I should, either, huh?"

"I don't *think*—I *know*. That stuff is *poison*. That's not grass; it's poison, babe. Shit," I concluded with a dismayed shake of the head.

"Maybe I'll just try a little with Terri."

She bought the damn stuff. I knew she wasn't going to throw it away.

"You said you hadda stay home tonight, anyway, didn't you?" she pushed, reinforcing her case.

"Yeah, I gotta stay home tonight," I said with reluctance. "I've got some things I gotta do."

"So, maybe I'll do some with Terri—just a little. I'll be careful, really, hon, I will."

Terri was Ann's loyal but flaky friend, just spacey enough to indulge Ann's whim to try a little cocaine, just crazy enough to try a little anything. Terri was one of the few people Ann eventually had taken into her confidence about us—no feuding, this time, over the matter of trust. Terri's knowledge of us was an asset. Her willing cooperation as an agent of our conspiracy provided Ann with an explanation of her whereabouts to satisfy her parents' questions from time to time, an excusing cover for late hours and unknown destinations.

Not much mention of Terri had been made since Ann's return from camp, although I somehow knew that often, when I dropped Ann off at night, she went to Terri's to talk and smoke for a while before going home, continuing a friendship that went back years. Before the summer, however, Terri had joined Ann and me for an occasional pizza, a joint, or an ice cream cone with sprinkles at Dairy Queen. It had been friendly contacts such as these that had given rise to a very strange succession of ideas which had emanated from Ann before she left for New Hampshire.

What began as a simple suggestion that, while she was away, maybe some night I'd go to the track with Terri, ultimately evolved to the bizarre suggestion that I execute the ceremonious deflowering of Terri's virginal centerpiece. I was shocked. I pried Ann with questions, seeking some understanding, some clarifying explanation, some insight into how her mind could possibly author a proposal which I considered to be nothing less than preposterous.

Was this some kind of weird means of pardoning her absence for the summer, an apologetically offered compensation for her going away? She said it wasn't. Was it a scale-balancing overture to make right the felt wrong of *her* non-virginal status at the time of our beginnings? Again she offered a negative response. Was it some kind of syrupy and sympathetically bestowed outlet to ensure that my hornies be turned in a safe, non-threatening direction while she was away? She shook her head in denial. Was it a consent extended to obtain reciprocity, the freedom to broaden *her* sexual experiences in the event of an opportunity at camp?

We previously had addressed this latter issue, agreeing we each were to be on our own for the summer with no obligations, no strings, and no restraints. Shit, that's not what *I* wanted, but in what kind of a position was I—a married man—to argue or negotiate? My possessive nature wanted her to pledge fidelity—I mean, friends, okay, but don't fuck. But, I wasn't dumb. With her three hundred miles away, what could I say? There wasn't anything I could do about anything she did. So, I agreed. She was free to do whatever she wanted, and so was I. She sure as hell didn't have to throw Terri in to get license for herself. So, where was this absurd idea coming from?

"How the hell did this get into your head?"

I was looking for a *good* answer, a response to which I could grant some credit, some reasonable explanation, something logical—not some wishy-washy "I don't know….." or "What's wrong with that?….." reply that lacked substance or thought. I leaned forward intently and listened as she sequenced, in crisp, terse statements, an established rationale to which she obviously had given much considered preparation. I found her answer to be fully candid and forthright, evidencing not a trace of deceit or ulterior motive.

"Terri's a virgin. But only because she has strong knees. Every experience she's had with a guy has been a bummer. They don't give two shits about her; they just want to fuck her. She's been mauled like a piece of meat. She's into guys, but she needs someone to treat her decently. She needs someone to be caring and gentle. I'm her friend; I'm her best friend. I know what it's like to be treated like shit. I don't want it to happen to her. She knows you, and she likes you. She knows what kind of person you are to me. You'd be good to her and good for her. I love you very much, and I know you love me, and it's okay. That's it."

She folded her hands deliberately on her lap and stared out the window at the cars streaming down Route 17 as we sat in the front of the van, parked in the bowling alley lot.

"That's it, huh? And what about Terri?" I asked, breaking the silence of what seemed like an eternity in which I, too, had focused concentration on the onrush of headlights on the far side of the dividing island and the race of blazing red taillights, diminishing in the distance, of automobiles and trucks heading north in the adjacent lanes.

"What *about* her?" she challenged back.

"Does she know about this?"

"We've talked enough. She'd go with it."

Her answer was evasive. Firm, but evasive. Talked? About what? About me? About this asshole plan? She *would* go with it? She *will* go with it? *When—if*—Ann told her? Ann *thought* she'd go with it? Ann, stoned Ann, *thought*—shit, that didn't make any difference, did it? I didn't push for any answers.

I thought about it a lot. Not a lot, but, you know, often. And then Ann left for camp. So, maybe I thought about it a little more often after that. Look, I'm human. I couldn't *not* think about it. It didn't go away. It just kept coming back, the way fantasies do.

I called the first week in August.

"Oh, yes—Hi, Charlie."

"Hi, Terri. Ya wanna go to the track."

"Surrrrre. Want me to bring some weed?"

"Surrrrre."

We smoked before we went in. I bought programs for the both of us. I gave her a quick run-down. She said she'd been to the track before and knew how to read it, but it must've been a while ago. I was hotter than a pistol. I had four winners in the first six races. It always happens that way when I'm betting two or four bucks a race instead of a wad. But this was a fun night, and I was stoned and as excited as hell—winning does that—jumping up and down with each finish—yelling, laughing, hugging, and then racing through the crowd of losers to the cashier's window.

"We shouldn't push our luck. Wanna go now?" I suggested.

We trekked back to the van in high spirits.

"Wanna smoke some more?"

"Why not?" she whooped excitedly. "Why not?"

We climbed through the curtain to the back and got wasted, but good. Was she naïve, or was she wise and following the script? Had Ann told her? Hinted? Told her outright? Was she waiting? Was it my move? We were talking, laughing, and smoking our way along an innocent pathway leading—where? Was she ready? Shit, man, suppose she didn't know what the fuck was going on? She was playing it like she had rehearsed it a hundred times, going right along for the ride, but, who knows what she was thinking? I was ripped, my mind as thick as the shag rug upon which we sat, the moment for ritual at hand. She spoke of something humorous and trivial, too complicated for my head to grasp, what remained of my conscious state engaged in intent examination of her facial features and her body.

The fantasies had been sublime. Christ, a virgin—slip her panties off, see her bush, open her wide, see the pink, and be the first one in, the first one! So gentle I could be and would be—the caressing pluck of a sweet maraschino, honeysuckled with proper respect for the first rites of womanhood in deflowering transport from maid to "made."

And then, it was gone. The fantasy evaporated. I deliberately had parked beneath one of the tall light stanchions that rose at intervals from the parking lot pavement, and now, in the *so* well planned dimness but not darkness, I retreated and recoiled, turned back by the paucity of softness, fervor, passion, and allure. She just wasn't my type—she wasn't like Ann. I couldn't do it, not even if it were her most fervent wish, not even for the charity of a friend. I couldn't. We laughed together, she at whatever she had just said, me at the mental recall of one of Ed Richards' favorite quotations from Shakespeare:

All things that are
Are with more spirit chased
Than enjoyed.....

.....from the first or second act of *The Merchant of Venice,* I think he had said. I wasn't sure.

Terri either went home delightfully happy for the rollicking good time we had had or sadly disappointed that she was still in firm possession of her maidenhood, whether she wanted the bloody thing or not.

"I went to the track with Terri last night," I told Ann on the telephone when I called the next day.

"That's neat. You guys have a good time?"

"Yeah, yeah—had four winners in six races. We laughed, we smoked....." blah-blah, blah-blah, blah-blah.

That's all I said. And she knew. She didn't have to ask, and she didn't comment. When I didn't say anything else had happened, she knew it hadn't. The communication we employed between us—our letters and phone calls included—represented our best efforts at non-delayed disclosure, with nothing held back, nothing retained, nothing reserved or put off, no lies, no deceit, no half-truths, and no bullshit excuses. Between us, there was only honesty. Maybe because we were lying to the rest of the world, we spared each other the cruel punishment of falsehoods. The hurt of the truth was enough. Her last letter had contained her confession of not running to the shower for relief when, again, she was turned-on by the kitchen dishwasher. In her own shaky hand she told me everything—the physical and emotional feelings of going to his bunk, the arousal, the play, the tease, the fun, the hesitation, the fright, the submission, the climax, the satisfaction, the guilt, the fear—the truth. I was glad she could tell me, glad she had. What could I do—except cry and hate her fucking, fucking, fucking, fucking, FUCKING guts? I had to remind myself, over and over again, a hundred times over, that the only reason I was even privy to the truth was because she loved me so much, and she knew I loved her so much, that she trusted she could tell me. And then I was okay.

CHAPTER 31

We broke the Twelfth Commandment, mortal sin the penalty, double mortal for doing it during the school day.

"Terri got a buzz, but the damn stuff didn't do anything for me," she said with consternation as she slumped into the chair by the side of my office desk. "Nothing. I didn't feel a thing."

"Ya didn't feel anything?" I asked, unsure if I felt sorry for her or relieved. "How much did you do?"

"Not much, but enough that I shouda felt something."

It was a quarter past eleven, a slow moving morning for her. She already had finished the two deliveries she had to make before noon. On her way back to the store she had stopped at school to relate, with the dismay and alarm of a child finding out there isn't a Santa Claus, the story of her drive with Terri the night before to a rest area on Route 80 and her disappointing first experience with snorting coke.

"Maybe ya got ripped off," I suggested as a possible explanation, leaning back in my swivel chair and putting my feet up on the desk like a big shot executive. "All I need is a good cigar."

"No, I think it's good stuff. Other people have told me it's fairly common *not* to get high the first time, just disappointing. I don't know if that's true or not. Whaddya want a cigar for? You don't smoke cigars."

"I know, I know, I just—"

"But, ya know," she interrupted. "I got up this morning horny as hell. I was thinkin' it might have somethin' to do with last night—the coke, ya know."

"You're always horny."

"No, really," she said, trying to run past my bland statement. "You love it, you know you do, but, really. I'm drivin' back this morning, and I'm wigglin' around on the front seat, all hot and itchy—"

"So you're in heat and ya come here to tease me, huh?" I needled.

"No, I can take care of myself, thank you," she retorted, unhappy with my poking fun. "I don't need you."

"Ya don't need me, huh? Try lickin' yourself and then tell me ya don't need me."

I gave her the business, but I didn't want to provoke her further; I didn't want her upset. One difference of opinion about the coke was enough. Besides, she was right. I loved it when she was horny. Her arousal turned me on like a light bulb—too good to waste—and it was almost time to go to lunch.

"Ya wanna go out?"

I pulled my feet back from the desk top and leaned forward, rearranging the shuffled papers on the blue desk blotter, putting things in order, preparing to leave.

I turned to her, an assortment of scribbled notes from students still in my hands.

"Maybe," she pouted. "You really hurt my feelings, you know?" she said with crispness, before I could speak, as she straightened herself stiffly in the blue vinyl-covered chair, her hands gripping the wooden arms of the contemporary design. "I didn't come here to tease you."

"I know. I'm sorry," I said soothingly. "C'mon, we'll go have lunch. Then we can fool around some, and take care of those hornies."

"I don't wanna fool around," she said, her conflicting statement catching me half way out of my seat.

"Oh, I thought—"

I plunked back down. What the hell *did* she want?

"I wanna make love."

"Yeah, well, that's what I meant. We can go—"

"I don't wanna go to lunch. I don't wanna go out."

"We can—"

"I wanna do it here….."

"We could, uh—"

"…..then my feelings won't be hurt."

I sat frozen in place.

"Ya say, here?" I laughed in disbelief.

"Here, right here. Let's."

"Let's not, and say we did," I countered quickly, offering a little levity to buy some time.

"I…..am…..so…..fucking…..horny, Charlie," she said as she stood up. "Let's, and say we didn't."

My levity had no purchasing power. It wasn't going to buy any time at all.

"Don't be an ass. We can't—"

"Of course we can," she interrupted with huff, if not with conviction. "Mrs. Bermingham knows I'm in here, so whatcha worryin' about. She's not gonna let anyone else in, the door's closed, and nobody knows from nothin'. I was here for a half hour yesterday, and the phone didn't even ring. I am *soooo* wet."

There was no stopping her, no way to call a halt. She was like a volcano ready to erupt, a bubbling, percolating, flowing river of molten lava burying every obstacle in the path of her irreversible sweep. Threats of the dire consequences of being found out weren't going to stem the tide. My pleadings were in vain, my protests falling on deaf ears and on a bare ass as she dropped her jeans and stepped out of her underpants, boldly dangling the flimsy, pink, bikini undergarment on the door knob.

"Christ, Ann, you're not gonna be able to make a peep. We hafta be *so* fuckin' quiet."

"Fuckin' quiet, yeahhhhh."

"Listen, I'm not kidding," I warned gravely. "No noise. Oh, this is stupid! We're not gonna be able to—"

"Shhhhh," she halted my objection.

I wondered if there wasn't a *Twelfth* Commandment: "Thou shalt not fuck in the Guidance Office," mortal sin the penalty, double mortal for doing it during the school day. Crazy, I know, but no more absurd than what was happening here, this hot tamale doing the Mexican Hat Dance in the raw, patting her tuft, as furry, soft, and fluffy as a newborn kitten—now I knew how it got its cute little nickname—her rump showing the goose flesh of sudden exposure.

I gawked in disbelief at what I had not been forceful enough in opposing. She slipped between my chair and the desk and hopped her behind to a bare-ass sit on the front edge, her feet not quite to the floor.

"Pull your chair in here. C'mon, let's take care of this desk work."

It wasn't the kind of invitation one could easily refuse or summarily dismiss, even when scared shit.

I stood, letting my jeans fall in a crumpled heap around my ankles, as she leaned back on her elbows and forearms and raised her knees, planting her heels on the edge of the desk.

I remember the scene; it wasn't a scene one is likely to forget, its offering so compelling and voluntary. I remember moving to her. I remember the whiteness of her lower lip as her teeth bit sharply into it, her face screwed up in the agony of containment. I remember clamping my mouth to hers, each of us taking turns bursting the other's lungs with the blowing, heaving exhales of our exercise, our eyes blazing the silent fear that one of us would fail and explode the secret of our fucking foolishness. I remember the two of us, returned to full dress and normal blood pressure, leaving the office and passing my secretary's desk.

"Got any extra blotters stashed away, Joan?" I asked with no show of undue concern or urgency. "I hadda chuck the old one. It's really seen better times."

"Green or yellow?"

"I have a choice?"

Why was I surprised? Either in her pocketbook, under her desk, or secreted away in a bottom file drawer or an unlikely corner, Joan possessed any office supply item for which there ever could be a requisition. What she couldn't produce with an immediate turn of her chair or reach of her hand, she was able to extort with the twist of an arm, using her good natured personality and wily creativeness to call in the return of previous favors from those who had access to the school's supply room. A blotter? Nothin' to it—a piece of cake!

"Green, Joan, thanks," I called over my shoulder as Ann and I headed through the door and into the hallway.

We turned right toward the big double doors beneath the exit sign, with Ann twittering under her breath, "You bastard. That blotter never saw better times."

****

A week later I stood at the curb and waited for Ann, the midday sun surprisingly warm for the season. I watched the delivery car make the turn off Queen Anne Road and race—Jesus, she knew it was a school zone—up the hill, jolting to a quick stop in front of me.

"Look at this, will you!" she demanded angrily, pointing to her chin as I slid onto the front seat next to her. "Just look!"

I focused a concerned gaze on the inflamed swelling on the right side of her chin, turning her face to the light of the window.

"Don't *look at it!"* she snapped in contradiction.

"Ya just said—"

"Oh, shit, what am I gonna do," she whined. "It just came outta nowhere. Fuckin' zit! Got up this morning, looked in the mirror, and there it was. Where we goin'?"

"I know," I said with sympathy, motioning my hand for her to move the car. I didn't mind her picking me up in the delivery car, but I didn't like sitting in front of the school. "I get 'em, too, every once in a while. Would you believe I could get a zit at my age? Let's go to the deli."

"I have a rehearsal; I have a tryout this weekend—shit. I have a voice lesson in Tenafly—"

"Too much pizza."

"Yeah, too much pizza, too much sweet stuff, too much junk food."

"Isn't there somethin' ya can put on it—somethin' good? Your father's gotta have something in the store that you can use on it, no? Go to the left, and circle around," I prompted.

"Yeah, a prophy. I can pull a rubber over my fuckin' head so nobody can see it," she retorted with exasperation.

"That reminds me of a great joke."

"Oh, shut up, Charlie," she huffed. "This isn't a joke. There's not a damn thing I can put on it that's any good. It's all garbage. Ya can't hide it. It's *there,* so the whole fuckin' world can see I'm a pig. What deli we goin' to?"

"You're not a pig," I said, leaning over for a kiss now that we were away from the school. "Over at the Plaza so we can get stuff for a picnic."

She maneuvered the small car deftly, swinging around turns and springing along the blacktop straightaway toward the Plaza section of town with little patience for the changing traffic light through which she sped.

"Hi, hon, how are ya?" she bubbled with an abrupt change of spirit. "Sorry for the crummy greeting. I didn't mean to say 'hello' by shovin' a zit in your face. I'm just so pissed."

We stopped at the delicatessen and bought some sandwiches. The Greek deli on the *other* side of town had the best ham and swiss, sliced extra thin and stuffed between two fresh pieces of seeded Jewish rye, so I ordered my second favorite here—roast beef, lettuce, extra mayo, on a hard roll. Ann picked up a bag of potato chips to go with her turkey hero, but I caught her eye and moved my finger to the right side of my chin in reminding caution, and she placed the bag back on the rack with heart-rending reluctance and a sour puss pout. We pointed through the glass display case, first at the large tray of German potato salad, then to the coleslaw, and finally to the macaroni salad with its colorful dices of red and green peppers sprinkled throughout. We watched the woman behind the counter fill three small containers with our choices, we added two cans of soda and a bag of Pepperidge Farm goldfish, and we were off—a U-turn, up the block to the gravel parking lot at the end of Votee Park, and a quick hand-in-hand run across the grass to the bench facing the tennis courts.

"Probably the last picnic of the year, babe," I said sadly as we sat and unpacked the brown paper bag between us. "Oh, napkins and everything."

"No straws."

"There're straws. I saw her put 'em in," I assured.

"I got 'em. Last picnic—yeah, I'm sure. That's a shame, huh?"

"Yeah."

Even now there was a chill in the air, but the sun was bright and warm, and neither of us regretted stretching the season for a final outing.

"You remember Julia?" Ann asked with a mouthful of sandwich. "Oh, this is delicious."

"Julia? Of course. See if there's a spoon in there, will ya, hon? How could I forget Julia?"

"You knew she was gay, right?"

"Yeah, I knew—so?"

"Know what I heard?" she asked in a whisper.

"What did ya hear?"

"Ya remember I told you about the two teachers at the junior high who were lesbians?"

"Yeah."

"They lived together?"

"Yeah, I remember."

"Well, they broke up. They had a fight or something, a lover's quarrel—more than that, I guess. They split. Julia's movin' in with one of them."

I stared at the container of potato salad I had just opened, then licked the top of the snap-on plastic cover.

"Holy Christmas," I muttered in amazement.

"I don't know if she's already in, or if she's *gonna* move in, but—" she continued.

"Whew," I whistled. "That's wild. That's *really* wild."

"Yeah, I know."

I looked out at the fenced tennis courts strung side by side, one behind the other in front of us, the green ball in the near enclosure being stroked left to right, and returned right to left, by two women in tennis outfits. They were trying to stretch the season, too. Their volley continued without a miss as I sat in mesmerized stare, my thoughts shuffling left to right, right to left. Julia living with a teacher. I hated those new green balls. Tennis balls are supposed to be white. Julia, a kid—Oh, nice shot—living with a teacher, probably twice her age. Wow.

"That's fucked up, man," I sighed eventually.

"Is that news, sports, or an editorial comment?" she questioned with a laugh.

"No, I know. I meant, it really blows my mind."

"What part, the age difference or the same sexes? Or that it's a teacher and a former student?"

I thought for a while and then shook my head.

"I don't know, hon. Eat your macaroni."

CHAPTER 32

Surviving, overcoming, enduring, and persisting continued as our routine.....A teaching colleague stunningly admits to breaking commandments poor Moses hadn't even thought of writing.....

As fall turned to winter—not by the calendar, yet, but certainly by the temperature—I found myself in established patterns of times before. Counseling teenage kids was ever challenging, yet ever invigorating, each day a unique experience unto itself. Never the kind of counselor who maintained an appointment calendar with bookings through the end of the week, other than those absolutely necessary, I handled things one at a time as they arose. I seldom knew what the day held in store when I walked into my office to "open shop" each morning. I never knew which or how many of my two hundred and forty kids were going to pop in or what they would bring with them. Every day I was born again into an unpredictable world of new excitement, new problems, new people, new adventure, and new learning—always, new learning. I said for years, that should a day end without me having *learned* something from my kids, *that* was the day I would retire.

At home, existing from day to day in a situation, mostly of my own making, that I knew had to end, was burdensome and bittersweet. My children, Jayne and Sandra, neglected though they may have been by the amount of time I spent away, especially in the evenings, were constant sources of enjoyment, pride, and happiness. Knowing as I did, that the time remaining for us as a family was closing, made the too infrequent hours I spent with them treasured moments stored on memory's microfilm for replay in the lonely days without them I knew were sure to come. Try as I did not to bring the hurt of deliberate confrontation or direct rejection upon Pam, I caused her to suffer the greater anguish of feeling suspicion and of standing in helpless witness of the painfully slow deterioration of our marriage. My growing involvement with Ann caused me to abandon any lingering thought of reconciliation and moved me from temptation to transgression, and then from benefit-of-the-doubt half-truths to foolishly transparent fabrications. My wife was nothing but a decent and loving woman who deserved none of this.

With Ann, all remained as it had been. Our relationship flowed with the natural smoothness of one hundred percent pure Vermont maple syrup over a stack of buckwheat flapjacks hot from the griddle. It had survived the boiling caldron into which the fragile innocence and non-possessive caring of its beginnings had been stirred with false accusation and controversy. It had overcome the differences of our ages, our roles, our situations, and our values. It had endured the constant threat of exposure, humiliation, embarrassment, and punishment. It had persisted in the face of adversity and instant catastrophe, behind the backs of her parents, under the nose of my wife, and within the reach of authority.

Surviving, overcoming, enduring, and persisting continued as our routine, as natural as breathing, living, and loving. All remained as it had been, except she did get the nose job she had promised herself she would get, and she did continue her long established love affair with weed despite promises and attempts at moderation.

When I visited her in the hospital on the occasion of her nose surgery, I was shocked by the brutality of the operation which left her with purplish-black bruises around each of her bloodshot eyes, a heavily bandaged nose, and a swollen face. When she told me she felt so beaten up that she had to have a smoke, I thought she was delirious.

"You're kidding, right? They're not gonna let ya smoke a cigarette in here," I lectured.

"I'm not talkin' about a cigarette, silly, and I'm not askin'."

"Well, ya certainly can't do a joint in here. Are you nuts?"

Did she really think she could pull that off, or was she too doped up on painkillers not to think she couldn't?

"I can, I can. Help me outta bed, will ya. Gimme your hand. I did one yesterday."

"Ya did one yesterday? Holy shit, you're outta your fuckin' mind."

She hobbled from the side of her bed to the bathroom door, holding the hospital robe—six sizes too large—around her, and, as if by magic, she produced a firmly wrapped joint and a book of matches. We went into the small bathroom, and she closed the door behind us before hopping to a barefoot stand on the toilet seat.

"Hold on to my legs so I don't fall in," she begged.

Now I've seen everything, I thought to myself.

"You are outta your fuckin' mind," I repeated in astonishment.

When she lit the joint and exhaled upward toward the vent in the ceiling directly above the toilet, I said it again, this time not in astonishment, this time with a howling laugh that I feared would bring the room nurse bursting through the door with eye-bulging alarm.

"You *are* out of your fuckin' mind!"

* * * * * * *

The A-School? I almost had forgotten. How easily things slip.

Away from the A-School, I barely gave it a thought. I wasn't curious about seeing their new set-up, I didn't visit, I didn't miss it, and I didn't care. It was the furthest thing from my mind—until Mark stood in the doorway of my office.

"You know who I mean—the girl from the A-School last year, the cute one, you know," he said, a little more insistence in his voice than I liked to hear. "Ya ever see her, or still see her?"

I measured him with careful scrutiny. I knew he was bluffing. Right away, I knew it. He didn't know anything; he was fishing.

"Yeah, every now and then," I replied casually.

"I've seen her here a coupla times," he taunted.

Mark wasn't dumb. But he didn't know as much as he wanted me to think he did. Of that I was certain. He just didn't know as much as he *wanted* to know. That's the kind of guy he was—not obnoxiously nosey, just eager to be in the know, and usually successful in manipulating himself into positions of confidence in which the behind-the-scenes exchange of rumor and scuttlebutt flowed freely among those who were privy to inside information. A classroom teacher—about my age, maybe a half dozen years older—he enjoyed an easy-going relationship with students, faculty colleagues, and several administrators, close personal alliances which often included subtle this-for-that and favor-for-favor understandings for mutual live-and-let-live, one-hand-washes-the-other, survival. Mark and I weren't close, but we got along fine, and it wasn't unusual for us to engage in light banter or friendly commiseration. We weren't close enough, however, for me to allow him to set me up or take advantage of me.

"Yeah, she stops by," I acknowledged glibly.

"Ann, right?"

"Yeah."

"Anything heavy?" he inquired as he edged into the office.

"Not really," I lied. "Why?"

"No reason—you know, ya hear things, sometimes true, sometimes not," he said as he sat down and pushed the door closed with his foot. "You know what this place is like. There's always a story if there's someone to listen."

"And you listen, right?" I smiled. "There's always someone to listen, if there's a story."

"I listen," he nodded smugly. "Yeah, I listen."

"And ya hear what?"

"Oh, nothin' specific, nothin' much. Just, you know, just talk."

The bastard was bluffing. He was flying on nothing but a wing and a prayer, trying to put two and two together—a little gossip, he saw her here a few times, he adds it all up, and he gets—

"Just bullshit, right, Mark? Just talk, just bullshit."

"Wellll, ya can never tell," he said with a stretch. "There's a lotta nice pussy around here, a *lotta* nice stuff. You tappin' her?"

He didn't know anything. Had he known, he would have been all over me. He would have nailed me and put me on the defensive. That's the way he was. He wouldn't ask if he already knew. Finesse and diplomacy weren't his style. He was blunt, just like his question.

"That's the talk, huh? That's what ya hear? I'm gettin' a little?" I laughed. The challenge was as good as a denial, and it was the best idea I could come up with on short notice. "If ya listen to all the talk, you'd think *everybody* was gettin' a little. If I believed everything I heard around here, I'd think this was pussy heaven," I bluffed, now my turn to bullshit a little, my turn to zing.

"You hear things, too, huh?"

"Yeah, I listen. I hear things. You gettin' any?"

Fuck, let's see how *he* likes it.

"You didn't hear anything about *me*, did ya?" he questioned with too much concern, too quickly.

Ah, ha! I knew I had touched a sensitive nerve. That's what I thought. No, I hadn't heard a lot of talk, just a little, just some whispers, just a few snide remarks, and everything I had heard—all of it—had been about Mark.

"Not *me*, not about *me*?" he repeated, his thumb to his chest in pointing identification each time he referred to himself.

"You can talk to me, Mark," I said in an assuring manner, dismissing his vehemence as not very convincing. "Shit, man, you asked *me* if I was tappin' Ann, right? So, who have *you* been tappin'?"

I hated that word; I hated his use of it in reference to Ann. Tappin' was something one might properly do to a shoe, a keg of beer, a telephone line, or a sewer pipe, not a woman. But I fed it back to him for the sake of communication mutuality, equals on an equal plane, about as high as a snake's belly. I tried to make it sound like he owed me, although I had admitted to nothing. The son-of-a-bitch—I'd *never* admit to tappin' Ann.

"Kathy Sanders," he stated boldly. "Not now—when she was a senior."

His candid reply stunned me. Like the swift, clean slice of a razor, it cut to the heart of the game, the blood an oozing afterthought. The admission stunned me. The name stunned me.

"Kathy Sanders? Holy shit! You were screwin' around with Kathy Sanders?" I whispered in amazement as I leaned forward in my chair.

Kathy, a honey of a kid, had been my counselee. When I became Acting Director of Guidance the year before the Alternative School opened, my counselees had been reassigned to other counselors in the department. But I had kept for myself Kathy and a handful of other seniors with whom I had grown close, seeing them through their senior year. Kathy and I had spent many,

many hours together talking about her classes, colleges, her applications, and her boyfriend.

"What about her fuckin' boyfriend?"

"That was part of her trouble," he smiled. "Seth wasn't her fuckin' boyfriend. He was her boyfriend, but he wasn't fuckin', not enough to keep her happy, anyway. She was gettin' very little, if any, as far as I could figure. I think there was something wrong there. I don't know what it was. I don't think he could get it up, or keep it up, or somethin'."

The bastard was telling the truth. At least *that* part I knew was true. Kathy hadn't been as blunt, but on more than one tearful occasion she had made mention of "disappointing" aspects of her relationship with Seth, hinting that they had sexual problems. I could check the rest of Mark's story, later. I still was in contact with Kathy.

"I don't know why. She didn't have any trouble turnin' me on," he continued. "She was some piece—nice cunt; tight, man. Whatta fuckin' body. She got it on with my wife, too."

"Your wife?" I gasped.

"Yeah, the three of us. I think she was more into my wife than she was into me," he blustered. "So, you can talk to me, Charlie boy, anytime," he winked maliciously as he got up and put his hand on the door knob.

I felt like someone had thrown a bucket of ice water in my face. I took the slap shot coldly. The puck hit me squarely in the gut, knocking me on the seat of my pants, sprawling me at the goal mouth as the missile slid into the open net. Scooooore! One to nothing, his favor. He played dirty, looking for me to trade scores and tie the game. It stunk. He could stand there as long as he wanted. I wasn't gonna play.

"By the way," he said as he opened the door and looked back. "Kathy's mother? You know her, right? I had her, too. The kid was better than her mother was. Whaddya think of that?"

He left me sitting in shock. Jesus Christ, I thought it was a 1-0 shutout, but it was twice as bad—Kathy Sanders *and* her mother. I wondered how he missed Louise, Kathy's younger sister, by two years or so. He could have fucked her, too, and made it a 3-0 rout—maybe win the Stanley Cup.

He was either the world's biggest bullshitter or—

A few days later I knew the truth. The son-of-a-bitch had broken commandments poor Moses hadn't even thought of writing: "Thou shalt not have your wife fuck around with a student you are fucking," and "Thou shalt not fuck the mother of a student you are fucking."

Holy Moses!

****

I told Ann, but not immediately. I sat on it for a day or two, staring out the window often, shaking my head in disbelief. Things were starting to get to me.

"Ya look a little rattled," she observed with narrowed eyes when I completed my accounting of the bizarre tale.

"No, I'm just—I guess I—Okay, okay, I'm rattled," I confessed, flatly. "It's so fuckin' unbelievable, it's—it's just….."

".....unbelievable," she concluded, filling in the blank left by my stammering. "I guess if ya can't take the heat, ya shouldn't be in the kitchen, huh?"

"Oh, c'mon, get off it! You're not tryin' to compare that shit to us, are you? You and me—that's one thing. I'm not sayin' it's right, but—"

"What's not right with you and me?" she challenged, failing to get my point. "Is something wrong?"

"No, nothing's *wrong*, no more than with Ed and Susan or with that Thomson guy and Katie, or whatever her name was. Don't you understand? Those—they don't upset me. They were love relationships. Even Sal from Northern Valley. At least he married the girl he was bangin'. Ya understand what I mean?" I frowned, as she acknowledged my pleading question with an unconvincing nod. "But look at the shit," I continued. "The other shit ain't like you and me, sweetheart. The other shit is *shit*—the other teachers Ed knows about, the pussy-chasers—and how many *doesn't* he know about? How many doesn't *anybody* know about?"

Ann nodded again, with more conviction this time, more understanding.

"Christ, Sarah and the other broad from Long Island—you know, from camp, takin' pictures—ain't that a piss! Ya think *that's* like you and me?"

"Julia," Ann added, solemnly.

"Yeah, Julia. Right, and now, this—Kathy, Mark, his wife, her mother. Now, *that's* shit. Christmas, I think I've heard it all. Then my mind is blown away with the next thing I find out about. Ya shoulda seen his face when he was tellin' me—as happy as a pig in shit. It hasta rattle ya. It hasta make ya think. And it's right in my own back yard."

The telephone rang on my desk, and I swiveled in my chair to take the call. It was a parent wanting to talk with a teacher about a report card grade her son had received in biology for the first marking period. I made arrangements to leave a note for the teacher to call the mother and hung up, looking at Ann as if there had been no interruption of our conversation.

"It does make ya think, doesn't it?" she acceded.

"It makes me wonder how many other back yards there are."

"It makes me think I should practice crossing my fingers and holding my breath."

"What's that supposed to mean?"

"It means I'm glad I'm not a mother with daughters," she said quietly. "I don't know how I could stand at the front door every morning and wave them off to school without crossing my fingers and holding my breath."

Strange it was to hear her talk like the guardian of American youth or the protector of America's mothers. But I shared her peculiar sympathy.

"That's a desolate thought. Is that the way you feel abut us? Ya sorry we ever got involved?" I plied cautiously.

"Us?" she squinted.

I don't know why I asked such a damn fool question. She wasn't sorry. Neither was I. Sorry? For cryin' out loud—maybe I just needed the reassurance.

"Yeah, us?"

"Well, I did think it was gonna be somethin' a little more than you just bein' after my body," she needled. " 'Are you after her body?' " she mimicked Fran with a prim, Victorian glare that distanced her from the dowdy words. "Why didn't the bitch just ask, 'Are you fuckin' Ann?' "

"You little—" I leaped, putting my hands in a strangle hold around her neck. "You thought it was gonna be something more than me bein' after your—"

"See, see, right away you're grabbin'," she teased with a squirm. "You're always grabbin' my body. Maybe Fran was right. If I had known—"

"Shhhhh, ya wanna have the whole school in here. I'm grabbin' your neck; I'm not grabbin' your body."

"After all this time, *now* you're gonna be shy? C'mon, sweet, a little lower, grab here—grab this."

CHAPTER 33

The changing nature of our relationship.....our "flip-flop" period.....Why try to force a traditional ending on a non-traditional relationship? We just loved each other. Period.....a convulsive seizure and the tragic diagnosis and prognosis.....

Some things change, and some things stay the same.

The changes that took place in the relationship Ann and I shared were divergent and gradual, yet the essence of our consensual affiliation remained resolute. Our physical liaison, our grabbin', and our lovemaking, continued for more than two years after her graduation, most of that time being known as our "flip-flop" period.

We took turns suggesting marriage, but each time the issue was gingerly forwarded by one of us, it was delicately side-stepped with a lighthearted, noncommittal response from the other.

"Whaddya think about us gettin' hitched?" she asked as she zipped her racket into its vinyl carrying case.

"I don't know. What *about* us getting hitched?" I returned the question. I stuffed my towel into the top of the bulging grip. "Where's the third ball? I only see two—Aren't we pretty well hitched, already?"

"I don't—oh, damn! I think it's still outside the fence. We didn't get the one we hit over, did we?"

"No, *we* didn't get the one *we* hit over," I chided, playfully, "but I'll be a nice guy and get it."

"No, you stay off your ankle. I'll get it. If you were such a nice guy, ya wouldn't have gotten me so pissed, and I wouldn't have slammed the ball over the fence."

"I didn't get you pissed," I retorted. "If you had made the shot in the first place—"

"I know, I know," she interrupted with a grimace as she painfully recalled the easy shot she had muffed and her subsequent burst of anger at herself. "Don't rub it in. Get the other two by the net, and I'll go around. It's really bothering you, isn't it?"

"The fuckin' thing," I muttered as I looked with disgust at my left ankle. The lack of any outward evidence of injury was almost as distressing as the pain I felt each time I put pressure on my foot. I hadn't twisted or sprained it. I just had played too long in cheap sneakers on a chronically weak underpinning that always gave me trouble on hard macadam courts.

"I'll get the ball. See if ya miss me enough when I'm gone to think about gettin' married," she chirped as she hurried across the court and let herself out the side gate.

Damn, she knew I loved her more than anything else in the whole world. Why the hell was she pressing marriage? How could she even talk about it? I wasn't even divorced yet.

I hobbled to the net to retrieve the two green balls that baked in the sun at center court and then shuffled back to the painted hurricane fencing that enclosed the playing area. I watched as Ann poked through the tall grass outside the fence in search of the missing ball.

"Over to the left more and back a little, I think," I called out.

"I'd be able to see the fuckin' thing if it was white," she yelled back with exasperation. "I hate these new green balls, damn it."

Of course I'd marry her. We agreed on everything!

"Back a little more, and bend over a little. Gimme a little look."

"I got it, I got it," she cut me short. "I didn't realize I had hit it so hard."

She picked up the elusive ball and jogged to the fence behind which I leaned, waiting, arms hanging from the grip of my hands on the latticed, steel wiring.

"Give you a little look," she derided. "Why should I give you a little look? I want ya to miss me enough to marry me. Hey, you look like a monkey in there," she laughed, flopping against the fence, her hands covering mine.

"So, how come ya wanna marry a monkey?"

"To make little monkeys," she said, laughing, as she pressed her face against the wire fence.

Her nose poked through, and I grabbed it lightly with my teeth, making her jump back.

"C'mon, cut the monkey business. I'm not even divorced, yet. It's gonna be months before I'm done with all that nonsense. It's hard to even think about marriage—remarriage—whatever. Right now, marriage seems sorta unnecessary—not very important. I don't know, maybe I'll feel differently about it later. Maybe we can just live together for awhile."

"And make little monkeys?"

"You never give up, do you?"

"I'll give you a little look," she bribed.

"What about a little lick?"

"Here comes the bride, all dressed in white."

On later occasions, it was I who made the overture of marriage and she who joshed the offer aside. We went back and forth, taking turns, every two months or so, flip-flopping along, each serious proposal and its subsequent declination in strange antithesis to the stance we each had assumed only a short time before, the two of us never being at the same point at the same time.

* * * * * * *

Ann returned to camp as a counselor and water ski instructor, as I had expected she would, the second summer after her high school graduation. On each of my two visits to New Hampshire, one in July and the other in August, we showed each other the little knickknacks and trinkets we each were buying and stashing away in tissue wrap for "our" apartment. One almost would have thought we were serious, but we continued to fudge the issue, making a playful game of our "let's get married" routine and finding amusement in playing devil's advocate. Only once, the following winter, did we confront the matter squarely. It scared the crap out of us—both of us. She wasn't ready to get married, and I wasn't ready to get remarried.

We never had a serious talk about it again. We didn't have to. The pressure was off. It was the best thing that ever could have happened to us. We knew—our relationship was lifelong. It didn't need to embrace any other qualities or characteristics. It was a love relationship without end. Once we got beyond attempting to force a *traditional ending* on a *non-traditional relationship,* we were better able to realize and appreciate that we had a truly special bond that was timeless and unconditional. The need to own or possess was gone. We each, with the encouragement of the other, emerged from social isolation, meeting new people, making new friends, and seeing and dating others. We held on to each other, and we let go of each other, at the same time. Khalil Gibran would have been so proud of us!

"Oh, we'll get married. We'll get married, someday. It may be when we're sixty-five, but, we'll get married," Ann said, her statement reflecting more the characteristics of determination and resolution than lament or jest.

"When you're sixty-five or when I'm sixty-five?" I asked with a laugh.

"Geez, that's somethin', isn't it?" she replied with genuine amazement. "I really don't ever think of the difference."

With the passage of time, physical intimacy gave way to this more elevated level of intimacy, always within a framework of love but with more focus on the love and caring of one human being for another than on a romantic involvement. Our relationship didn't cool; it matured and grew as we matured and grew. It purged itself of its contradictions. It brought itself into consonance with reality. It established a consecution of movement to a higher plane. Its new character was as sacred as our physical loving had been—as important, as powerful, as natural, and as beautiful. Pure and simple, we just loved each other. Period.

As our lives turned in different directions, more and more of Ann's time became devoted to drama classes, voice and dance lessons, auditions, and rehearsals for an ever increasing calendar of showcase presentations and theatre group performances. Her successes in summer stock playhouses began with the New London Barn Players in her beloved New Hampshire, where I remember her telling me, "Someday, someday I'm gonna be on that stage." Later, with Actor's Workshop & Repertory Company in West Palm Beach, Florida, she starred in a two-hour one-woman show, playwright William Luce's *The Belle of Amherst*, in which she portrayed the private life, thoughts, and poetic genius of Emily Dickinson. She moved from summer stock to dinner theatres in New York City, including showcase performances at The Bushes on West 73rd Street, and at the famed Copacabana.

Ann's career was on the move. After an appearance at the Nevele Hotel in the Catskill Mountains of New York State, Ann herself was on the move, west to California where, with a boyfriend, she shared a pad close to the Hollywood movie lots and sound stages that nourished her soul, entreated her imagination, and fired her determination.

I, over the same seven or eight year period, followed through with my divorce, continued in my counseling position at the high school, resurrected my interest in my stamp collection, became newly excited about camping, rafting, and photography, became a flea market and antique nut, did the single's scene, and finally remarried. Pam remarried as well, to another man named Charlie, divorced him shortly thereafter, and then married him a second time.

Ann's move to Los Angeles, unfortunately, was more than just a career stepping-stone in her search for recognition of her talent and success in her performances. It was more than just the pursuit of a dream and the quest to spend her life doing the only thing she ever really wanted to do—sing. It was an unexpected race against the clock, a bittersweet journey of life toward death, a weighty denial of an uncertain future, an ominous cloud that hovered over her head and followed her from New Jersey to the sunshine of the Golden State. While appearing on the Stardust Room stage of the Nevele Hotel in the Borscht Belt community of Ellenville, New York, Ann had suffered a major convulsive seizure. Shaken and perplexed, she had returned home to New Jersey where her parents, of course, immediately sought the nature and cause of her debilitating episode.

The medical diagnosis was not good. It was a disaster, so devastating that denial was a much easier concept for everyone—Ann, her parents, and me—to grasp than the harsh reality. The doctors had discovered an inoperable brain tumor. The prognosis was worse than the diagnosis. At twenty-six years of age, she had two years—three at most—to live, the doctors said. But what the hell do doctors know?

Ann wasn't the kind of person who would accept the dismal news, fold up her tent, and quit. At one point in her life she would have accepted her fate with resignation, but that was a long, long, long seven or eight years ago. Not now. Now she would fight it with tenacious vigor, not in any overt or demonstrative manner, but in a resolute commitment to her aspirations, her intentions, her hopes, her never-say-die attitude, and her nobody's-gonna-stop-me-now plans.

"Can you come over to the house tomorrow afternoon, hon, just for a little while?" she inquired on my office phone early one morning.

"Sure, babe," I answered without hesitation.

"I want you to help me cut my hair and take some pictures," she offered in explanation.

"Sure, babe," I repeated.

"I start my chemo in a few days, and I'm gonna lose my hair, anyway."

Oh, God, her beautiful, long, shiny, silky hair. Oh, my God. Oh—

There were to be no *before* and *after* pictures. When I got to her house after school the next afternoon and she opened the front door, it was more than obvious that the dirty deed already had been addressed and completed.

"I'm sorry, Charlie; I just had to get this over with. There was no sense dragging it out. Did you bring your camera, hon?"

"Yeah," I sighed, somewhat relieved that I hadn't been obliged to be a part of what must have been an extremely difficult and heavyhearted endeavor for her.

"You look really good," I acknowledged with honest surprise. "It looks good. Whadda *you* think, sweet?"

"Yeah, it's not too bad—not as bad as I thought it was gonna be. I'm happy with it. I still look like me, right?" she laughed.

I don't know what she did to it, but it did look good. There still was a lot of hair on her head. It was just cut short, in a bob of sorts, buy wavy and layered. Anyone who didn't know that once she had had long hair certainly would have thought she had an appropriately fashioned, natural, and cutely attractive hair treatment. I never asked her if she had cut it herself or if her mom had done it or if she had gone to a beauty parlor and had it professionally cut and shaped, but I suspected the latter.

"You still look like you. You look great, babe. Still want some pictures?"

"Yeah, come into the living room," she motioned, and I followed her the short distance into the house to a side window in the tastefully furnished living room.

"What about here? This okay, or is it too bright?"

"No, that's fine. I can use that light."

I took several pictures of her standing in front of the window in her light colored, coarsely knit, wool sweater with the wide turtle-neck collar. She managed to smile, but I knew she was having a tough time coping. As beautiful as she looked and as much as her new hair style was appealing, she was crushingly aware, as was I, that the loss of her long hair was but a prelude to the more tragic future loss of all of her hair as her chemo treatments would exact their cruel consequences.

The photos turned out to be great, capturing not only the bright highlights of her new coiffure but the gray and subdued mood of the occasion. The poor creature. When was Misfortune going to leave this poor soul alone?

Considering the circumstances, however—she had lost her long hair and it was only a matter of time before she would lose the rest—she handled the photo-op session pretty well. Me, too. I didn't cry a single tear until I was back in my car and heading home. Then the flood gates opened.....

* * * * * * *

Ann and I shared a closeness not affected by time, distance, or circumstance. Greeting cards, notes, and phone calls kept us in constant contact, and, in uncanny, unexplainable fashion, we sensed each other's presence, as two bodies of kindred spirit, when she came back to New Jersey. There were times when I knew she was on her way home before the plane ever landed, times when I knew it was her call before I answered the phone, times when I began looking for her car on the highway, *and spotted it*, although I had every reason to believe she was three thousand miles away in California. It was wacky and unbelievable, but it was true.

Ann's greeting cards, in particular, constituted an endless chain of unbroken love from her to me over eight years, my letter and note responses serving a like purpose from me to her. She rarely missed a holiday, seizing each as an opportunity to mail a card with a loving printed message and her distinctively own handwritten addendum: a Valentine's Day card in which she wrote, "I have so much to thank you for, including my sanity. You're the tops! Always, Ann;" a Christmas greeting addressed to "Charlie baby" and concluding with, "Wishing you sunshine, Love, Ann;" a birthday card inscribed, "You're still the tops, baby, Love ya, Ann;" a card for no particular reason or season to "My love," and signed, "Love, Sunshine;" and another "You're the tops, Charlie," birthday card; and more, and more, and so many more.

Our individual circumstances and involvements with other people made no difference and had no affect on our communication with each other or our feelings for each other. Our relationship with each other was separate and apart from our relationships with others, and posed no threat to others. I was aware that she was dating regularly and that her sexual liaisons ranged from random to committed. When she moved to Los Angeles, I knew she was living with a boyfriend. Ann knew that I was active in various singles' groups and that I had lived with three different women, each for more than a year, over an eight year period. In one of my letters to Ann soon after she relocated to California, I told her that my third live-together experience was, at last, for real, and that I would be marrying my present wife—ironically named *Ann*—in January, 1983. Ann's immediate response from the west coast came in the form of a beautiful Christmas card to the both of us:

> **Dear Ann and Charlie,**
>
> **Well, I guess by the time this arrives you will be pretty close to being married. I am so sorry to have to miss that occasion. I know it will be beautiful. I recognize the love in Charlie's handwriting. Ann, I look so forward to meeting you. It's funny. For some reason, I feel as if I know you well.**
>
> **Peace, love, happiness, Merry Christmas, Happy New Year, congratulations, Mazel tov!**
>
> **Love,**
> **Ann**

Ann flew from Los Angeles to New Jersey every three months so she could get her chemo treatment and the best available advice and counsel in New York City.

Each time she returned, we'd get together for a game of Scrabble at her kitchen table at her parents' apartment in Hackensack where they had moved after selling their house in Teaneck. She could play as well stoned as anyone I ever played straight. Sometimes we'd reminisce about the times we had spent together. Sometimes she'd mention one of our more unusual lovemaking episodes, but we never lingered on it long enough to revive for more than a fleeting moment the surge of feelings that accompanied the recollection. It was too powerful, too dangerous. On one occasion, she made a suggestion that perhaps we should "do it" one more time, for "old time's sake," but she quickly repealed the thought with a sobering observation.

"If we did, I'd be flying back from California every *week* to get more," she said, "and I can't do that, and you're married—It's best we leave things where they are, with the beautiful memories. Sex with you was the best sex I ever had, right up to now."

Her comment gave me a lot to think about, but I didn't have much time to think. I had to respond. I'll never know if I made the right decision. I do know that all I had to say was, "Let's do it, Sunshine," and she would have.

"Really? That's so nice; thank you, babe. That really makes me feel good. But, you're right. We'll stick with the beautiful memories. They'll never go away. I love you, pure and simple. You know I still love you, don't you?"

"Of course I know you still love me. And you know I still love you, too. That's the way it is, and that's the way it'll always be."

I never had the heart to tell her that the cinder road next to the park in Bergenfield had been paved, that town house condominiums covered our once secluded picnic hideaway near the stream in the woods in Mahwah, that the Route 17 drive-in theatre was closed and gone, that high-rise apartments now stood where the parking lot used to be across the street from Yonkers Raceway, that the red chair was gone—probably back on the street for rubbish collection whence it had come—and, finally, inevitably but propitiously, that the A-School had closed after a ten-year run. She never knew, either, that as the years passed, I had learned of more "back yard" teacher-student playing—a physical education teacher who had to pay a student for a hush-hush abortion; an audio-visual aids teacher who lost his job overnight—there on Friday, gone on Monday—when a girl he had gone after went to the principal; a science teacher who, after dating a student for a year and a half, climbed on his motorcycle with her holding on in back and headed for California, leaving his wife, his house, and his job behind. And that was just in *my* "back yard," *my* school!

At the end of the evening, Ann and I would say goodbye as we did for years. We'd hug each other briefly in loving embrace and kiss lightly, holding close but freezing lest any small movement hurdle us back to times and events past, times and events remembered with heart-pounding emotion and never to be forgotten fondness, but times and events past.

"I love you, Charlie. Thank you for saving my life," she would whisper softly in my ear. Every time, without fail. She said it and meant it like nothing else she had ever told me.

"I love you, Ann. Thank you for saving my life," I would respond always, saying it and meaning it like nothing else I had ever told her.

It was the height of our intimacy. We each knew..... *no distance between*..... We never said goodbye. We just turned and walked away in opposite directions until the next time.

CHAPTER 34

My little friend was—is—gone. She fought Misfortune's degradation like a bitch, but she lost the battle, and she died. A part of me died with her. Ann died the same year the Alternative School closed.....

Ann died on Saturday morning, November 24, 1984, eleven and a half years after I first met her, and just two and a half years after her doctors predicted she had between two and three years to live. But what the hell do doctors know?

During those two and a half years under threat, neither Ann nor I ever discussed her dying. We never even mentioned the words *die* or *death*—not once. There was never a countdown—six months to go, three months, one—and I never *thought* about Ann dying. I'm not aware of Ann ever *thinking* about dying. Even in the face of the obvious deterioration of her physical condition as time passed, we seemed to share an unspoken yet eternal belief that everything was going to be made right, that the chemo was going to destroy the cancer that was assaulting her life and squashing her dreams. With not one shred of factual substantiation, with not one iota of evidence to the contrary, we just assumed that Ann was going to get better and be well. But, that didn't happen. She didn't get better. She got worse.

I got the message I dreaded ever getting. The note, a scribbled telephone message in my wife's handwriting, was on my desk in the den when I got home. I had gone to the Meadowlands to play the trotters. Funny, in the swirl of odd-ball thoughts that crossed my mind that very night as I had studied the race program between the second and third races, I wondered what ever had become of Miss Jordan, the two-year old filly Ann and I had followed and bet on years before simply because it was her namesake. And now, home at twelve-thirty in the morning, I read in the dim light of the desk lamp the tragic news of the real Miss Jordan, my little sunshine friend:

> **Sloan Kettering.....scheduled for treatment.....started dragging foot..... CAT scan saw some spots.....think tumor may have spread.....**

A room number and a telephone number were noted, but there was no name on the message. There didn't have to be a name—I sat down on the couch, held my head in my hands, and cried like a baby. I knew it was over. I'm crying now, as I write.

The next afternoon, I made the drive into the City. I stood alone at her hospital bedside. I said "goodbye" to my little friend and held her hand in mine for two hours before whispering a last "I love you" into her ear. She didn't hear. She didn't know I was there. She was only breaths away from her final sleep. The two hours seemed like a moment, the almost twelve years a lifetime, each crammed with treasured thoughts that nobody and nothing, not even the tumorous growth which fatally swelled her brain into morbid senselessness, could ever steal from me.

This special person, undeserving of such an end—her prone, comatose body trailing tubes from her nostrils, arm, and groin, her lifeless room pervaded by the pungent odor of hospital beds and sickly people—was but an employed plaything in Misfortune's vexatious hands, a human yoyo, at times spun out and down to the lowest possible point and at times reeled in and up to the height of triumph. No matter at what level, however, it was Misfortune's cursed finger to which the end of the string remained damnedably attached.

At the lowest points, Misfortune deafened Ann's ear, deformed her leg, mocked her body, scorned her affection, humiliated her sexuality, threatened her womanhood, belittled her intelligence, ridiculed her talent, betrayed her trust, questioned her innocence, suspected her behavior, accused her honor, and sent her walking down the center line of a highway in pursuit of her own destruction. When she rose above each obstacle—as she did—to love and sing and live—which she did—it was Misfortune who made each triumph brief and cut each—her loving, her singing, her living, and then her very life—too short, catching her at the top of the string in those abominable and merciless hands and flinging her back down.

Her final unwinding to the bottom of the string, to rest in unconscious stillness in Death's bed, Misfortune unwilling to yank her up just one more time, had come from the top of her career in the middle of an engagement at the Nevele Hotel. Struck by seizure, she had returned home to begin two and a half years of radiation treatments, chemotherapy, and medication in a futile struggle to survive.

She fought Misfortune's ultimate degradation like a bitch! With bulldog tenacity, she disregarded the humiliating side effects of her disease and her treatment—the convulsive vomiting, the loss of her beautiful hair, the lapses of memory, the headaches, the pain, the slow atrophy of her once lithe body—hiding their severity from even some of her closest friends, to continue her life in "normal" fashion.

She flew back and forth between her parents' Hackensack apartment and her own apartment in Los Angeles, picking up "bit" parts in movies and commercials, auditioning and trying out, ever hopeful, constantly in search of "the one big break" that would propel her beyond the role of a *crowd artiste*, an extra, to that of a card-carrying Equity performer.

When she was back home in New Jersey, the two of us would go to Sandy Hook together for a day at the beach, go for a walk in the park, play tennis, have lunch together at Libonoti's where, surprisingly, the waitress remembered us from years before, or play Scrabble until one o'clock in the morning. She'd meet her friends in New York, replenish her pot supply—now a medical necessity—go to the hospital for her treatment, and be off again to California, carrying so much luggage over her shoulder that it practically bent her frail body in half.

Then she was home again for the last time, limping on one leg and dragging the other one behind her. Then she was in a wheelchair. Then she was in bed. Then she was in the hospital, for the third and last time.

She fought Misfortune like a bitch, to the end never believing she would die, never thinking it was a possibility, never knowing it was inevitable. But it was. She died. A part of me died with her.

The shock was enfeebling, the pain excruciating. I hadn't prepared myself. I wasn't ready. Never had I lost anyone close, and then, in a flash, I was without the person with whom I had been closest for almost a dozen years. I was totally devastated and heartbroken. I still am. I'll never get over it. My little friend was—is—gone.

Ann died the same year the Alternative School closed.

I am sure that with her final breath, when she slipped for the first and last time beyond Misfortune's grasp, she celebrated her eternal freedom and bid farewell to her lifelong Nemesis in characteristic Alternative School fashion: "Fuck you, asshole."

EPILOGUE I

I offer no excuses for my behavior. I was wrong—legally, ethically, and morally. No contrived excuses and no swift running or long hiding can right the wrong of the trusts I violated, the falsehoods I told, and the lie I lived. My behavior—perverse, irresponsible, and inexcusable—was as wrong as the relationship between Ann and I was right. The relationship was positive rather than negative, constructive rather than destructive, lifting rather than degrading, genuine rather than false, strengthening rather than debilitating, and wholesome rather than diseased. And that is why I feel no shame, embarrassment, guilt, or regrets.

Both of us knew what we were doing, and both of us knew it was wrong. We just couldn't stop doing it.

If things could have happened two years later than they did, they at least would have been blessed with the social proprieties. Two years later I wouldn't have been married; I would have been divorced. Two years later I might have met her behind the counter at the drug store; she wouldn't have been a student in school. Two years later we could have told anyone who didn't like it to shove it. And by what magic were we to hold ourselves at distance for two years to accommodate the standards of good behavior?

We talked often, probably not seriously enough, about writing a book together.

"A book?" I gasped. "No one would believe it."

A book? Was she serious?

"Ya know, we *should* write a book!" she continued, warming to her own suggestion.

"Sure," I said acrimoniously. "Spill the beans about us and have your mother fall over with a heart attack when she reads it."

"My mother wouldn't fall over," she defended, stiffly.

"Are you kiddin'? You want your mother to read about you running around the stage with your pants down, screwin' in the back of the van, playin' with yourself, and all the other stuff?"

"That's shitty, Charlie."

"What?"

"That's pretty shitty, ya know?" she bristled.

"What's shitty?"

"C'mon."

"No, what?"

"You're makin' it sound shitty on purpose. It's not shitty. Why are you makin' it sound so awful? I'm not ashamed of anything. My mommy loves me. She wouldn't have a heart attack if she knew everything, if she knew the whole story. The one thing I know for certain is that if my mom knew I was happy, she'd be happy. Christ, I can remember when I wanted to kill myself. Ya think she would have been happy with that?"

Today, I hope Ann was right, then. Actually, at the time of Ann's death, I was fairly certain that her mother, a very dear person for whom I came to have much affection, knew the extent of the relationship between her daughter and me. Ann had made several comments to me that indicated she had told her mother, certainly not all the lurid details, but—

And then there were the pictures. I don't recall the particulars, but Ann's mother had some pictures of Ann, professional photos taken for her resume. They must have been taken during her chemotherapy treatments because she was wearing a wig. There were two stunning 8 x 10 head and shoulder photographs, and her mother thought I'd like to have them—or copies of them. She may have given them to me at the funeral. I was there with my wife, but I was so broken up that I don't remember much. Perhaps she mailed them to me shortly thereafter, or maybe she gave them to me when I picked her up and we went to the cemetery together in early December. My memory fails me, but, actually, that is the most likely time I got the photographs. I was absolutely thrilled to have such beautiful "grown-up" photos of my little Sunshine. No matter, on December 23, a month after Ann's death, I returned the originals to her with this note:

> **Dear Mrs. Jordan,**
>
> **Thank you so much for the loan of the photos. I had copies made, but, unfortunately, it took longer than usual processing because negatives had to be made first. Anyway, I now have negatives, so if you should ever want more copies you can let me know.**
>
> **I've been back to the cemetery a few more times, just to spend a few quiet minutes each time. I still miss her so much, and I know you do, too, but I**

know she's at peace.....out of harm's way.

I'm sure it's a lot warmer in Florida than it is here now, and I hope you're feeling better. Enjoy the sunshine, and give your body and your heart and your mind a chance to relax.

Let me know when you get back, and I'll see you then. Give my regards to David.

Love,
Charlie

She responded shortly afterwards.

Dear Charlie,

I received Ann's pictures a few days ago. I am so happy to have them here. Thank you, and thank you for your visits to the cemetery, and thank you for all the love and care you gave Ann.

I am brokenhearted over her passing, and hope time will lessen the hurt....

I had a nice conversation over the phone with your Ann just before we left New Jersey.....

If you ever come down our way, I'd love to see you both.

Take care, have a good winter, and I will talk to you when I come back in April.

Love,
Eileen

She knew. She knew I was more than just Ann's teacher of eight years ago.

And then there was her father. Soon after Ann graduated, her father began calling me at the high school at the beginning of each school year. He was in search of a senior, a driver he could employ as a part-time delivery person for his drug store. I always was willing to oblige. It was good to be able to provide one of my counselees with a not always easily found part-time job opportunity. One year, however, I had a difficult time with his request.

"I don't know if I'll be able to get you a driver this year," I explained when he called. "I don't have any seniors this year; my freshmen and sophomores don't have driver's licenses yet."

"Oh?" he responded with surprise.

"I'll do the best I can," I promised.

"Uh—" he started. "Don't forget, uh, you owe me—"

"I *owe* you?" I asked quizzically. "What does that mean? What do I owe you for?"

"Ann—" he said coldly, stabbingly. "You know what."

He knew, too. He knew, and now he was going to use what he knew to extort a favor.

I never felt I owed him a thing. I got him his driver that year, but that was the last time he called. I hoped it was because he realized that *he* owed *me*. I know how egotistical and self-indulgent that might sound, but, with all due respect, there's more truth in that than there is in the idea that I owed him a driver in return for loving his daughter.

Ann's father may or may not ever understand, but I hope her mother can take comfort in knowing that her daughter, initially tormented by the cruelty, ignorance, and uncaring attitude of those who abused and humiliated her sexuality, was happy to discover that she was a physically normal young woman with natural and instinctive sexual drives and needs. Ann was happy to be able to express herself as a sexual being, finding pleasures which brought fulfillment and satisfaction to her and hurt to no one. Bedridden at home before entering the hospital for the last time—despondent, depressed, and feeling alone and helpless—she confided to me that one of the few, small enjoyments that remained was feeling herself, thinking of me, stroking her genitals, and bringing herself to climax before closing her eyes and drifting off to sleep each night, not knowing if she would see the light of another morning.

"The problem with writing a book isn't my mother, Charlie-nut. It's your job. You'll get fired, sure as hell. What would you do if that happened? Could ya handle it?"

I wouldn't—couldn't—answer her questions. Hell, I knew she was right. She was right then, and nothing has changed since. Yes, this book will cost me my job. My career as a professional educator is finished. *Persona non grata* is the label the local, county, state, and national educational associations will pin on me. They'll call me the bad apple. Hell, I'll be called a lot of things by a lot of people—*not sweet man,* that's for sure—maybe *Charlie-nut*, but *not sweet man.*

Yes, I'll be upset about losing my job. No, I'll not be happy with the epitaphs with which I'll be tagged by pious and provincial moralists and all the goodie-goodies of the world—all the tax cheats, the housewife shoplifters, the adulterers and adulteresses, the gossipers with lying tongues, those riddled with jealousy and envy, those who trade in shady dealings, the cheaters, thieves, and liars of all stripes, and those involved in questionable affairs, dirty affairs, and illicit affairs, past and present. They'll all have a field day with their name calling, finger pointing, and talking behind my back, forgetting their own not-too-innocent status as they seek absolution for themselves and their transgressions at my expense. Well, if that's their pleasure, so be it. Despite all, I'll still consider myself a very, very lucky man, a very fortunate person, fortunate for having known Ann and having had her be a part of my life.

Of all the people who ever touched my life—of all the people who ever had the potential of having their formal schooling, their life experiences, or their street-wise knowledge impact me—it was the fragile innocence of an insecure teenager—a Barbra Streisand wanna-be with a "little girl's" voice, a stage in her head, and a stash of weed allowing her to fly free—who lived in a past of summer camp memories and wanted nothing more for the future than to be able to stand center stage and sing her lungs out, who changed my life.

In the course of my lifetime, I have done things that would be considered odd and kooky by many, strange and bizarre by some, and wild and crazy by others, certainly not the standard fare of sterile activities usually associated with the conservative and predictable behavior that most people seem to expect of a school teacher. The salient feature of each of my experiences has been the *people* I have encountered along the way. I have hobnobbed with kooky, bizarre, and crazy people perfectly matched to the experiences in which I came to know them, as well as beautiful, caring, thoughtful, sensitive, and humane individuals of wisdom, thought, introspection, astuteness, and insight whom I often found in the same unlikely situations as well as in more traditional settings.

Each one of these people, in ways and manners characteristically unique and circumstantially compelling and illuminating, has contributed to the development of my being, and each one of them has assisted me in better understanding myself and discerning the inner nature of my person. To each one I owe an unpayable debt. With no ingratitude or disrespect to any of these dear people—people whom I knew, loved, lived with, worked with, or otherwise shared either a brief interlude or an extended component of my personal or professional life—none had the effect on me that Ann had.

The love story which I have recounted in this book is but half a story, for at the same time that the reported temporal movements of the heart and pleasures of the flesh were taking place as I impacted my influence on Ann, Ann was impacting her influence on me, orchestrating a metamorphic transformation of my personality, perception, and thought process, inexorably linked to the love relationship we shared, yet distinguishably disconnected and worthy of independent treatment in a future writing effort.

I said I feel no shame, embarrassment, guilt, or regrets regarding my involvement with Ann, but, of course, it is difficult to look back on events which precipitated such a drastic alteration of my lifestyle and subsequently required such a start-from-scratch reconstruction of my life without admitting to some degree of disappointment in two areas.

First, I have regrets that are peripheral, consequentially related to the relationship Ann and I shared. My involvement with Ann was not the cause of my divorce, but it was the catalyst which accelerated the process and the eradicating agent which precluded any possibility for reconsideration and dissolved any chance of reconciliation. It made me lie to and deceive a wife who deserved a better fate. It cost me my role as a father, denying me the day-to-day enjoyment and excitement of watching my two beautiful daughters grow up, causing me to miss sharing in their childhood delights and pleasures, their Halloweens and birthdays, their report cards and school photographs, their fun and tears. It forced me to lead a secretive and shrouded existence, forsaking friends and colleagues to whom I dared not reveal my activities.

Second, I regret that it took Ann's death to motivate me to produce the book she and I so often had talked about writing together. For reasons unknown, it was she more than I who wanted a book written, the story told. Even years later, after our sexual intimacy had terminated, she prodded me to make time for the effort.

"C'mon, Charlie, it wouldn't take that long. Once you got started, it would come easy. Remember all the poems you use to write? You could do it. I'd help ya, too. You still write poetry?"

"Roses are red, daisies are white; I need my job, so I ain't gonna write."

"Oh, pooh!" she berated with genuine dismay. "If that's the best ya can do, maybe ya *shouldn't* write a book."

"And you can do better?" I confronted with bravado.

She fiddled with the Scrabble tiles on the rack in front of her as if readying her next move, her eyes cast downward to avoid contact, but I knew her mind was assembling a response. Never would she allow such a challenge to stand. She damn well should have been assembling a word to play. She was fifty-two points down with only a handful of unselected tiles remaining face down in the cover of the box.

"Roses are red, violets are blue; if you feared for your job, why did you screw?"

"Cute. Crude, but cute," I laughed. "Ya had to zing me, right? I'll start on the book tomorrow. Will that make you happy?"

But, of course, I didn't. What was the rush?

"And, ya know, if we did write a book," Ann pushed again the next time we got together, "Ya know what we could do, like at the end—?"

It was June, 1984. We had just spent the evening at the kitchen table in her parents' high rise apartment on Prospect Avenue in Hackensack, bringing each other up to date on the past three months and playing two games of Scrabble to completion. We had sat for a few minutes, too, on the outside balcony off the living room to share a joint between games, watching cars pull in and out of the parking lot below, talking about what was happening in our respective lives and about her two brothers and her sister, discussing how tough it was for her to get into the City for grass, and reminiscing about "our" parking lots of years ago.

Now, as she was seeing me down the second floor hallway toward the stairs, the late hour and the lingering effects of the smoked weed made me rub my tired eyes with little energy or enthusiasm for discussing a book that probably never would be written anyway.

"What's that, babe?" I asked wearily, covering a yawn.

How the hell was I supposed to know that the time for talking about anything was quickly slipping away? How the hell was I supposed to know that the Scrabble box and the dictionary I carried tucked under my arm had made their last trip to Hackensack? How the hell was I supposed to know that my next poem would say goodbye forever to my little friend, that I'd place the farewell words under glass in a small frame and rest it on her grave site, where it remains today and where I will maintain it until the day I die? How the hell was I supposed to know that on that raw Wednesday afternoon in November when I was to leave a note for her on the table at the foot of her hospital bed that she'd never wake to read it, that when I was to take the elevator down from the seventh floor of Sloan Kettering and make my exit onto chilly York Avenue between 67th and 68th Streets that the car I would find parked directly in front of mine would bear an out-of-state license plate, the so familiar green and white tag of the State of New Hampshire, the plate's ominous slogan, *Live free or die,* reducing me to tears?

"At the end of the book, we could ask everyone who reads it, you know, if they like it, to send a few bucks to the American Academy of Dramatic Arts in New York. They could set up a scholarship for kids who couldn't pay by themselves….."

Jesus, she must have hurt like hell not to have been able to go.

"…..for kids who wanted to be actors or actresses or singers but—"

I reached over, pulled her close, and held her to my chest. I felt her body quiver. I heard her quiet words muffled by my shirt.

"It would give them a chance, anyway, right? You *did* tell me a few months ago that you *were* gonna start writing. Ya gonna promise?"

"That's really nice, babe," I whispered. "Yes, I promise; I'll start the book."

I kissed the back of her neck.

"Sleep tight. Have a good flight out tomorrow. I'll see ya when you're back in the fall."

I released her and turned to the stairway door.

"Hey, sleepy eyes, I love you. Thank you for saving my life. Sweet dreams, hon," she clucked like a contented hen.

"Yeah, babe, I love ya, too," I said as I turned back with a wink. "Thank you for saving my life. Sweet dreams, Sunshine."

She smiled warmly, bashfully. She started to say something, then hesitated before stepping back a few paces, grinning broadly, and turning back down the corridor toward the apartment door.

EPILOGUE II

This book was written twenty-five years ago, two years after Ann died. She began urging me to write it sometime before that. In March, 1984, I finally told her, half joking and half promising, "Okay, I'll start tomorrow."

It took two years for that "tomorrow" to come, another twenty-five years before publication. So, why should the story of this book be any less unusual than the story it tells?

I don't know why I made only a halfhearted attempt at publication twenty-five years ago. Just lazy, I guess. The writing took everything out of me, and just getting it down on paper satisfied *my goals* at the time, even if it didn't fulfill *my promise* to Ann. Even now, I don't know why I have a revived interest in seeing my work in print, except it is something I said I was going to do and something I promised Ann I would do.

Although I pulled out my manuscript every five years or so to rework the writing and add some new information when I happened upon a quantity of additional notes from Ann, I never mounted any serious effort to publish. I did retire ten years ago, so my job is no longer at stake, but that is the only significant change that has occurred over time. The story now is the same as the story was then. My love for Ann is as deep and as enduring as it ever was, despite her death and despite my being happily married and very much in love with my wife of the last twenty-eight years. My thanks to Ann is on-going and never-ending, for it was her influence that caused me to change my view of love and relationships, helping me to develop my personal qualities and making me the person I am today. Ann's impact on me, referred to in Epilogue I, has allowed me to eliminate the shackles of expectations, possessiveness, traditionalism, male chauvinism, jealousy, manipulation, and the need to control more lives than the *one* the good Lord gave me to control. It has permitted me to choose my feelings rather than to feel I must be a victim of them, to be an open rather than a closed person, and to be bold, assertive, outgoing, optimistic, and unafraid to take risks, to seek adventure, to fly free, to live each day to its fullest, and to be the master of my own destiny. I can't explain the fact that many of these characteristics and perspectives were the basis of the lessons *I* started out teaching *her*.

* * * * * * *

Ann and I knew our situation was not unique. We naively thought it was unique at first, but as we learned of other teacher-student liaisons, we realized that I was neither the first nor the last of my profession, she neither the first nor last student, to attach new meaning to the term *co-education,* and stretch it beyond the bounds of morality.

Were Ann here today, I'm not sure what she would think of the headlines that have played across the newspapers and the television screen over the past two decades: the New York City gym teacher and the fifteen-year old junior high school student who spent two months motel-hopping through seven states on their way to finally being caught in Las Vegas; the school guard who allegedly arranged trysts with a fifteen-year old in school and at a motel; the thirty-year old male faculty advisor to the Future Business Leaders of America Club who was arrested for allegedly having a ten-month affair with a fifteen-year old female club member; and the more recent saga of Mary Kay Letorneau who went to jail for having sex with Billy, her teenage student lover, and having his baby. Before that there was Debra Lafave with a fourteen-year old male student; a twenty-seven-year old Cliffside Park, New Jersey, high school teacher arrested for having a seven-month sexual relationship with a seventeen-year old female student; and a twenty-five-year old female math teacher and basketball coach from Lexington Middle School in Nebraska charged with sexual activity with a thirteen-year old eighth grade boy.

My first thought was that Ann would be stunned. But, of course, she wouldn't have been, any more than I was. She certainly would have bristled with dissent at having all teacher-student liaisons blanket-painted with the victim brush used by many journalists and news reporters who relish in the sensationalism of such juicy stories and by legal officials and local prosecutors eagerly intent on securing a popular public conviction.

Aware, as she was—as we both were—that the nature of many, if not most, teacher-student affairs was not only unhealthy but was sick and depraved, she would have pleaded only for each situation, including ours, to be judged independently, on its own merits or demerits.

As for us and our relationship, she didn't see herself a victim, she didn't see herself sexually harassed or put upon, she didn't see herself violated, she didn't see herself sexually assaulted, she didn't see me as a sexual predator, she didn't see me as a pedophile, she didn't see me as a sex offender, she didn't see me as a sexual abuser, and she didn't see our relationship as sick or perverse. Neither did she see the relationship between Ed and Susan Richards as negative or sick—indeed, they still are together, stable, happily married with three grown children and two grandchildren of their own, now *forty years* after their in-school intrigue began.

We knew some of what was happening—in our own back yards, locally, and across the country—and, as one instance after another came to our attention, we strongly suspected more was happening than what we knew. I suspected it was a case of a *lot* more. Subsequent events supported my suspicions.

Ann wasn't here in the late 1980's and the early-to-mid 1990's when a host of surveys and studies brought to light staggering statistics about one of the public schools' dirty little secrets: teacher-student sex. A 1993 national survey found twenty-five percent of girls and ten percent of boys in grades eight to eleven said they had been sexually harassed by a member of the faculty or staff during high school. In an earlier North Carolina survey of high school graduates, an incredible thirteen and a half percent said they had had *intercourse* with a teacher.

Carol Shakeshaft, a Hofstra University professor, and her co-author Audrey Cohan, conducted a study of more than two hundred cases of teacher-student sex, finding, among other things, that teachers most likely to fall into relationships with their students were those who spent time with them after school in extracurricular activities, and that many school districts lack a clear policy in handling teacher-student sex cases and fail to investigate and prosecute those involved.

New York City school officials admit to investigating more than a hundred cases of alleged sexual abuse by adult staff members from January 1991 to September 1994, twenty-five of those cases involving *pre*-teens.

A 2010 South Florida newspaper chronicled a full page history of teachers "crossing the line," reporting that one hundred and seventy-five Florida teachers had had their teaching licenses revoked over the past five years for sexual misconduct. Numerous others have been accused or arrested for alleged sexual misdeeds, their cases still winding their way through school disciplinary proceedings and the courts. The majority of the revoked license cases involved teachers and students of the opposite sex, but some were same-sex offenses. Teachers were not always the initiators; in some cases, flirtatious students made the first move.

And these surveys, studies, and reports include only those cases that somehow have come to see the light of exposure. What about the God-only-knows-how-many other cases that no one has ever known or heard about?

A shocking chain of events which has progressed to epidemic proportions over the past fifteen or twenty years? I think not. Rather, I now believe illicit teacher-student sex—without a spotlight on it, absent media coverage, without anyone wanting the issue surfacing, without anyone wanting to disturb the shroud of secrecy that has kept it beyond the eyes and ears of the willing ignorant—has been going on extensively in this country since the days of the old one-room schoolhouse.

There are those—mostly teacher union leaders, school board members, officials of the National Education Association, stodgy teachers, and local principals and school superintendents—who will challenge that belief. They will insist that teacher-student sex is not prevalent or widespread and that my belief is simply self-serving and an effort on my part to minimize my personal transgression. To those who take such a head-in-the-sand position, I have only this to say: I took full responsibility for my errant actions in my original writing twenty-five years ago. I admitted I was wrong then, and I now, again, acknowledge my guilt. My admission is unequivocal. Just as clear to those who choose to wear blinders, however, should be my contention that teacher-student sex is rampant. How rampant? With no proof, no ability to substantiate, no evidence to corroborate, nothing whatsoever to support my view, I would not be surprised to find that teacher-student sex was occurring every year in every co-educational public high school, rural or urban, with a population of more than six hundred students, from one end of the country to the other. *One* student out of *six hundred*, sexually involved in some way with a teacher, would be an ultra-conservative guesstimate. Impossible? Only if one *chooses* to think so.

One must be wary of what one thinks is impossible. I wonder if Annie would have thought it was impossible that shortly after I retired from Teaneck High School in 2001, my former Principal would be accused, arrested, tried, convicted, and go to jail for *his* sexual escapes with a student? I bet *he* thought it was impossible! But it wasn't. That's what happened.

Maybe my guesstimate should be one out of every *three* hundred.....

****

Sometimes the line that separates the possible from the impossible is very thin. I always thought it would be possible for me to maintain the poem, framed under glass and wrapped in clear plastic, that I left tucked behind the shrubbery at the base of Ann's gravestone. From the time of her death in 1984, I visited Ann's grave every two or three weeks, sometimes more frequently. After the unveiling in late 1985, I always left a small stone remembrance on top of the monument. I usually made the short drive from school to the cemetery in Paramus, off Forest Avenue, less than a mile from the park entrance and the children's zoo, during my lunch hour. Had anyone ever told me that someday I would be going to a virtually deserted cemetery so frequently, giving up my cherished lunch hour to stand alone in front of a gray gravestone and having a hushed one-way conversation with a long-deceased person, I would have told them they were nuts. But that's exactly what I did, shaking my head in disbelief that the "older I" was the survivor while the "younger she" was gone. I'd talk to Ann as if she were beside me, tell her I still thought she was sunshine, look above the sea of headstones that stretched far behind hers, shake my head still again, look at the sky beyond, raise my gaze to the heavens, and set my jaw firmly, pressing my lips together so hard that they hurt, trying to hold back the wetness that blurred my vision, and saying, "I love you, babe," before turning away in silence and walking slowly back to my van.

Twice a year, I'd remove the clear plastic wrapped packet and bring it home with me to clean the glass and replace the typed poem. I'd return to the cemetery the next day and carefully slide the restored packet beneath the base of the headstone and the low-cut, stiff-branched, green-leafed shrubbery that had been planted over the gravesite. No one could see the packet. It wasn't meant as a display. It wasn't meant for anyone to see. It was there for me—and for Ann.

After my retirement, my wife and I sold our New Jersey house and moved to what had been our summer home in Pennsylvania, outside of Milford. Shortly thereafter, we bought a small villa in Delray Beach, Florida, becoming snowbirds and pursuers of senior discounts and Early Bird specials. Then, a few years ago, we sold both the villa and our house in the northern section of the Poconos and bought a Florida house in Boynton Beach, becoming full-time Florida residents. Although we still made trips back North to reunite with family and friends, each move further away from New Jersey decreased the number of my visits to Ann's grave. Before our final move South, I made a special trip to the cemetery. I wanted, once more, to clean and refresh the poem packet.

I knelt down by the side of the gravestone and slid my hand between the base and the shrubbery, as I usually did. But this time something was wrong. I didn't feel anything. There was nothing there.

I held still, paralyzed. I couldn't believe there was nothing there. Where was it? What happened to it? This was the right gravestone, wasn't it? Where could it have gone? Where was my poem?

I stood up quickly and looked around. What the hell was going on? I looked down. Everything looked normal. What could have happened to it? Nobody—nobody—knew it was there. Had the landscape gardeners who regularly trimmed the shrubbery in the cemetery found it and taken it away? Nothing like that had happened in twenty years. The shrubbery in front of Ann's gravestone wasn't the kind of leafy shrubbery that ever needed trimming, anyway. It was a twisting kind of low-cut evergreen that clung to the ground and never seemed to grow.

Again, I knelt down by the side of the gravestone, and I pulled the stiff branches away from the base. As hard as I pulled, I barely could back the shrubbery away more than a few inches. But a few inches was all I needed to confirm that the packet wasn't there. What *was* there was a hole, a hole that extended under the concrete base—maybe six inches under, perhaps a little more—upon which the weighty gravestone stood.

The hole was about a foot and a half wide; it extended about a foot out in front of the monument. The depth of the hole appeared to vary from six to twelve inches around the sides and from a foot to a foot and a half in the middle. It was hard to tell, exactly. The hole was dark because the tight twist of the shrubbery's branches had formed a close-knit roof of sorts over the opening.

I stood again and looked down. The hole wasn't visible from the top—not at all.

I have no idea how the hole got there. I don't know if natural erosion or settling caused it, or if an animal had hollowed it out, or if, maybe—nah, I mean, I knew it really couldn't be that she—

As impossible as that possibility was, however, it was both exciting and entertaining to fantasize on my drive back home that the little one I called Sunshine, knowing that I wouldn't be coming back anytime soon, simply swallowed my poem to hold it close. It made me feel warm and comfortable to think that's what happened. The little cumquat stole my poem to get even with me for stealing her cosmetic pouch full of weed and smoking paraphernalia when I was trying to get her off the stuff. I still have that cosmetic pouch, and I bet she still has my poem!

Impossible? Yeah, of course—couldn't happen. It wasn't possible—but only if one *chooses* to think so, only if one *chooses* not to think of *alternative* explanations.

* * * * * * *

Goodbye, my little friend.
Once we held hands and walked together our
separate ways;
Now we hold hands and die together our
separate ways.
Goodbye, my kindred spirit.
Only I have heard the songs you never sang;
Only you have heard the poems I never wrote.

Someday, my little Sunshine,
beyond Misfortune's grasp,
We'll hold hands again
and sing songs and write poems together
and play Scrabble until four o'clock in the
morning.

Anyone wishing to make a scholarship donation in memory of Ann Jordan may do so with my heartfelt thanks.

American Academy of Dramatic Arts
Scholarship Committee
120 Madison Avenue
New York, NY 10016
(or on-line)